THE WEAKEST LINK
QUIZ BOOK

BUMPER EDITION

THE WEAKEST LINK
QUIZ BOOK

BUMPER EDITION

PENGUIN BOOKS

Published by the Penguin Group
Penguin Books Ltd, 27 Wrights Lane, London W8 5TZ, England
Penguin Putnam Inc., 375 Hudson Street, New York, New York 10014, USA
Penguin Books Australia Ltd, Ringwood, Victoria, Australia
Penguin Books Canada Ltd, 10 Alcorn Avenue, Toronto, Ontario, Canada M4V
3B2
Penguin Books India (P) Ltd, 11 Community Centre, Panchsheel Park,
New Delhi – 110 017, India
Penguin Books (NZ) Ltd, Cnr Rosedale and Airborne Roads,
Albany, Auckland, New Zealand
Penguin Books (South Africa) (Pty) Ltd, 5 Watkins Street, Denver Ext 4,
Johannesburg 2094, South Africa
Penguin Books Ltd, Registered Offices: Harmondsworth, Middlesex, England

First published 2001
1 3 5 7 9 10 8 6 4 2

Printed in England by Clays Ltd, St Ives plc

CONTENTS

HOW TO PLAY

THE RULES

So you've come this far, but are you smart enough to handle the Bumper Edition? Weakest Link is the quiz game with a difference - in order to win, the players must act as a team, working together to build chains of correct answers and round by round getting rid of the person who they think is the weakest link. The aim is to reach the 1000 point target, and the fastest way to do this is to answer a chain of nine correct answers in a row. To become the strongest link you'll need to use both your general knowledge and your strategic skills: should you 'bank' the points in the chain or risk losing them all by failing to answer your question correctly? Can you spot who is the weakest link in the team? Will you crumble under the pressure? Remember, you may leave with nothing. Are you too slow to stay? Will it be you taking the 'walk of shame' as you are voted the weakest link?

Once more you can experience the excitement, tension and sometimes embarrassment of the TV quiz show by playing the game at home, with *The Weakest Link Bumper Edition*. Here's a reminder of how to play:

What You Need

Weakest Link can be played by any number of players but ideally there should be four or more, one of whom will be the quiz master (see page 9 for playing with two or three players or on your own).

Each player will need a pencil and a sheet or pad of paper. The quiz master may also want a pencil and paper to keep a tally of the scores. If you want to give each round a time limit, you will need a watch with a second hand or a stopwatch.

The Rounds

The quiz master takes the book and opens it to the Questions section. At the beginning of the first round the quiz master asks the first question to the player whose initial is the earliest in the alphabet, the second question to the player on his or her left, and so on, asking each player a question in turn. In the following rounds the person to the left of the last player to answer a question in the previous round is the first to be asked.

The length of each round can be determined in a number of ways:
Timing: As in *The Weakest Link* TV programme, each round can have

a time limit, starting with 3 minutes for the first round, and cutting off 10 seconds with each further round. Round two would therefore be 2 minutes 50 seconds, round three 2 minutes 40 seconds, round four 2 minutes 30 seconds, and so on. In this case you may use up the questions of more than two pages in each round. In the first round the quiz master will have to keep watch on the time; in later rounds one of the eliminated players could be responsible for timing.

20 Questions: You could limit each round to 20 questions (two pages of the book).

Questions Per Player: Alternatively you could decide to ask each player three, four or five questions in each round. Again, the quiz master might use up the questions on more than two pages and would have to carry the scoring over.

Scoring

The quiz master is responsible for keeping a tally of the team's score for each round, using the points chain on each right-hand page. At the beginning of the round, he or she puts a finger on the bottom link of the chain, the 20. This is the amount that the first question is worth. If the question is answered correctly, the quiz master will move his or her finger up to the next link – 50. If the second question is answered correctly he or she moves it up to the third link – 100, and the team has gained 50 points. Scoring continues in this manner either until the end of the round or when the target is reached.

The aim of the players is to work together as a team to win as many points as possible during the round. To do this they must bank the points before the chain is broken by a wrong answer or before the round comes to an end. They do this by calling 'bank' when it comes to their turn to answer a question, but before the question has been asked. When 'bank' is called it is the amount of points that is below the quiz master's finger that actually goes into the bank. So if his/her finger is on 100 when 'bank' is called, the team has banked 50. The quiz master writes down the points banked either in the spaces provided or on a separate piece of paper. The quiz master then puts his or her finger back on 20 to start a new chain and asks the player who has banked the points his or her question. If the players reach their 1000 point target the round finishes early. They cannot exceed 1000 points per round.

It is up to the skill and judgement of each player whether to bank the points, thereby securing the points but breaking the chain, or to carry on and try to build the chain higher, but risk losing it all if they can't answer correctly. The question is, will you cope? Are you better off watching the show on TV rather than actually attempting to play the game?

If the last person to be questioned in the round does not call 'bank' before his or her question, the points on the current chain are lost. The players cannot see the chain, but to help them keep track of how the points are building, the quiz master should shout out 'chain broken' at the beginning of each chain (that is, whenever a question is answered incorrectly, or the points are banked). At the end of each round, only points that have been banked will go through to the next round.

At the end of the first round the quiz master adds up all the points banked. This balance is then brought forward to the next round, and can be written in the space at the top of the next right-hand page to keep a running total of the points for the game.

The Weakest Link

At the end of each round, each player must decide who has been the weakest link, answering the fewest questions correctly or failing to bank points. The players write their selection on their pieces of paper, which they hold up at the same time. The player with the most votes is the weakest link and is sent off with the words 'You are the weakest link... Goodbye!'

In the event of a draw, responsibility for naming the weakest link lies with those who have already been voted off as weakest links. These players should continue to keep track of the game so that they can cast their votes if necessary. And maybe settle some old scores!

Once the weakest link has been decided, the quiz master starts a new round with the remaining players.

The Last Round

In the last round, when there are only two players left, they have the opportunity to increase their points by trebling their total for the round. This is then added to the running total for the previous rounds. It is these points that the players will then play for in the final.

Head to Head

After the last round the two remaining players go head-to-head in a final battle to establish, once and for all, who is the strongest link. The players take it in turns to answer five questions each. The quiz master should mark each question with a tick if it is answered correctly, or a cross if it is answered incorrectly, in the spaces provided. The player who was the strongest link in the previous round (as decided by either the quiz master or the players who are no longer in the game) can decide whether to answer first or second.

The player who answers the most questions correctly is the winner, and the strongest link. If there is a tie after five questions, 'sudden death' questions are asked until there is a winner.

Sudden Death

The questions continue in pairs. If player A gets their question correct then player B will have to answer their question correctly to win. If player A gets their question wrong then player B will have to answer their question correctly to win.

Playing with Two or Three Players

You can use *The Weakest Link Bumper Edition* to test the general knowledge and skill of two or three players. In this case, players should take it in turns to ask a round of questions to one opponent. After each question the player has the chance to bank his or her points or continue and try to build up the chain of points.

After 20 questions, or if you wish to time the rounds three minutes, the round ends and the player's points are counted. That player then becomes the quiz master for the next round. If there are three players, he will question the third player, who will then test the first quiz master in the next round. If there are two players they simply take it in turns to be quiz master. After a set number of rounds, decided before the beginning of the game, the player with the most points is the winner.

Testing Your Own Knowledge

Of course, you can also use *The Weakest Link Bumper Edition* on your own to test your general knowledge. Try to answer 20 questions, then check to see how many you got right. Cover up the answers until the end of the round! Allocate yourself one point for each question answered correctly and see if you can improve your score with the next round.

Remember . . .

You have to be ruthless to be rich. Are you up to it? It's time to find out. Let's play The Weakest Link . . .

Round 1

1 According to the saying, going from a bad situation to an even worse one is like getting 'out of the frying pan and into the . . .' what?

2 Complete the name of the BBC soap opera that began in the 1980s: *East . . .* what?

3 In science, which two letters are used to abbreviate the words 'alternating current'?

4 In the nursery rhyme, which bridge is falling down?

5 According to superstition, what are you entitled to do when blowing out the candles on your birthday cake?

6 In the bible, during the crucifixion, Jesus was forced to wear a crown of what?

7 In astronomy, the letters HST stand for Hubble Space . . . what?

8 Which religion was reinstated in England by Mary I in the sixteenth century?

9 In maths, if you drive 80 miles on a round trip, how many miles is it one way?

10 In nature, which *L* is a variety of flower that can be prefixed by 'tiger' or 'water'?

11 In fashion, jeans are normally made from which fabric?

12 In film, complete the title of the 1986 John Hughes movie: *Ferris Bueller's . . .* what?

13 In food, from which part of the chicken does the drumstick come: the leg or the wing?

14 What kind of animal is the children's TV puppet Kermit?

15 The casino card game with the object of scoring 21 is known as black . . . what?

16 In science, what name is given to someone who studies ecology?

17 In computers, what does the 'e' in email stand for?

18 In space, constellations are groups of what?

19 Which ex-Spice Girl went on to release the singles 'Bag It Up' and 'Lift Me Up'?

20 In children's TV, what type of bird is Pingu?

Previous Total

1,000

800

600

450

300

200

100

50

20

Banked

Total

Answers

1 Fire
2 *Enders*
3 AC
4 London
5 Make a wish
6 Thorns (thorny branches)
7 Telescope
8 Catholicism (Roman Catholicism)
9 40
10 Lily
11 Denim (accept cotton)
12 *Day Off*
13 Leg
14 A frog
15 Jack
16 An ecologist
17 Electronic
18 Stars
19 Geri Halliwell (Ginger Spice)
20 Penguin

Round 2

1 In Roman numerals, which letter represents the number five?

2 In music, what name is given to a written symbol representing the pitch and duration of a musical sound?

3 In law, what *E* is the name given to the documents or objects used to prove or disprove someone's case?

4 In art, who painted the *Mona Lisa*?

5 In a game of darts, what is the highest score you can achieve with three darts?

6 In fashion, what *T* is a woollen fabric, commonly used to make men's sports jackets?

7 Blackfriars is a district in which city in the south-east of the UK?

8 In which 1964 children's film did Dick Van Dyke star as a chimney sweep named Bert?

9 In the animal kingdom, which animal is usually larger: the wallaby or the kangaroo?

10 In music, singer Axl Rose featured in which American rock band, formed in 1985?

11 In TV, Cybill Shepherd featured in the series *Moon . . . what*?

12 In food, consommé and gazpacho are types of what?

13 In which sport is the ball made of cork and twine and covered in red leather?

14 In geometry, how many right angles does a right-angled triangle have?

15 What character did Leonardo DiCaprio play in the 1996 film *Romeo and Juliet*?

16 In nature, 'common house' and bluebottle are both types of which insect?

17 In athletics, in which event did Linford Christie win a 1992 Olympic gold medal?

18 The art of planning the decoration and furnishings of a room or building is called 'interior . . .' what?

19 In money, what is the official currency of Australia?

20 In travel, which country would you be flying to if you were arriving at Indira Gandhi International Airport?

Previous Total

1,000

800

600

450

300

200

100

50

20

Banked

Total

Answers

1 V	**12** Soup
2 Note	**13** Cricket
3 Evidence	**14** One
4 Leonardo Da Vinci (accept Leonardo)	**15** Romeo
	16 Flies (accept fly)
5 180	**17** 100 metres (100
6 Tweed	metres sprint)
7 London	**18** Design
8 *Mary Poppins*	**19** Australian dollar
9 Kangaroo	(accept dollar)
10 Guns 'N' Roses	**20** India
11 *Lighting*	

Round 3

1 In film, Brad Pitt stars as Tyler Durden in which 1999 action movie: *Fight Club* or *End of Days*?

2 In nature, counting what on a tree's trunk can enable you to calculate its age?

3 In TV, Mel Blanc provided the voice for Barney in which prehistoric cartoon series?

4 In food, which is larger: a hen's egg or a quail's egg?

5 In pop music, which British artist performed the hit song 'Stan' with Eminem at the 2001 Grammy Awards?

6 In history, what was the first name of the eighteenth-century British explorer Captain Cook?

7 Swedish pop group Europe had a UK number-one single in 1986 with a song entitled 'The Final . . .' what?

8 In popular culture, which famous British entrepreneur opened his first record shop in 1971?

9 In UK geography, Kingston upon . . . what is a town in Surrey?

10 Pines are members of which large family of trees?

11 In criminology, what term applies to the scientific investigation of a crime?

12 In the animal kingdom, what G is a grazing antelope also known as a wildebeest?

13 In which year did the first non-stop and non-refuelling aeroplane flight around the world take place: 1972 or 1986?

14 In TV, Lawrence Tureaud played B. A. Baracus in *The A-Team*. By what name is the actor more commonly known?

15 In fashion, what *B* is a single flower worn on a jacket lapel?

16 In food, ghee is a cooking fat originating from which country?

17 In theatre, . . . [what] *on the Roof* is the title of a 1964 musical featuring a character called Tevye?

18 What is a peccadillo: a petty sin or a type of cigar?

19 In music, 'Raindrops Keep Falling on My Head' re-entered the UK singles charts four times in 1970 for which French singer?

20 Name the 1995 film based on an Irvine Welsh novel about a group of drug addicts.

Previous Total

1,000

800

600

450

300

200

100

50

20

Banked

Total

Answers

1 *Fight Club*	**11** Forensics (forensic science)
2 The rings	**12** Gnu
3 *The Flintstones*	**13** 1986
4 Hen's egg	**14** Mr T
5 [Sir] Elton John	**15** Buttonhole
6 James	**16** India
7 'Countdown'	**17** *Fiddler*
8 Richard Branson	**18** A petty sin
9 Thames	**19** Sacha Distel
10 Conifers	**20** *Trainspotting*

Round 4

1 In British history, what was the name given to the intense air attack on southern England by the Luftwaffe between 1940 and 1941?

2 In the animal kingdom, to which family of fish does the haddock belong?

3 In which country of the UK was physicist and chemist Michael Faraday born?

4 In literature, in which country of the UK was the writer Frederick Forsyth born?

5 In the animal kingdom, is the coyote a carnivore or a herbivore?

6 According to the theory of relativity, what is the highest speed possible?

7 In the 1975 film, what type of shark was 'Jaws'?

8 In human biology, where does digestion start: in the stomach or the mouth?

9 In football, for which Premiership team did David Seaman play at the beginning of 2001?

10 In nature, what type of animal is a sea cow: a mammal or fish?

11 In TV, in which decade did *Monty Python's Flying Circus* first appear on British TV?

12 In the USA, for what do the initials of the press agency AP stand?

13 In nature, apiculture is the practice of keeping which sort of insects?

14 In which city is the Marais district: Paris or Brussels?

15 In tennis, which country did Gabriela Sabatini represent?

16 In New Zealand, is Auckland on the North or South Island?

17 In a standard game of gin rummy, how many cards are dealt to each player at the beginning?

18 In which year did the UK National Lottery start: 1994, 1995 or 1997?

19 In science, which element was formerly called 'Inflammable Air'?

20 In TV, what was the original occupation of Su Pollard's character, Peggy, in the BBC sitcom *Hi-De-Hi!*?

Answers

1 The Blitz	**11** 1960s (in 1969)
2 Cod	**12** Associated Press
3 England	**13** Bees
4 England	**14** Paris
5 Carnivore	**15** Argentina
6 Speed of light	**16** North (Island)
7 Great White (*Carchardon carcharias*)	**17** Ten
	18 1994 (14 November)
8 Mouth	**19** Hydrogen
9 Arsenal	**20** Chalet maid (*accept maid or cleaner*)
10 Mammal	

Previous Total

1,000

800

600

450

300

200

100

50

20

Banked

Total

Round 5

1 In US history, was John Adams the first or second president of the USA?

2 In art, what R is a movement in painting which attempts to represent the world in an accurate way?

3 In UK politics, the Representation of the People Act of 1918 gave the vote to most men over what age?

4 The magazine *Four Four Two* is devoted to the coverage of which sport?

5 In geography, where is the city of Perth: Western or South Australia?

6 In 1986, which former page 3 girl had a UK top-ten hit single with 'Touch Me'?

7 In sport, which boxer is known as 'Iron Mike'?

8 In the animal kingdom, the emu is native to which country?

9 In maths, how many even numbers are there between one and 1,001?

10 In sport, in which country was former champion jockey Pat Eddery born?

11 In film, which birds feature in the 1996 movie *Fly Away Home*, starring Jeff Daniels?

12 What name is given to the study of coats of arms?

13 In travel, the world's first passenger railway was built in which century: the eighteenth or nineteenth?

14 In film, what is the name of the female star of *Pretty Woman* and *The Pelican Brief*?

15 In economics, which stock exchange is older: Hamburg or London?

16 In nature, which S is a brown pigment which can be made from the ink of cuttlefish?

17 Affiliated to the United Nations, in which country is the World Bank located?

18 In world geography, in which Middle Eastern country is the Negev Desert?

19 In US history, Spiro T. Agnew was vice-president in whose administration in the 1970s?

20 In science, what is the opposite of centrifugal force?

Previous Total

1,000

800

600

450

300

200

100

50

20

Banked

Total

Answers

1 Second	**11** Geese
2 Realist (accept Realism)	**12** Heraldry
3 21	**13** Nineteenth
4 Football	**14** Julia Roberts (accept Julie Fiona Roberts)
5 Western	**15** Hamburg
6 Sam Fox (Samantha Fox)	**16** Sepia
7 Mike Tyson	**17** USA
8 Australia	**18** Israel
9 500	**19** Richard Nixon
10 Ireland	**20** Centripetal

Round 6

1 In history, which city state came into existence in 1929, after a treaty between Mussolini and the Pope?

2 Which US city is closer to New York by road: Boston or Los Angeles?

3 Which fictional Spanish character attacked windmills, believing them to be giants in Cervantes's 1605 novel?

4 What D is a British cathedral city on the River Wear?

5 In Jordan, is the head of state a monarch, president or prime minister?

6 Which US-born DJ released the album *Play* in 1999, featuring the tracks 'Porcelain' and 'Natural Blues'?

7 In biology, enamel, dentine and pulp are all part of which T found in the mouth?

8 What year saw the deaths of Elvis Presley, Charlie Chaplin and Bing Crosby: 1973 or 1977?

9 What was the full name of the American comic strip which inspired the musical and film *Annie*?

10 Which British male fashion designer co-presented the TV programme *The Clothes Show*?

11 In history, William Bligh captained which ship, whose crew mutinied against him on 28 April 1789?

12 In religion, which archangel revealed the message of the Koran to Prophet Muhammad?

13 In music, Jimmy . . . who had a 1967 UK hit single with 'The Wind Cries Mary'?

14 In TV, what O is the name of the long-running BBC arts programme that started in 1967?

15 What is the name of the small muscular sac that stores and concentrates bile?

16 In film, who directed *Taxi Driver*, *Mean Streets*, *Raging Bull* and *Goodfellas*?

17 Mannheim is an industrial port at the confluence of the Rhine and the Neckar rivers in which European country?

18 In which century did Bonnie Prince Charlie live?

19 What was the nickname of Melvyn Hayes's character in the UK TV sitcom *It Ain't Half Hot Mum*?

20 In literature, which author wrote the 1854 novel *Hard Times*?

Previous Total
1,000
800
600
450
300
200
100
50
20
Banked
Total

Answers

1 Vatican City (accept The Vatican)
2 Boston
3 Don Quixote (Don Quixote de La Mancha)
4 Durham
5 Monarch
6 Moby (Richard Melville Hall)
7 Tooth (accept teeth)
8 1977
9 *Little Orphan Annie*
10 Jeff Banks
11 HMS *Bounty*
12 Gabriel (accept Jibril/ Jibra'il)
13 Jimi Hendrix
14 *Omnibus*
15 Gall bladder
16 Martin Scorsese
17 Germany
18 Eighteenth century (1720–88)
19 Gloria
20 Charles Dickens

Round 7

1 In American politics, for how many years was J. Edgar Hoover director of the FBI: 28 or 48?

2 In the human body, what C, associated with feeding difficulties and common among babies, can be caused by wind in the intestine?

3 Which pop artist's studio was called The Factory?

4 In religion, one of the 'Pillars of Islam' is to make a pilgrimage to which city?

5 In which country in 1388 did the Battle of Otterburn take place, between Scottish and English forces?

6 In geography, which C is a Mediterranean island that is divided in two by the Attila Line?

7 Which sporting legend was the first cricketer to score a test century for England?

8 The national airline of which country is named after the mythical bird-god Garuda: Indonesia or Malaysia?

9 In modern literature, what N was the surname of the Russian writer Vladimir . . ., author of the novel *Lolita*?

10 In film, which drama starring Dustin Hoffman and Meryl Streep was voted Best Picture of 1979?

11 In the human body, in which organ are the ciliary muscles situated: the eye or the liver?

12 With which sport would you associate Nelson Piquet?

13 In modern history, in which country did the 'Great Purge' take place between 1936 and 1938?

14 What *N* was a movement in theatre that aimed to present ordinary life as accurately as possible?

15 Complete the title of the 1851 novel by Nathaniel Hawthorne: *The House of the Seven . . .* what?

16 In TV, whose *Big Impressions* have included David Beckham and the 'royal' Royle Family?

17 What was the title of Ken Loach's 1969 film adaptation of the novel *A Kestrel for a Knave*?

18 Which British military service has bases at Brize Norton and Northolt?

19 Born in 1922, Lucian Freud is famous in which profession: painting, writing or music?

20 In UK geography, Matlock is the administrative centre of which county?

Previous Total

1,000
800
600
450
300
200
100
50
20

Banked

Total

Answers

1 48
2 Colic
3 Andy Warhol
4 Mecca
5 England
6 Cyprus
7 W. G. Grace (William Gilbert Grace)
8 Indonesia
9 Nabokov
10 *Kramer vs Kramer*
11 Eye
12 Motor racing (*accept* Formula One)
13 Soviet Union (*accept* Russia/USSR)
14 Naturalism
15 *Gables*
16 Alistair McGowan
17 *Kes*
18 Royal Air Force (*accept* RAF)
19 Painting
20 Derbyshire

Round 8

1 In Greek legend, Andromache was the wife of which chief Trojan warrior?

2 In the opera *The Magic Flute*, what is Papageno's job: a dog-catcher or a bird-catcher?

3 In pop music, *We Can't Dance* was a 1991 UK hit album by which British band?

4 In sport, who won the 1980 Grand National: Ben Lomond or Ben Nevis?

5 In politics, which French leader said of Margaret Thatcher, 'She has the mouth of Marilyn Monroe and the eyes of Caligula'?

6 Built by the Romans, the Antonine Wall ran from the Firth of Clyde to which other Scottish Firth?

7 In music, which composer, famous for waltzes, composed the operetta *Die Fledermaus*?

8 In England, the 1611 translation of the Bible was named after which king?

9 Is Loki the Roman or Norse god of mischief and evil?

10 In children's literature, what is the surname of William, the mischievous schoolboy created by Richmal Crompton?

11 In geography, the prison of Robben Island is located in which country?

12 The Vasa dynasty was a royal family in which European country from the 1500s to 1818?

13 In biology, which muscle is responsible for the pumping action of the human heart?

14 To which family of animals does the alpaca belong?

15 Eric Arthur Blair, who wrote the novel *1984*, is better known by what pen-name?

16 Which singer married fashion designer Jeff Banks in 1968?

17 Which British painter, sculptor and engraver painted *The Monarch of the Glen*?

18 In music, how many planets were included in Gustav Holst's *The Planets Suite*?

19 Which type of deer was introduced into the Scottish Highlands in the 1950s?

20 Which British Impressionist, famous for his paintings of music-hall interiors, died in 1942?

Previous Total

1,000
800
600
450
300
200
100
50
20

Banked

Total

Answers

1 Hector
2 Bird-catcher
3 Genesis
4 Ben Nevis
5 François Mitterrand
6 Forth
7 Johann Strauss (accept Strauss/Johann Strauss the Younger)
8 King James (James I; The King James Version)
9 Norse
10 Brown
11 South Africa
12 Sweden
13 Cardiac muscle
14 Camel
15 George Orwell
16 Sandie Shaw
17 Landseer (Sir Edwin Landseer)
18 Seven
19 Reindeer
20 Walter Sickert

Round 9

1 In the nursery rhyme 'It's raining, It's pouring', what is the Old Man doing?

2 According to tradition, which foodstuff must be thrown over your shoulder when spilt?

3 In religion, in the northern hemisphere, Easter takes place during which of the four seasons?

4 In snooker, what colour is the 'cue' ball?

5 In food, what *I* is a sugar-based mixture used to decorate cakes and pastries?

6 In film, in the 1996 movie *Flipper*, what type of animal is Flipper?

7 In nature, what *C* is a strongly scented flower, used to make herbal teas?

8 In sport, how many events are there in a decathlon?

9 In children's literature, which of the following was written by Hans Christian Andersen: *The Snow Queen* or *Snow White*?

10 In the animal kingdom, what *P* is the low, vibrant sound made by a contented cat?

11 Is Mandarin a Chinese or Japanese language?

12 In politics, with which party is Norman Lamont associated?

13 In food, what is the main vegetable ingredient of coleslaw?

14 Which TV cartoon features Homer, Marge, Bart and Lisa?

15 In the animal kingdom, which A is a mammal with an armour of bony plates on its back?

16 Britain uses British Summer Time in the summer, and *what* in the winter?

17 According to the proverb, 'If you marry in Lent, you'll live to . . .' what?

18 Which G is a branch of mathematics concerning the properties of shapes?

19 In geography, in which continent is Libya?

20 In nature, are tomatoes categorised botanically as vegetables or fruits?

Previous Total

1,000

800

600

450

300

200

100

50

20

Banked

Total

Answers

1 Snoring	**13** Cabbage
2 Salt	**14** *The Simpsons*
3 Spring	**15** Armadillo
4 White	**16** Greenwich Mean
5 Icing	Time (accept
6 Dolphin	GMT/Greenwich
7 Camomile	Observatory Mean
8 Ten	Time/Standard Time)
9 *The Snow Queen*	**17** Repent
10 Purr	**18** Geometry
11 Chinese	**19** Africa
12 Conservative	**20** Fruits

Round 10

1 In language, 'whistle and flute' is cockney rhyming slang for which item of clothing?

2 In science, name either of the two elements which combine to make water.

3 In politics, Jimmy Carter was president of which country in the late 1970s and early 1980s?

4 Which festive birthday is shared by Kenny Everett, Annie Lennox and Sir Isaac Newton?

5 In nature, what type of animal is a mongoose: a bird or a mammal?

6 In maths, if a TV programme started at 8.35 and finished at 10.15, how long did it last?

7 In nature, 'monocots' are seedlings that sprout with how many leaves?

8 In geography, Manitoba and Ontario are provinces of which North American country?

9 In film, the actor Alfredo James Pacino is more commonly known by which name?

10 Who invented the electric battery in 1800: Alessandro Volta or Robert Bunsen?

11 Which comic-strip dog was drawn by cartoonist Charles Schulz?

12 In the animal kingdom, what G is the smallest member of the ape family?

13 Actor Ralph Little plays Antony in which TV sitcom?

14 In science, in which hemisphere would you find the *Aurora Australis*: northern or southern?

15 In motoring, what is the American term for a manually operated transmission?

16 In geography, in which European country is the town of Edam?

17 In pop music, which singer won Best British Male at the 2001 Brit Awards?

18 In food, what *M* is a cheese traditionally made from buffalo milk?

19 In which country was fashion designer Gianni Versace born?

20 Which country was the first to develop and use tanks during the First World War: Britain or Germany?

Previous Total

1,000

800

600

450

300

200

100

50

20

Banked

Total

Answers

1 A suit
2 Hydrogen/oxygen
3 United States (accept USA, the US, America)
4 Christmas Day (25 December)
5 Mammal
6 1 hour 40 mins (accept 100 mins)
7 One
8 Canada
9 Al (accept Al Pacino)
10 Alessandro Volta
11 Snoopy
12 Gibbon
13 *The Royle Family*
14 Southern
15 Stick shift
16 Holland (accept Netherlands)
17 Robbie Williams
18 Mozzarella
19 Italy
20 Britain

1 In TV, Tim Vincent, Peter Duncan and Simon Groom have all been presenters on which children's programme?

2 What *H* is an inert gas, safer than hydrogen, used to fill children's balloons that float away when released?

3 In sport, what is the name of the golf club that is usually used to knock the ball into the hole when on the green?

4 What *T* is the name for a group of monkeys?

5 In TV, complete the title of the 1960s music show: *Ready, Steady* . . . what?

6 In which country would you find Le Mans, where the annual 24-hour motor race takes place?

7 In film, Bing Crosby and Danny Kaye starred in which 1954 festive musical?

8 Viscose is a fabric derived from the pulp of what?

9 In history, how many years did the French revolution last: ten or twenty?

10 In sport, in which country is Park City, one of the venues of the 2002 Winter Olympics?

11 In TV, Kym, Noel, Suzanne, Myleene and Danny were picked to perform in which band on a reality-TV programme?

12 Which 1996 Tom Cruise film features the line 'Show me the money'?

13 In physics, what *E* is the form of energy created by charged particles?

14 In literature, the title of E. M. Forster's first novel is *Where Angels Fear to* . . . what?

15 In 1862, which American president said 'In giving freedom to the slave, we assure freedom to the free'?

16 What was the first name of the famous painter father of Paloma Picasso?

17 In nature, what name is given to the atmospheric layer above the Earth's surface which filters most of the sun's ultraviolet rays?

18 Complete the title of Bruce Springsteen's 1985 UK hit, 'Dancing in the . . .' what?

19 In sport, kabaddi is a seven-a-side team game originally played in which country?

20 Are agoutis native to Australia or South America?

Previous Total

1,000

800

600

450

300

200

100

50

20

Banked

Total

Answers

1 *Blue Peter*
2 Helium
3 Putter
4 Troop
5 Go
6 France
7 *White Christmas*
8 Wood
9 Ten
10 United States (accept US/USA/United States of America/America)
11 Hear'Say
12 *Jerry McGuire*
13 Electricity/electrical
14 Tread
15 Abraham Lincoln
16 Pablo
17 Ozone layer (accept ozone)
18 Dark
19 India
20 South America

Round 12

1 What type of sea creatures are the focus of the 1999 film *Deep Blue Sea*?

2 In food, what solid fat was invented in the late 1860s as an alternative to butter?

3 In which sport do 'end zones' make up part of the field of play?

4 Which city, on the Tigris river, is the largest in Iraq?

5 Which is further: 40 miles or 58 kilometres?

6 In medicine, what C is a state of deep unconsciousness from which the patient cannot be woken?

7 In music, Neil . . . who had a UK top-ten hit in 1962 with 'Breaking up is Hard to Do'?

8 In the USA, which major city stands on the left bank of the Potomac river?

9 The Roman Catholic Church, the Orthodox Churches and the Protestant Churches are all branches of which religion?

10 In the animal kingdom, which species of squirrel was introduced to Britain from North America: grey or red?

11 Which comedy improvisation show, hosted by Clive Anderson, had Richard Vranch as resident pianist?

12 In which decade did the *Des O'Connor Show* first appear on British TV?

13 To which country would you be flying if you were arriving at Marco Polo International Airport?

14 Complete the title of this Alan Bennett play: *The Madness of George the ...* what?

15 In geography, Dublin is on which coast of Ireland: east or west?

16 In nature, what *S* is an evergreen tree with hard, sharp leaves, or needles and cones which hang from the branches?

17 In maths, if you bought five books at £4.99 each, what would the total cost be?

18 In language, what is the literal translation of the expression *'vis-à-vis'*?

19 In politics, who was elected First Minister of the Northern Ireland Assembly in 1998?

20 In geography, what *P* on the River Ribble is the administrative centre of Lancashire?

Previous Total

1,000

800

600

450

300

200

100

50

20

Banked

Total

Answers	
1 Shark	**12** 1960s (1963)
2 Margarine	**13** Italy
3 American football	**14** *Third*
4 Baghdad	**15** East coast
5 40 miles	**16** Spruce
6 Coma	**17** £24.95
7 Sedaka	**18** Face to face (do *not*
8 Washington (accept	accept head to head)
Washington, DC)	**19** David Trimble
9 Christianity (Christian	**20** Preston
Church)	
10 Grey	
11 *Whose Line Is It Anyway?*	

Round 13

1 In which country was the car manufacturer BMW founded?

2 In music, for what is Kiri Te Kanawa famous: singing or playing the violin?

3 Which 1939 movie starring Clark Gable and Vivien Leigh was based on a novel by Margaret Mitchell?

4 In politics, the deliberate breaking of a law through non-violent direct action is known as 'civil . . .' what?

5 In popular culture, what was Dawn French's profession before she became an actress: teacher or secretary?

6 In history, in which century was approximately 30 per cent of the English population killed by the Black Death?

7 What colour pigment is made from the metal cobalt?

8 In geography, where is the Isle of Skye situated: the Inner or Outer Hebrides?

9 In film, which actress plays Tom Cruise's wife in the 1999 movie *Eyes Wide Shut*?

10 In which modern country was Christopher Columbus born?

11 In music, which patriotic song title is given to the finale of Elgar's *Coronation Ode*?

12 In which decade was the comedy series *Last of the Summer Wine* first broadcast on British TV?

13 The first American satellite, Explorer 1, was launched into orbit in which year: 1952 or 1958?

14 Which ancient European capital is home to the Parthenon?

15 In nature, the *Prunus domestica* is more commonly known as which fruit?

16 According to Matthew's gospel, who was arrested in the Garden of Gethsemane after being kissed by Judas?

17 In maths, what fraction is a half plus a third?

18 Which of the following was the first to be nationalised in the 1940s by the Labour government: the Bank of England or the National Coal Board?

19 In music, the viola is the alto member of which family of instruments?

20 In which country did the first Commonwealth Games take place in 1930?

Previous Total

1,000

800

600

450

300

200

100

50

20

Banked

Total

Answers

1 Germany
2 Singing
3 *Gone with the Wind*
4 Disobedience
5 Teacher
6 Fourteenth century
7 Blue (accept navy/ dark blue/deep blue)
8 Inner
9 Nicole Kidman (accept Nicole Mary Kidman)
10 Italy

11 'Land of Hope and Glory'
12 1970s (accept 70s) (1973)
13 1958
14 Athens
15 Plum (accept prune)
16 Jesus (accept Christ, Jesus Christ)
17 Five-sixths
18 The Bank of England
19 Violin
20 Canada

Round 14

1 Who painted *The Garden of Earthly Delights*: Bosch or Botticelli?

2 In which decade was it made compulsory to wear a seatbelt in the front seat of a car in the UK?

3 Which ancient civilisation is associated with Homer?

4 In UK geography, what *R* is an English city in North Yorkshire on the River Ure?

5 Which James Bond star played the character Trooper Joe Roberts in the 1965 film *The Hill*?

6 In literature, Holden Caulfield is the sixteen-year-old narrator of which 1951 J. D. Salinger novel?

7 In pop music, who has been The Rolling Stones's drummer since 1962: Charlie Watts or Bill Wyman?

8 In literature, which Nick Hornby novel reveals the intricacies of British football?

9 In TV, Lindsey . . . who played Jaime Sommers in the action programme *The Bionic Woman*?

10 What *M* is the surname of Charles, the Scottish chemist who took out a patent for waterproof clothing in 1823?

11 In geography, which city stands near the mouth of the River Eden in Cumbria?

12 In classical music, tabla are drums from which country?

13 Which American singer had UK number-one singles with 'Magic Moments' and 'Don't Let The Stars Get In Your Eyes' during the 1950s?

14 Which supermodel played Bruce Wayne's girlfriend in the film *Batman and Robin*?

15 On which of the Spanish 'Costas' are the resorts of Marbella and Torremolinos?

16 In TV, which actress played the character Michelle Fowler in *EastEnders*?

17 In theatre, the play *A Man For All Seasons* is about Sir Thomas More, the Lord Chancellor to which English monarch?

18 In which British city is Holyrood House, associated with Mary, Queen of Scots?

19 In football, which West Midlands club is nicknamed 'The Blues'?

20 According to the Roman calendar, which month was the tenth month of the year?

Previous Total

1,000

800

600

450

300

200

100

50

20

Banked

Total

Answers

1 Bosch (*accept* Hieronymus Bosch)
2 1980s
3 Greek
4 Ripon
5 (Sir) Sean Connery
6 *The Catcher in the Rye*
7 Charlie Watts
8 *Fever Pitch*
9 Lindsey Wagner
10 (Charles) Macintosh
11 Carlisle
12 India (*accept* Pakistan and Bangladesh)
13 Perry Como
14 Elle Macpherson
15 Costa del Sol
16 Susan Tully
17 Henry VIII
18 Edinburgh
19 Birmingham City (*accept* Birmingham)
20 December

Round 15

1 Which Labour MP was disgraced after borrowing money from Paymaster General Geoffrey Robinson?

2 Which controversial women's magazine, revived in the US in 1965 by Helen Gurley Brown, was first published in Britain in March 1972?

3 Which senior Nazi poisoned himself after being condemned to hang at Nuremberg in 1946?

4 In art, which famous sculptor and painter designed the Medici Chapel in Florence?

5 What A is a strict Protestant group in the USA, who reject the influences of modern industrial society?

6 What was the first name of Rocky's girlfriend in the 1976 film starring Sylvester Stallone?

7 In rugby union, which country does Scott Gibbs represent?

8 Which former British intelligence officer wrote the novels *The Confidential Agent* and *The Human Factor*?

9 In pop music, complete the title of Bob Dylan's 1966 UK hit album: *Blonde On . . .* what?

10 In the US, 'OH' is the abbreviation for which state?

11 In TV, Gerry . . . who created the *Thunderbirds* series?

12 In music, 'Lemmy' is the lead singer of which British heavy-metal band?

13 Which 1850 novel by Nathaniel Hawthorne features an adultress in seventeenth-century New England?

14 Who married Aristotle Onassis in 1968?

15 Complete the title of the 1987 movie starring Steve Martin: *Planes, Trains and . . .* what?

16 Which football manager was the first man to score a hat-trick against Rangers at Ibrox in 1963?

17 In theatre, in which country was the dramatist and poet Henrik Ibsen born?

18 In the King James Version of the Bible, how many books are there in the Old Testament?

19 In the US, the military post and gold reserve Fort Knox is named after a general from which American war?

20 Which American actress provided the voice for the character Princess Bala in the 1998 animated film *Antz*?

1,000

800

600

450

300

200

100

50

20

Banked

Total

Answers

1 Peter Mandelson
2 *Cosmopolitan*
3 Hermann Goering
4 Michelangelo
5 Amish
6 Adrian
7 Wales
8 Graham Greene (accept Graham Henry Greene)
9 *Blonde*
10 Ohio
11 Gerry Anderson
12 Motorhead
13 *The Scarlet Letter*
14 Jackie Kennedy (Jacqueline Lee Bouvier Kennedy)
15 *Automobiles*
16 Alex Ferguson (Sir Alex Ferguson)
17 Norway
18 39
19 American War of Independence
20 Sharon Stone

Round 16

1 In music, which composer wrote the 'Water Music', thought to be for King George I's procession down the River Thames in 1717?

2 Which international organisation established the International Court of Justice?

3 Where in the body would you find the 'sylvian fissure'?

4 In the animal kingdom, what is the common term for domesticated cavies?

5 In world politics, Mohandas Gandhi was a leader of the National Congress of which country?

6 In TV, what was the name of the US legal drama series starring Corbin Bernsen and Jimmy Smits?

7 Viticulture is the growing of which fruit?

8 In 1993, which British athlete set the 110 metres hurdles world record in Stuttgart?

9 In theatre, for what does the abbreviation FOH stand?

10 Omaha is the largest city in which American state?

11 Who painted Sunday Afternoon on the Island of La Grande Jatte?

12 In human biology, what V describes the two lower chambers of the heart?

13 Which Norwegian city is located on the Aker river?

14 In football, Kenny Dalglish is the most capped player for which country?

15 In the animal kingdom, a 'murder' is the name given to which group of birds?

16 In literature, complete the title of the 1953 Raymond Chandler novel *The Long . . .* what?

17 What is the name of the religious order for men founded in the thirteenth century by St Francis of Assisi?

18 In computing, what is the name of the material that is most commonly used in the manufacture of microchips?

19 Who became king of Spain following Franco's death in 1975 and returned the country to democracy?

20 In geography, what W is a port on the coast of Cumbria in north-west England?

Previous Total

1,000

800

600

450

300

200

100

50

20

Banked

Total

Answers

1 Handel (George Frederic Handel)
2 United Nations (accept UN)
3 Brain (accept head or skull)
4 Guinea pigs
5 India
6 *LA Law*
7 Grapes (accept growing vines)
8 Colin Jackson
9 Front of House
10 Nebraska
11 Georges Seurat
12 Ventricles
13 Oslo
14 Scotland
15 Crows
16 *Goodbye*
17 Franciscans (accept OFM, Order of Friars Minor)
18 Silicon
19 Juan Carlos (Juan Carlos I)
20 Workington

Round 17

1 According to the saying, moving fast or wildly is moving 'like a bat out of . . .' where?

2 In food, a chipolata is what form of meat product?

3 In the children's nursery rhyme, how many fiddlers did Old King Cole call for?

4 In which TV programme, later a film starring Tom Cruise, did tapes 'self-destruct in five seconds'?

5 In science, what natural force makes all falling bodies on Earth accelerate at around 9.8 metres per second squared?

6 In language, does the French word 'beau' translate as 'ugly' or 'beautiful' in English?

7 In football, which colour shirts do Liverpool wear for their home league matches?

8 With which religion would you associate a rabbi?

9 Which country invaded the Falkland Islands on 2 April 1982?

10 Which fruit is the main ingredient of the drink scrumpy?

11 In computing, binary numbers are always made up of zero and which other digit?

12 In the animal kingdom, what M is the name given to the long hair found on the head and shoulders of a male lion?

13 In the children's novel *The Wind in the Willows*, who lives in Toad Hall?

14 In which European country would you find Düsseldorf?

15 In TV, the name of the American sitcom about a talking horse was *Mister . . .* what?

16 On a standard Monopoly board, the four corner squares are 'Go', 'Jail', 'Go To Jail' and what else?

17 What type of oven was inspired by wartime radar technology in the 1940s?

18 According to superstition, what will a person not cast if they have sold their soul to the devil?

19 With which scientific discipline is Albert Einstein associated: chemistry, physics or biology?

20 In music, what *R* is a small woodwind instrument often taught to children at school?

Previous Total

1,000

800

600

450

300

200

100

50

20

Banked

Total

Answers

1 Hell	**11** One
2 Sausage	**12** Mane
3 Three	**13** Toad (*accept* Mr Toad)
4 *Mission: Impossible*	**14** Germany
5 Gravity	**15** *Ed*
6 Beautiful	**16** 'Free Parking'
7 Red (*accept* red and white)	**17** Microwave
8 Judaism	**18** A shadow
9 Argentina	**19** Physics
10 Apples	**20** Recorder

Round 18

1 In which sport do you have 'fly halves' and 'hookers'?

2 What is the popular name for the Royal Canadian Mounted Police?

3 In history, which young Jewish girl's diary was originally published in 1947?

4 How many livers are there in the human body?

5 In which country in the British Isles would you find the town of Dunfermline?

6 In art, which V is a resinous transparent solution that solidifies into a protective glossy coating?

7 In the animal kingdom, a termitarium houses colonies of which insect?

8 In history, 'sink or swim' was a trial to test the innocence of women suspected of being what?

9 Which two words are the title of a Bob Hoskins film, a Nat King Cole song and a small picture in the Louvre in Paris?

10 In biology, what O is a major part of a living body that has a distinctive vital function?

11 In science, the alteration of genetic material by technical means is known as genetic . . . what?

12 For a wedding, the invitations are traditionally sent out by the parents of whom: the bride or the groom?

13 In the animal kingdom, how many babies do apes normally have at a time?

14 Which section of the Bible has more books, the Old Testament or the New Testament?

15 In American politics, who replaced George Bush Senior as president?

16 According to their marketing, which children's dolls sprouted from a garden of cabbages in 1983?

17 Which Greek battle gave its name to a race that is just over 26 miles long?

18 In one day cricket, for how many innings does each team have to bat?

19 In which 1997 film does the character Jack Dawson say 'I'm the king of the world'?

20 In food, which part of the mustard plant is used to make mustard?

Previous Total

1,000

800

600

450

300

200

100

50

20

Banked

Total

Answers

1 Rugby (rugby union)
2 Mounties
3 Anne Frank
4 One
5 Scotland
6 Varnish
7 Termites
8 Witches (accept a witch)
9 *Mona Lisa*
10 Organ
11 Engineering (accept modification)
12 (The) Bride
13 One
14 Old Testament
15 Bill Clinton (accept President Clinton/ William Jefferson Clinton)
16 Cabbage Patch Kids
17 Marathon
18 One
19 *Titanic*
20 The seeds

Round 19

1 In TV, what colour was Lady Penelope's car 'FAB One' in the *Thunderbirds* series?

2 In medicine, what *B* is the term meaning 'not malignant'?

3 In nature, palm oil is obtained from the fruit of which tree?

4 In football, which TV presenter set a goal-scoring record for Arsenal during the 1990s?

5 In geography, the Arc de Triomphe is at the western end of which famous street in Paris?

6 Which American TV soap featured JR and Sue Ellen?

7 In Indian cooking, what *B* is an appetiser consisting of vegetables mixed with batter and deep fried?

8 What is the generic name for news and information which is broadcast through TV sets in the form of text and graphics?

9 In music, what is a sonata? A piece of music or a female vocalist?

10 In the animal kingdom, which plant forms the main part of a giant panda's diet?

11 In science, what underwater location device takes its name from the words 'Sound Navigation and Ranging'?

12 In which country would you find the port of Alexandria?

13 In film, who played the character Vivian Ward in the 1990 romantic comedy *Pretty Woman*?

14 In music, what type of instrument is a ukelele: stringed or wind?

15 In the TV programme *Changing Rooms* what nickname is given to the celebrity odd job man?

16 The council of which British city includes the wards of Didsbury, Chorlton and Whalley Range?

17 In horse riding, which is faster, trot or canter?

18 In nature, aspen, box and monkey puzzle are all types of what?

19 What is the official language of Vatican City, Italian or Latin?

20 In food, what C is the traditional cuisine of the French-speaking Caribbean?

Previous Total

1,000
800
600
450
300
200
100
50
20

Banked

Total

Answers

1 Pink	**11** Sonar
2 Benign	**12** Egypt
3 Palm tree	**13** Julia Roberts
4 Ian Wright	**14** Stringed
5 Champs Elysées	**15** Handy Andy
6 *Dallas*	**16** Manchester
7 Bhaji	**17** Canter
8 Teletext	**18** Tree
9 Piece of music	**19** Latin
10 Bamboo	**20** Creole

Round 20

1 In the BBC sitcom *Red Dwarf*, what was the computer played by Norman Lovett and Hatty Hayridge called?

2 In maths, if a sack weighs four and a half kilos, how much would four sacks weigh?

3 In history, the Roman emperor Vespasian ordered the construction of which famous amphitheatre in Rome?

4 In sport, what do sumo wrestlers throw into the ring before they engage in combat?

5 In human biology, what G is a unit of inherited material that controls a particular characteristic?

6 USA for Africa was the US equivalent of which group?

7 Italy, Austria, Hungary and what other country formed a 'Triple Alliance' in 1882?

8 In science, what word, with the abbreviation C, is the measurement of electric charge?

9 In music, Benjamin Britten composed the opera *Gloriana* in 1953 to celebrate which royal occasion?

10 In which year was American singer, songwriter and guitarist Neil Diamond born: 1941 or 1951?

11 In film, the actors Steve Guttenberg, Tom Selleck and Ted Danson starred together in which 1987 comedy?

12 In British geography, where is the city of Sheffield: North or South Yorkshire?

13 Which *H* is a species of gull associated with coastal areas and rubbish tips?

14 What name was given to robbers on horseback who plagued Britain's main roads during the seventeenth and eighteenth centuries?

15 In music, with which song did All Saints have their first UK number-one hit single in 1998?

16 In which decade was *The Simpsons* first broadcast on American TV?

17 Which *L* is an institution in which you might find the Dewey decimal classification system?

18 In modern history, which aged Chinese leader died on 9 September 1976?

19 In nature, which garden flower comes in varieties called damask, tea and climbing?

20 In the TV soap *EastEnders*, what is the name of Martin Fowler's older brother?

Previous Total

1,000
800
600
450
300
200
100
50
20

Banked

Total

Answers

1 Holly	**12** South Yorkshire
2 18 kilos	**13** Herring
3 Colosseum	**14** Highwaymen
4 Salt	**15** 'Never Ever'
5 Gene	**16** 1980s (in 1987)
6 Band Aid	**17** Library
7 Germany	**18** Chairman Mao
8 Coulomb	(*accept* Mao
9 Coronation of	Zedong)
Elizabeth II (*accept the*	**19** Rose
Coronation)	**20** Mark Fowler (*accept*
10 1941	Mark)
11 *Three Men and a Baby*	

Round 21

1 In fashion, what *S* is a sample of cloth?

2 Simon Archer and Jo Goode won Britain's first ever Olympic medal in which racket sport in Sydney?

3 In astronomy, when is a black hole created: when a star is born or when it collapses?

4 In geography, what *L* is an English city on the right bank of the Mersey Estuary?

5 In maths, what is 60 per cent expressed as a fraction, in its lowest possible terms?

6 In which country was the actress Juliette Binoche born?

7 Mexico City is built on the ruins of which empire's capital?

8 In TV, what former *Neighbours* character was played by Alan Dale: Jim Robinson or Scott Robinson?

9 In which 1981 Hollywood film did Sylvester Stallone and Michael Caine appear alongside the footballers Pele and Bobby Moore?

10 What *S*, running through the buttocks and the back of the thigh, is the longest and thickest nerve in the body?

11 In pop music, with which British rock group are the Knopfler brothers associated?

12 In which city in south-east England would you find the Trinity College of Music?

13 In film, who starred as Kevin in the 1990 comedy movie *Home Alone*?

14 In Australia, is the official head of state a monarch, president or prime minister?

15 In literature, complete the name of the Charles Dickens novel: *Barnaby* . . . what?

16 On which British island is the town and port of Cowes?

17 In which English county is the Bank of England's printing works, where all English banknotes are produced?

18 In music, 'Three Coins in the Fountain' was a 1954 number-one UK hit single for which famous American singer?

19 In the TV comedy *The Good Life*, what was Tom and Barbara's surname?

20 In history, in which country was the fifteenth-century explorer Vasco da Gama born?

Previous Total
1,000
800
600
450
300
200
100
50
20
Banked
Total

Answers

1 Swatch	**10** Sciatic nerve
2 Badminton	**11** Dire Straits
3 When it collapses	**12** London
4 Liverpool	**13** Macaulay Culkin
5 Three fifths (*accept* three over five; *do not accept* six tenths)	**14** Monarch
	15 *Rudge*
	16 Isle of Wight
6 France	**17** Essex
7 The Aztec empire	**18** Frank Sinatra
8 Jim Robinson	**19** Good
9 *Escape to Victory* (*accept Victory*, the US title)	**20** Portugal

Round 22

1 Which S is plaster mixed with powdered marble and applied to the exterior of buildings?

2 In the USA, in the late 1960s and 1970s, to what were the Strategic Arms Limitation Talks abbreviated?

3 In pop music, which New Romantic band had a 1986 UK hit album entitled *Through The Barricades*?

4 In fashion, which tennis star, nicknamed 'The Crocodile', invented the short-sleeved polo shirt in 1934?

5 In biology, where would you find the terminal bud? At the tip or the base of a plant?

6 In which decade did King Edward VIII abdicate?

7 On 5 May 1961, Alan Shepherd became the first American to go where?

8 In TV, James Herriot and Tristan Farnon were characters in which British drama?

9 In which city was an assassination attempt made on President Ronald Reagan in 1981?

10 In sport, which county cricket team play home matches at The Oval and Guildford?

11 Which C is the largest city in South Island, New Zealand, and shares its name with an English town?

12 In TV, Roger Moore and Ivor Dean starred in which 1960s adventure crime series?

13 In music, which famous Austrian composer wrote the opera *The Magic Flute*?

14 What G is the most southerly of the Windward Islands in the Caribbean?

15 Born in 1716, was Capability Brown a violinist, a clown or a landscape gardener?

16 The Sunni and the Shi'ites are the main branches of which religion?

17 In football, for which London club did Glenn Hoddle make his professional debut in 1975?

18 In literature, complete the title of Edgar Doctorow's 1989 novel: *Billy . . .* what?

19 In which year did the rocket *Pioneer 10* become the first man-made object to fly beyond our solar system: 1982 or 1995?

20 In the human body, lipase and tripsin are types of what *E* used to regulate metabolic reaction?

Previous Total

1,000

800

600

450

300

200

100

50

20

Banked

Total

Answers

1 Stucco
2 SALT
3 Spandau Ballet
4 René Lacoste (*accept* Lacoste)
5 Tip
6 1930s (1936)
7 Space
8 *All Creatures Great and Small*
9 Washington, DC
10 Surrey
11 Christchurch
12 *The Saint*
13 Mozart (Wolfgang Amadeus Mozart)
14 Grenada
15 Landscape gardener
16 Islam (*accept* Muslim)
17 Tottenham Hotspur
18 *Bathgate*
19 1982
20 Enzymes

Round 23

1 In history, which Chancellor of the Exchequer, later Prime Minister, introduced old-age pensions in 1909?

2 Which football club did goalkeeper Mark Bosnich leave to join Chelsea in January 2001?

3 Who wrote the novel *The Testament*, about a 78-year-old multibillionaire called Troy Phelan?

4 St David's in Pembrokeshire is the smallest place in Britain to have what sort of place of worship?

5 In the animal kingdom, how many varieties of poisonous lizard are there in the world: two or twelve?

6 The paper used to make manila envelopes was originally made from plants grown in which country?

7 The flower *Helleborus niger*, which flowers in winter, is better known by what festive name?

8 In which country was the athlete Merlene Ottey born?

9 In British geography, the rivers Nene, Welland and Great Ouse flow into which shallow bay of the North Sea between Norfolk and Lincolnshire?

10 By what name is the punk singer and musician John Lydon better known?

11 In history, which US general was in command of the United Nations forces in the 1950 Korean War?

12 In which country was air conditioning invented?

13 In language, what does the name 'Cairo' mean in Arabic: 'victorious' or 'big city'?

14 Which team play their home games at Filbert Street and are nicknamed 'The Foxes'?

15 In biology, what name is given to the basic building blocks for DNA and RNA?

16 Which member of the Spice Girls has the word 'Angels' tattooed across her stomach?

17 In literature, Miss Prism is a character in which 1895 play by Oscar Wilde: *The Importance of Being Earnest* or *Lady Windermere's Fan*?

18 In which country in the UK was theoretical physicist and cosmologist Stephen Hawking born?

19 In the TV series *Frasier*, from which British city does the character Daphne come?

20 The Taleban is an Islamic group which controls much of which Asian country?

Previous Total
1,000
800
600
450
300
200
100
50
20
Banked
Total

Answers

1 Lloyd George (David Lloyd George)
2 Manchester United (accept Man United/ Man U)
3 John Grisham
4 Cathedral
5 Two
6 Philippines
7 Christmas Rose
8 Jamaica
9 The Wash
10 Johnny Rotten
11 (Douglas) McArthur
12 USA (accept United States of America, etc.)
13 Victorious
14 Leicester City (accept Leicester)
15 Nucleotides (accept nucleic acid)
16 Mel C (accept Sporty Spice/Melanie Chisholm)
17 *The Importance of Being Earnest*
18 England
19 Manchester
20 Afghanistan

Round 24

1 In sport, which British tennis player won the Copenhagen Open in February 2001?

2 In modern literature, which female author wrote the 1950 novel *The Grass Is Singing*?

3 In art, what *P* is the name given to the technique of painting with small dabs rather than long brushstrokes?

4 In maths, if a clock gains twelve minutes a day, how many days will it take for it to gain two hours?

5 In literature, who wrote the novels *Bear Island* and *The Guns of Navarone*?

6 In Formula One, in which European country would you find the track at Imola?

7 In pop music, what female name features in the titles of songs by Paul McCartney, Snap and The Boomtown Rats?

8 On which island in the South Atlantic did Ernest Shackleton die while on his fourth Antarctic expedition: South Georgia or West Falkland?

9 In literature, the historical novel *The Virginians* by Thackeray was set during which revolution?

10 Mossad is the foreign intelligence agency in which Middle Eastern country?

11 In music, Anne-Sophie Mutter is associated with which instrument?

12 In which Asian country are the Ellora Caves?

13 In politics, what *F* was the nickname of the nineteenth-century prime minister Lord Palmerston?

14 In the animal kingdom, what is the name given to a baby lynx?

15 In which city of Thailand are the Democracy Monument and the Palace Buildings found?

16 What nationality was the inventor of the Zeppelin airship?

17 Which Charles Dickens novel features the characters John Harmon, Bella Wilfer and Mr Boffin?

18 The Indus river in present-day Pakistan gave its name to which religion?

19 In history, the Sage kings were legendary rulers of which Eastern country?

20 In pop music, Nick Rhodes plays the keyboards with which British band?

Previous Total

1,000

800

600

450

300

200

100

50

20

Banked

Total

Answers

1 Tim Henman	**12** India
2 Doris Lessing	**13** Firebrand
3 Pointillism	**14** Kitten
4 Ten	**15** Bangkok
5 Alistair Maclean	**16** German
6 Italy	**17** *Our Mutual Friend*
7 Mary	**18** Hindu
8 South Georgia	**19** China
9 American	**20** Duran Duran (accept
10 Israel	Arcadia)
11 Violin	

Round 25

1 According to the saying, when mistaken, you are barking up the wrong . . . what?

2 In science, what *B* is the study of life and all living things?

3 In sport, in which year are the next Summer Olympic Games due to be held?

4 In music, The Beatles were commonly referred to as 'The Fab . . .' what?

5 In politics, Saddam Hussein became president of which country in 1979?

6 What *C* is the name given to a gambling hall, common in places like Las Vegas?

7 In the Bible, what did Jesus turn into wine?

8 In law, capital punishment is also known as the . . . *what* penalty?

9 In biology, the stem of a plant usually grows in which direction?

10 In music, Buddy Holly sang about which Peggy in 1957?

11 In tennis, how many players are on court during a doubles match?

12 In TV, which actor plays Mr Bean in the comedy series of the same name?

13 What type of food is ricotta?

14 In which of Perrault's fairy tales does a princess prick her finger on a spindle and fall into a deep sleep?

15 Tiger Woods is famous for playing which sport?

16 In human biology, the tiredness associated with travel across time zones is known as 'jet . . .' what?

17 In fashion, a stiletto is a type of what: heel or hat?

18 In geography, what name is given to a large, usually slow-moving mass of ice?

19 In British politics, Robin Cook is associated with which party?

20 What B is the name given to American whiskey made from at least 51 per cent corn?

Previous Total

1,000

800

600

450

300

200

100

50

20

Banked

Total

Answers

1 Tree
2 Biology
3 2004
4 Four
5 Iraq
6 Casino
7 Water
8 Death
9 Upwards (accept towards the light/ towards the sun)
10 (Peggy) Sue
11 Four
12 Rowan Atkinson (Rowan Sebastian Atkinson)
13 Cheese
14 *Sleeping Beauty* (accept *La Belle au Bois Dormant*)
15 Golf
16 Lag (accept jet lag)
17 Heel
18 Glacier
19 Labour (accept New Labour)
20 Bourbon

Round 26

1 In the animal kingdom, in which continent are tigers still found in the wild?

2 At the start of a game of chess, does white or black move first?

3 In TV comedy, which elderly character's catchphrase is 'I don't believe it!'?

4 In our solar system, which planet orbits closest to the sun?

5 In maths, add the number of days in a week to the number of months in a year.

6 In UK geography, where is the town of Oldham situated: in Greater London or Greater Manchester?

7 In politics, who was British prime minister when the Maastricht Treaty was signed in 1992?

8 In sport, what is the official called in a game of field hockey: an umpire or a referee?

9 Which two-piece item of women's beachwear was first modelled in Paris in 1946?

10 In football, Atlético Madrid is a team in the domestic league of which European country?

11 In children's literature, what was the name of Dr Seuss's famous feline creation?

12 What would you expect to buy at Hamleys, in London's Regent Street?

13 In human biology, what O is an unhealthy excess of body weight?

14 In the Bible, the prophet Daniel survives a night in a den of which kind of animal?

15 In England, which is further east: Bournemouth or Portsmouth?

16 In the Bible, which giant was the champion of the Philistine army?

17 In pop music, complete the title of Sandie Shaw's 1964 number-one hit single: 'There's Always Something There To . . .' what?

18 In science, what F is a term given to harmful radioactive debris from a nuclear explosion that drops to earth?

19 In cricket, which international team is known as the 'Windies'?

20 In the USA, which state uses the postal abbreviation 'TX'?

Previous Total
1,000
800
600
450
300
200
100
50
20
Banked
Total

Answers

1 Asia
2 White
3 Victor Meldrew
4 Mercury
5 Nineteen
6 Greater Manchester
7 John Major
8 Umpire
9 Bikini
10 Spain
11 The Cat in the Hat
12 Toys (accept games)
13 Obesity (accept obese)
14 Lions
15 Portsmouth
16 Goliath (of Gath)
17 'Remind Me'
18 Fallout
19 The West Indies
20 Texas

Round 27

1 In TV, what number did the Thunderbirds International Rescue Space Station have: 1 or 5?

2 In which sport would you compete in the Tour de France?

3 What *B* is also known as a naevus or strawberry mark?

4 Are leeches herbivores or carnivores?

5 In comic books, which superhero is known as the 'Dark Knight of Gotham City'?

6 In which decade was the original *Grease* film released?

7 Which famous magazine is known as *Hola* in Spain?

8 In music, the cello, violin and double bass all belong to which family of instruments?

9 What name is given to the type of electric current which reverses direction at regularly recurring intervals?

10 In geography, what *H* is a mountain range in Asia which means 'Abode of Snow' in Sanskrit?

11 Of which religion is the six-pointed Star of David a symbol?

12 In biology, what *U* is the use of sound waves to form a picture of internal tissues?

13 In rugby union, for which country did Jonny Wilkinson score 35 points against Italy in February 2001?

14 In the animal kingdom, which animal is considered to be more endangered: the giant panda or the black bear?

15 In art, what is the name for a profile image or portrait, usually in black on a white background or vice versa?

16 In modern history, which nationalist Indian leader developed a form of nonviolent resistance which he called 'Satyagraha'?

17 In music, which rock 'n' roll singer's backing group was called The Comets?

18 Which airline is owned by Richard Branson?

19 Which British triple jumper won the BBC Television Sports Personality of the Year Award in 1995?

20 In comic strips, Florrie is the wife of which lazy character created by Reg Smythe?

Answers

1 5
2 Cycling
3 Birthmark
4 Carnivores
5 Batman/the Batman
6 1970s (accept 70s)
7 Hello
8 String
9 Alternating (AC, alternating current)
10 Himalayas
11 Judaism (accept Jewish)
12 Ultrasound
13 England
14 Giant panda
15 Silhouette
16 Mahatma Gandhi (accept Gandhi/Mohandras Gandhi)
17 Bill Haley
18 Virgin Atlantic (accept Virgin/Virgin Airways)
19 Jonathan Edwards
20 Andy Capp

Round 28

1 In music, which instrument of the brass family plays higher-pitched notes: the trumpet or trombone?

2 In the animal kingdom, what *P* is a large, herbivorous, spiny rodent?

3 In film, which English actor played leading roles in both *Elizabeth* and *Shakespeare in Love* in 1998?

4 Actress Sarah Jessica Parker stars in the TV series *Sex and the. . .* what?

5 In science, what is the term for the transfer of heat in a solid object: conduction or convection?

6 In nature, sea lettuce and bladderwrack are what type of marine plant?

7 In English football, how many leagues are there above the first division?

8 In UK geography, where is the city of Bradford: South Yorkshire or West Yorkshire?

9 Who is the mother of John Lennon's son Julian?

10 In the song from the musical *Oklahoma*, what *S* has a fringe on top?

11 According to superstition, staring at what type of moon will turn you into a lunatic?

12 Is cable stitch used in knitting or embroidery?

13 São Paulo is the largest city in which South American country?

14 In which American TV series did the starship *USS Enterprise* first appear?

15 In maths, if a circle is divided into three sections and one is 180 degrees and one is 90 degrees, how big is the last section?

16 In the British peerage, which is the higher degree of nobility: viscount or earl?

17 In geography, in which Latin American country would you find Tijuana?

18 Ragtime is a style of music principally associated with which instrument?

19 In TV, what is the surname of the American talk-show host Montel?

20 In science, fast breeder and thermal are both types of what kind of reactor?

Previous Total

1,000

800

600

450

300

200

100

50

20

Banked

Total

Answers

1 Trumpet
2 Porcupine
3 Joseph Fiennes (*if answer Fiennes, be more specific*)
4 City
5 Conduction
6 Seaweed
7 One
8 West (Yorkshire)
9 Cynthia Lennon (Cynthia Powell)
10 Surrey

11 Full moon (*accept full*)
12 Knitting
13 Brazil
14 *Star Trek* (*accept original series, Star Trek*)
15 90 degrees
16 Earl
17 Mexico
18 Piano
19 Williams
20 Nuclear

Round 29

1 Which famous American actor was nicknamed 'Bogie'?

2 In science, the *Magellan* spacecraft mapped 99 per cent of which planet's surface in the early 1990s: Earth or Venus?

3 Which famous doll's boyfriend, called Ken, was created by Ruth and Elliot Handler in 1961?

4 In which decade was former prime minister Margaret Thatcher born?

5 With which sport would you associate Lindsay Davenport?

6 In maths, if petrol costs 80 pence per litre, how much would you pay for ten litres?

7 According to the title of the classic 1947 Christmas movie, there was a *Miracle on* . . . which *Street*?

8 In theatre, 'The Last Supper' is a song from which Andrew Lloyd Webber musical?

9 In which decade was the American sitcom *Taxi*, starring Danny De Vito, first seen on British TV?

10 In geography, the Place des Vosges and the Place de la Concorde are found in which European capital city?

11 In UK politics, for which party was Diane Abbott elected MP for Hackney North and Stoke Newington in 1987?

12 In mammals, a 'proboscis' is a long, flexible what?

13 Which country's civil war began in 1861 with the Battle of Bull Run?

14 In pop music, which American singer was born Anthony Benedetto in 1926?

15 In football, in which position did Peter Shilton play during his professional career?

16 Mr Micawber and Mrs Gamp are characters created by which nineteenth-century novelist?

17 In which 1968 film does a scientist called Julius say 'You know the saying: "human see, human do"'?

18 In the Bible, how many people did Jesus feed with just two fish and five loaves of bread?

19 Which is the world's second largest ocean?

20 Who played the character Doctor Peter Venkman in the 1984 movie *Ghostbusters*?

Previous Total

1,000

800

600

450

300

200

100

50

20

Banked

Total

Answers

1 Humphrey Bogart (Humphrey DeForest Bogart)

2 Venus

3 Barbie

4 1920s (1925; accept 20s)

5 Tennis

6 £8 (800 pence)

7 34th

8 *Jesus Christ Superstar*

9 1980s (1980)

10 Paris

11 Labour

12 Nose (accept trunk)

13 America's (United States/USA)

14 Tony Bennett

15 Goalkeeper

16 Charles Dickens

17 *Planet Of The Apes*

18 Five thousand

19 Atlantic

20 Bill Murray

Round 30

1 In the USA, which state has the postal abbreviation 'UT'?

2 In the animal kingdom, the Iberian imperial eagle is native to which European country?

3 In science, what M is the study of microbes?

4 In politics, which Conservative prime minister said 'The lady's not for turning'?

5 In pop music, which British male artist's 1994 'Best of' album was entitled *Fields of Gold*?

6 In music, complete the title of the 1934 musical by Cole Porter: *Anything . . . what*?

7 In which year was the 'Model T' Ford car first introduced: 1908 or 1915?

8 Dennis Quaid is the younger brother of which American actor?

9 In art, in which century did Leonardo Da Vinci paint the *Mona Lisa*?

10 In science, which metallic element in the Periodic Table is given the symbol Ni?

11 In which American sport does lay begin with a 'tip-off'?

12 In heraldry, three feathers of which bird appear on the badge of the Prince of Wales?

13 In history, the Post Office in which Irish city was the central point of the 1916 Easter Rebellion?

14 In music, what is the first name of female pop singer . . . Abdul, who had a UK hit in 1990 with 'Opposites Attract'?

15 In history, Thomas . . . who was the third president of the USA?

16 Oliver . . . who directed the films *Wall Street* and *JFK*?

17 In sport, a game of polo consists of six periods called what?

18 In modern literature, under what name does Harry Patterson write thrillers: Jack Higgins or George Milton?

19 In film, name the 1957 Second World War epic starring Alec Guinness, about the plight of British POWs in a Japanese prisoner-of-war camp.

20 In theatre, Anton Chekhov wrote a play called *The* . . . what *Orchard*?

Previous Total

1,000
800
600
450
300
200
100
50
20

Banked

Total

Answers

1 Utah	**11** Basketball
2 Spain (accept Portugal)	**12** Ostrich
3 Microbiology	**13** Dublin
4 Margaret Thatcher	**14** Paula
5 Sting (Gordon Sumner)	**15** Jefferson
6 Goes	**16** Stone
7 1908	**17** Chukkas
8 Randy Quaid	**18** Jack Higgins
9 The sixteenth century	**19** *Bridge on the River Kwai*
10 Nickel	**20** *Cherry*

Round 31

1 In pop music, who did U2's Bono sing with on the 1993 UK hit single 'I've Got You Under My Skin'?

2 Wesley . . . who played the lead role in the 1992 film *Passenger 57*?

3 In geography, in which country is the Mount of Olives situated?

4 In literature, which of Homer's epic poems records the adventures of Odysseus?

5 In Australia, which enormous stone, called 'Uluru' by the Aborigines, is named after an Australian prime minister?

6 In art, in which county in eastern England was painter John Constable born?

7 In world geography, New York City is situated at the mouth of which major river?

8 In nature, what is the name of the fossil that looks like a large flattened snail shell?

9 In TV, which ex-*EastEnders* character was the eldest daughter of the character Carol Jackson?

10 In biology, which *K* is a protein found in rhinoceros horns and human hair?

11 The United States became involved in which major conflict in Asia in 1950?

12 In literature, who wrote the novels *The French Lieutenant's Woman* and *The Magus*?

13 What was the occupation of Edmund Halley, who devised one of the first practical diving bells in 1717?

14 In Greek mythology, Icarus was imprisoned in Crete by which king?

15 In history, which duke and general, born in 1769, was nicknamed 'Old Conky'?

16 Which city in the south of France was named after Nike, the Greek goddess of victory?

17 In geography, the Sulu Sea is a part of which ocean?

18 In the TV cartoon *Secret Squirrel*, what type of animal was his Moroccan sidekick?

19 David Kotkin is the real name of which world-famous magician?

20 In science, in 1714 the mercury thermometer was invented by Daniel . . . who?

Previous Total

1,000
800
600
450
300
200
100
50
20

Banked

Total

Answers

1 Frank Sinatra (Francis Albert Sinatra)	**10** Keratin
2 Snipes	**11** Korean War
3 Israel	**12** John Fowles
4 The *Odyssey*	**13** Astronomer (accept mathematician)
5 Ayers Rock	**14** Minos
6 Suffolk	**15** Duke of Wellington
7 The Hudson	**16** Nice
8 Ammonite	**17** Pacific
9 Bianca Butcher (accept Bianca/ Bianca Jackson)	**18** A mole
	19 David Copperfield
	20 Fahrenheit

Round 32

1 In motor racing, who won the Australian Grand Prix in March 2001?

2 In economics, what does IMM stand for?

3 In film, which actor played Jonathan Harker in the 1992 horror film *Bram Stoker's Dracula*?

4 Which make of motor scooter was first produced in 1946 in Italy?

5 Which famous Conservative politician married Norma Johnson in 1970?

6 In Greek mythology, who was held by the heel and dipped into the water of the Styx?

7 In science, what jelly-like substance is used as a culture medium to grow bacteria in a petri dish?

8 In which American state would you find the cities of Philadelphia and Pittsburg?

9 In which Scottish city are Heriot-Watt and Napier Universities located?

10 Which publishing company famous for romance novels was founded in 1908?

11 What is the longest-running children's comic in the UK?

12 In film, soul singer Aretha Franklin appeared in which 1980s action comedy with Dan Aykroyd and John Belushi?

13 In which decade was the long-playing record invented?

14 In geography, which country, consisting of a chain of coral islands, is the smallest in Asia?

15 What *A* is the second largest city in Belgium?

16 In a British orchestra, the leader normally plays which instrument?

17 In TV, what was the surname of Kevin, the character played by Fred Savage in the US sitcom *The Wonder Years*?

18 In the children's programme *Tweenies*, what is the name of the dog?

19 The four colours that make up the Kenyan flag are red, black, white and which other colour?

20 Who wrote the play *Habeas Corpus*?

Previous Total

1,000

800

600

450

300

200

100

50

20

Banked

Total

Answers

1 Michael Schumacher
2 International Money Market (accept International Monetary Market)
3 Keanu Reeves
4 Vespa
5 John Major
6 Achilles
7 Agar (Agar-Agar)
8 Pennsylvania
9 Edinburgh
10 Mills and Boon (Harlequin Mills and Boon)
11 *Dandy*
12 *The Blues Brothers*
13 1940s (accept 40s)
14 Maldives
15 Antwerp
16 Violin
17 Arnold
18 Doodles
19 Green
20 Alan Bennett

Round 33

1 Earl Grey, Assam and Ceylon are all varieties of which beverage?

2 According to the saying, having an obsessive preoccupation is like having a bee in your what?

3 In music, what *H* is a song in praise of God?

4 In science, a lunar month is a unit of time based on the motion of what around the Earth?

5 In film, complete the title of the 1987 movie starring Robin Williams: *Good Morning . . .* what?

6 In racing, what *J* is the name given to a professional who rides horses?

7 In pop music, complete the 1978 Rod Stewart song title: 'Do Ya Think I'm . . .' what?

8 In England, at what age can you marry without your parents' permission?

9 According to the nursery rhyme, 'Simple Simon met a pieman, going to the . . .' what?

10 By road, which is further from London: Aberdeen or Glasgow?

11 In football, AC Milan is a team in the domestic league of which European country?

12 What *S* is a book with blank pages that is used to keep newspaper cuttings, pictures and other memorable things?

13 In food, how is the technique of working dough by stretching and folding until it achieves the required consistency known?

14 In children's TV, is Sooty's girlfriend Soo a badger or a panda?

15 In TV, comedian Alan Davies stars in the drama *Jonathan . . .* who?

16 In the animal kingdom, what *S* is a mammal with a woolly coat, kept for its wool and meat?

17 In music, a harmonica is also known as a 'mouth . . .' what?

18 What do fortune tellers 'read' in the bottom of teacups, to see the future?

19 In maths, express one-fifth as a percentage.

20 In science, what *F* is a structure in which fuel such as coal, coke or oil is burned to produce heat?

Previous Total

1,000
800
600
450
300
200
100
50
20

Banked

Total

Answers	
1 Tea	**11** Italy
2 Bonnet	**12** Scrapbook
3 Hymn	**13** Kneading
4 Moon	**14** Panda
5 *Vietnam*	**15** *Creek*
6 Jockey	**16** Sheep
7 Sexy	**17** (Mouth) Organ
8 Eighteen	**18** Tea leaves
9 Fair	**19** 20 per cent
10 Aberdeen	**20** Furnace

Round 34

1 In money, what is the name of the British government's bank?

2 What is the flavour of the liqueur Tia Maria?

3 Southwark is a borough on the South Bank of which UK city?

4 In England, the pole outside a barber's shop was traditionally red and what colour?

5 In literature, complete the title of this Shakespeare play: *The Winter's . . .* what?

6 What is the literal meaning of the cinematic term '*film noir*'?

7 In religion, what N is a member of a religious community of women who has made life vows of poverty, chastity and obedience?

8 If a car park has a capacity of 200, how may cars are there if it is three-quarters full?

9 The wax from which insect is used in the manufacture of lipstick, candles and polishes?

10 In music, Brian Epstein was the manager of which famous Liverpool band in the 1960s?

11 In TV, Angus Deayton played Victor and Margaret's neighbour in which BBC sitcom?

12 In which country of the UK is Powis Castle?

13 In maths, if you bought eight dozen eggs, how many would you have?

14 In the Hans Christian Andersen story, who was tricked into parading naked in public?

15 What is the first name of US president George W. Bush's wife: Tipper or Laura?

16 Complete the title of the 1987 film starring Nicolas Cage: *Raising . . .* what?

17 In TV, on which of the Channel Islands was the detective series *Bergerac* set?

18 In nature, what *F* is a powder usually made by grinding the edible parts of cereal grains?

19 In politics, MPs who do not hold an office in government or opposition are referred to as '. . . [what]-benchers'?

20 In earth science, fresh water makes up what percentage of all water on the earth: 3, 13 or 30 per cent?

Previous Total

1,000

800

600

450

300

200

100

50

20

Banked

Total

Answers

1 The Bank of England
2 Coffee
3 London
4 White
5 *Tale*
6 Black film (do *not* accept dark film)
7 Nun (do *not* accept novice, as they haven't made life vows)
8 150
9 Bee
10 The Beatles
11 *One Foot in the Grave*
12 Wales
13 96 eggs
14 The emperor
15 Laura
16 *Arizona*
17 Jersey
18 Flour
19 Back-[benchers]
20 3 per cent

Round 35

1 In TV, which former docu-soap star now presents the BBC talent show *Star For a Night*?

2 In which country would you find the county of Galway?

3 In the Bible, how many sons did Jacob have?

4 At which athletics event did Jonathan Edwards set a new world record in 1995?

5 In which Russian city is the famous Red Square situated?

6 In the animal kingdom, is the 'Kori bustard' a bird or a large beetle?

7 In TV, who starred as Norman Stanley Fletcher in the sitcom *Porridge*?

8 In history, which country was Great Britain fighting during the first 'Opium War', in the nineteenth century?

9 In geography, which European country is unofficially known as Holland?

10 Which American intelligence organisation was investigated following the failure of the 'Bay of Pigs' invasion in 1961?

11 With which industry would you associate American Spike Lee: film or sport?

12 In the children's TV programme *Teletubbies*, what colour is Tinky Winky?

13 In nature, the common name for the plant that feeds on insects and small animals is a 'Venus . . .' what?

14 Horology is the art of making what: clocks or tools?

15 What G is a museum of art opened in New York in 1959?

16 With which football position are Seaman, Barthez and Van Der Gouw associated?

17 How is Sir Malcolm Sargent best known: as a conductor, explorer or actor?

18 In the human body, the windpipe, diaphragm and which pair of organs form the respiratory system?

19 Christchurch is the largest city on the South Island of which country?

20 What colour is the crown of the last hoop or wicket on a croquet field: red or yellow?

Previous Total

1,000

800

600

450

300

200

100

50

20

Banked

Total

Answers

1 Jane McDonald
2 Republic of Ireland (*accept* Ireland/Eire/ Southern Ireland)
3 Twelve
4 Triple jump (*accept* hop, step and jump; *do not accept* long jump)
5 Moscow
6 Bird
7 Ronnie Barker
8 China
9 The Netherlands
10 CIA
11 Film
12 Purple
13 (Venus) Fly trap
14 Clocks
15 Guggenheim
16 Goalkeepers (*accept* goalies)
17 Conductor
18 Lungs
19 New Zealand
20 Red

Round 36

1 With which band did Midge Ure have a UK hit single in 1981 with the song 'Vienna'?

2 In science, what name is given to the process of causing chemical change in a solution, using an electric current?

3 In TV, how many contestants were there at the start of the first UK series of *Big Brother*?

4 Which rock 'n' roll singer had a UK number-one single in 1981 with 'This Ole House'?

5 In food, which of the following is a type of bread: feta, pitta or pancetta?

6 The two main political parties in the United States are the Democratic Party and which other?

7 In literature, complete the title of Geoffrey Chaucer's collection of stories: *The Canterbury . . . what*?

8 In the Roman Catholic and Anglican Churches, what D is the name given to an ordained minister who ranks immediately below a priest?

9 In US politics, which president was re-elected in 1792: George Washington or Abraham Lincoln?

10 Who had a UK number-one hit single in 1986 with 'When The Going Gets Tough, The Tough Get Going'?

11 A poor urban settlement on the outskirts of a city is known as a '. . . [what] town'?

12 In food, finnan haddie is the Scottish name for which smoked fish?

13 In which country is the popular seaside resort and fishing port of Trouville?

14 In film, which trio starred in the 1937 comedy *A Day at the Races*?

15 In which continent is the River Limpopo?

16 In popular culture, which actor famously has 'Scotland Forever' and 'Mum and Dad' tattooed on his arm?

17 Leonard Bernstein wrote the music for which musical based on *Romeo and Juliet*?

18 In 1983, which famous actress began a fitness fad when her keep-fit video first appeared in the early 1980s?

19 In Rudyard Kipling's *The Jungle Book*, which animals brought up Mowgli as a child?

20 With which sport is Pat Eddery associated?

Previous Total

1,000
800
600
450
300
200
100
50
20

Banked

Total

Answers

1 Ultravox
2 Electrolysis
3 Ten
4 Shakin' Stevens (accept Shaky/ Michael Barrett)
5 Pitta
6 Republican (Party)
7 *Tales*
8 Deacon
9 George Washington
10 Billy Ocean (Leslie Sebastian Charles)
11 Shanty (town)
12 Haddock
13 France
14 Marx Brothers (accept Groucho, Chico and Harpo Marx/Julius Henry, Leonard and Adolph Marx)
15 Africa
16 Sean Connery
17 *West Side Story*
18 Jane Fonda
19 Wolves
20 Horse racing

Round 37

1 Which American actor portrayed the criminal Robert Stroud in the 1962 film *Birdman of Alcatraz*?

2 In pop music, the musician Damon Gough is otherwise known as Badly Drawn . . . what?

3 In geography, in which country of the UK would you find the River Ouse?

4 In film, Ralph Fiennes starred as a dying cartographer in which romantic drama?

5 In London, Poet's Corner is part of which religious building?

6 In the human body, in which organ would you find the glomerulus?

7 In literature, who wrote the 1974 novel *Tinker, Tailor, Soldier, Spy*?

8 What *L* is a city in eastern Egypt, on the east bank of the Nile?

9 Woodrow Wilson was president of the United States during which world war?

10 In cricket, what does 'lbw' stand for?

11 Architect Jorn Utzon designed which famous public building in Sydney?

12 Kurt Russell starred as a fireman in which 1991 film?

13 Etymology is the study of the origin of what?

14 Which leading Hollywood actress played the role of Karen Blixen in the 1985 film *Out of Africa*?

15 What *A* is the name given to one of the three main breeds of horse recognised by its superior beauty and elegance?

16 The Battle of Pinkie in 1547 was fought just to the east of which major Scottish city?

17 With which sport would you associate Niki Lauda?

18 In science, how many joules of energy does a 60-watt light bulb use per second?

19 What *M* is a word for a bacterium, derived from the Greek for 'little life'?

20 What is the capital of Finland?

Previous Total
1,000
800
600
450
300
200
100
50
20
Banked
Total

Answers

1 Burt Lancaster (Burton Stephen Lancaster)
2 Boy
3 England
4 *The English Patient*
5 Westminster Abbey
6 Kidney
7 John Le Carré (David John Moore Cornwell)
8 Luxor
9 (World War) One (accept First)
10 Leg before wicket
11 Sydney Opera House (accept Opera House)
12 *Backdraft*
13 Words (accept morphemes)
14 Meryl Streep (Mary Louise Streep)
15 Arab (accept Arabian)
16 Edinburgh
17 Formula One (accept motor racing)
18 60
19 Microbe
20 Helsinki

Round 38

1 Which country is the leading supplier of gold?

2 With which branch of the armed forces would you associate the Coldstream Guards, Green Howards and Blues and Royals?

3 What O is a three-act opera by Handel that shares its name with a popular holiday destination in Florida?

4 In which decade of the twentieth century did Persia become known as Iran?

5 Morpeth is the administrative centre of which northern county in the UK?

6 In religion, which A is the traditional founder of the Hebrew priesthood?

7 With which US sport would you associate Dennis Rodman?

8 Which religious relic does Indiana Jones attempt to find in the 1989 film *Indiana Jones and the Last Crusade*?

9 Roy Scheider played the lead role in which 1975 film, adapted from a Peter Benchley novel?

10 In TV, David Hyde Pierce plays Niles Crane in which American sitcom, set in Seattle?

11 T.Rex lead singer Mark Field was better known as what?

12 In boxing, which fellow Briton did Lennox Lewis defeat in a 1993 World Heavyweight Title fight?

13 In the animal kingdom, 'Manx' cats are native to which British island?

14 In modern literature, Salman Rushdie won the Booker Prize in 1981 for which novel?

15 In human biology, what J is a yellow discolouration of the skin caused by an excess of bile pigments in the blood?

16 Which musical hall of fame and museum is in Cleveland, Ohio?

17 In Shakespeare's play, who does Othello jealously kill when he sees Cassio in possession of her handkerchief?

18 Shrewsbury is a town in which UK county?

19 In which century did Henry VIII become head of the Church of England after breaking away from Rome?

20 Who starred as Holly Golightly in the 1961 movie *Breakfast at Tiffany's*?

Previous Total

1,000
800
600
450
300
200
100
50
20

Banked

Total

Answers

1 South Africa (Republic of South Africa)
2 Army
3 *Orlando*
4 1930s (1935)
5 Northumberland
6 Aaron
7 Basketball
8 The Holy Grail (accept San Grail/San Grael)
9 *Jaws*
10 *Frasier*
11 Marc Bolan
12 Frank Bruno
13 Isle of Man
14 *Midnight's Children*
15 Jaundice
16 Rock 'n' roll
17 Desdemona (accept his wife)
18 Shropshire
19 Sixteenth
20 Audrey Hepburn (Audrey Kathleen Ruston/Edda Kathleen van Heemstra Hepburn-Ruston)

Round 39

1 In which country was the actor Omar Sharif born?

2 In pre-decimal currency, how many farthings were there in a penny?

3 In sport, which London football club unexpectedly beat Liverpool in the 1988 FA Cup final?

4 In literature, in which century did Alfred, Lord Tennyson live and work?

5 Designer Robin Day is famous for developing stacking versions of which type of furniture?

6 In human biology, what name is given to the thin piece of skin that is found between the middle ear and outer ear?

7 In film, who produced *Midnight Express*, *Chariots of Fire* and *The Killing Fields*?

8 The Badminton Horse Trials in Gloucestershire are held in which month each year?

9 In which country was the diarist and naval administrator Samuel Pepys born?

10 For what do the initials ANC stand, when referring to the South African political organisation founded in 1912?

11 Which famous US basketball star appeared alongside Bugs Bunny in the 1996 film *Space Jam*?

12 In which decade were microwave ovens invented?

13 Which member of the *Popstars* band was revealed to have two children?

14 Complete the title of Jack London's 1903 novel: *The Call of the . . .* what?

15 Myxomatosis is a virus associated with which animal?

16 In Greek mythology, which Ethiopian princess was chained to a rock as a sacrifice to a sea-monster?

17 In the Bible, the name of which character from the Book of Genesis means 'life-giving'?

18 The video artist Steve . . . who won the 1999 Turner Prize for his film *Deadpan*?

19 In sport, a Greek shepherd called Spyridon Louis was the first-ever winner of which long-distance modern Olympic event in 1896?

20 In Moscow, Red Square is next to which famous citadel?

Previous Total

1,000

800

600

450

300

200

100

50

20

Banked

Total

Answers

1 Egypt	**11** Michael Jordan
2 Four	**12** 1940s (1947)
3 Wimbledon	**13** Kym (Kimberley; Kim Marsh; Kimberley Marsh)
4 Nineteenth century	
5 Chairs	
6 Ear drum (*accept* tympanic membrane)	**14** *Wild*
	15 Rabbit (*accept* hare)
7 David Puttnam	**16** Andromeda
8 May	**17** Eve
9 England (*accept* UK/ Britain)	**18** (Steve) McQueen
	19 Marathon
10 African National Congress	**20** The Kremlin

Round 40

1 In film, which comedian is associated with the catchphrase 'Another fine mess you've gotten us into'?

2 Bengali is the state language of which country?

3 Robert Wagner and Stephanie Powers starred as millionaire detectives in which 1980s US series?

4 In the nursery rhyme, what was the name of the piper's son who stole a pig and ran away?

5 According to the Bible, who committed the first murder?

6 What mathematical aid was patented by William Burroughs in 1885?

7 The father of which BBC2 presenter wrote the novel *The Mosquito Coast*?

8 In which country was the Akita dog originally bred?

9 In politics, which Denis was Chancellor of the Exchequer in Britain from 1974 to 1979?

10 What is the name of the cathedral-like railway station in New York City, which was opened in 1913?

11 What is the name of the son in the 1960s series *The Munsters*?

12 In which famous room was the Treaty of Versailles signed?

13 In literature, what is the nickname of the character Arthur Radley in Harper Lee's 1960 book *To Kill A Mockingbird*?

14 In children's TV, what name was given to the cartoon about vegetable escapees from a greengrocer's shop?

15 Which famous French fashion designer was nicknamed the 'enfant terrible de Paris' in the 1970s?

16 In the Old Testament, who pulled down the pillars of a house in Gaza, killing himself and 3,000 Philistines?

17 In which ocean are the Nicobar Islands?

18 Since the Norman Conquest, how many kings of England have been called Edward?

19 Which is the largest beetle native to Britain?

20 A string quartet usually consists of two violins, a viola and which instrument?

Previous Total

1,000

800

600

450

300

200

100

50

20

Banked

Total

Answers

1 Oliver Hardy (Laurel and Hardy)
2 Bangladesh
3 Hart To Hart
4 Tom (accept Tom, Tom)
5 Cain
6 Calculating machine (calculator)
7 Louis Theroux
8 Japan
9 Denis Healey
10 Grand Central Station

11 Eddie
12 The Hall of Mirrors
13 Boo (Boo Radley)
14 The Munch Bunch
15 Jean-Paul Gaultier
16 Samson
17 Indian
18 Eight
19 Stag beetle
20 Cello (accept violoncello)

Round 41

1 In space, which blue planet was discovered in 1846?

2 Brisbane is the capital of which Australian state?

3 In rugby union, how many players are there in the 'backs'?

4 The world's first large iron bridge was built in 1779 in Shropshire, across which river?

5 In the animal kingdom, which term is used to describe a black-and-white horse?

6 In pop music, which male artist had his first solo hit song with 'Spread a little Happiness' in 1982?

7 In food, which many-seeded fruit is the Christian symbol of the Resurrection?

8 In geography, in which North American country is the Slave river found?

9 In TV, who is the presenter daughter of Nanette Newman and film director Brian Forbes?

10 Sergio Leone's film *For A Few Dollars More* was the follow-up to which 1964 western starring Clint Eastwood?

11 Which Lerner and Loewe musical became associated with President Kennedy's thousand days in office?

12 In TV, what is the name of the US drama series which is set in County General Hospital?

13 Which 1995 cult film features the mysterious character Keyser Soze?

14 In nature, the seed pods of cotton plants are called what?

15 In geography, Bridgetown is the capital of which West Indian country?

16 In history, what present-day country ruled the Ottoman Empire?

17 What sort of lung was invented by doctors Philip Drinker and Louis Shaw in 1927?

18 In film, which famous singer starred opposite Nick Nolte in the 1991 movie *The Prince of Tides*?

19 Which former pop star presented the 1980s children's cookery show *Eggs and Baker*?

20 In the 1540s, Michelangelo was appointed architect of which famous church in Rome, but died before its completion?

Previous Total
1,000
800
600
450
300
200
100
50
20
Banked
Total

Answers

1 Neptune	**11** *Camelot*
2 Queensland	**12** *ER*
3 Seven	**13** *The Usual Suspects*
4 (River) Severn	**14** Bolls
5 Piebald	**15** Barbados
6 Sting (accept Gordon Sumner)	**16** Turkey
7 Pomegranate	**17** Iron lung
8 Canada	**18** Barbra Streisand
9 Emma Forbes	**19** Cheryl Baker
10 *A Fistful Of Dollars* (accept *Per un Pugno di Dollari*)	**20** St Peter's

Round 42

1 In the nursery rhyme 'Rub a Dub Dub', how many men were in the tub?

2 In literature, from which country does Hellenistic writing come?

3 What *P* is the name of a person who operates puppets?

4 In science, the two poles of a magnet are known as north and what?

5 In the animal kingdom, which very large mammal has a long, muscular trunk and can be either African or Indian?

6 According to tradition, which popular colour for a wedding dress symbolises virtue and innocence?

7 What type of food is Edam?

8 In biology, how many senses do humans traditionally have?

9 In religion, complete the name of this commemorative day in the Christian calendar: Palm . . . what?

10 In music, a harmonica is also known as a mouth . . . what?

11 Michael Jackson gave a speech to the Union of which university in March 2001?

12 If there are twelve bottles of wine in a case, and you need 36 bottles for a party, how many cases must you buy?

13 In pastimes, what is made by repeatedly dipping a prepared wick into wax?

14 In football, Barcelona is a team in the domestic league of which European country?

15 In fashion, in the saying 'top hat and tails', to which item of clothing does the word 'tails' refer?

16 In food, tortilla is a type of bread originating from which North American country?

17 In pop music, from which country did the Spice Girls come?

18 From which London station does the Eurostar leave?

19 What is the popular name for the type of gas used in riot control, because of the effects it has on the eyes?

20 In the USA, AFL stands for the American Federation of . . . what?

Previous Total

1,000
800
600
450
300
200
100
50
20

Banked

Total

Answers

1 Three	**12** Three
2 Greece	**13** A candle
3 Puppeteer	**14** Spain
4 South	**15** Jacket (accept coat)
5 Elephant	**16** Mexico
6 White	**17** Britain (accept
7 Cheese	England/UK)
8 Five	**18** Waterloo (do not
9 Sunday	accept Ashford)
10 (Mouth) organ	**19** Tear gas
11 Oxford	**20** Labour

Round 43

1 Which nineteenth-century Danish author is famous for the fairy tales *The Little Mermaid* and *The Ugly Duckling*?

2 What sort of animal is a barbel: a monkey or a fish?

3 According to the saying, you should be careful not to throw what out with the bath water?

4 In geometry, how many sides of equal length does an isosceles triangle have?

5 In film, what is the stage name of Carlos Estevez, star of *Platoon* and *Hotshots*?

6 In food, what is the main meat ingredient in moussaka?

7 In language, Afrikaans is one of the official languages of which country?

8 If an aerosol can contains propellants other than CFCs, it often has the words 'ozone . . .' what printed on it?

9 In maths, how many grams are there in 2.5 kilograms?

10 In which country is the resort of Benidorm located?

11 What type of car features prominently in the 1969 film *The Italian Job*?

12 In maths, express three-quarters as a percentage.

13 Is the first name of defeated US presidential candidate Al Gore short for Albert or Alistair?

14 In classical music, which word comes from the Italian word meaning 'alone' and denotes a piece of music that should only be played by one performer?

15 In the TV comedy *Only Fools and Horses*, which character had the nickname Del Boy?

16 In geography, which ocean has the larger area: the Atlantic or the Pacific?

17 In human biology, what *S* is a series of small bones that protects the spinal cord and allows the body to twist and turn?

18 In nature, what is the name of the soft-bodied, legless fly larvae that are often found in decaying matter?

19 When laying a table, should cutlery for the first course be on the outside or the inside of a place setting?

20 In the musical *Grease*, what type of vehicle was being sung about in the song 'Greased Lightning'?

Previous Total

1,000

800

600

450

300

200

100

50

20

Banked

Total

Answers

1 Hans Christian Andersen
2 Fish
3 The baby
4 Two
5 Charlie Sheen
6 Lamb
7 South Africa
8 Friendly (accept safe)
9 2,500 grams
10 Spain
11 Mini Cooper (accept Mini)
12 75 per cent
13 Albert
14 Solo
15 Derek Trotter (Derek)
16 Pacific
17 Spine (accept spinal column)
18 Maggots
19 Outside
20 A car

Round 44

1 In geography, what C is a country in south-east Asia, situated between Thailand and Vietnam?

2 What is the path of a planet around its sun called?

3 In which county is the district of Torbay: Devon or Somerset?

4 Which war, involving Britain, took place in 1982?

5 In politics, how many general election victories did John Major achieve as prime minister?

6 In pop music, which artist released an album entitled *The Immaculate Collection* in 1990?

7 In food, what C is the name for a selection of raw vegetables served with a dip?

8 In which country was the actress and model Isabella Rossellini born?

9 Which US civil rights leader came to prominence in 1956, by leading and organising a bus boycott?

10 Which American footballer and movie star is nicknamed 'Juice'?

11 What is the name of the outer hairy cellulose covering of seeds and grains, commonly associated with coconuts?

12 In which country did the ancient language of Sanskrit originate?

13 In TV, *Perry* . . . who was the title and main character of the US legal drama of the 1950s and 1990s?

14 One of the earliest types of water pumps was known as an Archimedes . . . what?

15 In sport, what is the surname of Paul, the English footballer who joined the Italian club Lazio in 1992?

16 In maths, what is 99 plus 199?

17 In space exploration, how many nations have contributed to the construction of the International Space Station: sixteen or 60?

18 What *P* is the name of the Italian fashion house founded in Milan in 1913?

19 In which decade did Nirvana have a UK top-ten hit single with 'Come As You Are'?

20 What was the surname of Benjamin, the US scientist, author and philanthropist who invented the bifocal lens in 1784?

Previous Total

1,000

800

600

450

300

200

100

50

20

Banked

Total

Answers

1 Cambodia
2 Orbit
3 Devon
4 Falklands War
5 One
6 Madonna
7 *Crudités*
8 Italy
9 Martin Luther King (Jnr)
10 O. J. Simpson (Orenthal James Simpson)
11 The husk (*accept* coir)
12 India
13 *Mason*
14 Screw
15 Gascoigne
16 298
17 Sixteen
18 Prada
19 1990s (1992)
20 Franklin

Round 45

1 The term 'hibernation' refers to an animal's period of inactivity in what type of climate: warm or cold?

2 In food, what *M* is a fiery soup whose name means 'pepper water'?

3 In geography, Hertford is the administrative centre of which county in the UK?

4 According to the title, who . . . *Calls* in the J. B. Priestley play?

5 Singer Adam Rickitt, who had a 1999 UK top-ten hit single with 'I Breathe Again', was formerly an actor in which TV soap opera?

6 What *P* is the small dried berry of the pepper plant?

7 Who played the character Mickey Saxe in the 1986 film *Hannah and Her Sisters*?

8 In history, in which century did the American War of Independence take place?

9 In the TV comedy *Frasier*, what is Martin's dog called?

10 Which BBC children's TV programme began each episode with the words 'Here is a house. Here is a door. Windows – one, two, three, four'?

11 With which sport would you associate Rod Laver?

12 Which 1990s boy band became the first group since The Beatles to have four consecutive UK number ones?

13 In science, what *D* is the name given to quantities of information that are processed by a computer?

14 In Australia, which is further east: Brisbane or Melbourne?

15 In which country was silent film actor and comic Buster Keaton born?

16 In literature, in Spenser's *The Faerie Queene*, published in the sixteenth century, what type of creature was Orgoglio: a giant or an elf?

17 In science, hexose is a simple sugar with how many carbon atoms?

18 In TV, actor Stephen Tompkinson starred in which award-winning comedy as a ruthless reporter?

19 In the children's Mr Men stories, what colour is Mr Bounce?

20 In history, in which century did Abraham Lincoln die?

Previous Total

( )

1,000

800

600

450

300

200

100

50

20

Banked

Total

Answers

1 Cold
2 Mulligatawny
3 Hertfordshire
4 *An Inspector*
5 *Coronation Street*
6 Peppercorn
7 Woody Allen
8 Eighteenth (century)
9 Eddie
10 *Play School*
11 Tennis
12 Take That
13 Data
14 Brisbane
15 United States (accept US/USA/America/ United States of America)
16 Giant
17 Six
18 *Drop The Dead Donkey*
19 Yellow
20 Nineteenth

Round 46

1 In which American sport was Mickey Mantle famous?

2 In geography, in which county is the cathedral city of Chichester?

3 In music, the Savoy Operas refer to the operettas of which musical duo?

4 Donna . . . who had a UK top-ten hit single in 1976 with the disco song 'Love To Love You Baby'?

5 In which sport do England play Scotland for the Calcutta Cup: rugby league or rugby union?

6 In warfare, bis sulphide is also known as what type of gas, first used in the First World War?

7 In biology, the epidermis is the outer layer of which part of the body?

8 In geography, in which country would you find the Ural mountains and the Ural river?

9 Which *Dirty Dancing* actor had a 1988 UK hit single with 'She's Like the Wind'?

10 Which American city housed the first skyscraper buildings: Chicago or Los Angeles?

11 In sport, with which British boxer did Evander Holyfield draw in a 1999 World Title fight?

12 In UK politics, the Representation of the People Act of 1928 gave the vote to women over what age?

13 In food, what type of food is the Turkish dish baklava: a stew or a sweetmeat?

14 In geography, the village of Marathon is located in which European country?

15 In which country was the rock singer Chris Rea born?

16 Bournville is a residential and industrial district in which British city?

17 In which South American country is Punta Arenas, one of the southernmost cities in the world?

18 Does the Geffrye Museum in east London specialise in exhibiting toys, clothes or furniture?

19 In sport, what is the maximum number of players allowed in a game of croquet?

20 In pop music, which group had a UK number-one single with 'Make it Easy on Yourself' in 1965: The Walker Brothers or The Everly Brothers?

Previous Total

1,000
800
600
450
300
200
100
50
20
Banked
Total

Answers

1 Baseball
2 West Sussex
3 Gilbert and Sullivan
4 Summer (LaDonna Gaines)
5 (Rugby) Union
6 Mustard gas
7 Skin
8 Russia
9 Patrick Swayze (Patrick Wayne Swayze)
10 Chicago
11 Lennox Lewis
12 21
13 Sweetmeat
14 Greece
15 England (accept UK/ Great Britain)
16 Birmingham
17 Chile
18 Furniture
19 Four
20 The Walker Brothers

Round 47

1 In film, complete the title of the 1987 Richard Attenborough film about the life of South African activist Steve Biko: Cry . . . what?

2 In UK geography, on which island off the coast of Wales would you find Beaumaris Castle?

3 In science, what invention of the 1950s contains thousands of tiny transistors on a piece of material smaller than a stamp?

4 In pop music, which former member of Wham! released the 1990 song 'Shake'?

5 In medicine, which blood-sucking creatures are used to extract blood and reduce severe bruising?

6 In sport, who succeeded Terry Venables as England's football coach on 1 July 1996?

7 In Greek mythology, Orpheus's wife, Eurydice, died from the bite of what kind of reptile?

8 Which type of music did pianist Jelly Roll Morton claim to have invented?

9 In athletics, with which event would you associate arch-rivals Steve Backley and Jan Zelezny?

10 Which Italian city is known as Venezia by locals?

11 In the TV comedy The Royle Family, which character is the mother of David Keanu Ronan Best?

12 In human biology, what P describes the soft, moist matter beneath the enamel and dentine of a tooth?

13 In rugby league, how many points is a drop-goal worth?

14 In which American state is the winter-sports resort of Aspen?

15 In marine life, the terms 'cycloid' and 'placoid' refer to which part of a fish?

16 In music, Schubert composed the song 'Death and the . . .' what in 1817?

17 In the Bible, how many fish did Jesus use to feed the five thousand?

18 In which country of the UK is Radnor Forest?

19 In film, who starred in the title role of the 1992 comedy *My Cousin Vinny*?

20 In the animal kingdom, what is the name given to a group of dolphins?

Previous Total

1,000

800

600

450

300

200

100

50

20

Banked

Total

Answers

1 (Cry) *Freedom*
2 Anglesey (Ynys Mon)
3 Microchip (accept integrated circuit/ silicon chip)
4 Andrew Ridgeley
5 Leeches
6 Glenn Hoddle
7 Snake
8 Jazz
9 Javelin
10 Venice
11 Denise Best (née Royle; accept Denise)
12 Pulp
13 One
14 Colorado
15 Scales
16 'Maiden'
17 Two
18 Wales
19 Joe Pesci
20 Pod

Round 48

1 Which 1961 film, written by Arthur Miller, starred Marilyn Monroe and Clark Gable?

2 In art, in the title of the famous portrait by Frans Hals, what is the Cavalier doing?

3 In William Shakespeare's *Hamlet*, what relation is Ophelia to Laertes?

4 Which one of the following is the name of a military aircraft: Tigercat or Wolfcat?

5 A 'get' is a bill of divorce in which religion?

6 In ancient history, the Punic Wars took place in the second and third centuries BC, between the Carthaginians and which empire?

7 In geography, the island of Staffa off the coast of Scotland is part of which chain of islands?

8 Hailie Selassie became emperor of where in 1930?

9 The university city of Berkeley is in which American state?

10 The French writer and soldier Cyrano de Bergerac was born in which century?

11 In medicine, a phlebotomy is an incision into what *V*?

12 In literature, what is the name of the weaver character in Shakespeare's *A Midsummer Night's Dream*?

13 Which Britpop group released the album *Moseley Shoals* in 1996?

14 The Khyber Pass connects Afghanistan to which country?

15 The 1950 novel *A Town Like Alice* is set against the backdrop of which war?

16 Which American beat Arnaud Clement to win the men's singles at the Australian Open tennis championship in January 2001?

17 In which 1994 British film does John Hannah's character read the W. H. Auden poem 'Funeral Blues'?

18 In modern history, which Soviet leader published his first major work in 1914, called *Marxism and the Nationality Question*?

19 In jazz, which instrument was big band leader Buddy Rich famous for playing?

20 In music, Mungo . . . who had a 1970 UK number-one hit single with 'In the Summertime'?

Previous Total

1,000

800

600

450

300

200

100

50

20

Banked

Total

Answers

1 *The Misfits*
2 Laughing
3 Sister (*accept* sibling)
4 Tigercat
5 Judaism (*accept* Jewish religion)
6 Roman (Empire)
7 Hebrides (*accept* Inner Hebrides, *but not* Outer Hebrides or Western Isles)
8 Ethiopia (*accept* Abyssinia)
9 California
10 Seventeenth (1619)

11 Vein
12 Bottom
13 Ocean Colour Scene
14 Pakistan
15 Second World War (*accept* World War II)
16 Andre Agassi
17 *Four Weddings and a Funeral*
18 Joseph Stalin (*accept* Stalin/Iosif Stalin)
19 Drums
20 (Mungo) Jerry

Round 49

1 In science, the point when the moon is at its closest to Earth is known as what?

2 For what do the D and H stand in D. H. Lawrence?

3 Which member of Boyzone married Yvonne Connolly in 1998?

4 What was the name of the tax, abolished in 1640, raised by English monarchs in times of emergency to strengthen the navy?

5 In which African country would you find Mombasa?

6 Which Russian composer wrote *Swan Lake* and *The Nutcracker Suite*?

7 In January 2000, which former German Chancellor resigned as honorary chairman of the Christian Democratic Union Party in the wake of a corruption scandal?

8 Which Christmas accessory was invented by Tom Smith in the 1800s?

9 The comic actor Dudley Moore is also known for playing jazz on which instrument?

10 Which canal in Central America allows ships to travel between the Pacific and Atlantic oceans?

11 Where in Sweden is the Nobel Prize Foundation located?

12 Otology is the study of the what?

13 Which sculptor, with the first name Henry, was born the son of a miner in Castleford, Yorkshire in 1898?

14 Which *T* was the president of Yugoslavia who established an independent Communist state in 1945?

15 In the Bible, what instrument was David playing when Saul hurled a spear at him?

16 Benjamin Disraeli and William Gladstone were prime ministers during which century?

17 Which London landmark was designed by Richard Rogers and consists of a Teflon canopy suspended on twelve masts?

18 What is the name of the dramatist who wrote the play *The Real Inspector Hound* and the screenplay for *Shakespeare in Love*?

19 What is the name of the cat character who appeared on *Dandy's* first cover?

20 In rugby union, what nationality is the 2001 British Lions coach Graham Henry?

Previous Total

1,000

800

600

450

300

200

100

50

20

Banked

Total

Answers

1 Perigee	**11** Stockholm
2 David Herbert	**12** Ears
3 Ronan Keating	**13** Henry Moore
4 Ship money	**14** Tito (Josip Broz Tito)
5 Kenya	**15** Harp
6 Tchaikovsky (*accept* Peter Ilyich Tchaikovsky)	**16** Nineteenth (century)
	17 The Millennium Dome (*accept* The Dome)
7 Helmut Kohl	**18** Tom Stoppard
8 Christmas cracker	**19** Korky (Korky the Cat)
9 Piano	**20** New Zealander
10 Panama Canal	

Round 50

1 According to the saying, wasting energy on a lost cause is like flogging a dead . . . what?

2 What would you be lacking if you were dehydrated?

3 Complete the line of this song from a famous musical: 'The hills are alive with the sound of . . .' what?

4 What is the name of the highest mountain peak in the world?

5 In the children's stories by Jean de Brunhoff, what kind of animal is Babar?

6 In the Bible, which future king of Israel killed Goliath?

7 In the animal kingdom, how many cells does a unicellular organism have?

8 What *L* is the name for the type of nonsense verse which shares its name with an Irish town?

9 In money, what kind of card is referred to as plastic money?

10 Add together the number of sides that three triangles have in total.

11 In science, which element appears in charcoal, coal and diamonds?

12 In food, 'nouvelle cuisine' was developed in which country?

13 In the animal kingdom, what O is an edible mollusc that is known to produce pearls?

14 In human biology, which hollow, muscular organ has contractions that pump blood throughout the body?

15 In geography, Tiananmen Square is in which country?

16 The word 'tripartite' means divided into how many parts?

17 In which European country would you find the resort of Marbella?

18 In science, on the Richter scale, which of the following is classed as 'catastrophic': one or twelve?

19 In which country would you kiss the Blarney stone?

20 In politics, Margaret Beckett is associated with which party?

Previous Total

1,000
800
600
450
300
200
100
50
20

Banked

Total

Answers

1 Horse	**11** Carbon
2 Water (accept fluid[s]/liquid[s])	**12** France
	13 Oyster
3 'Music'	**14** Heart
4 (Mount) Everest	**15** China
5 Elephant	**16** Three
6 David	**17** Spain
7 One	**18** Twelve
8 Limerick	**19** Ireland (accept Eire/ Republic of Ireland)
9 Credit card (accept debit card)	**20** Labour (accept New Labour)
10 Nine	

Round 51

1 Friesian and Jersey are types of what?

2 In human biology, what is the name for the reflex by which the eyelids close quickly to protect or lubricate the eye?

3 Which famous waxwork modeller was born in 1761 in Switzerland?

4 What S is a species of bird whose name means 'rapid' or 'fast moving'?

5 On a 24-hour clock, what time is it four hours after midday?

6 Which TV comedy of the 1970s and 80s originally featured 'The Fonz'?

7 In history, what type of creature did coal miners use to provide a warning of low oxygen?

8 In history, Neil Armstrong was the first human to set foot where?

9 Kleptomania is a compulsion to do what?

10 Officer Dibble and Benny the Ball were characters in which cartoon series, first shown in the 1960s?

11 In food, guacamole is a dip or spread which originates from which country?

12 In racket sports, which is heavier: a badminton racket or a tennis racket?

13 Which American film actor has the nicknames 'The Italian Stallion' and 'Sly'?

14 What *F* is a large bird with pink feathers, webbed feet, a long neck and long, thin legs?

15 In pop music, with which singer is Art Garfunkel most associated?

16 In geography, Arkansas and Delaware are states in which country?

17 What *M* is a species of weasel that has a rich brown fur used in fashion?

18 Toto was the name of Dorothy's dog in which 1939 film?

19 In TV, *Fawlty Towers* was written by Connie Booth and which co-star?

20 In nature, what type of area would be described as arid: a dry or wet area?

Previous Total

1,000

800

600

450

300

200

100

50

20

Banked

Total

Answers

1 Cattle (*accept cow*)
2 Blinking (*accept blink reflex/winking/nictitating*)
3 Madame Tussaud (Marie Tussaud Grosholtz)
4 Swift
5 1600 (hours)
6 *Happy Days*
7 Bird (*accept canary*)
8 On the moon
9 Steal (*accept thieve*)
10 *Top Cat* (*accept Boss Cat*)
11 Mexico
12 Tennis
13 Sylvester Stallone
14 Flamingo
15 Paul Simon
16 United States (*accept US/USA/America/United States of America*)
17 Mink
18 *The Wizard of Oz*
19 John Cleese
20 Dry

Round 52

1 In geography, which European country's name means 'low-lying land'?

2 Which of the Minogue sisters played Emma Jackson on the Australian soap opera *Home and Away*?

3 In politics, in which year did Tony Blair become prime minister?

4 In medicine, tinnitus affects which organ of the body?

5 In England, which city is further north: Leicester or Nottingham?

6 In film, which actress won a Bafta and an Oscar in 2001 for her leading role in *Erin Brockovich*?

7 What is the name of the electronic device which treasure-hunters use to pinpoint the location of underground metal?

8 Mortality rate is usually recorded as the number of what per thousand population per year?

9 In professional boxing, which is heavier: a bantamweight or a super-bantamweight?

10 In the animal kingdom, what term is used for animals with four feet?

11 In the Bible, who, as a baby, was placed in a basket among the rushes in the Nile?

12 Which UK radio station transmits *Woman's Hour*?

13 In human biology, what *T* is another name for the shin bone?

14 In the Royal Navy, what type of ship is HMS *Invincible*: a destroyer or an aircraft carrier?

15 With which sport would you associate the New Zealander Jonah Lomu?

16 How many seconds are there in a third of a minute?

17 In clothing, on which part of the body would you wear a 'jabot': your neck or your head?

18 In the animal kingdom, what S is the smallest breed of British pony?

19 In American football, former Chicago Bears player William Perry was nicknamed after which kitchen appliance?

20 In film, actor David Prowse is famous for playing the Green Cross Code Man and which *Star Wars* character?

Answers

1 The Netherlands (*accept* Holland)
2 Dannii (Dannielle Jane Minogue)
3 1997
4 Ear
5 Nottingham
6 Julia Roberts (Julie Fiona Roberts)
7 Metal detector
8 Deaths (accept people dying/fatalities)
9 Super-bantamweight
10 Quadrupeds
11 Moses
12 Radio 4
13 Tibia
14 Aircraft carrier
15 Rugby union (*accept* rugby; *do not accept* rugby league)
16 20
17 Neck
18 Shetland
19 'The Fridge' (refrigerator)
20 Darth Vader

Previous Total

1,000
800
600
450
300
200
100
50
20

Banked

Total

Round 53

1 In nature, what *F* is the name given to the group of organisms that includes mushrooms and toadstools?

2 In Japan, what is 'ikebana': a form of martial art or flower arranging?

3 What is the name for a military force consisting of mounted troops trained to fight from horseback?

4 What *P* is the name given to the process of searching for gold using a circular dish in a stream of water?

5 Which Mr Men character talks all the time?

6 In music, the song 'Oh, Pretty Woman' was a UK number-one hit in 1964 for Roy . . . who?

7 In history, South African prime minister Doctor Malan instituted which system meaning 'apartness' or 'separate development'?

8 In the animal kingdom, is a cat a carnivore or a herbivore?

9 Which Boyzone singer's second child was born in February 2001 and named Marie?

10 Which fictional doctor, created by Hugh Lofting, was able to understand the language of animals?

11 In which decade of the twentieth century was the aerosol can invented?

12 In which ocean are the Falkland Islands situated?

13 In nature, wolves, jackals and coyotes are all from which family of animals?

14 In science, what *H* is a chemical element that is always present in acidic compounds?

15 What is the name of the system, similar to radar, which detects underwater objects by reflected sound?

16 With which group did Gerry Marsden have a UK number-one single in 1963 with the song 'You'll Never Walk Alone'?

17 In nature, what is the natural habitat of the halibut: fresh or salt water?

18 In UK politics, who was on the throne when Labour won the 1950 general election?

19 What *A* is a group of islands in the North Atlantic Ocean settled by the Portuguese in the fifteenth century?

20 In which English county is the town of Basildon?

Previous Total

1,000

800

600

450

300

200

100

50

20

Banked

Total

Answers

1 Fungi (accept fungus)
2 Flower arranging
3 Cavalry
4 Panning
5 Mister Chatterbox
6 Orbison
7 Apartheid
8 Carnivore
9 Ronan Keating
10 Doctor Dolittle
11 1920s (1926)
12 Atlantic
13 Dogs (accept Canidae/canine)
14 Hydrogen
15 Sonar (accept ASDIC)
16 Gerry And The Pacemakers (accept The Pacemakers)
17 Salt (water)
18 George VI
19 Azores
20 Essex

Round 54

1 What C is the name given to the high-ranking officials of the Roman Catholic Church who are also given the title of 'Eminence'?

2 In pop music, which actress and singer had a UK number-one in 1980 with 'Xanadu'?

3 In music, the tango, samba and bossa nova all originated in which continent?

4 What B was the name the Romans gave to the tribes who invaded their empire from the north-east?

5 Which fictional detective has been played by actors Basil Rathbone and Peter Cushing?

6 In the USA, which state uses the postal abbreviation 'WA'?

7 In geography, the constitutional republic of India consists of how many states: fifteen or 25?

8 In TV, in which decade was the sitcom *Up Pompeii* first shown on British TV?

9 In sport, which British woman athlete won the Olympic 400 metres hurdles gold medal in Barcelona in 1992?

10 In pop music, actor Richard E. Grant starred in which 1997 film alongside the Spice Girls?

11 Which language has also been called the speech of Canaan and Judaea?

12 Which city was the capital of Finland until 1812: Oulu or Turku?

13 In which 1999 film did Johnny Depp play a detective hunting a headless horseman?

14 In music, which Liverpool pop legends had their first UK number-one single with 'From Me to You' in 1963?

15 In geography, which is the largest of the Canary Islands?

16 What was the name of the children's game show in which presenter Christopher Biggins's catchphrase was 'Safari, So Goody'?

17 In which continent is Lake Victoria?

18 In sport, which famous English footballer wore the number-seven shirt during the 2000 to 2001 season for Manchester United?

19 Admiral Nelson lost his eye and arm on which side of his body?

20 In the animal kingdom, what *H* is the name given to a new-born alligator?

Previous Total

1,000

800

600

450

300

200

100

50

20

Banked

Total

Answers

1 Cardinals (do not accept curia)	**11** Hebrew
2 Olivia Newton John	**12** Turku
3 South America	**13** *Sleepy Hollow*
4 Barbarians	**14** The Beatles
5 Sherlock Holmes	**15** Tenerife
6 Washington	**16** *On Safari*
7 25	**17** Africa
8 1960s (1969)	**18** David Beckham (accept Beckham)
9 Sally Gunnell	**19** Right
10 *Spice World*	**20** Hatchling

Round 55

1 In science, *Sputnik One* was the name of the first what?

2 In geography, what is the largest county in the Republic of Ireland?

3 Christopher . . . who won an Oscar for his role in the 1978 film *The Deer Hunter*?

4 In history, the battles of Bull Run and Gettysburg took place during which civil war?

5 In sport, which famous British boxer is nicknamed 'the Prince'?

6 In literature, from which town did Shakespeare's *Merry Wives* come?

7 In film, complete the title of the 1962 thriller starring Frank Sinatra: *The Manchurian* . . . what?

8 In geography, in which European country is the city of Padua?

9 In literature, which of J. R. R. Tolkien's books was published in three volumes?

10 The Palio is a race in Siena involving which type of animal?

11 In which American city was Martin Luther King assassinated in 1968?

12 The 1961 film *Breakfast at Tiffany's* starred George . . . who as Paul Varjak?

13 In nature, what type of animal is a pied wagtail?

14 In fashion, the level to which a skirt or dress hangs is referred to as the 'hem-. . .' what?

15 In TV, in which school was Mrs McCluskey the headmistress?

16 Which Lincolnshire town on the River Witham is adjacent to the A1 and is the birthplace of Margaret Thatcher?

17 In astrology, if your birthday falls on 1 March, under which sign of the zodiac were you born?

18 What was the surname of Alphonse, the notorious Chicago gangster born in Brooklyn in 1899 who died in 1947?

19 In film, who starred as Jane Hudson in the 1962 movie *What Ever Happened to Baby Jane*?

20 In biology, what *B* is a word used to describe the division of something into two halves?

Previous Total

1,000
800
600
450
300
200
100
50
20

Banked

Total

Answers

1 Artificial satellite (accept satellite/ Russian satellite)
2 Cork
3 Walken
4 American Civil War
5 Naseem Hamed
6 Windsor
7 *Candidate*
8 Italy
9 *The Lord of the Rings*
10 Horse
11 Memphis
12 Peppard (accept George Peppard)
13 Bird
14 (Hem-)line
15 Grange Hill
16 Grantham
17 Pisces
18 Capone (Al Capone)
19 Bette Davis
20 Bisection (accept bisecting/bisect)

Round 56

1 In theatre, Grace Stansfield was the real name of which 1930s and 40s Lancashire singer and comedienne?

2 In Greek myth, Icarus had wings of wax and what?

3 In film, which *Friends* actress co-starred with Jim Carrey in the 1994 comedy *Ace Ventura, Pet Detective*?

4 Who wrote *Howard's End* and *A Passage To India*?

5 In theatre, which Gilbert and Sullivan light opera, first produced in 1879, features the song 'I am the Very Model of a Modern Major-General'?

6 In pop music, which ex-member of the Commodores released the year 2000 album entitled *Renaissance*?

7 In which European capital city would you find the Theatre of Dionysus?

8 In Formula One, in which country is the Albert Park racetrack?

9 In TV, who stars as Carrie Bradshaw in the US comedy series *Sex and the City*?

10 What Z is a German term, meaning 'spirit-time', which is used to suggest the general mood or spirit of an era?

11 In the Bible, what did Matthew collect for the Romans before becoming a disciple?

12 In pop music, which singer's 1983 UK hit album was entitled *An Innocent Man*?

13 If a clock loses three minutes a day, how many days will it take for it to lose an hour?

14 In literature, who wrote *The Secret Life of Salvador Dalí*, published in 1944?

15 In sport, which Spanish football club won the Champions League in 1998 and 2000?

16 Who played the character Henry Gondorff in the 1973 film *The Sting*?

17 In travel, which city in New Zealand has a parliamentary building known as 'The Beehive'?

18 In Shakespeare's play *Romeo and Juliet*, who does Paris offer to marry?

19 In pop music, Ian Broudie is the lead singer of which Liverpool-based band?

20 What *B* is the name for the upward force exerted by a fluid on a body immersed in it?

Previous Total

1,000

800

600

450

300

200

100

50

20

Banked

Total

Answers

1 Gracie Fields
2 Feathers
3 Courteney Cox (accept Courteney Cox-Arquette)
4 E. M. Forster (Edward Morgan Forster)
5 *The Pirates of Penzance*
6 Lionel Richie
7 Athens
8 Australia
9 Sarah Jessica Parker
10 Zeitgeist
11 Taxes (accept money)
12 Billy Joel (William Martin Joel)
13 20
14 Salvador Dalí (Salvador Felipe Jacinto Dalí y Domenech)
15 Real Madrid
16 Paul Newman (Paul Leonard Newman)
17 Wellington
18 Juliet
19 The Lightning Seeds
20 Buoyancy

Round 57

1 Which US sport features in Don DeLillo's 1972 novel *End Zone*?

2 In art, which sculptor's Trewyn Studio in St Ives, Cornwall, is now a memorial museum to her?

3 What was the first new town designated under the New Towns Act of 1946?

4 In the animal kingdom, what *A* is the name of the heaviest living snake?

5 In geography, which city is the chief sea port of Cuba?

6 Who played James Bond in the 1979 film *Moonraker*?

7 In art, Botticelli's works *The Birth of Venus* and *Primavera* hang in the Uffizi Gallery in which Italian city?

8 Lanolin is fatty matter from the wool of which animal?

9 Which children's TV series about a 5ft tall magical robot was produced by former Monkee Mickey Dolenz?

10 The Protestant and Roman Catholic cathedrals in Armagh are both dedicated to which saint?

11 Which 1876 Mark Twain novel tells the tale of an orphan growing up on the Mississippi?

12 Which emperor was defeated by Wellington at the Battle of Waterloo?

13 How are the Conservative MPs Nicholas and Ann Winterton related?

14 In music, with which song did The Animals have a 1964 UK number-one hit single?

15 In geography, in which county in southern England is the market town of Aylesbury?

16 Which Scottish actor portrayed Nick Leeson in the 1999 film *Rogue Trader*?

17 In literature, which author wrote the children's book *The Happy Prince and Other Tales*?

18 Which former Master of the Royal Mint appeared on the reverse of the old one-pound note?

19 On the coast of which ocean is the port and holiday resort of Acapulco?

20 Which children's book, made into a film in 1999, tells the tale of a human family who adopt a mouse as their son?

Previous Total

1,000
800
600
450
300
200
100
50
20
Banked
Total

Answers

1 American football
2 Barbara Hepworth
3 Stevenage
4 Anaconda
5 Havana
6 Roger Moore (Roger George Moore)
7 Florence
8 Sheep
9 *Metal Mickey*
10 (Saint) Patrick
11 *The Adventures of Tom Sawyer* (accept *Tom Sawyer*)
12 Napoleon (accept Napoleon Bonaparte/ Napoleon I)
13 Husband and wife (accept married, etc.)
14 'House of the Rising Sun'
15 Buckinghamshire
16 Ewan McGregor (Ewan Gordon McGregor)
17 Oscar Wilde (Oscar Fingal O'Flahertie Wills Wilde)
18 Sir Isaac Newton
19 Pacific
20 *Stuart Little*

Round 58

1 What *R* is the name of the list of ingredients and procedure required for preparing a meal?

2 In sport, which type of flower is on the badge of England's rugby union shirts?

3 The three colours that make up the American flag are blue, white and what?

4 In which sporting arena would you find a matador?

5 What *K* is both a term in computer science and a green frog-puppet created by Jim Henson?

6 According to the saying, a person in a completely unsuitable environment is a 'fish out of . . .' what?

7 In nature, 'earth', 'round', 'flat' and 'wire' are all types of which creature?

8 In TV, what is the surname of the American talk-show host Oprah?

9 In football, Tottenham Hotspur are based in which city?

10 In physics, how many terminals does a 'diode' have?

11 The hobby of observing trains and recording railway locomotive numbers is known as what?

12 In food, on a French menu, what are *champignons*?

13 The children's book *Through the Looking Glass and What Alice Found There* is the sequel to which famous Lewis Carroll novel?

14 What *A* is an alcoholic beverage brewed from malt and hops?

15 In travel, when arriving at a UK airport, which colour customs channel is used if a passenger has goods to declare?

16 What is singer Victoria Adams's nickname?

17 In nature, what *S* is a black powder formed by the incomplete burning of coal?

18 Add together the number of sides that three squares have in total.

19 Who was the US president between 1993 and 2001?

20 In music, which percussion instrument consists of a pair of metal discs that are held in each hand and struck together?

Previous Total
1,000
800
600
450
300
200
100
50
20
Banked
Total

Answers

1 Recipe
2 Rose
3 Red
4 A bullring (bullfighting ring)
5 Kermit
6 Water
7 Worms
8 Winfrey
9 London
10 Two
11 Trainspotting (accept gricing)
12 Mushrooms
13 *Alice's Adventures In Wonderland* (accept *Alice in Wonderland*/ *Alice's Adventures Underground*)
14 Ale (accept alegar)
15 Red
16 'Posh Spice' (accept 'Posh')
17 Soot
18 Twelve
19 Bill Clinton (William Jefferson Clinton; William Jefferson Blythe III)
20 Cymbals

Round 59

1 What K is a craft in which the practice of making the first stitches is called 'casting on'?

2 In politics, Mo Mowlam is associated with which party?

3 In TV, from which presenter would you have expected to receive a 'Jim Fixed It For Me' badge?

4 In food, what general term can be applied to domestic birds such as chickens, turkeys, ducks and geese?

5 In nature, what H is grass that has been cut and dried for fodder?

6 In sport, what is a tennis ball made of: rubber or leather?

7 In history, Australia and which other country's armed forces comprised the Anzacs?

8 In TV, which Saturday night programme was based in a mock stately home in the fictional village of Crinkley Bottom?

9 In the animal kingdom, what type of animal is a bushbaby: a rodent or a primate?

10 In the Bible, who instructed Noah to build the ark?

11 Which country widely used the guillotine during its revolution?

12 In music, which comedian had a UK top-ten hit single in 1988 with 'Loadsamoney, Doin' Up The House'?

13 What is the Republic of Ireland's largest city?

14 In nature, which insect is so called because its front legs are folded up under its head as if it is praying?

15 In TV, the sitcom *Yes, Minister* was continued as the programme *Yes . . .* what?

16 In the USA, who eventually conceded defeat on 13 December 2000 in the last presidential election?

17 Is short-sightedness corrected using a converging or diverging lens?

18 In pop music, which American artist won Best International Female at the 2001 Brit Awards: Madonna or Britney Spears?

19 Merlot, Burgundy and Shiraz are types of which drink?

20 In science, what is the name for the strong shockwave generated by an aircraft when it is flying at supersonic speeds?

Previous Total

1,000

800

600

450

300

200

100

50

20

Banked

Total

Answers

1 Knitting
2 Labour (accept New Labour)
3 (Sir) Jimmy Saville
4 Poultry (accept fowl)
5 Hay
6 Rubber
7 New Zealand
8 *Noel's House Party*
9 Primate
10 God
11 France
12 Harry Enfield
13 Dublin
14 Praying mantis
15 *Prime Minister*
16 Al Gore (accept Gore)
17 Diverging
18 Madonna
19 Wine (accept red wine)
20 Sonic boom

Round 60

1 With reference to time, for what do the initials GMT stand?

2 What type of animal is an eel: a worm or a fish?

3 In sport, which British athlete won the Olympic decathlon gold medal in 1980 and 1984?

4 In TV, *The Thin Blue Line* was a comedy series about which profession?

5 In the New Testament, what was the name of the archangel who foretold Jesus's birth to Mary?

6 In England, which town is further south: Blackpool or Southport?

7 What is the world's largest man-made structure?

8 In biology, toxaemia is the poisoning of what liquid found in the body?

9 In which continent was the actor Richard E. Grant born: Africa or Asia?

10 In art, which part of his body did Vincent Van Gogh cut off?

11 In science, incandescence describes the emission of what from a substance due to its high temperature?

12 In the animal kingdom, what A is the name given to the class of cold-blooded animals that can live both on land and in the water?

13 In pop music, which American singer and writer is known as the 'Piano Man'?

14 What *B* is the name given to the soft mass of nervous tissue within the skull that controls and coordinates the nervous system?

15 In film, how many monkeys feature in the title of the 1995 futuristic thriller starring Bruce Willis and Brad Pitt?

16 In music, 'Peggy Sue' was a UK top-ten hit single for which solo artist in 1957?

17 In nature, the Mercalli Scale measures the intensity of which natural phenomenon?

18 In travel, which international airport in New Zealand has the code 'AKL'?

19 In pop music, at what type of function is the Steps video 'Tragedy' set: a wedding or a christening?

20 Complete this motto, coined by Emmeline Pankhurst: 'Deeds, not . . .' what?

Previous Total
1,000
800
600
450
300
200
100
50
20
Banked
Total

Answers

1 Greenwich Mean Time
2 Fish
3 Daley Thompson (Francis Morgan Thompson)
4 The police (force)
5 Gabriel
6 Southport
7 Great Wall of China
8 Blood
9 Africa (Swaziland)
10 His ear

11 Light
12 Amphibians (accept amphibia)
13 Billy Joel (William Martin Joel)
14 Brain
15 Twelve
16 Buddy Holly
17 Earthquake
18 Auckland International Airport
19 Wedding
20 'Words'

Round 61

1 In film, who replaced first choice Tom Selleck in the role of Indiana Jones in *Raiders of the Lost Ark*?

2 In the Bible, whilst on hallowed ground which item of clothing did God instruct Moses to remove at the burning bush?

3 In anatomy, the bones in the fingers and which other part of the body are called phalanges?

4 On the TV show *Popstars*, how many people were in the final band?

5 In which English county would you find Oxford, Banbury and Henley-on-Thames?

6 In nature, what G is the first stage in the growth of a seed into a seedling?

7 Who made the first royal Christmas broadcast in 1932: George V or Elizabeth II?

8 According to the proverb, 'Half a . . . *what* is better than no bread'?

9 In music, according to the title of the Bangles' 1986 UK hit single, which day of the week was 'manic'?

10 In chemistry, nitric acid consists of hydrogen, oxygen and which other chemical element?

11 In history, King Paul was head of state of which country from 1947 to 1964: Spain or Greece?

12 What is the name for the anchored floats in the sea that mark channels and indicate dangers to navigation?

13 In which 1992 film did Mike Myers play Wayne Campbell, the presenter of a popular public-access TV show?

14 In fashion, what name is given to a sweater with a high, turned-over collar?

15 In science, a substance dissolved in another substance is known as what?

16 In human biology, the term 'cardiovascular' refers to which internal organ?

17 To which tennis player was Barbara Becker married, until their divorce in January 2001?

18 What kind of animal is a deerhound?

19 In motor racing, the Indianapolis 500 takes place in which country?

20 What is the name of the short-handled farming tool with a curved blade used for cutting corn since medieval times?

Previous Total

1,000
800
600
450
300
200
100
50
20

Banked

Total

Answers

1 Harrison Ford	**12** Buoys
2 His shoes (footwear/ sandals)	**13** *Wayne's World*
3 Toes	**14** Polo-neck (accept turtle-neck)
4 Five	**15** Solute
5 Oxfordshire	**16** Heart
6 Germination	**17** Boris Becker
7 George V	**18** Dog
8 Loaf	**19** United States (accept US/USA/America/ United States of America)
9 Monday ('Manic Monday')	
10 Nitrogen	**20** Sickle
11 Greece	

Round 62

1 In science, what does a 'manometer' measure: pressure or voltage?

2 In which decade was the Humber Bridge first opened to traffic?

3 In the American TV series, in which city did Cagney and Lacey work as detectives?

4 In film, complete the title of the 1999 Anthony Minghella thriller: *The Talented Mr . . .* who?

5 In language, which day of the week is *'Tisdag'* in Swedish?

6 In literature, the character Georgiana Podsnap appears in which Charles Dickens novel: *Oliver Twist* or *Our Mutual Friend*?

7 In which African country might you visit Benin city, Kano and Lagos?

8 In music, what *T* means 'to put into a different key'?

9 In pop music, who replaced Peter Gabriel as lead singer of Genesis in 1975?

10 In customs, what *F* is the name given to the traditional legends, customs and beliefs of a group of people?

11 In geography, in which Asian country are the Narmada and Godavari rivers situated?

12 In history, when did the Thracian gladiator Spartacus die: the first century BC or the first century AD?

13 Who wrote the novel *Shirley*: Jane Austen or Charlotte Brontë?

14 In money, before the decimalisation of the British currency in 1971, the penny was represented by which letter?

15 In which Italian city do the Spanish Steps lead up to the church of the Trinita dei Monti?

16 In TV, what was the nickname of the *Thunderbirds* character Hiram K. Hackenbacker?

17 In the Bible, the queen of where tried to impress Solomon with her riches?

18 In the animal kingdom, the 'Landrace' is a breed of what farm animal?

19 In history, the General Strike of 1926 was called in support of which national union?

20 In football, who replaced Graham Taylor as England coach in 1994?

Previous Total

1,000
800
600
450
300
200
100
50
20

Banked

Total

Answers

1 Pressure	**11** India
2 1980s (1981)	**12** (First century) BC
3 New York	**13** Charlotte Brontë
4 *Ripley*	**14** d.
5 Tuesday	**15** Rome
6 *Our Mutual Friend*	**16** Brains
7 Nigeria	**17** (Queen of) Sheba
8 Transpose	**18** Pig
9 Phil Collins (Philip Collins)	**19** NUM (accept mineworkers/miners)
10 Folklore	**20** Terry Venables

Round 63

1 In politics, what *D* is the word that describes the process of powers being delegated from a higher level of government to a deputy or substitute?

2 How many months of the year have only thirty days?

3 Which noted British composer died in 1934 aged 76: Vaughan Williams or Sir Edward Elgar?

4 Bill Paxton starred alongside Helen Hunt in which 1996 film about tornadoes?

5 What *V* means clothing worn by ecclesiastics at ceremonial functions?

6 Henry IV, Henry V and Henry VI were all kings from which royal house: York, Lancaster or Plantagenet?

7 John McEnroe and which famous Australian tennis player formed a band called the Full Metal Rackets?

8 Which American actor co-starred with Nicole Kidman in the 1997 film *The Peacemaker*?

9 In which country did the credit card industry originate?

10 Which British artist painted *A Bigger Splash* in 1967?

11 In film, Dean . . . who starred opposite Jerry Lewis in the 1956 comedy *Hollywood or Bust*?

12 In football, which English team did not compete in the 1999/2000 FA Cup tournament because they were playing in the World Club Championships?

13 In political history, Bob Hawke and Malcolm Fraser have been prime ministers of which country?

14 In which year did Iraq invade Kuwait, thereby precipitating the Gulf War?

15 In music, which famous jazz trumpeter wrote the tunes 'Milestones' and 'So What'?

16 In history, which *B* was a leader of the conspiracy to assassinate Julius Caesar?

17 In which decade did France's long-serving president François Mitterrand retire?

18 What is the surname of fashion designer Issey, born in April 1938 and based in Tokyo?

19 Dunedin is a city and port on which island in New Zealand?

20 In pop music, complete the title of Seal's 1995 UK hit single 'Kiss From a . . .' what?

Previous Total

1,000
800
600
450
300
200
100
50
20

Banked

Total

Answers

1 Devolution
2 Four
3 (Sir Edward) Elgar
4 *Twister*
5 Vestment
6 Lancaster
7 Pat Cash
8 George Clooney (George Timothy Clooney)
9 United States (accept US/USA/America/ United States of America)
10 David Hockney
11 Martin
12 Manchester United (accept Man United/ Man U)
13 Australia
14 1990
15 Miles Davis (Miles Dewey Davis)
16 Brutus (Marcus Junius Brutus)
17 1990s
18 Miyake
19 South Island
20 'Rose'

Round 64

1 In film, which actress played the role of Clarice Starling in the *Silence of the Lambs* sequel, *Hannibal*?

2 What name is given to the beak of a bird as well as to an American banknote?

3 In TV, Frank Bough and Anneka Rice have both presented which long-running BBC travel programme?

4 Which US state uses the postal abbreviation 'OK'?

5 In pop music, which British heavyweight boxer entered the UK charts in December 1995 with 'Eye of the Tiger'?

6 What is the name given to a vessel specifically adapted to keep open a navigable passage through ice?

7 Which 1961 Joseph Heller novel is set on an island airforce base towards the end of World War II?

8 What is the name of the Gaelic sport in which a stick called a 'hurley' is used to hit a small ball?

9 'Cabbage White', 'Red Admiral' and 'Painted Lady' are all types of which insect?

10 Edwin Budding and John Ferrabee invented which labour-saving gardening tool in 1830?

11 In which London building is the tomb of writer Geoffrey Chaucer?

12 Pasta envelopes filled with minced meat, known as 'Kreplach', are associated with which religion?

13 In football, for which Premiership team did Dennis Bergkamp play at the beginning of 2001?

14 In mythology, which Greek god was represented as a young, winged archer, shooting his arrows at gods and men?

15 In astronomy, 'spiral', 'barred' and 'elliptical' are all types of what?

16 Who wrote *The Bonfire of the Vanities*?

17 In the TV comedy series *Friends*, what is Rachel's surname?

18 In which European civil war was the Falange a political movement?

19 In religion, the Kaaba is the cube-shaped shrine at the heart of which city sacred to Muslims?

20 Which famous British heavyweight boxer was knighted in February 2000?

Previous Total

1,000

800

600

450

300

200

100

50

20

Banked

Total

Answers

1 Julianne Moore (Julie Anne Smith)
2 Bill
3 *Holiday*
4 Oklahoma
5 Frank Bruno
6 Ice-breaker
7 *Catch-22*
8 Hurling
9 Butterfly
10 Lawnmower
11 Westminster Abbey (accept South Transept of Westminster Abbey)
12 Judaism (accept Jewish)
13 Arsenal
14 Eros (*do not accept* Cupid)
15 Galaxy
16 Tom Wolfe (Thomas Kennerly Wolfe Junior)
17 Green
18 Spanish (Civil War)
19 Mecca
20 Henry Cooper

Round 65

1 What is the name of the rich substance similar to honey which bees feed to the larvae that become queens?

2 In science, gunpowder is an explosive made from a mixture of potassium nitrate, charcoal and which yellow chemical element?

3 In the British Isles, what S is the largest of the Inner Hebrides islands?

4 The characters Doctor Frank Bryant and Rita appear in which 1983 British comedy film written by Willy Russell?

5 In which century did the poet Robert Browning live?

6 In geography, the Isle of Sheppey is an island connected by road to which English county?

7 Which well-known French Impressionist painter is reported to have said 'If the world really looks like that, I will paint no more'?

8 What is the name of the prehistoric period occurring directly before the Jurassic period?

9 In which Russian city was the Saviour Gate Tower built in 1491?

10 Which nineteenth-century prime minister wrote the novels *Sybil* and *Coningsby* before taking office?

11 In 1983, Konrad Kujau and Gerd Heidermann were jailed in West Germany for forging whose diaries?

12 In politics, what H is the name given to the dominance of one state over a group of other states?

13 In the TV series *All Creatures Great and Small*, who did Robert Hardy play?

14 In which US state is Minneapolis?

15 Which London museum houses the National Art Library?

16 In which UK city is Aston University based?

17 In athletics, which country does 400 metres runner Cathy Freeman represent?

18 Complete the title of this Bertolt Brecht play: *Mother Courage and Her . . .* what?

19 In travel, which European country would you be visiting if you flew to Faro airport?

20 In history, Ramses II was the pharaoh of which country during the thirteenth century BC?

Previous Total

1,000
800
600
450
300
200
100
50
20

Banked

Total

Answers

1 Royal jelly
2 Sulphur
3 Skye
4 *Educating Rita*
5 Nineteenth (century)
6 Kent
7 Monet (Claude Monet)
8 Triassic (period)
9 Moscow
10 Disraeli (Benjamin Disraeli/Earl of Beaconsfield/ Viscount Hughenden of Hughenden)
11 Adolf Hitler's (*accept* Hitler's)
12 Hegemony
13 Siegfried Farnon (*accept* Siegfried)
14 Minnesota
15 Victoria and Albert Museum (*accept* V & A)
16 Birmingham
17 Australia
18 *Children*
19 Portugal
20 Egypt

Round 66

1 What *F* is the name of the artificial light source used in photography?

2 In human biology, the navel is more commonly known as the 'belly . . .' what?

3 In the nursery rhyme, 'It's Raining, It's Pouring', who was snoring?

4 A 'goatee' is what type of facial feature?

5 In the animal kingdom, what is an osprey: a bird or a fish?

6 With which sport would you associate Englishman Nasser Hussain?

7 According to the saying, something that enjoys a short period of fashion is the 'flavour of the . . .' what?

8 Women put on trial in Salem in 1692 were accused of participating in what kind of occult practice?

9 In travel, what *T* is a person who visits places away from home for pleasure?

10 How many weddings did Hugh Grant attend, according to the title of a film in which he starred?

11 In literature, complete the title of this classic novel by Victor Hugo: *The Hunchback of* . . . where?

12 In science, what is the freezing point of water at normal pressure on the Celsius scale?

13 In geography, which country is known as the 'Land of the Rising Sun'?

14 What *I* is a coloured liquid used for writing, drawing and printing?

15 In the animal kingdom, after the tiger, what is the second largest of the big cats?

16 In nature, what is the name for a large mass of ice that has broken away from a glacier and floats in the sea?

17 In politics, which colour is associated with the Conservative Party?

18 In fashion, during the Second World War many women drew a seam on to their bare legs to imitate what item of clothing?

19 In the 1939 film *The Wizard of Oz*, what gift did the Scarecrow want from the Wizard?

20 In human biology, the pains and efforts of childbirth are known as what *L*?

Answers

1 Flash (*accept* flash photography/ flashgun/flashbulb)
2 Button
3 The Old Man
4 Beard (*accept* facial hair/tuft/chin hair)
5 Bird
6 Cricket
7 Month
8 Witchcraft
9 Tourist (*accept* traveller)
10 Four
11 *Notre Dame*
12 Zero degrees (*accept* zero)
13 Japan
14 Ink
15 Lion
16 Iceberg
17 Blue
18 Stockings (*accept* nylon or silk stockings)
19 A brain
20 Labour

Previous Total

1,000
800
600
450
300
200
100
50
20

Banked

Total

Round 67

1 In music, 'penny' and 'tin' are types of which instrument?

2 In food, what is the principal ingredient of the Italian dish risotto?

3 In travel, which international airport has the code 'LHR'?

4 In fashion, what *P* was a style of high-soled shoe popular in the 1970s which caused numerous ankle injuries?

5 In science, which colour comes between orange and green in the rainbow?

6 In France, if you were asked to 'asseyez vous', what should you do?

7 In biology, how many cells are there in a bicellular organism?

8 In football, Roma is a team in the domestic league of which European country?

9 A short poem which is alliterative and very difficult to say quickly is known as a 'tongue . . .' what?

10 In which country of the UK is the city of St David's?

11 In science, what *M* is a device for looking at things that are normally too small for the human eye to see?

12 Complete the well-known saying: 'More haste, less . . .' what?

13 In film, Demi Moore and Patrick Swayze starred in which supernatural romance of 1990?

14 On a violin, which produces lower notes: a thick string or a thin string?

15 In a chicken run, there are 28 hens and two cockerels. How many hens are there to each cockerel?

16 Complete the name of the world-famous Italian fashion designer: Giorgio . . . who?

17 In law, what Q is to make void or annul a judgement?

18 In food, which strong-smelling member of the onion family has a bulb consisting of between six and two dozen cloves?

19 In food, what colour is a ripe Granny Smith apple?

20 What D is a spring flower with a single, yellow, trumpet-shaped bloom?

Previous Total

1,000

800

600

450

300

200

100

50

20

Banked

Total

Answers

1 Whistle	**11** Microscope
2 Rice	**12** Speed
3 London Heathrow (accept Heathrow)	**13** *Ghost*
	14 Thick
4 Platforms (accept platform)	**15** Fourteen
	16 Armani
5 Yellow	**17** Quash
6 Sit down	**18** Garlic
7 Two	**19** Green
8 Italy	**20** Daffodil
9 Twister	
10 Wales	

Round 68

1 According to the proverb, there is what among thieves?

2 In science, is water that contains a large proportion of dissolved calcium ions said to be hard or soft?

3 What is the name given to the person in charge of an orchestra who directs the musicians?

4 In comic books, which character was known as the 'Boy Wonder'?

5 In economics, complete this saying: 'Bad money drives out . . .' what?

6 What name is given to the upper chamber of the British Parliament?

7 In history, at which harbour on the island of Oahu was the American fleet attacked in 1941?

8 In fashion, the end of a sleeve is commonly known by what name?

9 In science, which of the following is a renewable energy source: wood or coal?

10 In music, a large jazz ensemble popular in the 1930s is known as a 'big . . .' what?

11 Where in the eye is the cornea situated: front or back?

12 In the Bible, who spoke to Moses from the burning bush?

13 In human biology, what C is the formation of a sticky mass to stop the flow of blood?

14 In TV, which character did Leslie Grantham play in *EastEnders*?

15 In the animal kingdom, which flying mammal has a scientific name meaning 'hand wing'?

16 If a farmer plants 200 seeds and exactly 30 per cent grow, how many plants will he have?

17 In food, what *B* is a sweet French bread roll?

18 Which US city is the largest in the state of Alabama and shares its name with the second largest city of the UK?

19 In biology, what colour is the albumen of an egg when cooked?

20 What was the name of Jim Henson's Muppet-style TV show which had characters called Doozers and Fraggles?

Previous Total

1,000

800

600

450

300

200

100

50

20

Banked

Total

Answers

1 Honour	**13** Clot
2 Hard	**14** Den Watts (accept Den/Dirty Den)
3 Conductor	**15** Bats
4 Robin	**16** 60 plants
5 Good	**17** Brioche
6 House of Lords	**18** Birmingham
7 Pearl Harbor	**19** White
8 Cuff	**20** *Fraggle Rock*
9 Wood	
10 (Big) Band	
11 Front	
12 God (accept The Lord/Jehovah/Yahweh)	

Round 69

1 In which country was the actress Sophia Loren born?

2 In human biology, blood cells which help the body to fight disease are what colour: red or white?

3 In TV, complete the title of the 1973 BBC sitcom starring James Bolam: *Whatever Happened to the . . .* what?

4 In Greek mythology, for what colour fleece did Jason and the Argonauts go in search?

5 In nature, what *M* is an area of wetland without trees or shrubs?

6 In pop music, which Minogue sister released a single in 1991 entitled 'Love and Kisses'?

7 In which sport would you find spikes, blocks and a starting pistol?

8 In geography, in which country would you find the city of Nancy?

9 In science, what name is given to the study of immunity and the immune system?

10 In history, which 'Age' followed the Bronze Age?

11 In which year was the Empire State Building opened in New York: 1931 or 1942?

12 In biology, what is the scientific Latin name given to human beings?

13 In music, what is the first name of the blind Italian male opera singer Bocelli?

14 In fashion, a skirt that flares wider at the bottom than the top is commonly known as an 'A-...' what skirt?

15 Which Monty Python comedian played Q's assistant R in the 1999 James Bond film *The World Is Not Enough*?

16 What is the name for a glass case containing a metal filament which provides light when an electric current is passed through it?

17 In the Elizabethan public theatre, what *P* was the central unroofed area of the auditorium that offered the cheapest tickets?

18 In rugby, Australia plays against which nearby country for the Bledsoe Cup?

19 In maths, how many times does four go into 36?

20 In film, in which 1982 science-fiction movie did Henry Thomas play the character Elliot?

Previous Total

1,000
800
600
450
300
200
100
50
20
Banked

Total

Answers

1 Italy
2 White
3 *Likely Lads*
4 Golden (Fleece)
5 Marsh
6 Dannii
7 Athletics (*accept* running/sprinting)
8 France
9 Immunology
10 Iron Age
11 1931
12 *Homo sapiens*
13 Andrea
14 (A-)Line
15 John Cleese (John Marwood Cleese)
16 Light bulb (*accept* bulb)
17 Pit
18 New Zealand
19 Nine
20 *ET: The Extra Terrestrial* (*accept* ET)

Round 70

1 Where is the Italian city of Siena: Tuscany or Umbria?

2 In sport, the Harlem Globetrotters are a basketball team from which country?

3 What was the name of the 1986 comedy musical film, starring Rick Moranis and Steve Martin, about a giant man-eating plant?

4 In pop music, complete the title of George Michael's 1990 UK hit album: *Listen Without . . .* what?

5 In geography, what M is a country in Asia, bordered on the north by Russia and on the south by China?

6 From what is rum distilled?

7 Which racket sport was reintroduced as a full medal event to the Olympics in 1988?

8 Which biblical figure's name is the title of a 1968 UK top-ten hit single by Tom Jones?

9 In politics, by what name is an Act of Parliament known before it is passed by the House of Commons and House of Lords and has received royal assent?

10 Was artist Joan Miró an Impressionist or a Surrealist?

11 Which of the following is a species of lemur native to Madagascar: Aye-Aye or Nay-Nay?

12 In geography, Free State and Western Cape are both provinces of which African country?

13 The world's first atomic-powered ship was launched in which decade?

14 Residents of which Spanish city are called 'Madrilenos'?

15 Rocky Marciano is associated with which sport?

16 What English name is given to the group of islands in the English Channel which the French call the *Iles Normandes*?

17 Who was the last US president to serve two terms in office before Bill Clinton?

18 In chemistry, what *P* is a metal that bursts into flame when in contact with water?

19 Which American actress starred in the 1998 romantic comedy *Sliding Doors*?

20 The first public railway equipped for steam-powered engines was a twenty-mile track built in which country in the 1820s?

Previous Total

1,000

800

600

450

300

200

100

50

20

Banked

Total

Answers

1 Tuscany
2 United States (accept US/USA/America/ United States of America)
3 *Little Shop of Horrors*
4 *Prejudice*
5 Mongolia
6 Sugar cane (accept molasses/dunder)
7 Tennis
8 Delilah
9 A bill
10 Surrealist
11 Aye-Aye
12 (Republic of) South Africa
13 1950s
14 Madrid
15 Boxing
16 The Channel Islands
17 Ronald Reagan (Ronald Wilson Reagan)
18 Potassium
19 Gwyneth Paltrow (Gwyneth Kate Paltrow)
20 England (accept Britain/Great Britain/ UK)

Round 71

1 In sport, in which year did the Frenchman Eric Cantona retire from football: 1995 or 1997?

2 Wollongong is a city in which Commonwealth country?

3 If your shopping costs £7.27, how much change would you get from a £10 note?

4 In London, the National Gallery is on the northern side of which famous square?

5 Complete the title of the 1961 wartime adventure film: *The Guns of . . .* where?

6 In science, slaked lime is calcium oxide that has been chemically combined with which liquid?

7 In TV, what was the name of the holiday camp on the sitcom *Hi-De-Hi*?

8 In which American sport do you score 'touchdowns' and 'field goals'?

9 In modern history, which country won the Battle of Stalingrad in 1943?

10 In 1990, which famous Newcastle-born footballer had a UK top-ten hit single with 'Fog On The Tyne'?

11 In economics, what M is the exclusive possession of a market by a supplier of a product?

12 In geography, the Great Lakes of Canada and the USA consists of how many lakes?

13 In which century was Darwin's *The Origin of Species* published?

14 In TV, what character had friends including Oswald the Ostrich and Mr Peregrine the Penguin?

15 In pop music, which band, led by singer Errol Brown, had their only UK number one in 1977 with the single 'So You Win Again'?

16 Which British security service was established in 1909?

17 In history, on which country's side did China fight during the Korean War?

18 In US politics, which president resigned in 1974?

19 What *L* is the third-largest city in France?

20 In pop music, what is the surname of Leo, who had a 1977 UK hit single with 'When I Need You'?

Previous Total

1,000

800

600

450

300

200

100

50

20

Banked

Total

Answers

1 1997	**11** Monopoly
2 Australia	**12** Five
3 £2.73	**13** Nineteenth
4 Trafalgar Square	**14** Muffin the Mule
5 *Navarone*	(accept Muffin)
6 Water	**15** Hot Chocolate
7 Maplins	**16** MI5
8 American football	**17** North Korea
9 Soviet Union (accept	**18** Nixon
Russia/USSR)	**19** Lyon
10 Paul Gascoigne	**20** Sayer
(accept Gazza)	

Round 72

1 In the Bible, Saul took the road to where following Stephen's martyrdom in Jerusalem?

2 In TV, in which American detective drama did Edward Woodward play the role of Robert McCall?

3 In which 1950 Billy Wilder film did Gloria Swanson star as Norma Desmond?

4 In which pop band were brothers Matt and Luke Goss?

5 Which train station was London's first mainline terminus?

6 Who preceded Neil Kinnock as Labour Party leader?

7 In TV, in which decade was the American sitcom *MASH* first aired on British TV?

8 In religion, John Wyclif and his followers were the first to translate the Bible into which language?

9 In the USA, which amendment to the Constitution provides freedom from self-incrimination?

10 In history, which famous British sailor led a surprise attack on the Spanish fleet in Cadiz in 1587?

11 Which US detective drama was about an ex-policeman who becomes a radio presenter: *Midnight . . .* what?

12 In agriculture, what L is a type of soil ideal for cultivation due to its mix of clay and sand?

13 In pop music, Abs, Jay, Sean, Rich and Scott are members of which boy band?

14 Which famous British actor played Bill Sykes in the 1968 musical film *Oliver!*?

15 Which Scottish football manager won the League Championship twice with Arsenal before becoming manager of Spurs, in 1998?

16 In the USA, who wrote the famous 'Letter from Birmingham City Jail', when he spent nine days in prison in 1963?

17 In pop music, Chris Martin is the lead singer of which band, winners of a 2001 Brit Award for Best British Album?

18 In politics, Likud is a political party in which Middle Eastern country?

19 What M was the atomic bomb project which US physicist Robert Oppenheimer directed in 1942?

20 Which term describes a scissor-like device or the convergence by two wings of an army on an enemy?

Previous Total

1,000

800

600

450

300

200

100

50

20

Banked

Total

Answers

1 Damascus
2 *The Equalizer*
3 *Sunset Boulevard*
4 Bros
5 Euston
6 Michael Foot
7 1970s (1973)
8 English
9 Fifth (Amendment)
10 (Sir) Francis Drake
11 *Caller*
12 Loam

13 Five
14 Oliver Reed (Robert Oliver Reed)
15 George Graham
16 Martin Luther King (Reverend Martin Luther King Junior)
17 Coldplay
18 Israel
19 Manhattan
20 Pincer (pincer movement)

Round 73

1 At which sport do the Chester Jets play the Manchester Giants?

2 In which Shakespeare play are Caliban and Ariel principal characters?

3 In literature, who wrote the science-fiction classics *The Time Machine* and *The Invisible Man*?

4 In literature, which book published in 1980, by Douglas Adams, is about an Earthman called Arthur Dent?

5 Don Henley was the drummer with which 1970s US band?

6 In history, by what name were the French Protestants who were slain in the 1572 St Bartholemew's Day Massacre known?

7 In which Jane Austen novel does Mr Knightley marry the heroine?

8 In TV, who played the character Hannibal in the 1980s action comedy *The A-Team*?

9 In heraldry, which member of the British royal family has the motto 'Ich Dien', meaning 'I Serve'?

10 How many quavers equal a semibreve?

11 Which *A* is the island to which King Arthur's body was carried after he was mortally wounded?

12 In which English county is the town of Lyme Regis?

13 Which 1994 Robert Altman film was set in the fashion industry?

14 In 1999, artist Tracey Emin was shortlisted for the Turner Prize with her representation of which piece of furniture?

15 In the nursery rhyme 'The House that Jack Built', what did the rat eat?

16 In western Germany, which city and port on the River Rhine is noted for its art academy?

17 The carol 'Silent Night' is translated from words originally written in which language?

18 In sport, which American women's tennis player won the Australian Open in 2000 without losing a set?

19 The US multi-millionaire industrialist who was born in 1839 was called John D. . . . . what?

20 The first two-pound coin was issued in 1986 to commemorate which international sporting event?

Previous Total

1,000
800
600
450
300
200
100
50
20

Banked

Total

Answers

1 Basketball
2 *The Tempest*
3 H. G. Wells (Herbert George Wells)
4 *The Hitchhiker's Guide to the Galaxy*
5 The Eagles
6 Huguenots
7 *Emma*
8 George Peppard
9 The Prince of Wales (accept Charles/ Prince Charles)
10 Eight
11 Avalon
12 Dorset
13 *Pret à Porter*
14 Bed
15 The malt
16 Düsseldorf
17 German
18 Lindsay Davenport
19 Rockefeller
20 Commonwealth Games

Round 74

1 According to the saying, when in good health, one is as fit as which musical instrument?

2 In human biology, what *T* is the top of the leg between the knee and the hip?

3 In the title of a well-known fairy tale, which character is associated with a beanstalk?

4 In nature, what is the common name for the insect that makes honey?

5 In TV, who is Dawn French's comedy partner?

6 The game of chance in which players pull out a concealed prize from a large bran tub is known as a 'lucky . . .' what?

7 In the animal kingdom, the 'black . . .' what had fleas that transmitted the outbreak of plague in the Middle Ages?

8 Which American city is referred to as 'The Big Apple'?

9 In music, what *H* is a song of praise to God or a saint?

10 In human biology, which organ in the skull is the coordinating centre of the nervous system?

11 In which athletics event do competitors attempt to clear a high crossbar with the aid of a pole?

12 In the TV soap *EastEnders*, which character was shot on the day of Melanie and Steve's wedding?

13 In nature, what is the fruit of an oak tree called?

14 At which annual racing event are there fences called 'Becher's Brook' and 'The Chair'?

15 Which member of the royal family married Sophie Rhys Jones?

16 Which biblical character wore a coat of many colours?

17 In the stage musical, what was Sweeney Todd's profession?

18 Whose backing group was called The Pips during the 1960s and 1970s?

19 What *L* is the name given to a natural area of fresh water surrounded by land?

20 In the UK, which birds are raced over long distances because of their homing instincts?

Previous Total

1,000
800
600
450
300
200
100
50
20
Banked
Total

Answers

1 Fiddle
2 Thigh
3 Jack
4 Bee (accept honeybee)
5 Jennifer Saunders
6 Dip
7 (Black) Rat
8 New York
9 Hymn
10 Brain
11 Pole vault
12 Phil Mitchell (accept Phil)
13 Acorn

14 Grand National (Martell Grand National Handicap Steeple Chase)
15 Prince Edward (accept The Earl of Wessex)
16 Joseph
17 Barber (accept hair stylist/hairdresser/ 'Demon Barber')
18 Gladys Knight (Gladys Maria Knight)
19 Lake (accept loch/ lochan)
20 Pigeons (accept homing pigeons/ racing pigeons)

Round 75

1 In biology, the abbreviation CNS stands for Central Nervous . . . what?

2 In music, Paul, John, George and Ringo were all members of which Liverpool band?

3 In Arabian mythology, which word was adopted to describe the spirit who emerged from a lamp to come to Aladdin's aid?

4 In politics, Jack Straw is associated with which party?

5 In maths, if three children share 33 sweets equally, how many do they have each?

6 What C is the name given to a professional cook?

7 In film, the correct name for the Oscars is the 'what Awards'?

8 In pop music, who was Paul Simon's regular musical partner?

9 In travel, a habitual worldwide traveller is known as a 'globe . . .' what?

10 In the animal kingdom, what type of creature is a meerkat: a mongoose or cat?

11 In nature, what L is the name given to an area of closely mown grass, often part of a garden?

12 The card game Rummy has a variation which shares a name with which alcoholic drink?

13 Cessna and Boeing are makes of which sort of transport?

14 According to superstition, which small, yellow flower is said to detect a liking for butter, when held under the chin?

15 What *A* is the name given to a system intended to increase fitness and change body shape by fast, strenuous exercises?

16 In food, gnocchi and tagliatelle are both types of what?

17 In geography, the Great Indian Desert is in which continent?

18 In biology, where in the eye is the retina located: front or back?

19 Which sporting event was first held in Athens in 1896?

20 In the military, what *P* is the name given to the optical instrument designed to observe from a submerged submarine?

Previous Total

1,000

800

600

450

300

200

100

50

20

Banked

Total

Answers

1 System
2 The Beatles
3 Genie (*accept* jinn/ jinnee)
4 Labour (*accept* New Labour)
5 Eleven
6 Chef
7 Academy (Awards)
8 Art Garfunkel (Arthur Ira Garfunkel)
9 Trotter
10 Mongoose
11 Lawn
12 Gin
13 Aeroplane
14 Buttercup
15 Aerobics
16 Pasta
17 Asia
18 Back
19 Olympic Games (*accept* Modern Olympic Games/The Olympics)
20 Periscope

Round 76

1 Which 1966 film, based on a true story, featured a lion cub called Elsa?

2 Which queen featured on the Penny Black stamp in 1840?

3 Which country is known to its inhabitants as 'Nippon'?

4 According to the title of the Tremeloes' 1967 UK number-one single, 'Silence Is . . .' what?

5 In food, 'arran pilot' and 'desiree' are varieties of which vegetable?

6 In TV, Charlie . . . who stars in the BBC series *Ground Force*?

7 What name is given to the piece of iron nailed to the bottom of a horse's hoof?

8 In maths, which is greater: five sixths or 90 per cent?

9 Which famous model-train manufacturer produced its first toy in 1920?

10 In which skiing event do competitors zigzag downhill through a series of markers?

11 In which European city would you find the Sorbonne University?

12 In fashion, which Vivienne won the British Designer of the Year Award in 1990 and 1991?

13 In science, to which group of organic compounds do sugars belong: proteins or carbohydrates?

14 Which British celebrity couple agreed to be interviewed by Ali G for Comic Relief in February 2001?

15 In the USA, how many cents are there in a quarter?

16 With which sport would you associate Mike Atherton and Shane Warne?

17 In geography, which north-eastern Italian city is made up of more than one hundred islands?

18 In the animal kingdom, what *T* is another name for an eagle's claw?

19 In which country of the UK are the Cambrian Mountains?

20 In pop music, complete the title of Gerry And The Pacemakers' 1964 UK hit single 'Ferry Across the . . .' what?

Previous Total

1,000

800

600

450

300

200

100

50

20

Banked

Total

Answers

1 *Born Free*	**12** Westwood (Vivienne Isabel Westwood)
2 (Queen) Victoria	**13** Carbohydrates
3 Japan	**14** David and Victoria Beckham (accept Posh and Becks/the Beckhams)
4 Golden	
5 Potato	
6 Dimmock	
7 Horseshoe (accept shoe)	**15** 25
8 90 per cent	**16** Cricket
9 Hornby	**17** Venice
10 Slalom (accept slalom race/giant slalom)	**18** Talon
	19 Wales
11 Paris	**20** Mersey

Round 77

1 Complete the title of the 1986 film starring Sean Penn and Madonna: *Shanghai . . .* what?

2 In modern history, what was the surname of Idi, the Ugandan president between 1971 and 1979?

3 In science, the living system that represents the relationship between plants and animals in a habitat is called a what '. . . system'?

4 In the Shakespeare play *Julius Caesar*, a Soothsayer warns Caesar about the ides of which month?

5 What C was a fashionable dance of the 1920s named after a town in South Carolina, USA?

6 How many sporting events are there in the heptathlon?

7 In pop music, which group of Irish sisters had a 1979 UK hit single with 'I'm In The Mood For Dancing'?

8 Which Welsh-born Oscar-winning actor portrayed the writer C. S. Lewis in the 1993 film *Shadowlands*?

9 On which river does the Henley Regatta take place?

10 In literature, the writer Terry Pratchett is most commmonly associated with which type of novel: fantasy or horror?

11 In science, based on nitro-glycerine, what *D* is an explosive invented by Alfred Nobel in 1866?

12 In the US, which Californian city is also know as 'Frisco'?

13 In the Bible, Sodom and which other city were destroyed because of the depravity of their inhabitants?

14 In theatre, which hero of English folk-tales and pantomime is a poor country boy who eventually becomes Lord Mayor of London?

15 In food, what is traditionally served around the rim of a margarita glass?

16 In film, which famous blonde actress starred with Jane Russell in the 1953 comedy *Gentlemen Prefer Blondes*?

17 Which *W* is a relative of the dog, commonly found in packs and known for its howling?

18 What is a damson: a plum or a pear?

19 Which British admiral had an illegitimate daughter called Horatia with Lady Hamilton?

20 What *P* is the name for the building that houses the dressing rooms at a cricket ground?

Previous Total
1,000
800
600
450
300
200
100
50
20
Banked
Total

Answers

1 (*Shanghai*) *Surprise*
2 Amin (accept Amin Dada)
3 Eco(system)
4 March
5 Charleston
6 Seven
7 The Nolans
8 (Sir) Anthony Hopkins (Philip Anthony Hopkins)
9 (River) Thames
10 Fantasy
11 Dynamite
12 San Francisco
13 Gomorrah
14 Dick Whittington
15 Salt
16 Marilyn Monroe (Norma Jean Baker)
17 Wolf
18 Plum
19 Nelson (accept Admiral Nelson/Lord Nelson/Viscount Nelson/Horatio Nelson/Baron Nelson of the Nile)
20 Pavilion

Round 78

1 In the Bible, the book which tells of the early days of the Christian Church is called the 'Acts of the . . .' what?

2 In music, what was the first name of the female member of The Carpenters?

3 In TV, complete the title of the Saturday morning children's show from the 1970s and 80s, presented by Noel Edmonds: *Multi-Coloured* . . . what?

4 In science, to the nearest hour, how many hours does it take for the Earth to rotate around its own axis once?

5 Chamonix is a winter holiday resort in which country?

6 In film, what type of creature did Daryl Hannah play in the 1984 comedy *Splash*?

7 In the animal kingdom what M is a group of land animals that carry their young about in pouches?

8 In biology, where in the body is the temporal artery: the head or hands?

9 Which French expression, meaning 'false step', is used to describe a breach of manners or good conduct?

10 In modern history, the term 'McCarthyism' arose in which decade in American politics?

11 The name of which dinosaur means 'three-horned face'?

12 In football, which English club play their home matches at Anfield?

13 The game of Brag is an early version of which card game?

14 What C is the old measure of energy, which is still used in the study of food?

15 In which 1993 film does Tommy Lee Jones play a US marshal trying to track down Harrison Ford?

16 Who was the US president when Iraq invaded Kuwait in 1990?

17 In history, Henry VIII's sixth wife was Catherine . . . who?

18 In which game do players compete in the Melody Amber tournament, held in Monte Carlo?

19 In science, what club-shaped instrument is used to pound or crush substances that are placed in a mortar?

20 In language, 'lapin' is the French word for which animal?

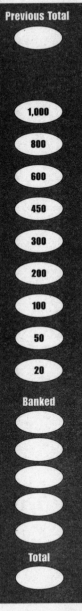

Previous Total

1,000

800

600

450

300

200

100

50

20

Banked

Total

Answers

1 Apostles	**12** Liverpool
2 Karen	**13** Poker
3 *Swap Shop*	**14** Calorie
4 24 (hours)	**15** *The Fugitive*
5 France	**16** George Bush
6 Mermaid	(George Herbert
7 Marsupials	Walker Bush)
8 Head	**17** Parr
9 *Faux pas*	**18** Chess
10 1950s	**19** Pestle
11 Triceratops	**20** Rabbit

Round 79

1 What M is an alcoholic drink made by fermenting a solution of honey?

2 Apart from the euro, what is the monetary unit of Austria?

3 Which of the Marx Brothers played Rufus T. Firefly in the 1933 film *Duck Soup*?

4 In the animal kingdom, what C is a stout-bodied scavenging insect which infests buildings, especially kitchens?

5 In music, on which instrument was the composer George Gershwin an accomplished performer?

6 In the TV soap *Coronation Street*, which character is played by actor Johnny Briggs?

7 In biology, the condition miliaria is more commonly known as 'prickly . . .' what?

8 In film, actor John Goodman played which character in the 1994 comedy *The Flintstones*?

9 In human biology, the tendon of the heel is named after which Greek war hero?

10 Name the female star of the films *The War of the Roses* and *Romancing the Stone*.

11 In science, in which country was the psychologist Ivan Pavlov born?

12 What C can be the number of eggs laid at one time or one of the foot-pedals in a car?

13 In the UK, by what acronym is the Campaign for Real Ale known?

14 Which poisonous gas has the chemical symbol CO?

15 Which famous British social reformer opened a boy's home in the East End in 1867?

16 In TV, in which BBC science-fiction sitcom did Danny John-Jules play 'Cat'?

17 In which Austrian city is Gustav Klimt's most famous work, *The Kiss*, exhibited?

18 In botany, what *F* is the common name for the leaves of plants such as ferns and palms?

19 Which actor starred as the autistic Raymond Babbitt in the 1988 film *Rain Man*?

20 In firearms, what *C* is the name for the internal diameter of a gun barrel?

Previous Total

1,000

800

600

450

300

200

100

50

20

Banked

Total

Answers

1 Mead (accept metheglin/mulsum/mulse)
2 Schilling
3 Groucho (Julius Henry Marx)
4 Cockroach
5 Piano
6 Mike Baldwin
7 Heat
8 Fred Flintstone (accept Fred)
9 Achilles
10 Kathleen Turner (Mary Kathleen Turner)
11 Russia (accept Soviet Union/ USSR)
12 Clutch
13 CAMRA
14 Carbon monoxide
15 Doctor Barnardo (Thomas John Barnardo)
16 *Red Dwarf*
17 Vienna
18 Frond(s)
19 Dustin Hoffman
20 Calibre

Round 80

1 In which European country is the port of Malmo?

2 In literature, Frances Hodgson Burnett wrote which children's book about an American child who turns out to be an English lord?

3 What is the popular name of the V-shaped bone above the breastbone of a chicken, which is traditionally snapped apart after the meal?

4 In which country does the annual Sundance Film Festival take place?

5 In marine life, what is the common name for the orca?

6 Which sport would you see at the Three As Indoor Championships?

7 In history, what term meaning 'horseman' was given as a nickname to Charles I's supporters during the English Civil War?

8 In TV, which viewer response programme was first hosted by Robert Robinson in 1961?

9 What C is the part of a petrol engine in which liquid fuel is converted into a vapour?

10 In the Bible, the tomb for Jesus was provided by Joseph of where?

11 In which US sport do you have to stay on a horse for as long as possible without being thrown off?

12 In music, how many crotchets equal a whole note or semibreve?

13 What *D* is the slang name given to an aerial battle, particularly during the World Wars?

14 What was the full title of the third instalment of the *Die Hard* films?

15 The *Asian Age* and *Hindustan Times* are national newspapers in which country?

16 In TV, for what do the initials 'OB' stand?

17 Which weapon has the same name as the cement mixture used for bonding bricks?

18 Which sport is also known as 'pugilism'?

19 In Greek mythology, what was the name given to the goddesses who presided over arts and sciences?

20 In which English county is the city of Portsmouth?

Previous Total

1,000

800

600

450

300

200

100

50

20

Banked

Total

Answers

1 Sweden
2 *Little Lord Fauntleroy*
3 Wishbone (accept furcula/merrythought)
4 United States (accept US/USA/America/ United States of America)
5 Killer whale
6 Athletics
7 Cavalier
8 *Points of View*
9 Carburettor
10 Arimathea
11 Rodeo (accept bucking bronco/ bronc or bronco riding/rodeo riding)
12 Four
13 Dogfight
14 *Die Hard With A Vengeance*
15 India
16 Outside broadcast
17 Mortar
18 Boxing
19 Muses
20 Hampshire

Round 81

1 The name of which Jewish ceremony means 'Son of the Commandment'?

2 In football, which Spanish club did England international Steve McManaman join in 1999?

3 In literature, from which country of the British Isles did poet Geoffrey Chaucer come?

4 In pop music, which American singer had a UK hit single in 1980 with 'Love On The Rocks'?

5 Which term meaning 'openness' was used to describe Gorbachev's policy of allowing greater freedom of speech in the Soviet Union?

6 Retsina is a dry white wine originating from which European country?

7 Which American director made the films *Do The Right Thing* and *Malcolm X*?

8 In geography, what is the name for the crescent-shaped lakes which are formed when a meander of a slow-flowing river is cut off from the main channel?

9 In the children's TV programme *Teletubbies*, what colour is Dipsy?

10 What is the name of the London concert venue in South Kensington built in memory of the Prince Consort?

11 In which country was actor Gary Oldman born?

12 In literature, complete the title of Alan Paton's 1948 novel *Cry, the Beloved* . . . what?

13 Which Rodgers and Hammerstein musical named after an American state was originally called *Away We Go!*?

14 Which part of the body contains around seven hundred million alveoli?

15 In the 1937 children's film, how many of the Seven Dwarfs could speak?

16 In which English county is Deal Castle?

17 In politics, which tax replaced the Community Charge in 1993?

18 Which British city has the postcode prefix 'NG'?

19 In biology, an allergy is also known as hyper . . . what?

20 What was the surname of Tony, the lead singer with the 1980s band Spandau Ballet?

Previous Total

1,000

800

600

450

300

200

100

50

20

Banked

Total

Answers

1 Bar Mitzvah
2 Real Madrid
3 England
4 Neil Diamond (Neil Leslie Diamond)
5 Glasnost
6 Greece
7 Spike Lee (Shelton Jackson Lee)
8 Ox-bow lake (accept ox-bow/ox-bow bend/ox-bow cut-off)
9 Green
10 Royal Albert Hall
11 England (accept United Kingdom/UK/ Britain/Great Britain)
12 *Country*
13 *Oklahoma!*
14 Lungs
15 Six
16 Kent
17 Council Tax
18 Nottingham
19 Sensitivity
20 Hadley

Round 82

1 In pastimes, what *K* is the name of a light framework covered in thin material which is flown on the end of string?

2 According to the saying, goods acquired illegally have fallen off the back of which type of vehicle?

3 In heraldry, what colour is denoted by the term 'vert'?

4 In film, which superhero has a girlfriend called Lois Lane?

5 In the animal kingdom, what type of creature is a bass?

6 In food, what is the traditional flavour of a humbug sweet: peppermint or strawberry?

7 In football, Valencia is a team in the domestic league of which European country?

8 In language, what is the American word for a handbag?

9 In politics, which party won the 1997 General Election?

10 In biology, what name is given to the terminal digits of the foot?

11 In art, mixing red and yellow paint together produces which colour?

12 In politics, ministers and shadow ministers in the House of Commons are referred to as '. . . [what] benchers'?

13 In sport, the home strip of the England rugby union team is mainly what colour?

14 In travel, what *C* is a type of holiday taken on a ship, usually stopping at a number of destinations?

15 In TV, complete the title of this US police drama: *Miami . . .* what?

16 In food, an orange is richest in which vitamin?

17 In human biology, what *F* is a type of break in a bone?

18 In fashion, during the 1970s, which garment came in styles called the 'mini', 'midi' and 'maxi'?

19 In the animal kingdom, in which continent are sloths native in the wild: Australasia or South America?

20 In which European country is the county of Kerry?

1,000

800

600

450

300

200

100

50

20

Banked

Total

Answers

1 Kite	**12** Front (benchers)
2 Lorry	**13** White
3 Green	**14** Cruise
4 Superman (*accept* Clark Kent)	**15** Vice
5 Fish	**16** Vitamin C
6 Peppermint	**17** Fracture
7 Spain	**18** Skirt
8 Purse	**19** South America
9 Labour (*accept* New Labour)	**20** Republic of Ireland (*accept* Ireland/ Southern Ireland/ Eire)
10 Toes	
11 Orange	

Round 83

1 Which animal did Dick Whittington send away on a merchant ship?

2 In nature, what *F*, used alongside the word 'fauna', refers to flowers and plants?

3 In science, which is nearest to the Earth's crust: the outer core or the upper mantle?

4 Yiddish is a language spoken by people of which religion?

5 In biology, how many leaves does a bifoliar plant have?

6 Which football comic strip appears in *The Sun* newspaper: *Striker* or *Defender*?

7 What *T* are wood-eating insects, also known as white ants, which are terrible pests in parts of the US?

8 In language, what do Americans call underground train systems?

9 In fashion, kitten-heel, slingback and mule are all types of what?

10 In science, what *P* is the word used to describe the table of chemical elements grouped according to their properties and structure?

11 In popular culture, what nickname did Clark Gable share with Elvis Presley?

12 In music, what instrument is a pair of small Afro-Cuban drums struck with the hands?

13 In men's fashion, what *T* is a short jacket without tails, used for formal wear and often worn with a bow tie?

14 In food, biscotti originate from which country?

15 What *A* describes a work of art which does not represent aspects of the material world?

16 In the animal kingdom, what type of animal is a mole: an insectivore or an omnivore?

17 Who played Catwoman in the 1992 film *Batman Returns*?

18 In science, what *A* is a mixture of gases that surrounds the earth?

19 In literature, what *N* is the fictional land featured in the series of seven 'chronicles' for children by C. S. Lewis?

20 In pop music, 'Father Figure' and 'Faith' were UK hit singles for which singer and songwriter?

Previous Total

1,000

800

600

450

300

200

100

50

20

Banked

Total

Answers

1 Cat	**11** 'The King'
2 Flora	**12** Bongo(s)
3 Upper mantle	**13** Tuxedo
4 Judaism (*accept* Jewish)	**14** Italy
5 Two	**15** Abstract
6 *Striker*	**16** Insectivore
7 Termite	**17** Michelle Pfeiffer
8 Subway(s)	**18** Air (atmosphere)
9 Shoe(s) (*accept* footwear)	**19** Narnia
10 Periodic	**20** George Michael (Georgios Kyriacos Panayiotou)

Round 84

1 In sport, in which country are the Headingly and Edgbaston cricket grounds?

2 How many back-boards are there on a basketball court?

3 What A is a term used to describe a region in which annual rainfall is less than 25 centimetres?

4 In TV, in which department of Holby City Hospital does Charge Nurse Charlie Fairhead work?

5 In politics, Helen Clark became prime minister of which country in 1999: Canada or New Zealand?

6 What R is the name for the long-handled tool with a row of teeth used for clearing grass cuttings and leaves?

7 In music, who had a UK number-one single with 'Ob-La-Di Ob-La-Da' in 1968: Marmalade or Jam?

8 In the Bible, who told Peter to look after his followers before he ascended to Heaven?

9 Who is the vice-president to George W. Bush?

10 In the title of the children's TV programme, what was the name of the steam engine that lived in a shed at the end of a railway in North Wales?

11 In food, from where does the dish of falafel originate: the Middle East or the Far East?

12 What common material is made from a mixture of calcium carbonate, sand and sodium carbonate?

13 Cary Grant and Grace Kelly starred in the 1955 Hitchcock movie *To Catch a . . .* what?

14 In nature, what type of tree is the sycamore: evergreen or deciduous?

15 Which admiral led the British to victory over the French in the 1798 Battle of the Nile?

16 In the human body, what type of blood cell is a lymphocyte: red or white?

17 TV presenters Donna Air and Declan Donnelly were in which children's drama?

18 In science, a polygraph is the technical name for what type of detector?

19 Polar bears are found in which polar region: North or South?

20 Which term refers to the earliest period of history, when tools and weapons were made of stone not metals?

Previous Total

1,000

800

600

450

300

200

100

50

20

Banked

Total

Answers

1 England (accept Great Britain or UK)
2 Two
3 Arid
4 Casualty (accept A and E/Accident and Emergency)
5 New Zealand
6 Rake
7 Marmalade
8 Jesus (Jesus Christ)
9 Dick Cheney
10 *Ivor the Engine* (accept Ivor)
11 Middle East
12 Glass

13 *Thief*
14 Deciduous
15 Nelson (Admiral Nelson/Lord Nelson/ Viscount Nelson/ Horatio Nelson/ Baron Nelson of the Nile)
16 White
17 *Byker Grove*
18 Lie detector
19 North
20 Stone Age (accept Palaeolithic/ Neolithic/Mesolithic)

Round 85

1 In 2001, Tom Hanks received a Golden Globe Award for Best Actor for which film?

2 In maths, if you can cycle 30 miles in an hour, how many miles could you cycle in twelve hours?

3 In food, from which country does chutney originate: India or China?

4 In geography, what V is a Canadian city in British Columbia, which shares its name with a nearby island?

5 In film, which British actor starred opposite Elizabeth Taylor as Mark Antony in the 1963 classic *Cleopatra*?

6 In education, for what do the initials IQ stand?

7 In Australia, which is further north: Darwin or Adelaide?

8 In 1983, which country did US president Ronald Reagan describe as 'a focus of evil in the modern world'?

9 In Elizabethan art, for what was Nicholas Hilliard best known: his miniature portraits or pastoral landscapes?

10 In geography, 'the sleeve' is the translation of the French name for which stretch of water?

11 In nature, what B is the term for gold or silver in the form of bars or ingots?

12 In which decade did Rolf Harris have a UK top-ten hit single with 'Sun Arise'?

13 In nature, halite is commonly known as what type of salt?

14 In religion, what *P* is the name given to a person who is divinely inspired to communicate God's will to the people?

15 Which town in southern Greece lends its name to a UK catalogue department store?

16 In science, the acronym CAD stands for 'Computer Aided . . .' what?

17 In popular culture, which former Radio One DJ is known as the 'Hairy Cornflake'?

18 In which country was jockey Frankie Dettori born?

19 In geography, which sea area of the Pacific Ocean takes its name from the formations which make up the Great Barrier Reef?

20 In pre-decimal currency, how many pence were there in a shilling?

Previous Total

1,000

800

600

450

300

200

100

50

20

Banked

Total

Answers

1 Cast Away
2 360 miles
3 India
4 Vancouver
5 Richard Burton (Richard Walter Jenkins Junior)
6 Intelligence Quotient
7 Darwin
8 Soviet Union (accept USSR)
9 Miniature portraits
10 English Channel (accept The Channel)
11 Bullion
12 1960s (1962)
13 Rock (salt)
14 Prophet
15 Argos
16 Design
17 Dave Lee Travis (accept DLT)
18 Italy
19 Coral Sea
20 Twelve

Round 86

1 Which British artist has produced works including a tiger shark in preserving fluid and a cow's head being eaten by maggots?

2 The year 2000 film *Thirteen Days* centres on which 1962 event in US history?

3 In Scottish football, how many leagues are there above the third division?

4 In literature, which award-winning actor is the son of the late poet and novelist Cecil Day-Lewis?

5 In which year was actor Sean Connery awarded a knighthood?

6 In TV, what is the first name of Ruth Rendell's Detective Chief Inspector Wexford?

7 What mythical creatures did Sir Arthur Conan Doyle famously believe two girls saw in a garden in Cottingley in 1917?

8 What has the Covent Garden Theatre been known as since it was dedicated to opera in the mid-nineteenth century?

9 What M is a species of tree said to bestow blessings of long life upon any child passed through its branches?

10 In tennis, what is the next point won after 'deuce' called?

11 Which political party did Abraham Lincoln represent?

12 Julianne Moore and Jodie Foster have both played which character in films about Dr Hannibal Lecter?

13 Fair Isle is off the coast of which UK country?

14 On a 24-hour clock, what time is it nine hours after midday?

15 In TV, which member of *The Young Ones* cast appeared as Flashheart in assorted episodes of *Blackadder*?

16 Which American First Lady was voted Arkansas's Woman of the Year in 1983 and Young Mother of the Year in 1984?

17 In science, what *R* did the French physicist Henri Becquerel discover in 1896?

18 What *R* is a town in Cheshire on the Manchester Ship Canal and the River Mersey?

19 Which musical by Lionel Bart features the song 'As Long as He Needs Me'?

20 What was the name of Henry VIII's first child?

Previous Total

1,000

800

600

450

300

200

100

50

20

Banked

Total

Answers

1 Damien Hirst
2 Cuban Missile Crisis
3 Three
4 Daniel Day-Lewis
5 2000
6 Reginald (Reg)
7 Fairies
8 Royal Opera House
9 Maple (maple tree)
10 Advantage
11 Republican
12 Clarice Starling

13 Scotland
14 2100 (hours)
15 Rik Mayall
16 Hillary Clinton (Hillary Rodham Clinton)
17 Radiation (accept radioactivity)
18 Runcorn
19 *Oliver!* (do not accept *Oliver Twist*)
20 Mary (accept Mary I/Mary Tudor)

Round 87

1 Which decade saw the birth-control pill first used in the UK?

2 Which baseball player was nicknamed the 'Bambino'?

3 Which *L* is an insect from North Africa that is often found in huge numbers and is related to the grasshopper?

4 In Formula One, in which country would you find the track at Hockenheim?

5 In maths, what is three multiplied by the number of degrees in a right angle?

6 Which Rodgers and Hammerstein musical is based on the play *Green Grow the Lilacs* by Lynn Riggs?

7 In the animal kingdom, what *L* are small nocturnal primates that live in the trees of Madagascar?

8 Which American actress starred in the film *Working Girl* and the *Alien* series?

9 In the thirteenth century BC, hoplites were foot soldiers from which ancient civilisation?

10 In music, which famous German composer was baptised in Bonn on 17 December 1770?

11 The English county of Berkshire is noted for rearing what type of farm animal?

12 By what name is the American actress Mary Elizabeth Spacek more commonly known?

13 In which sensory organ would you find the 'oval window' and the 'round window'?

14 In which century was the novel *The Fortunes and Misfortunes of the Famous Moll Flanders* first published?

15 In which 1994 film did Brad Pitt play the character Tristan Ludlow?

16 In politics, what *H* is the name of Tony Benn's son, who was elected MP for Leeds Central in the June 1999 by-election?

17 In music, which female artist had a UK number-one hit single with 'Orinoco Flow'?

18 In mythology, which Greek god invented the lyre, which he then gave to Apollo?

19 With what American sport would you associate Darryl Strawberry?

20 When in the 1980s were the last one-pound notes issued in England?

Previous Total

1,000

800

600

450

300

200

100

50

20

Banked

Total

Answers

1 1960s (1962)
2 Babe Ruth
3 Locust
4 Germany
5 270
6 *Oklahoma!*
7 Lemurs
8 Sigourney Weaver (Susan Alexandra Weaver)
9 Greek (Greece)
10 Beethoven (Ludwig Van Beethoven)
11 Pigs
12 Sissy (Spacek)
13 Ear (*accept* middle ear)
14 Eighteenth
15 *Legends of the Fall*
16 Hilary
17 Enya (Eithne Ni Bhraonain)
18 Hermes
19 Baseball
20 1984

Round 88

1 Which Shakespeare play features Caliban?

2 In fashion, the designer Lady Hare, born in July 1946, is better known as Nicole . . . who?

3 On which sea are the Bulgarian resorts of Burgas and Varna?

4 In tennis, Frenchman Yannick Noah won which Grand Slam championship in 1983?

5 Which *E* is the city in Holland where England played their opening football match of Euro 2000 against Portugal?

6 In music, in which country was the composer Dmitri Shostakovich born?

7 In geography, the River Ravi, in southern Asia, is one of the 'Five Rivers of the . . .' what?

8 Which species of bird has young known as peachicks?

9 Which famous Suffolk-born landscape artist shares his surname with a rank of police officer?

10 In football, Kenneth Wolstenholme said 'They think it's all over. It is now' when which England player scored?

11 In which European city are the headquarters of UNESCO based?

12 A carbohydrate is an organic compound containing carbon, hydrogen and which other chemical element?

13 Which US intelligence agency was established in 1947?

14 Which diminutive *EastEnders* actress wrote an autobiography called *All of Me*?

15 In pop music, which New Zealand model is the former wife of rock star Rod Stewart?

16 Which South African city in Gauteng Province was founded in 1886, following the discovery of gold?

17 In which sport was Louise Latimer the British number one in the year 2000?

18 With whom does Audrey Hepburn co-star in the 1961 romantic comedy *Breakfast At Tiffany's*?

19 Which writer/comedian played Melchett in the TV comedy series *Blackadder*?

20 Which government department deals with the management of the national economy?

Previous Total
1,000
800
600
450
300
200
100
50
20
Banked
Total

Answers

1 The Tempest
2 Farhi
3 Black Sea
4 French Open
5 Eindhoven
6 Russia
7 Punjab
8 Peacock
9 Constable (John Constable)
10 Geoff Hurst (accept Hurst)
11 Paris
12 Oxygen
13 The CIA (Central Investigation Agency)
14 Barbara Windsor (accept Babs Windsor/Barbara-Ann Deeks)
15 Rachel Hunter
16 Johannesburg
17 Tennis (accept lawn tennis)
18 George Peppard
19 Stephen Fry (Stephen John Fry)
20 The Treasury

Round 89

1 In the animal kingdom, what M is the specific name given to any mammal that carries its young in a pouch?

2 With which sport is Carnoustie in Scotland associated?

3 In literature, which Charles Dickens novel features the school Dotheboys Hall?

4 Which film and stage musical tells the story of Anna Leonowens, who travels to Siam to be a tutor to the king's children?

5 What is the capital city of Iceland?

6 What T is a nickname for a birdwatcher whose aim is to collect sightings of rare birds?

7 In music, according to the 1956 UK hit single, on which hill did Fats Domino find his 'thrill'?

8 What is the name of the large nerve which carries visual information from the eye to the brain?

9 In UK geography, in which county are the Quantock Hills?

10 In the nursery rhyme, what sort of animal did Tom, the piper's son steal?

11 To which political party do the twin MPs Angela and Maria Eagle belong?

12 In the animal kingdom, the giraffe can only be found wild in which continent?

13 In religion, what is the name of the official publication of the Salvation Army?

14 In football, with over ninety international appearances, Jim Leighton is which country's most capped goalkeeper?

15 In theatre, which musical is an adaptation of George Bernard Shaw's play *Pygmalion*?

16 Otopeni International Airport is located just to the north of which Romanian city?

17 Which character did Adrian Edmondson play in the BBC sitcom *The Young Ones*?

18 Who became the president of the United States after JFK's assassination?

19 In geography, Mont Pelée is a volcano on which French island in the Caribbean?

20 In literature, which 1994 best-selling novel by Louis de Bernières features the characters Pelagia and Mandras?

Previous Total

1,000

800

600

450

300

200

100

50

20

Banked

Total

Answers

1 Marsupial	**12** Africa
2 Golf	**13** *The War Cry*
3 *Nicholas Nickleby*	**14** Scotland('s)
4 *The King and I*	**15** *My Fair Lady*
5 Reykjavik	**16** Bucharest
6 Twitcher	**17** Vivyan
7 Blueberry (Hill)	**18** Lyndon B. Johnson
8 Optic nerve	**19** Martinique
9 Somerset	**20** *Captain Corelli's*
10 A pig	*Mandolin* (accept
11 Labour Party (accept	*Corelli's Mandolin*)
New Labour)	

Round 90

1 According to the saying, 'Finders keepers, losers . . .' what?

2 In science, a battery has a positive and what other type of terminal?

3 In which sport is a 'bull' worth 50 points?

4 In clothing, what *B* is the jacket worn as part of a school uniform?

5 In food, what colour is the skin of a ripe courgette?

6 In nature, what *P* is the soft, white lining inside an orange?

7 What is the name of the small device, made from a length of bent wire, which is used to keep papers together?

8 In nature, on which group of flying animals would you find beaks?

9 In cockney rhyming slang, what are your 'mince pies'?

10 In geography, in which country of the United Kingdom is the River Thames?

11 According to tradition, who led rats away from Hamelin by playing his flute?

12 In dentistry, what C is the common name for a hole in a tooth caused by decay?

13 According to boxing rules, it is illegal to punch below the what?

14 In the animal kingdom, which is usually larger: a rabbit or a hare?

15 In science, what M is the process which brings a frozen material to an unfrozen state by heating?

16 In the animal kingdom, *Ovis aries* is the Latin name for which wool-producing animal?

17 In pop music, Rod Stewart had a UK number-one hit single in 1983 singing about 'Baby . . .' who?

18 Who was president of Iraq during the Iran–Iraq war between 1980 and 1988?

19 Which B is an alcoholic beverage brewed from malt, hops and water?

20 In football, Lyon is a team in the domestic league of which European country?

Previous Total

1,000
800
600
450
300
200
100
50
20

Banked

Total

Answers

1 Weepers
2 Negative
3 Darts
4 Blazer
5 Green
6 Pith
7 Paperclip (accept staple)
8 Birds
9 Eyes
10 England
11 The Pied Piper
12 Cavity (accept caries)
13 (The) Belt
14 Hare
15 Melting
16 Domestic sheep (accept sheep)
17 Jane
18 Saddam Hussein
19 Beer (accept bitter)
20 France

Round 91

1 A piano trio is written for how many instruments?

2 In the Bible, who gained his strength from a vow never to cut his hair?

3 In sport, what S is a game in which you use a cue and a rest?

4 In American politics, what was the surname of the assassinated president known as JFK?

5 What H is the name for a vigorous long walk, or recreational walking tour?

6 According to the saying, someone's brief success is just a 'flash in the . . .' what?

7 In TV, what is the name of the police drama series which is set in Sun Hill?

8 In football, Stuttgart is a team in the domestic league of which European country?

9 In music, which famous female singer was married to Ike Turner?

10 In human biology, what N is a word used to describe feeling sick?

11 In the American TV series, how many million dollars did it cost to turn Steve Austin into a bionic man?

12 What is the name of the Irishman who created *Riverdance* and *Lord of the Dance*?

13 In music, complete the title of this hymn: 'Onward Christian . . .' what?

14 What is the national speed limit in the UK for a car on a single carriageway?

15 Which famous American tennis player defeated Tim Henman in the Wimbledon semi-finals in 1998 and 1999?

16 In biology, what A is another word used to describe the feelers found on an insect's head?

17 In maths, a taxi journey costs £31. How much change would you get from a £50 note?

18 Which town in the Netherlands is famous for its round cheeses covered in red wax?

19 In which country did karaoke originate?

20 What name is given to the pork that is cured, sometimes smoked and then cut into strips called rashers?

Previous Total

1,000

800

600

450

300

200

100

50

20

Banked

Total

Answers

1 Three
2 Samson
3 Snooker
4 Kennedy
5 Hike (hiking)
6 Pan
7 The Bill
8 Germany
9 Tina Turner (accept Anna Mae Bullock)
10 Nauseous (accept nausea)
11 Six
12 Michael Flatley
13 Soldiers
14 60 miles per hour
15 Pete Sampras
16 Antennae
17 £19
18 Edam
19 Japan
20 Bacon

Round 92

1 With which American sport would you associate 'The Giants', 'The 40-Niners' and 'The Redskins'?

2 In England, which city is further north: Hull or Liverpool?

3 In pop music, which British band, named after a cocktail, had a UK number-one hit single in 1981 with 'The Land Of Make Believe'?

4 What *E* is the name used to describe the passing of the moon between the sun and the Earth?

5 In American history, Harry Longbaugh was a western outlaw better known as 'The Sundance . . .' what?

6 In the animal kingdom, which *P* has a long train of feathers and is India's national bird?

7 In the English language, what do we call the meal that the French know as *'petit déjeuner'*?

8 In religion, what was the last name of Pontius, the Roman governor of Judea?

9 In sport, what is the name given to the form of rugby union which is played with seven players on each side?

10 In which Scandinavian country is the city of Gothenberg?

11 A blue marlin is what type of creature?

12 In history, the Battle of Britain was fought between Britain and which other country?

13 In music, the clarinet has a small, thin piece of cane attached to the mouthpiece known as a what?

14 In music, who sang the theme tune to the James Bond film *Goldfinger* in 1964?

15 Which country was officially joined to England in the 1536 and 1542 Acts of Union?

16 In the animal kingdom, a herd of elephants is mainly made up of which sex?

17 In which 1997 film did Will Smith play a secret agent tracking down aliens?

18 In pop music, 'Bring it All Back' and 'Two In A Million' were 1999 UK hit singles for which group?

19 In science, what type of element is helium: metallic or non-metallic?

20 In classical music, which ex-wife of Andrew Lloyd Webber sang 'The Phantom of the Opera' when it was released as a single in 1986?

Previous Total

1,000

800

600

450

300

200

100

50

20

Banked

Total

Answers

1 American football	**10** Sweden
2 Hull	**11** Fish
3 Bucks Fizz	**12** Germany
4 Eclipse (accept solar eclipse)	**13** Reed
5 Kid	**14** Shirley Bassey
6 Peacock	**15** Wales
7 Breakfast	**16** Females
8 Pilate	**17** *Men in Black*
9 Sevens (Rugby Sevens/Seven-a-Side)	**18** S Club 7
	19 Non-metallic
	20 Sarah Brightman

Round 93

1 In science, methanol and ethanol belong to which group of liquids?

2 According to the title of the Shakespeare play, the Merchant came from which city?

3 In history, Charles Darwin's ship bore the name of which breed of dog: beagle or corgi?

4 In which English city is Headingly cricket ground?

5 In nature, what G is a family of plants including wheat and maize?

6 In science, which female scientist won a Nobel Prize for physics in 1903 with Pierre Curie?

7 In the USA, which state uses the postal abbreviation OH?

8 In pop music, Right Said Fred had their only UK number-one single with which song: 'Deeply Dippy' or 'Barbie Girl'?

9 In film, who played Benjamin Braddock in the 1967 movie *The Graduate*?

10 In travel, the resort town of Montreux is found in which European country?

11 In TV, in which decade did the American sitcom *Mister Ed* first appear on British screens?

12 In nature, what S is the name given to the watery fluid that circulates in plants?

13 In travel, the Grand Canal runs through which Italian city?

14 In politics, Alan Milburn is associated with which party?

15 In sport, the football club Queen's Park is based in which Scottish city?

16 By air, which city is closer to London: Copenhagen or Frankfurt?

17 Which diminutive American comedy actor married Rhea Perlman in 1982?

18 In maths, what is the total number of sides that three hexagons have?

19 The character Big Bird is from which American children's TV programme?

20 What name is given to either of the geographic north and south points of the axis about which the Earth rotates?

Previous Total

1,000

800

600

450

300

200

100

50

20

Banked

Total

Answers

1 Alcohols (accept monohydric alcohols)
2 Venice
3 Beagle
4 Leeds
5 Grass (accept Grimineae)
6 Marie Curie
7 Ohio
8 'Deeply Dippy'
9 Dustin Hoffman
10 Switzerland
11 1960s (in 1964)
12 Sap
13 Venice
14 Labour (accept New Labour)
15 Glasgow
16 Frankfurt
17 Danny Devito (Danny Michael DeVito/ Daniel Michaeli)
18 Eighteen
19 Sesame Street
20 Pole

Round 94

1 The safety pin was invented in which century: the eighteenth or nineteenth?

2 Which legendary Egyptian queen has been played in films by Claudette Colbert, Vivien Leigh, Sophia Loren and Elizabeth Taylor?

3 In geography, which sea port in Cornwall overlooks Mount Bay and the island of St Michael's Mount?

4 In TV, William Bodie and Ray Doyle were characters in which drama series?

5 Which of these insects has wings: cockroaches or fleas?

6 In travel, IST is the international airport code for which Turkish city?

7 In maths, if seven kiwi fruit cost £1.20, how much would 21 kiwis cost?

8 In science, the atomic symbol Kr stands for which element that shares a name with Superman's native planet?

9 In TV, in the children's animated series *Roobarb and Custard*, what type of animal was Roobarb?

10 In the animal kingdom, what J is South America's largest wild cat?

11 According to European legend, does the Flying Dutchman captain a sea plane or a ghost ship?

12 In Formula One, what is the first name of Ralf Schumacher's more famous brother?

13 What was the title of the 1996 film starring Tom Cruise as a sports agent who loses all but one of his clients?

14 In snooker, which country of the UK does the 1998 world champion John Higgins represent?

15 In which country is the Savannah river situated?

16 In the American TV series, which superheroine, played by Lynda Carter, flew an invisible jet?

17 Where would you usually find the enzyme pepsin: in the mouth or the stomach?

18 In marine life, what L has a single conical shell and attaches itself to rocks?

19 In which city would you find Stormont Castle?

20 In Luke's gospel, in which town in Galilee did Mary and Joseph live?

Previous Total

1,000

800

600

450

300

200

100

50

20

Banked

Total

Answers

1 Nineteenth (1849)	**11** Ghost ship
2 Cleopatra	**12** Michael
3 Penzance	**13** *Jerry Maguire*
4 *The Professionals*	**14** Scotland
5 Cockroaches	**15** USA
6 Istanbul	**16** Wonder Woman
7 £3.60	**17** Stomach
8 Krypton	**18** Limpet
9 Dog	**19** Belfast
10 Jaguar	**20** Nazareth

Round 95

1 In TV, Honor Blackman featured in the 1990s British sitcom *The Upper . . .* what?

2 Which famous American pop artist began his art career by making shoe advertisements?

3 If a Formula One racing car completes 60 laps of a two-mile circuit, how many miles has it done?

4 In London, Trafalgar Square was named in honour of which hero's last victory?

5 In English football, how many leagues are there above the second division?

6 In 1983, William Golding was awarded the Nobel Prize in which field?

7 In world geography, the largest town in Alberta, Canada is called Medicine . . . what?

8 In film, actor Tim Allen was the voice of which character in the 1995 comedy animation *Toy Story*?

9 With which sport would you associate Ben Crenshaw and Fred Couples?

10 What A is the name for the hobby of beekeeping?

11 In geography, which mountain range in northern Russia forms the boundary between Europe and Asia?

12 In the comic *The Beano*, Cuthbert Cringeworthy is the class swot in which school?

13 In TV, which female presenter hosted the BBC's Children in Need 2000 appeal with Terry Wogan?

14 In history, the Dawes Plan was drawn up in 1924 to alleviate the burden of reparations imposed on which country?

15 In nature, what G is the name for a deep and narrow opening between hills or mountains, which usually contains a river?

16 In geography, Lima is the capital of which South American country?

17 In sport, Clive Woodward took over as coach of which nation's rugby union team in 1997?

18 In pop music, whose 1975 UK hit album was entitled *Still Crazy After All These Years*?

19 In geography, in which European country are the rivers Arno and Po situated?

20 In food, what F is the name of a thin biscuit made of nuts and dried fruits and coated with chocolate?

Previous Total

1,000

800

600

450

300

200

100

50

20

Banked

Total

Answers

1 Hand
2 Andy Warhol (Andrew Warhola)
3 120 (miles)
4 Admiral Nelson (accept Nelson)
5 Two
6 Literature
7 Hat
8 Buzz Lightyear
9 Golf
10 Apiculture
11 Ural Mountains (accept Urals)
12 Bash Street
13 Gaby Roslin
14 Germany
15 Gorge (accept gully)
16 Peru
17 England
18 Paul Simon
19 Italy
20 Florentine

Round 96

1 Which playwright wrote *Love's Labour's Lost*?

2 In fashion, which designer, born in December 1959, is the son of Sir Terence Conran?

3 In the Bible, who was sold into slavery by his brothers, and became an adviser to a pharaoh?

4 In film, Susan . . . who played Janet Weiss in the 1975 musical *The Rocky Horror Picture Show*?

5 In history, the *Lusitania*, which was sunk in 1915, belonged to which nation?

6 In TV, what was the occupation of John Alderton's character in the sitcom *Please Sir!*?

7 Who beame America's 42nd president in 1993?

8 Lucky Eddie is the sidekick of which comic-strip Viking?

9 The Douro river rises in which European country?

10 Which UK violinist made his 1977 debut at 20 with the Philharmonia Orchestra at the Royal Festival Hall?

11 In which castle in 1969 did the investiture of the Prince of Wales take place?

12 What is the name of Zoe Ball's husband, who had a 1999 UK number-one single with 'Praise You'?

13 In football, for which country did Johan Cruyff play at international level?

14 Which 1944 Allied campaign in France was codenamed 'Operation Overlord'?

15 In a game of cricket, how many individual stumps would you find on the field of play?

16 In biology, what name is given to the structure that surrounds the cytoplasm of a cell?

17 The 1990 movie starring Tom Hanks and Meg Ryan was entitled *Joe Versus the* what?

18 What type of military vessels are *Theodore Roosevelt* and *Abraham Lincoln*?

19 In which religion is a 'mufti' a legal expert who guides the courts in interpretation?

20 Which UK artist/film-maker directed the 1993 film *Blue*?

Previous Total

1,000

800

600

450

300

200

100

50

20

Banked

Total

Answers

1 William Shakespeare
2 Jasper Conran (Jasper Alexander Thirlby Conran)
3 Joseph
4 Sarandon
5 Britain
6 Teacher
7 Bill Clinton (William Jefferson Clinton)
8 Hagar The Horrible
9 Spain
10 Nigel Kennedy (*accept* Kennedy)
11 Caernarvon (Castle)
12 Fatboy Slim (Norman Cook/Quentin Cook)
13 The Netherlands (*accept* Holland)
14 The Normandy Campaign (*accept* D-Day Landings/D-Day Invasion/Normandy Landings/Invasion of north-western Europe/ Invasion of Normany)
15 Six
16 Membrane (*accept* cell wall/cell membrane/plasma membrane)
17 *Volcano*
18 Ships (*accept* aircraft carriers)
19 Islam
20 Derek Jarman

Round 97

1 At which event did American Maurice Greene become Olympic champion and world record holder?

2 Which English Chancellor was executed for refusing to acknowledge Henry VIII as head of the Church?

3 In pop music, which Swedish duo had a 1991 UK hit album entitled *Joyride*?

4 Which Victorian novelist, born in 1812, wrote the books *The Battle of Life* and *The Haunted Man*?

5 A candela is a unit which measures the intensity of what?

6 In football, how many times was Kevin Keegan European Footballer of the Year?

7 Robert Carlyle and Emily Watson starred in which 1999 film adaptation of Frank McCourt's story set in Ireland?

8 In the TV series *The Man from UNCLE*, the character Napoleon Solo was played by Robert . . . who?

9 In the USA, the Bear Flag Revolt was a revolt against Mexican Rule by US settlers in which western state?

10 In pop music, which Scottish-formed rock band's name is Greek for 'from the womb'?

11 What is the title of Oscar Wilde's only novel?

12 Which UK film actress is married to film director Jim Threapleton?

13 In rugby union, which New Zealand player scored a record eight tries in the 1999 World Cup finals?

14 In boxing, in which country was the fighter Rocky Marciano born?

15 Which Ancient Greek discovered that the weight loss of an object placed in water is equal to the weight of the displaced water?

16 In the USA, which president signed the bill for the Civil Rights Act of 1964?

17 Which famous US band reached number one in the UK in 1966 with 'Reach Out, I'll Be There'?

18 Mount Everest is in which mountain range?

19 In food, osso . . . [what] is an Italian dish of braised veal knuckle?

20 What *D* is the removal of salt, usually from sea water, to produce water for drinking?

Previous Total

1,000
800
600
450
300
200
100
50
20

Banked

Total

Answers

1 100 metres (100 metres sprint)
2 (Sir) Thomas More (*accept* Saint Thomas More)
3 Roxette
4 Charles Dickens
5 Luminous intensity (*accept* light)
6 Twice
7 *Angela's Ashes*
8 Vaughn
9 California
10 Del Amitri
11 *The Picture of Dorian Gray*
12 Kate Winslet
13 Jonah Lomu
14 United States (*accept* US/United States of America/USA/ America)
15 Archimedes
16 Lyndon B. Johnson [Lyndon Baines Johnson] (*accept* LBJ/ Johnson)
17 Four Tops
18 Himalayas
19 *Buco*
20 Desalination

Round 98

1 Which author wrote the novel *A Separate Peace*, about two friends at boarding school during World War II?

2 In the children's cartoon series of the same name, what sort of creatures were the pop group members Alvin, Simon and Theodore?

3 In which British National Park would you find the mountain peaks Helvellyn and Skiddaw?

4 In music, which British rock band had a UK top-ten hit single in 1970 with 'Paranoid'?

5 *The Old Man And The Sea* was instrumental in gaining which author the 1954 Nobel Prize for Literature?

6 The Eurostar train route stops at Calais, Paris and which other French city?

7 In art, in which country of the UK was the painter Thomas Gainsborough born?

8 What is the first name of Professor Clare, who presents the Radio 4 series *In the Psychiatrist's Chair*?

9 In cricket, which English county won all three major one-day trophies in the year 2000?

10 Which novelist wrote the important feminist piece 'A Room of One's Own'?

11 In music, which British punk band had UK hits in 1979 with 'London Calling' and in 1980 with 'Bankrobber'?

12 In which European city is the Rembrandt Museum?

13 Which children's TV series featured ex-astronaut Jeff Tracy and his sons?

14 Which former Beatle composed an orchestral work entitled 'Standing Stone' that premièred in 1997?

15 In which American city is Yale University?

16 In which continent are the Altai mountains?

17 Which former leader of the Liberal Democrats was granted a knighthood in the Queen's Birthday Honours list in June 2000?

18 Canada and which country were divided up at the end of the French and Indian War in 1763?

19 In which county is Hurst Castle, separated from the Isle of Wight by a mile of water?

20 The city of Karachi in Pakistan is situated on the coast of which sea?

Previous Total

1,000
800
600
450
300
200
100
50
20

Banked

Total

Answers

1 John Knowles	**12** Amsterdam
2 Chipmunks	**13** *Thunderbirds*
3 Lake District	**14** Sir Paul McCartney
4 Black Sabbath	**15** New Haven (in
5 Ernest Hemingway	Connecticut)
(accept Hemingway)	**16** Asia
6 Lille	**17** Paddy Ashdown
7 England	(Jeremy John Durham
8 Anthony	Ashdown)
9 Gloucestershire	**18** USA (America)
10 Virginia Woolf	**19** Hampshire
11 The Clash	**20** Arabian (Sea)

Round 99

1 In the nursery rhyme, who had lost her sheep?

2 On which Australian soap opera did Jason Donovan appear?

3 New York City is often referred to as 'the Big . . .' what?

4 In which country would you find the city of Dijon, famous for its mustard?

5 What *K* is a species of bird, commonly found on riverbanks and renowned for its fish-catching abilities?

6 How many natural satellites orbit the planet Earth?

7 In entertainment, Russell Crowe won his first Oscar for Best Actor in which film?

8 In the Beatles song, Lucy was in the Sky with what?

9 In politics, Nelson Mandela became the president of which country in 1994?

10 In science, what is the name of the type of electrical power that comes from harnessing the sun's energy?

11 In which city is the TV soap opera *Brookside* set?

12 In human biology, nausea in the early stages of pregnancy is commonly referred to as 'morning . . .' what?

13 Dexter, Holstein and Durham are all breeds of which animal?

14 In literature, Johann David Wyss and his son wrote the novel *The Swiss Family . . .* who?

15 In geography, which Asian country has the largest population of any country in the world?

16 How many seats does a tandem usually have?

17 At which film festival could a film win the Palme d'Or?

18 In music, a sextet is a musical composition written for how many instruments?

19 In science, what is the name for the type of oven that uses electromagnetic waves to cook food?

20 In sport, what was added to football shirts for the first time in the 1933 FA Cup final to make the players easier to recognise?

Previous Total

1,000

800

600

450

300

200

100

50

20

Banked

Total

Answers

1 Little Bo-Peep	**11** Liverpool
2 *Neighbours*	**12** Sickness
3 Apple	**13** Cow (accept cattle)
4 France	**14** *Robinson*
5 Kingfisher	**15** China
6 One (the moon)	**16** Two
7 *Gladiator*	**17** Cannes
8 Diamonds	**18** Six
9 South Africa	**19** Microwave
10 Solar	**20** Numbers

Round 100

1 In which country is the state of Montana: USA or Canada?

2 In fashion, what *B* is the name given to a soft, brimless hat associated with the French?

3 In which 1980s time-travelling trilogy of films did Michael J. Fox star?

4 In religious art, what *H* is a circular symbol of holiness or enlightenment surrounding a saint?

5 In TV, complete this programme title: *Monty Python's Flying . . .* what?

6 In food, Brie and Camembert are both types of what?

7 How many queens are there on a chessboard at the beginning of a standard game?

8 Who is reported to have bought pop star Billie Piper a Ferrari in January 2001?

9 In pop music, complete the title of the 1981 Adam and the Ants UK number-one single: 'Stand And . . .' what?

10 Which metal is most commonly found in liquid thermometers?

11 What do Americans call the pavement?

12 In science, what happens to cooler air in a room: does it sink or rise?

13 In the animal kingdom, what *T* is the largest member of the cat family?

14 In music, Dionne who is a soul singer who shares her name with an English Midlands town?

15 What R is an exact copy or model?

16 In finance, interest is paid either net or . . . what?

17 In the human body, what do we call an injury to the body causing discolouration but no laceration of the skin?

18 To which country would you travel if you wanted to visit the Pyramids of Giza?

19 In language, what A is a word made up from the initial letters of other words?

20 In film, which Hollywood actor starred as both Rocky Balboa and John Rambo?

Previous Total

1,000

800

600

450

300

200

100

50

20

Banked

Total

Answers

1 USA
2 Beret
3 *Back To The Future*
4 Halo
5 Circus
6 Cheese
7 Two
8 Chris Evans (Christopher Evans)
9 Deliver
10 Mercury
11 Sidewalk
12 Sink
13 Tiger (Siberian tiger)

14 Warwick (Dionne Warwick)
15 Replica (accept reproduction)
16 Gross (accept whole, variants on 'without deductions')
17 Bruise (accept contusion)
18 Egypt
19 Acronym
20 Sylvester Stallone (Sylvester Enzio Stallone)

Round 101

1 In politics, Herbert Hoover was president of which country from 1929 to 1933?

2 In maths, if a video lasts for three hours, how many minutes is it?

3 By what name is the former member of The Beatles Richard Starkey more commonly known?

4 In the animal kingdom, is the male or female adult lion larger?

5 What is the highest value a letter is worth in the game of Scrabble when placed on a standard square?

6 In pop music, Bing who performed a duet with David Bowie on the single 'Peace on Earth' in 1982?

7 In transport, what *B* is a small post marking a traffic island?

8 In which European city is the Place de la Bastille located?

9 In biology, a cell usually contains how many nuclei?

10 In nature, what is the name for a tremor which occurs after an earthquake?

11 In food, what *H* is the outer covering of some fruits, nuts, and grains, for instance coconuts?

12 In the animal kingdom, a black leopard is more commonly known as what?

13 In geography, to which European country do the islands of Sardinia and Sicily belong?

14 In sport, what is the official called in a game of rugby union: an umpire or a referee?

15 Who, in June 1997, became the youngest Conservative Party leader since William Pitt?

16 In language, is a suffix placed at the beginning or the end of a word?

17 In the Bible, what did Moses receive from the Lord at the top of Mount Sinai?

18 In human biology, which fibrous sheets of tissue found in the larynx can produce sounds by vibrating?

19 Complete the name of this country in the West Indies: Trinidad and what?

20 In history, who invaded Britain first, the Vikings or the Romans?

Answers

1 United States (accept US/USA/America/ United States of America)
2 180
3 Ringo Starr
4 Male
5 Ten
6 (Bing) Crosby
7 Bollard
8 Paris
9 One
10 Aftershock
11 Husk (accept hull)
12 Panther
13 Italy

14 Referee
15 William Hague (William Jefferson Hague)
16 End
17 The Ten Commandments (stone tablets/the Law of the Tablets/Tablets of the Law/the Decalogue)
18 Vocal cords (accept vocal folds)
19 Tobago
20 The Romans

Previous Total

1,000
800
600
450
300
200
100
50
20

Banked

Total

Round 102

1 In physics, what *M* is anything that has mass which can be detected and measured?

2 What *T* is a Tahitian word which has entered the English language, meaning a form of personal decoration?

3 In TV, in which decade did *The Morecambe and Wise Show* first air on British TV?

4 In computing, the word 'bit' is a contraction of 'binary . . .' what?

5 To which country did actor Mel Gibson emigrate in 1968 at the age of twelve?

6 In fashion, on which part of the body would you wear a cummerbund?

7 In science, which Russian space station fell to Earth in March 2001?

8 How many strings does a ukelele have: four or six?

9 In the 1981 film *Raiders of the Lost Ark*, which character did Harrison Ford play?

10 In the animal kingdom, what is a 'honey-eater' – a type of bird or bear?

11 In British politics, which Labour leader resigned in 1992 and became a European Commissioner?

12 In pop music, complete the title of Sister Sledge's 1979 UK hit album: *We Are . . .* what?

13 In TV, by what name is the comedian Robert Alan Monkhouse better known?

14 In human biology, what B has a soft core known as marrow?

15 In movie serials, which hero had a girlfriend called Dale Arden?

16 Princess Diana and the footballer David Ginola have both campaigned on behalf of the UN to eradicate what type of weapon?

17 In a river, the word 'meander' refers to what – a waterfall or a bend?

18 Which entertainer plays Bob Martin in the TV comedy series of the same name?

19 In which country of the UK is the Forth Bridge?

20 In football, what is the name for the horizontal beam which forms the top of a goal?

Previous Total

1,000

800

600

450

300

200

100

50

20

Banked

Total

Answers

1 Matter
2 Tattoo
3 1960s (1961)
4 Digit
5 Australia
6 (Around the) Waist
7 Mir
8 Four
9 Indiana Jones
10 Bird
11 Neil Kinnock (Neil Gordon Kinnock)
12 Family
13 Bob Monkhouse
14 Bone
15 Flash Gordon
16 Land mines
17 Bend
18 Michael Barrymore (Michael Keiron Barrymore)
19 Scotland
20 Crossbar

Round 103

1 What term is used to describe a sheep, calf or foal that is between one and two years old?

2 Which actor sang on the single in 2000 about the children's TV show *Bob The Builder*?

3 In science, what does a Geiger counter measure?

4 In pop music, with which band was Shane MacGowan the lead singer, The Pixies or The Pogues?

5 For which political party was John Gummer elected MP for Suffolk Coastal in 1983?

6 In biology, what *S* is a carbohydrate which forms the main food element in rice?

7 In art, onto what surface are frescos painted?

8 In geography, the Black Forest is in which European country?

9 What head-dress, especially associated with Sikh men, consists of a long piece of fabric wrapped around the head?

10 In maths, if you bought something which cost £75 after a 25 per cent discount, what was the original price?

11 In the TV comedy *Friends*, what is the name of Phoebe's twin sister: Ursula or Janice?

12 In pop music, how many members are there in the boy band Westlife?

13 In science, what is the most common element found in the Earth's crust?

14 In Scottish football, how many leagues are there above the First Division?

15 Vespa and Lambretta are famous manufacturers of what type of vehicle?

16 Which European city was named after the Greek goddess Athene?

17 Which musical instrument was former US president Bill Clinton fond of playing?

18 In children's literature, which *H* was an orphan living in the Swiss Alps with her grandfather?

19 In which year was the famous cycling race the Tour de France first contested – 1903 or 1933?

20 If you buy a TV for £195 and a video player for £125, how much have you spent in total?

Previous Total

1,000

800

600

450

300

200

100

50

20

Banked

Total

Answers

1 Yearling
2 Neil Morrissey
3 Radiation (*accept* radioactivity)
4 The Pogues
5 Conservatives (*accept* Tories)
6 Starch
7 Walls (*accept* plaster)
8 Germany
9 Turban (*accept* Dastar)
10 £100
11 Ursula
12 Five
13 Oxygen
14 One
15 Scooters (mopeds)
16 Athens
17 Saxophone (*accept* tenor saxophone)
18 Heidi
19 1903
20 £320

Round 104

1 In mammals, how many chambers does the heart have?

2 In politics, which *D* is a system of government in which sovereignty rests with the whole people, who rule either directly or through representatives?

3 In the USA, which state uses the postal abbreviation AL?

4 Which sailor character first appeared in 1929 in a cartoon about Olive Oyl's family?

5 Which ecological organisation uses the name *Rainbow Warrior* for its ships?

6 What was the name of the inventor of the raised-point printing system for the blind that can be read by touch?

7 In film, complete the title of the 1990 science-fiction thriller starring Arnold Schwarzenegger, *Total* . . . what?

8 In pop music, The Fine Young Cannibals had a 1986 UK top-ten hit single with which Elvis Presley song?

9 In science, the phon is a unit for the measurement of what, loudness or brightness?

10 In the animal kingdom, what are pigs classified as – omnivores or herbivores?

11 Who played William Thacker in the 1999 film *Notting Hill*?

12 In design, the Model A replaced which famous Ford car in 1927?

13 In food, gefilte fish is a dish most commonly associated with which religion?

14 In UK politics, in which year of the 1990s did Gordon Brown become Chancellor of the Exchequer?

15 In the the TV programme *Thomas the Tank Engine*, by what name is Sir Topham Hatt better known?

16 In nature, which holly tree produces berries? The male or the female?

17 In film, in which 1993 romantic comedy did Meg Ryan star as Annie Reed, a woman who finds her perfect partner after listening to a radio talk show?

18 In pop music, Shakin' Stevens had a UK number-one hit single about what colour door?

19 In which American sport do you have quarterbacks and running backs?

20 Natural gas consists mostly of which gas?

Previous Total

1,000

800

600

450

300

200

100

50

20

Banked

Total

Answers

1 Four	**12** The Model T
2 Democracy	**13** Judaism (accept Jewish)
3 Alabama	**14** 1997
4 Popeye	**15** The Fat Controller
5 Greenpeace	**16** Female
6 Braille (Louis Braille)	**17** *Sleepless in Seattle*
7 Recall	**18** Green
8 'Suspicious Minds'	**19** American football
9 Loudness	**20** Methane (accept marsh gas, CH_4)
10 Omnivores	
11 Hugh Grant (Hugh John Mungo Grant)	

Round 105

1 In geography, what C are a group of mountains forming part of the Grampian system of central Scotland?

2 If a restaurant bill is £56, how much is a ten per cent tip?

3 In football, for which country did Franz Beckenbauer play at international level?

4 In which South American country are the cities of Manaus and Belo Horizonte?

5 In pop music, complete the title of this Rod Stewart 1971 UK number-one single, 'Maggie . . .' who?

6 Which 1986 Oliver Stone Vietnam war film had the tagline 'The first casualty of war is innocence'?

7 In geography, which Japanese city's name means 'eastern capital'?

8 At which sport did Nick Farr-Jones and David Campese represent Australia?

9 In TV, complete the title of the sitcom starring Donald Sinden and Windsor Davies as antique dealers: *Never The . . .* what?

10 In literature, complete the title of the 1914 Edgar Rice Burroughs novel *Tarzan of the . . .* what?

11 Which is faster, the heart rate of a child or an adult?

12 What A is a system of exercises designed to increase oxygen consumption?

13 In UK politics, which Labour MP published the first part of her memoirs, *The Castle Diaries*, in 1980?

14 In UK geography, in which English county is the seaside resort of Broadstairs?

15 Which British actress played Ophelia in the 1996 film version of *Hamlet* and then starred in *Titanic*?

16 In Russia, the rouble is made up of 100 what?

17 Which tiny people did Gulliver discover in the first part of Johnathan Swift's novel *Gulliver's Travels*?

18 In film, the 1995 thriller *Murder In The First* features which San Francisco island prison?

19 Which is further south, Bulgaria or Romania?

20 In the Gospel of John, with what did Mary wipe Jesus's feet after soothing them with ointment?

Previous Total

1,000

800

600

450

300

200

100

50

20

Banked

Total

Answers

1 Cairngorms	**12** Aerobic
2 £5.60	**13** Barbara Castle
3 West Germany	(accept Barbara Anne
(accept Germany)	Castle/Baroness
4 Brazil	Castle)
5 May	**14** Kent
6 *Platoon*	**15** Kate Winslet (Kate
7 Tokyo	Elizabeth Winslet)
8 Rugby union (accept	**16** Kopeks
rugby – do not accept	**17** The Lilliputians
rugby league)	**18** Alcatraz
9 *Twain*	**19** Bulgaria
10 Apes	**20** Her hair
11 Child	

Round 106

1 In history, which position in Franklin Roosevelt's government did Harry Truman hold before succeeding him as president in 1945?

2 Which county cricket club is based in Manchester?

3 In entertainment, British model Kimberly Stewart is the daughter of which rock star?

4 In film, what is the name of Ben Elton's directorial debut, about a childless couple desperate for a baby?

5 In travel, which Scandinavian country is primarily famous for its fjords?

6 In which Shakespeare play does the main character murder King Duncan, aided by his wife?

7 What V is the city in south-eastern Russia where the Trans-Siberian Railway terminates?

8 In history, what was the family name of Charles II?

9 Hepatitis A causes the inflammation of which organ?

10 Who directed the action film *Death Wish*?

11 The Aire Gap is an important route by rail, road and canal through which range of hills in northern England?

12 In the human body, which gland produces thyroxin?

13 Saul Hudson is the real name of which former lead guitarist of the band Guns N' Roses?

14 In UK geography, which Hampshire castle stands above Portsmouth Harbour and is enclosed by a Roman wall?

15 In pop music, Emerson, Lake and Palmer had a UK hit single in 1977 with 'Fanfare for the Common . . .' what?

16 In literature, Dante, Virgil and Beatrice are characters in which fourteenth-century poem by Dante Alighieri?

17 In history, by what name were the labour camps for dissidents in the Soviet Union known?

18 What *D* is Britain's smallest flowering plant, which grows on the surface of ponds and ditches?

19 In TV, with which children's programme was the gardener Percy Thrower associated?

20 In US politics, which American president was nicknamed 'The Great Communicator'?

Previous Total

1,000

800

600

450

300

200

100

50

20

Banked

Total

Answers

1 Vice-president
2 Lancashire
3 Rod Stewart
4 *Maybe Baby*
5 Norway
6 *Macbeth* (accept The Scottish Play)
7 Vladivostok
8 Stuart
9 Liver
10 Michael Winner
11 Pennines
12 Thyroid
13 Slash
14 Portchester Castle
15 Man
16 *The Divine Comedy* (accept *Divina Commedia*)
17 Gulags (Main Administration of Corrective Labour Camps)
18 Duckweed
19 *Blue Peter*
20 Ronald Reagan (Ronald Wilson Reagan)

Round 107

1 In nature, what colour is the ripe fruit of a lime tree?

2 In human biology, mouth-to-mouth artificial respiration is commonly known as 'the kiss of . . .' what?

3 What J is the name for a sale of miscellaneous second-hand articles, usually for charity?

4 Which famous American statue depicts a woman carrying a flaming torch?

5 According to tradition, what is broken against a ship when it is first launched?

6 In the children's book *Alice in Wonderland*, which animal does Alice follow at the beginning of the story?

7 In the US TV series, Sarah Michelle Gellar plays the part of Buffy the Vampire . . . what?

8 According to the saying, when pretending to be uninterested, you are 'playing hard to . . .' what?

9 What do British motorists call the part of a car known as the 'trunk' in the USA?

10 In 1982, which member of the royal family was born to Princess Diana and Prince Charles?

11 What was the name of the year 2001 TV show in which five people were selected to form a pop band?

12 In literature, who wrote the best-selling novel *Hollywood Wives*, published in 1983?

13 What S is the needle on a record player?

14 In the nursery rhyme, Jack Spratt could eat no fat and his wife could eat no . . . what?

15 In fashion, on what part of the body would you wear an espadrille?

16 Gamma rays caused Bruce Banner to turn into which large green character?

17 Pop stars Natalie Imbruglia and Kylie Minogue appeared in which Australian TV soap opera?

18 What O is an aquatic mammal commonly found on riverbanks, with partially webbed paws and waterproof fur?

19 A large, hard, spherical sweet designed for sucking is known as a 'gob . . .' what?

20 In which 1993 film did Robin Williams's character disguise himself as an elderly nanny?

Previous Total

1,000

800

600

450

300

200

100

50

20

Banked

Total

Answers

1 Green (accept yellow-green)
2 Life
3 Jumble sale
4 Statue of Liberty (accept Liberty Enlightening the World)
5 A bottle (bottle of champagne/wine/fizzy wine/sparkling wine)
6 (White) Rabbit
7 Slayer
8 Get
9 Boot
10 Prince William (Prince William Arthur Philip Louis/Prince William Windsor)
11 Popstars
12 Jackie Collins
13 Stylus
14 Lean
15 Foot
16 The Hulk (accept The Incredible Hulk)
17 Neighbours
18 Otter
19 Stopper
20 Mrs Doubtfire

Round 108

1 In the animal kingdom, what *L* is a species of marine crustacean with five pairs of legs?

2 In a class of 30 pupils, seventeen pupils had pets. How many did not?

3 Muslin is a type of fabric made from which fibre?

4 In pop music, Lionel Richie had a 1984 UK number-one single with which song: 'Hello' or 'Goodbye'?

5 In rowing, what C is the term that refers to an event in which there is no separate steersman in the boat?

6 What is the name of the UK TV game show in which members of the public or celebrities work with top chefs to produce a meal in twenty minutes?

7 In the animal kingdom, what *D* is the name given to the small, soft feathers that cover and insulate the whole body of a bird?

8 According to the Bible, it is easier for a camel to pass through the eye of a what, than for a rich man to enter the kingdom of God?

9 Robert Carlyle starred in which British film about unemployed Sheffield steelworkers?

10 Which animal is the hippopotamus more closely related to: the horse or the pig?

11 In human biology, what *H* is the name given to a succession of involuntary spasms of the diaphragm, causing a characteristic sound?

12 Which 1980 cartoon starred Evil Edna, Mavis and The Moog as inhabitants of a wood?

13 The Turin Shroud is the cloth thought by many to have covered whose body?

14 In sport, what *R* is the name for the playing area in ice hockey?

15 In a battery, out of which terminal do electrons flow: the positive or negative terminal?

16 Woodrow Wilson was president of which country between 1913 and 1921?

17 In architecture, what *D* is an evenly curved roof with a circular base?

18 In the animal kingdom, which *O* is an ape distinguished by its long red hair?

19 In human biology, the renal arteries supply which organs with blood?

20 In fashion, who was Donatella Versace's famous designer brother?

Previous Total

1,000

800

600

450

300

200

100

50

20

Banked

Total

Answers

1 Lobster
2 Thirteen
3 Cotton
4 'Hello'
5 Coxless
6 *Ready, Steady, Cook*
7 Down
8 Needle
9 *The Full Monty*
10 Pig
11 Hiccup
12 *Willow the Wisp*

13 Jesus Christ (accept Christ/Jesus)
14 Rink
15 Negative
16 USA (accept America/United States/the US)
17 Dome
18 Orang-utan
19 Kidneys
20 Gianni (Versace)

Round 109

1 In cartoons, which famous rabbit made one of his first appearances in *A Wild Hare* in 1940?

2 In music, whose backing group was called The Blockheads?

3 What, in cockney rhyming slang, are 'daisy roots'?

4 In food, macadamia nuts are native to which Antipodean country?

5 Which of the following rivers is longer: the Amazon or Orinoco?

6 What colour is the cross on the national flag of Greece?

7 In history, in which year was Guy Fawkes discovered attempting to blow up James I and Parliament: 1605 or 1705?

8 In the animal kingdom, 'hawk', 'cinnabar' and 'underwing' are types of which insect?

9 The All Saints single 'Pure Shores' was recorded for the soundtrack of which film in the year 2000?

10 In 1980 the formation of a national trade union known as Solidarity took place in which Eastern European country?

11 In food, which is larger: a goose's egg or a quail's egg?

12 With which sport do you associate Pat Rafter?

13 In geography, the Congo is the second largest river of which continent?

14 In the Shakespeare play, who told Macbeth that he would one day become king?

15 In geography, what *K* is the pass which runs for 33 miles, linking Afghanistan and Pakistan?

16 What is the surname of Aaron, the American TV executive who has produced series including *Charlie's Angels* and *Beverly Hills 90210*?

17 In which ocean would you find the China Sea?

18 In food, what *S* are ground-up grains of wheat that are by-products of flour milling and used to make couscous and puddings?

19 CB and short-wave are both types of which form of communication?

20 In TV, which Irish presenter has fronted *Auntie's Sporting Bloomers*, *Children in Need* and his own talk show?

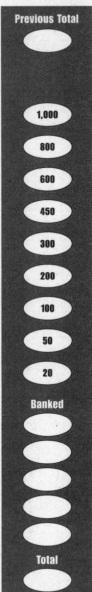

Previous Total

1,000
800
600
450
300
200
100
50
20

Banked

Total

Answers

1 Bugs Bunny	**12** Tennis
2 Ian Dury	**13** Africa
3 Boots	**14** The three witches
4 Australia	(accept three Weird
5 Amazon	Sisters/Weird Sisters)
6 White	**15** Khyber (Pass)
7 1605	**16** Spelling
8 Moth	**17** Pacific Ocean
9 *The Beach*	**18** Semolina
10 Poland	**19** Radio
11 Goose's egg	**20** Terry Wogan

Round 110

1 What *R* is the currency in Sri Lanka, Nepal and Pakistan?

2 At high altitude the body compensates for reduced oxygen by increasing production of which blood cells?

3 In pop music, complete the title of the year 2000 album by Robbie Williams: *Sing When You're . . .* what?

4 What *F* is the name for a decorated band running along the wall of a room, usually below the ceiling?

5 Which queen allegedly sent the Casket Letters to the Earl of Bothwell, which are regarded as evidence of her involvement in her husband's murder?

6 Which 1988 film starring Tom Cruise as a bartender had the tagline 'When he pours, he reigns'?

7 In science, which *K* is a unit of measurement that is used when describing an object's mass?

8 In TV, the diminutive actor Gary Colman played the character Arnold in which 1980s US sitcom?

9 In theatre, complete the title of the song from Irving Berlin's musical about Annie Oakley: 'You Can't Get a Man with a . . .' what?

10 Which *L* is a London theatre you would find in Wellington Street, off The Strand?

11 In politics, of which country did Lionel Jospin become prime minister in 1997?

12 In history, what was the name of Richard the Lionheart's brother, who followed him as king?

13 In 1920s fashion, the term 'Oxford bags' referred to what item of clothing?

14 In UK geography, in which English county would you find Bideford and Ilfracombe?

15 In rock music, which male singer and musician had a band called The Heartbreakers?

16 Where was designer Karl Lagerfeld born?

17 In religion, complete the name of the Afro-American movement led by Elijah Muhammad: The Nation of . . . what?

18 In TV, which cockney bigoted character returned to British screens in 1985 in the series *In Sickness and in Health*?

19 In medicine, an EEG measures electrical impulses in which specific part of the body?

20 In 1988, which *EastEnders* actor married singer Shirley Holliman, a former member of Wham's backing group?

Previous Total

1,000
800
600
450
300
200
100
50
20

Banked

Total

Answers

1 Rupee	**12** John (*accept* John Lackland)
2 Red (*accept* erythro-cytes/corpuscles)	**13** (Wide-legged) Trousers
3 *Winning*	**14** Devon
4 Frieze	**15** Tom Petty
5 Mary Queen of Scots	**16** Germany
6 *Cocktail*	**17** Islam
7 Kilogram	**18** Alf Garnett
8 *Diff'rent Strokes*	**19** Brain (*accept* head/skull)
9 Gun	
10 The Lyceum	**20** Martin Kemp
11 France	

Round 111

1 In maths, if there are 500 sweets in a jar and you eat 50, what percentage is left?

2 How many ventricles are there in a human heart?

3 In nature, what *F* is a term for all the animal life of a particular region or period?

4 In geography, the UK town of Gloucester is on which river?

5 In history, which military dictator took control of Spain in 1936?

6 Which former England cricketer, born in 1955, also played for Scunthorpe United Football Club?

7 In Roman mythology, which *P* was a beautiful princess who was loved by Cupid?

8 In 1661, Isaac Newton entered Trinity College at which university?

9 Pasadena and Long Beach are both found in which US city?

10 In which 1973 film did Robert Redford and Paul Newman cheat a fortune out of a criminal banker?

11 In modern history, Joseph Goebbels served under which European dictator?

12 Which cast member of the US TV series *Friends* starred as Major Don West in the 1998 movie *Lost in Space*?

13 In human biology, the female uterine tube is more commonly known as what?

14 In 1928, which Soviet leader announced the country's first five-year plan?

15 In Greek mythology, Hera was both the wife and which other relation of Zeus?

16 In a rugby union team, how many players act as prop forwards in a scrum?

17 Who starred as Johnny Utah in the 1991 action film *Point Break*?

18 In science, what *P* is the name for the art of making fireworks?

19 Which country built the first man-made object to strike the moon?

20 In world politics, who was the Cuban leader of the anti-Batista rebellion from 1953 to 1959?

Previous Total

1,000

800

600

450

300

200

100

50

20

Banked

Total

Answers

1 90 per cent
2 Two
3 Fauna
4 Severn
5 Franco (General Francisco Franco/ Francisco Paulino Hermenegildo Teodulo Franco Bahamonde)
6 Ian Botham
7 Psyche
8 Cambridge
9 Los Angeles
10 *The Sting*
11 Adolf Hitler
12 Matt Le Blanc
13 Fallopian tube (accept oviduct)
14 Stalin (Josef Stalin/ Josef Vissarionovich/ Iosif Dzhugashuili)
15 Sister
16 Two
17 Keanu Reeves (Keanu Charles Reeves)
18 Pyrotechnics (accept pyrotechny)
19 Soviet Union (accept USSR/Russia)
20 Fidel Castro (Fidel Castro Ruz)

Round 112

1 In sport, which country does Marcus Trescothick represent at cricket?

2 Which US president replaced Herbert Hoover in 1933, promising a 'New Deal' to combat the Depression?

3 In film, which actress played the character Princess Ann in the 1953 romance *Roman Holiday*?

4 In pop music, complete the title of the 1988 Midnight Oil UK hit single 'Beds Are . . .' what?

5 In maths, if you spend £30 per calendar month on your pet, how much do you spend per year?

6 How many points are there on each star of the US flag?

7 In UK politics, who succeeded John Smith as Shadow Chancellor in 1992?

8 In computing, what G is a measure of memory capacity equal to 1024 megabytes?

9 Queens and Staten Island are boroughs of which US city?

10 What F is an old type of gun which is fired by a spark from a stone?

11 In film, who starred opposite Dean Martin in the 1956 comedy *Pardners*?

12 In geography, which limestone plateau is a National Park at the southern end of the Pennines in Derbyshire?

13 Which country and western singer married Hollywood actress Julia Roberts in 1993?

14 In science, a 'bel' is a unit of intensity of sound equal to how many decibels?

15 In which South American country are the seaports of Belem and Recife?

16 In entertainment, what name did Zoe Ball and Norman Cook give their first child?

17 In film, the lines 'Do you expect me to talk?' and 'No, Mr Bond, I expect you to die' are from which 1964 James Bond film?

18 In religion, what is the name of the ancient Chinese religion which means 'the way'?

19 What was the name of Christopher Biggins's character in the BBC sitcom *Porridge*?

20 Which poem about the King Arthur legend was written by Walter Scott in 1810?

Previous Total

1,000
800
600
450
300
200
100
50
20

Banked

Total

Answers

1 England
2 Franklin D. Roosevelt (accept FDR/Franklin Delano Roosevelt – if answer is 'Roosevelt', ask which one)
3 Audrey Hepburn (Edda Van Heemstra Hepburn-Ruston)
4 Burning
5 £360
6 Five
7 Gordon Brown
8 Gigabyte
9 New York (City)
10 Flintlock
11 Jerry Lewis (Joseph Levitch)
12 Peak District
13 Lyle Lovett (Lyle Pearce Lovett)
14 Ten
15 Brazil
16 Woody (accept Woody Cook)
17 *Goldfinger*
18 Tao (Taoism)
19 Lukewarm
20 'The Lady Of The Lake'

Round 113

1 In film, who starred as Paul Maclean in the 1992 movie *A River Runs Through It*?

2 What famous landmark in Banbury was destroyed by Puritans in 1602 but replaced in the nineteenth century?

3 Who succeeded Golda Meir as prime minister of Israel in 1974?

4 In the animal kingdom, what animal is the only mammal, other than the spiny anteater, that lays eggs?

5 In physics, what *I* describes the tendency of an object to remain in a state of rest or uniform motion until external force is applied?

6 In which country was the twentieth-century Existentialist author Simone de Beauvoir born?

7 Which Devon town has given its name to a type of carpet with a long soft pile and complex patterns?

8 In Greek mythology, what *M* was a sorceress who fell in love with Jason and helped him obtain the Golden Fleece?

9 Which British band released the album *(What's the Story) Morning Glory* in 1995?

10 What *F* was a short-lived artistic movement led by French artist Henri Matisse?

11 In November 2000, which river flooded York?

12 In religion, which *M* was the city to which Muhammad fled, from Mecca, in AD 622?

13 In food, what type of nut is usually used to make a Waldorf salad?

14 Which British actress played Matt Damon's love interest in the 1997 Oscar-winning film *Good Will Hunting*?

15 If a jelly is made up of equal parts of lime, strawberry and lemon, what fraction is lemon?

16 In the British Army, what is the name of the national reserve force of volunteer soldiers?

17 In geography, the island of Sumatra is part of which south-east Asian country?

18 Which British-born world heavyweight boxing champion lost to Oliver McCall in 1994?

19 The book *Good Wives* by Louisa May Alcott was the sequel to which classic novel?

20 In which Midlands county is the group of stately homes known as The Dukeries?

Answers

1 Brad Pitt
2 The Banbury Cross (accept the Cross)
3 Yitzhak Rabin
4 Platypus
5 Inertia
6 France
7 Axminster
8 Medea
9 Oasis
10 Fauvism
11 (River) Ouse
12 Medina (accept Madinah/Al Medinah)
13 Walnut
14 Minnie Driver (Amelia Driver)
15 One third
16 Territorial Army (accept TA)
17 Indonesia
18 Lennox Lewis
19 *Little Women*
20 Nottinghamshire

Previous Total

1,000
800
600
450
300
200
100
50
20

Banked

Total

Round 114

1 What G is the state police force of the Republic of Ireland?

2 The 1989 Kevin Costner film about baseball was called *Field of . . .* what?

3 Lake Como is in which European country?

4 In science, what name is given to the coil of wire that is heated in a light bulb?

5 Which M was an ancient country east of the Dead Sea, now in Jordan, which was often at war with Israel?

6 In football, for which Premiership team did Robbie Fowler play at the beginning of 2001?

7 What E is the name given to an electrical connection between an appliance and the ground?

8 In pop music, complete the name of the group formed in Birmingham in 1978: Dexy's Midnight . . . what?

9 In religion, which C was the Chinese teacher and philosopher whose work is recorded in the Analects?

10 In mythology, which C was a prophetess who predicted that Paris's birth would lead to the Troy's destruction?

11 The Alps are in Switzerland, France, Austria and where?

12 Followers of which religion might pay the Purifying Tax, or Zakat, to the poor?

13 Which former England cricket captain had a row with umpire Shakoor Rana which led to the cancellation of a Pakistan tour?

14 Which famous mistress of Charles II was the mother of a Duke of Saint Albans?

15 In literature, which famous nineteenth-century author wrote *Northanger Abbey*?

16 'Don't You Forget About Me' was a 1985 UK hit single for which Scottish band?

17 In November 1999, which country joined Russia and the US as the only nations to put a spacecraft into orbit and then recover it?

18 In film, what is the name of the studios established in 1936 in Buckinghamshire?

19 In UK geography, in which country of the UK is Haverfordwest situated?

20 What *R* is the symbol used to represent a silence or pause?

Previous Total

1,000

800

600

450

300

200

100

50

20

Banked

Total

Answers

1 Garda (accept Garda Siochana)
2 *Dreams*
3 Italy
4 Filament
5 Moab
6 Liverpool
7 Earth
8 Runners
9 Confucius
10 Cassandra
11 Italy
12 Islam (accept Muslim)
13 Mike Gatting (Michael William Gatting)
14 Nell Gwynn
15 Jane Austen
16 Simple Minds
17 China (accept People's Republic of China)
18 Pinewood (Studios)
19 Wales
20 Rest

Round 115

1 To accept that someone is correct whilst not being entirely convinced is known as 'giving them the benefit of the . . .' what?

2 In sport, what is the common name for the stringed bats which are used in games such as tennis and badminton?

3 In entertainment, which top-selling pop singer, born in 1958, was nicknamed 'Jacko' by the press?

4 Complete the following term used in a game of poker: 'a royal . . .' what?

5 In film, who played Professor Henry Higgins in the 1964 musical *My Fair Lady*?

6 In geography, in which hemisphere is the United Kingdom: the northern or southern hemisphere?

7 In football, Marseilles is a team in the domestic league of which European country?

8 In food, what kind of meat product is a bratwurst?

9 In computing, for what do the initials IT stand?

10 In travel, what is the name given to an overland expedition to observe animals, especially popular in Africa?

11 In human biology, what S is a sac-like organ in which food is partially digested?

12 In UK politics, who became prime minister immediately after the 1997 General Election?

13 In an orchestra, who uses a baton?

14 At sea level, and standard pressure, what is the boiling point of water in degrees Celsius?

15 Which famous waxworks museum is located in London's Marylebone Road?

16 Which type of bridge, made up of boats, shares its name with a card game?

17 In terms of passenger numbers, which is the busiest UK airport?

18 In biology, nausea brought on by the motion of vehicles is commonly known as 'travel . . .' or 'motion . . .' what?

19 In rugby union, which country has a badge of a thistle on players' shirts?

20 In music, complete the title of the song from *The Sound of Music*: 'Sixteen Going on . . .' what?

Previous Total

1,000
800
600
450
300
200
100
50
20

Banked

Total

Answers

1 Doubt	**10** Safari
2 Rackets	**11** Stomach
3 Michael Jackson (Michael Joseph Jackson)	**12** Tony Blair (Anthony Charles Lynton Blair)
	13 Conductor
4 Flush	**14** 100 degrees
5 Rex Harrison	**15** Madame Tussaud's
6 Northern	**16** Pontoon
7 France	**17** Heathrow
8 Sausage	**18** Sickness
9 Information Technology	**19** Scotland
	20 'Seventeen'

Round 116

1 In maths, if a quiz show uses 1,000 questions per week, how many does it use in a year?

2 In Roman history, what *G* was the name given to the combatants who fought to the death in arenas?

3 According to the saying, when there is no need for further explanation, a nod is as good as a . . . what?

4 In UK geography, Lizard Point is at the southern tip of which English county?

5 In the animal kingdom, what *D* is a hollow space that an animal uses to live in and rear young?

6 What is the name of the handheld devices which convert sound into an electrical signal at concerts?

7 The Battle of Jutland was fought between Britain and which other European country in 1916?

8 Which tennis tournament did Pete Sampras win for the seventh time in the year 2000?

9 In science, the melting of the core of a nuclear reactor due to overheating is known as a 'melt . . .' what?

10 In the animal kingdom, what *M* is the name given to a dog of mixed breed?

11 Thomas Mapother the Fourth is the real name of which *Mission: Impossible* actor?

12 In nature, what *B* is the name commonly given to the head of an immature mushroom before its cap has expanded?

13 In biology, what species of mammal are *Homo sapiens*?

14 A bowling crease features in which sport?

15 In chess, which piece usually has a top formed in the shape of a battlement?

16 In religion, what *H* is a biblical expression literally meaning 'Praise the Lord'?

17 What is the name for the version of golf which has a series of comical obstacles in the way of the holes?

18 In food, ravioli and tortellini are both types of what?

19 In geography, in which country of the UK is the town of Bognor Regis?

20 In athletics, what is the name of the sixteen-pound ball on the end of a metre-long piece of wire that is used in a throwing event?

Previous Total

1,000

800

600

450

300

200

100

50

20

Banked

Total

Answers

1 52,000
2 Gladiators
3 Wink
4 Cornwall
5 Den
6 Microphones
7 Germany
8 Wimbledon
9 Down
10 Mongrel
11 Tom Cruise
12 Button

13 Human beings (accept man)
14 Cricket
15 Rook (accept castle)
16 Hallelujah (do not accept Hosanna)
17 Crazy golf (mini golf/ miniature golf/putt-putt)
18 Stuffed pasta (accept pasta)
19 England
20 The hammer

Round 117

1 Which is a species of whale: 'pilot' or 'captain'?

2 If you buy nine apples, seven bananas and six oranges from a greengrocer, how many pieces of fruit do you have?

3 In the United States, what *P* was the legal ban on the manufacture and sale of alcohol, which began on 16 January 1920?

4 In TV, Joanna Lumley played the character of Patsy Stone in which comedy series?

5 In film, the director of the 1992 film *Bram Stoker's Dracula* was Francis Ford . . . who?

6 In biology, hypermetropia is more commonly known as what '-sightedness': long or short?

7 A spinach company in Texas erected a statue in 1937 to honour which cartoon character?

8 In computing, what *B* is a program that allows the user to search and view data, especially on the Internet?

9 In TV, which former *Blue Peter* presenter was one of the celebrities in the *Big Brother* house for Comic Relief?

10 In which UK country is Blair Castle?

11 In science, illumination and illuminance means the intensity of what on a surface?

12 Which Oasis band member married Patsy Kensit in 1997?

13 In biology, where do reptiles lay their eggs: on land or in water?

14 In musical theatre, complete the title of the Gilbert and Sullivan song from the operetta *The Pirates of Penzance*: 'I Am the Very Model of a Modern Major . . .' what?

15 In human biology, what name is given to the fluid surrounding a foetus in the womb?

16 In the USA, is the state of California known as the Silver or the Golden State?

17 Debbie McGee is married to which magician?

18 What *M* is a substance often used to make whisky that is obtained by allowing a grain to soften in water and germinate?

19 In TV, actress Lisa Faulkner played a doctor in which hospital-based drama set in Bristol?

20 What *V* is the unit of measurement of potential difference between two points on a conductor?

Previous Total

1,000

800

600

450

300

200

100

50

20

Banked

Total

Answers

1 Pilot	**11** Light
2 22	**12** Liam Gallagher
3 Prohibition	**13** On land
4 *Absolutely Fabulous*	**14** General
5 Coppola (*accept* Francis Ford Coppola)	**15** Amniotic fluid
6 Long	**16** Golden State
7 Popeye	**17** Paul Daniels
8 Browser	**18** Malt
9 Anthea Turner	**19** *Holby City*
10 Scotland	**20** Volt (*accept* voltage)

Round 118

1 In population terms, which is larger: Dorset or Devon?

2 With which style of American music would you associate Hank Williams?

3 In theatre, which former *Big Breakfast* presenter is starring as Roxie Hart in the West End musical *Chicago*?

4 In history, which Russian word meaning 'council' came to refer to the Union of Socialist Republics?

5 In music, Smokey Robinson and Miracles had a 1970 UK number one with 'The Tears of a . . .' what?

6 Which *H* is the name of a town in northern England and the capital city of Nova Scotia in Canada?

7 In modern history, of which country did Mao Zedong become ruler in 1949?

8 In human reproduction, what sex of baby do two X chromosomes produce?

9 In literature, complete the title of E. M. Forster's first novel: *Where . . . [what] Fear To Tread*?

10 In fashion, what type of short skirt was introduced by London designer Mary Quant in the 1960s?

11 At which English university did Charles Darwin study after leaving Edinburgh in 1828?

12 With which band did Holly Johnson have a 1984 UK number-one hit single with the song 'Two Tribes'?

13 In *EastEnders*, which of the Mitchell brothers fled to South America with his daughter Courtney?

14 Which birthday did David and Victoria Beckham's son, Brooklyn, celebrate in March 2001?

15 In literature, from which 1949 George Orwell novel does this quotation come: 'Four legs good, Two legs bad'?

16 Which of these cities is nearest to the equator: Moscow, New York or Sydney?

17 In music, what percussion instrument is a set of metal tubes suspended from a frame and struck with a hammer?

18 In the animal kingdom, what *A* is a South American mammal related to the llama?

19 In sport, which Sussex football league team has the nickname 'Seagulls'?

20 What was the name of Carrie Fisher's character in the original *Star Wars* trilogy?

Previous Total

1,000
800
600
450
300
200
100
50
20

Banked

Total

Answers

1 Devon
2 Country (accept country and western)
3 Denise Van Outen
4 Soviet
5 Clown
6 Halifax
7 China
8 Female (accept girl/girls)
9 *Angels*
10 Mini (skirt)
11 Cambridge
12 Frankie Goes To Hollywood
13 Grant
14 His second
15 *Animal Farm*
16 Sydney
17 Tubular bells (accept chimes)
18 Alpaca
19 Brighton and Hove Albion (accept Brighton)
20 Princess Leia

Round 119

1 In history, in which country did the October Revolution occur in 1917?

2 What Y was the nickname applied during the American Civil War by southerners to northern soldiers?

3 In TV, Betty Turpin and Hilda Ogden have been characters in which soap?

4 In food, what type of vegetable is asparagus: a leaf or stem vegetable?

5 In British politics, with which party was Roy Hattersley associated?

6 In film, which Australian actor, famous for his role in *Shine*, appeared in both *Elizabeth* and *Shakespeare in Love* in 1998?

7 In pop music, which famous singer had hits in 1978 and 1996 with the Scotland football squad?

8 In science, which metal is the better conductor of heat: gold or silver?

9 In nature, which is the tallest-growing tree, native to California?

10 In music, how many *Pomp and Circumstance* marches did Sir Edward Elgar complete: five or ten?

11 In which decade did *Lunik Two* become the first man-made object to strike the moon?

12 Which marine mammals are so called because, in some species, the adult males have a mane?

13 In business, what *A* refers to anything that a company owns that can be turned into cash?

14 When did the mesolithic period occur: during the Stone Age, Iron Age or Ice Age?

15 In TV, the 1980s programme *OTT* was an adult version of which children's show?

16 In 1954, who became the youngest jockey to win the Derby?

17 In the USA, which politician, who went on to become president, delivered the 'Checkers the dog' speech in September 1952?

18 For which political party was Kate Hoey elected MP for Vauxhall in 1989?

19 In sport, which country's cricket team famously wears baggy green hats?

20 In the TV soap *EastEnders*, which character is Jamie Mitchell's godfather?

| Previous Total |
| 1,000 |
| 800 |
| 600 |
| 450 |
| 300 |
| 200 |
| 100 |
| 50 |
| 20 |
| Banked |
| Total |

Answers

1 Russia
2 Yankee(s)
3 *Coronation Street*
4 Stem
5 Labour
6 Geoffrey Rush
7 Rod Stewart (Roderick David Stewart)
8 Silver
9 Redwood (accept California redwood/ sequoia/giant sequoia)
10 Five
11 1950s
12 Sea-lions
13 Asset
14 Stone Age
15 *Tiswas*
16 Lester Piggott
17 Richard Nixon (Richard Milhous Nixon)
18 Labour
19 Australia
20 Phil Mitchell

Round 120

1 Complete the title of the 1978 film starring Gregory Peck and Laurence Olivier: *The Boys From . . .* where?

2 Which 1930s prime minister was the son of Joseph Chamberlain?

3 In pop music, which group won Best British Group at the Brits in 2001: Coldplay or Orbital?

4 When an electric current flows in a metallic conductor, what *E* actually carry the current?

5 In art, which Italian word, meaning 'fresh', describes a method of wall painting on wet plaster?

6 In the USA, Louis Brandeis became the first Jewish man to be appointed to which court in 1916?

7 Sidney Poitier starred as Porgy in which 1959 musical?

8 In pop music, the Bee Gees were born in Britain but brought up in which Antipodean country?

9 Which market town in Devon, at the head of the River Teign estuary, has a National Hunt racecourse?

10 In geography, the Dead Sea is situated between Jordan and which other Middle Eastern country?

11 In music, which American actress and singer had a UK number-one hit single with 'Secret Love' in 1954?

12 What is the name of the German parliament building which was destroyed by fire in 1933?

13 Which US actor starred as the ex-cop Rick Deckard in Ridley Scott's 1982 science-fiction film *Blade Runner*?

14 In World War II, what was the long battle beginning in 1942, in which the German advance into the Soviet Union was halted?

15 The Tyrol is a province in which European country?

16 On which British island is Parkhurst Prison?

17 In which English county is the city of Rochester, which is at the mouth of the River Medway?

18 In which German city did U2 record most of their aptly titled 1991 album *Achtung Baby*?

19 Which blonde actress played Angela Phinlay in the 1950 film *The Asphalt Jungle*?

20 In football, Stan . . . who became the first man to play for six different Premiership clubs in the year 2000?

Answers

1 *Brazil*	**12** The Reichstag
2 Neville Chamberlain (Neville Arthur Chamberlain)	**13** Harrison Ford
	14 The Battle of Stalingrad
3 Coldplay	**15** Austria
4 Electrons	**16** Isle of Wight
5 Fresco	**17** Kent
6 Supreme Court	**18** Berlin
7 *Porgy and Bess*	**19** Marilyn Monroe (Norma Jean Baker)
8 Australia	
9 Newton Abbot	**20** Stan Collymore
10 Israel	
11 Doris Day (Doris Mary Ann von Kappelhoff)	

Previous Total

1,000

800

600

450

300

200

100

50

20

Banked

Total

Round 121

1 Which superheroine first appeared in 1941 in *All-Star* comics?

2 The resort of Santa Eulalia is on which of the Balearic Islands?

3 In film, who played Meredith Johnson in the 1994 thriller *Disclosure*?

4 In theatre, Malcolm is the rightful heir to King Duncan in which Shakespeare play set in Scotland?

5 In pop music, which group had a UK number-one hit single in 1994 with 'Things Can Only Get Better'?

6 What was the name of the queen of the Iceni, who led her people against Roman rule in AD 61?

7 In film, which American actor played Charlie in *Mean Streets* and George Baines in *The Piano*?

8 In which religion is Diwali a late-autumn festival?

9 In 1936, Japan signed the Anti-Comintern Pact with which European country?

10 What *H* is an artillery firearm which takes its name from the Dutch word for 'catapult'?

11 Who wrote the play *Waiting for Godot*?

12 Who wrote the novel *The House on Hope Street*?

13 In mythology, which of the knights of the Round Table was the son of Lancelot?

14 In nature, what *L* is a deciduous conifer of the northern hemisphere, with needles growing in bunches and small woody cones?

15 In sport, which American city is the home of the football team nicknamed 'The Forty-Niners' after the 1849 gold rush?

16 In UK politics, which nineteenth-century British prime minister was of Italian–Jewish descent?

17 In which Thomas Hardy novel does the character Angel Clare appear?

18 In theatre, the actress who famously played Desdemona to Paul Robeson's Othello was Dame Peggy . . . who?

19 Frank Bruno twice fought which American for the WBC Heavyweight Championship?

20 Who starred as Rooster Cogburn in the 1969 film *True Grit*?

Previous Total

1,000
800
600
450
300
200
100
50
20

Banked

Total

Answers

1 Wonder Woman
2 Ibiza
3 Demi Moore (Demetria Gene Guynes)
4 *Macbeth* (accept 'The Scottish Play')
5 D-Ream
6 Boadicea (Boudicca)
7 Harvey Keitel
8 Hinduism (accept Hindu)
9 Germany
10 Howitzer
11 Beckett (Samuel Barclay Beckett)
12 Danielle Steel
13 Galahad
14 Larch
15 San Francisco
16 Benjamin Disraeli (accept Disraeli/Earl of Beaconsfield/ Viscount Hughenden of Hughenden)
17 *Tess of the d'Urbevilles*
18 Ashcroft
19 Mike Tyson (accept Iron Mike Tyson/ Michael Tyson)
20 John Wayne (Marion Michael Morrison)

Round 122

1 In pop music, 'All I Wanna Do' and 'Everyday Is A Winding Road' have been UK hit singles for which American female singer?

2 West Point is a military academy in which country?

3 What was the name of the French cardinal who was made Louis XIII's chief minister in 1624?

4 In pop music, 'Always Come Back To Your Love' was a UK hit in 2001 for Samantha . . . who?

5 Which South American capital city is furthest north?

6 Which Hampshire city would you be entering if you crossed the city bridge over the River Itchen?

7 Which Japanese emperor, who died in January 1989, was an amateur marine biologist?

8 The forint is the monetary unit of which Eastern European country?

9 Which Oscar Wilde play, subtitled 'A Trivial Comedy for Serious People', was first performed in London in 1895?

10 In entertainment, which *Melrose Place* actress is married to Bon Jovi guitarist Richard Sambora?

11 With which East Midlands football club did Gary Lineker begin his professional career?

12 Which Irish rock star played the character Pink in the 1982 film *Pink Floyd: The Wall*?

13 South-west Africa is the former name of which African country?

14 In which Russian city is the Lenin mausoleum?

15 Complete this quote from *The Taming of the Shrew* by William Shakespeare: 'Come on and kiss me . . .' who?

16 In history, by what nickname was Alfred, the king of Wessex, known?

17 In film, which actor played the young Indiana in the 1989 adventure *Indiana Jones and the Last Crusade*?

18 Former World's Strongest Man winner Geoff Capes breeds which type of bird?

19 In which decade was the hovercraft invented?

20 In which English county is the town of Chester-Le-Street?

Previous Total

1,000
800
600
450
300
200
100
50
20

Banked

Total

Answers

1 Sheryl Crow
2 United States (*accept* US/USA/America/ United States of America)
3 Cardinal Richelieu (Armand Jean du Plessis de Richelieu)
4 Mumba
5 Caracas
6 Winchester
7 Hirohito (Showatenno)
8 Hungary
9 *The Importance of Being Earnest*
10 Heather Locklear
11 Leicester City (accept Leicester)
12 Bob Geldof (Robert Frederick Xenon Geldof)
13 Namibia
14 Moscow
15 Kate
16 Alfred the Great (*accept* 'The Great')
17 River Phoenix (River Jude Phoenix)
18 Budgies (budgerigars)
19 1950s
20 (County) Durham

Round 123

1 Complete this well-known saying: 'Rain, rain, go away, come again another . . .' what?

2 With which sport would you associate Monica Seles?

3 Complete the title of the 1993 film starring Tom Hanks and Meg Ryan: *Sleepless in . . .* where?

4 In the animal kingdom, what type of creature is a stingray?

5 In cookery, apple sauce is traditionally served with which meat?

6 Which legendary British figure robbed from the rich and gave to the poor?

7 In pop music, whose 1981 UK number-one album was entitled *Shaky*?

8 In nature, what S is the name given to marine plants found living in the sea or on the seashore?

9 In money, a regular payment made by a bank on a customer's behalf is known as a 'direct . . .' what?

10 Former prime minister Harold Wilson said: 'A week is a long time in . . .' what?

11 Through which of the following does sound travel faster: air or water?

12 In nature, what name is given to an artificial home for bees?

13 In music, which cockney duo had a UK top-ten hit in 1980 with 'Rabbit'?

14 In the Hans Christian Andersen story, which vegetable was placed beneath a stack of mattresses to test a princess?

15 According to tradition, the Pied Piper led which creatures away from Hamelin?

16 In the animal kingdom, what K is an Australian bird known for its laughing song?

17 The organisation FIFA is associated with which sport?

18 The UK TV programme about collectors of old artefacts and furniture is called *The . . .* [what] *Roadshow?*

19 In nature, a popular pancake syrup is extracted from the sap of which variety of tree?

20 Complete the title of the 1971 gangster film starring Michael Caine: *Get . . .* who?

Previous Total
1,000
800
600
450
300
200
100
50
20
Banked
Total

Answers

1 Day	**10** Politics
2 Tennis (*accept* lawn tennis)	**11** Water
	12 Hive (*accept* beehive)
3 *Seattle*	**13** Chas and Dave
4 Fish (*accept* ray fish)	**14** A pea
5 Pork (*accept* goose)	**15** Rats
6 Robin Hood (Robin of Locksley)	**16** Kookaburra
	17 Football (*accept* soccer)
7 Shakin' Stevens (Michael Barratt)	**18** *Antiques*
8 Seaweed	**19** Maple (sugar maple)
9 Debit	**20** Carter

Round 124

1 In food, what name is given to young pilchards that are normally sold in tins?

2 In politics, Sir Geoffrey Howe is associated with which party?

3 In maths, what is 25 per cent expressed as a fraction?

4 According to the saying, someone making a bad start has 'started off on the wrong . . .' what?

5 In the animal kingdom, what *F* is another term used to describe a herd of sheep?

6 According to tradition, which item of jewellery is given by a groom to his bride on their wedding day?

7 Stephen Mangan played which diarist in the 2001 TV series . . . *The Cappuccino Years?*

8 In the Roald Dahl book, what type of factory did Willy Wonka own?

9 In theatre, complete the title of the musical based on the play *The Matchmaker: Hello . . .* who?

10 In photography, what *E* is a print that has been 'blown up'?

11 The actor Aristotle Savalas was better known by which first name?

12 What type of animal is a red snapper?

13 In food, what is the main ingredient of hash browns?

14 In music, complete the title of Barry White's 1974 UK hit single: 'You're the First, the Last, My . . .' what?

15 In geography, in which country of the UK is the county of Gwynedd?

16 A small quantity of alcohol taken as a remedy for a hangover is known as 'hair of the . . .' what?

17 In which sport is the net higher: tennis or badminton?

18 What *B* is the name given to the tall fur hat worn by certain British soldiers?

19 According to tradition, which species of animal supposedly helps Santa to deliver presents to children all round the world?

20 In music, how many members of the Beatles were there?

Previous Total

1,000
800
600
450
300
200
100
50
20

Banked

Total

Answers

1 Sardines	**11** Telly
2 Conservative (accept Tory)	**12** Fish
3 One quarter	**13** Potato
4 Foot	**14** Everything
5 Flock	**15** Wales
6 A ring (wedding ring)	**16** Dog (accept dog that bit one/you)
7 Adrian Mole	**17** Badminton
8 Chocolate (factory)	**18** Busby (accept bearskin)
9 *Dolly*	**19** Reindeer
10 Enlargement (accept enlarged)	**20** Four

Round 125

1 In food, what is the name given to the American double-decker sandwich made with at least two fillings?

2 In politics, Jacques Chirac became president of which country in 1995?

3 In maths, how much would you spend on three boxes of chocolates at £4 each?

4 In the animal kingdom, are mites classified as arachnids or rodents?

5 What is the floral emblem of Switzerland?

6 In the TV comedy *Only Fools and Horses*, which character had the catchphrase 'Luvvly jubbly'?

7 The former British prime minister Margaret Thatcher was known as the 'Iron . . .' what?

8 In the USA, Idaho Falls is a city in which state?

9 In biological classification, what *F* is the family of mammals to which cats belong?

10 In pop music, *Welcome to the Pleasuredome* was a UK hit album in 1984 by which British band?

11 In science, what is the opposite of repulsion?

12 In the animal kingdom, what is the meaning of the Aboriginal word 'koala': 'no water' or 'small bear'?

13 In TV, which cockney comedian now hosts *The Generation Game*?

14 In fashion, what name refers to a set of rules regarding acceptable style of attire?

15 The Star of Africa and the Jubilee are types of which precious gemstone?

16 In Spain, which food is used in the fight at the annual La Tomatina Festival?

17 In tennis, which Swedish player won the Men's French Open every year between 1978 and 1981?

18 In biology, in which body fluid can plasma be found?

19 Which small dog takes its name from the German for 'badger dog'?

20 In pop music, Mick Fleetwood is the drummer with which band?

Previous Total

1,000

800

600

450

300

200

100

50

20

Banked

Total

Answers

1 Club sandwich (accept hero/poor boy)
2 France
3 £12
4 Arachnids
5 Edelweiss
6 Del Boy (accept Del/ Derek/Derek Trotter)
7 Lady
8 Idaho
9 Felines (accept Felidae)
10 Frankie Goes To Hollywood
11 Attraction
12 'No water'
13 Jim Davidson
14 Dress code
15 Diamonds
16 Tomatoes
17 Bjorn Borg
18 Blood
19 Dachshund
20 Fleetwood Mac

Round 126

1 In football, which position did Pat Jennings play during his professional career?

2 In language, which slang word for 'prison' is said to come from the name of a jail in Southwark?

3 In human biology, which are larger: capillaries or veins?

4 In the animal kingdom, what kind of creature is a nightjar?

5 In which country were the first modern Olympic Games held in 1896?

6 In fashion, what *M* is a fibre made from the long, silky hair of the Angora goat?

7 In UK politics, which Labour Prime Minister was in office from 1945 to 1951?

8 In Arthurian legend, which magician guided the destiny of King Arthur?

9 Which group of islands in the Mediterranean Sea includes Majorca, Minorca and Ibiza?

10 In nature, what *H* is Britain's largest wasp?

11 In music, Erasure released cover versions of which Swedish band's songs in 1992?

12 In which English county would you find the towns of Reading, Bracknell and Eton?

13 In Greek mythology, which *Z* was called the father of both gods and men?

14 In the Bible, who broke the original Ten Commandments tablets when he discovered the idolatry of the Israelites?

15 How many kilograms are there in three metric tonnes?

16 Which city is closer to London: Madrid or Berlin?

17 In the animal kingdom, what type of reptile is a 'Flying Dragon'?

18 In America, what was the surname of John Harvey, the food manufacturer famous for producing cereals?

19 In music, which US pop act had 1988 UK hit singles with 'Push It' and 'Twist and Shout': Salt 'n' Pepa or Salt 'n' Vinegar?

20 The 1996 film *The English Patient* is set at the end of which World War?

Previous Total

1,000

800

600

450

300

200

100

50

20

Banked

Total

Answers

1 Goalkeeper (accept goalie)
2 Clink
3 Veins
4 Bird (accept nocturnal bird)
5 Greece
6 Mohair
7 Clement Attlee
8 Merlin
9 Balearic Islands (accept Balearics)
10 Hornet
11 Abba
12 Berkshire
13 Zeus
14 Moses
15 Three thousand
16 Berlin
17 Lizard
18 Kellogg
19 Salt 'n' Pepa
20 Second (accept II)

Round 127

1 With which sport would you associate Leon Spinks?

2 In literature, who illustrated the first edition of *The Tale of Peter Rabbit* by Beatrix Potter?

3 In the animal kingdom, which mammal is known as the 'large cat bear' in China?

4 Which West End show features the songs 'Razzle-Dazzle' and 'All that Jazz'?

5 In geography, which South-east Asian island state is situated off the southern tip of the Malay Peninsula?

6 In the human body, which C is the hard connective tissue that is composed mainly of collagen?

7 In sport, which famous former West Indian cricketer hit more sixes than any other during his Test career?

8 In language, a 'Neddy' is another name for which four-legged animal?

9 In which country was the composer Sergei Rachmaninov born?

10 In TV, where was the Australian drama *The Flying Doctors* set: Cooper's Crossing or Summer Bay?

11 To which order of animals does the hamster belong: rodents or primates?

12 In nature, from which continent did potatoes originate?

13 In which city would you find La Guardia airport?

14 In 1857, the title of 'Prince Consort' was bestowed on whom by Queen Victoria?

15 Complete the title of Ernest Hemingway's 1952 work: *The Old Man and the . . .* what?

16 What type of shop did Hugh Grant's character own in the 1999 film *Notting Hill*?

17 The name of which fast-moving member of the cat family comes from the Hindi for 'having a speckled body'?

18 In pop music, which boy band released a cover of 'Uptown Girl' in aid of Comic Relief?

19 The actor Jean-Claude Van Damme is known as 'The Muscles from . . .' where?

20 What, in common law, is the worst classification of crime: misdemeanour, felony or treason?

Previous Total

1,000

800

600

450

300

200

100

50

20

Banked

Total

Answers

1 Boxing
2 Beatrix Potter (*accept* Helen Beatrix Potter/ Mrs William Heelis)
3 Panda
4 *Chicago*
5 Singapore
6 Cartilage
7 Viv Richards (Sir Vivian Richards)
8 Donkey
9 Russia
10 Cooper's Crossing

11 Rodents
12 South America
13 New York
14 Prince Albert
15 *Sea*
16 Bookshop (accept booksellers/travel book shop)
17 Cheetah
18 Westlife
19 Brussels
20 Treason

Round 128

1 In which country is Darjeeling tea grown?

2 Which British classical composer, famous for *The Planets*, was also a teacher at St Paul's Girls' School?

3 What C describes the code of behaviour followed by medieval knights?

4 What is the surname of Bryan, the Canadian rock star who released a greatest-hits album entitled *So Far So Good*?

5 In literature, in which century did the writer Graham Greene live and work?

6 In film, which actress co-starred with Michael Douglas in the 1984 comedy *Romancing the Stone*?

7 In which English county would you find Shrewsbury and Telford?

8 In which country was the artist Edgar Degas born?

9 In Norse mythology, what was stolen from Thor?

10 In which decade was Mahatma Gandhi assassinated?

11 In which American city might you travel from Union Square to Fisherman's Wharf by cable car?

12 In the British peerage, which is the higher degree of nobility: baron or viscount?

13 In TV, which *Men Behaving Badly* actor starred in the second series of *Jeeves and Wooster*?

14 Lionel Begleiter was the original name of which famous songwriter and composer?

15 Gwyneth Paltrow and Judi Dench both won Oscars for which 1998 film, set mainly in the theatre?

16 In law, was Interpol formed before or after the Second World War?

17 In sport, which car manufacturer provides the engines for the Formula One motor-racing team McLaren?

18 In music, which well-known duo wrote the operetta *The Sorcerer*?

19 A frittata is what type of Italian egg dish?

20 The conspiracy to kill King James I at the 1605 opening of Parliament is known as the '... [*what*] Plot'?

Answers

1 India (*accept* Republic of India)
2 Holst (Gustav Holst/ Gustavus Theodore von Holst)
3 Chivalry
4 Adams
5 Twentieth
6 Kathleen Turner (Mary Kathleen Turner)
7 Shropshire
8 France
9 His hammer
10 1940s (1948)
11 San Francisco
12 Viscount
13 Martin Clunes
14 Lionel Bart
15 Shakespeare In Love
16 Before (1923)
17 Mercedes
18 Gilbert and Sullivan (Sir William Schwenk Gilbert and Sir Arthur Seymour Sullivan)
19 Omelette
20 Gunpowder (Plot)

Round 129

1 In cockney rhyming slang, if you gave someone a 'goose's neck', what would it be?

2 In sport, which country does Kenny Logan represent at rugby union?

3 Originally called Bishop's Lynn in the Middle Ages, the town of King's Lynn is in which English county?

4 In film, what was the name of the 1983 sequel to *Saturday Night Fever*, starring John Travolta?

5 How many European cents make up one euro?

6 In science, in which century did Benjamin Franklin use a kite to prove that lightning was electrical?

7 In geography, what *P* is a dry, barren plateau extending over southern Argentina and Chile?

8 In literature, Matthew Kneale's novel, named as the 2000 Whitbread Book of the Year, is called *English . . . what*?

9 Chattanooga National Military Park in America commemorates which war?

10 What fraction is a sixth plus a half?

11 Which Edward was the first Yorkist king?

12 In history, Benjamin Disraeli and William Gladstone were prime ministers during which century?

13 In nature, what P is the collective name for minute organisms which drift with the currents in seas and lakes?

14 The name of which Jewish ceremony means 'Son of the Commandment'?

15 Which city was the capital of West Germany until unification in 1990?

16 Which music awards started in 1977 but didn't become an annual event until 1982?

17 As what was Frenchman Claude Debussy famous: a composer, artist or philosopher?

18 Who directed the Oscar-winning 1999 film *American Beauty*, starring Kevin Spacey?

19 In literature, from which country does Hellenistic writing come?

20 Which religion was reinstated in England by Mary I in the sixteenth century?

Previous Total

1,000

800

600

450

300

200

100

50

20

Banked

Total

Answers

1 A cheque
2 Scotland
3 Norfolk
4 *Staying Alive*
5 One hundred
6 Eighteenth
7 Patagonia
8 *Passengers*
9 American Civil War
10 Two thirds (*accept* four sixths)
11 Edward IV
12 Nineteenth
13 Plankton
14 Bar Mitzvah
15 Bonn
16 The Brit Awards (*accept* The Brits)
17 Composer
18 Sam Mendes
19 Greece
20 Catholicism (Roman Catholicism)

Round 130

1 What is the second-largest island in the British Isles?

2 In nature, a 'cob' is the male of which long-necked bird?

3 In science, the letters 'oz' are an abbreviation for which imperial measurement of weight?

4 In geography, Queensland is in which part of Australia: the north-east or south-west?

5 In religion, in which testament of the Bible does the story of the Garden of Eden feature?

6 In history, of which country was Macbeth king in the eleventh century?

7 In food, what type of dish is bisque: a soup or a dessert?

8 Which great Italian Renaissance artist and scientist is credited with the invention of the parachute?

9 In nature, which pungent herb is known by the Latin name *Thymus vulgaris*?

10 First elected as an MP in 1983, Chris Smith is associated with which party?

11 Which city was the intended destination of the ocean liner *Titanic*?

12 Which BBC TV show featured the accident-prone Frank Spencer?

13 What is the capital of Austria?

14 In the animal kingdom, is the crocodile a reptile or an amphibian?

15 In the Second World War, two conferences were held between Roosevelt and which British leader in Quebec in 1943 and 1944?

16 In theatre, what is the surname of Elaine, the British singer and actress who starred in the musicals *Evita*, *Cats* and *Chess*?

17 On which coast of England is the seaside resort of Bridlington: west or east?

18 In the Hindu religion, Krishna is often depicted with a herd of which animals?

19 Is English musician Emma Kirkby famous as a clarinettist or a singer?

20 In the animal kingdom, what *P* is a rodent that, when threatened, charges backwards and drives its spines into its attacker?

Previous Total

1,000
800
600
450
300
200
100
50
20

Banked

Total

Answers

1 Ireland
2 Swan
3 Ounce
4 North-east
5 Old (Testament)
6 Scotland
7 Soup
8 Leonardo da Vinci (accept Leonardo/ Leonardo di Ser Piero da Vinci)
9 Thyme
10 Labour (accept New Labour)
11 New York
12 *Some Mothers Do 'Ave 'Em*
13 Vienna
14 Reptile
15 Winston Churchill (Winston Leonard Spencer Churchill)
16 Paige
17 East
18 Cows (accept cattle)
19 Singer
20 Porcupine

Round 131

1 In which US state are the UCLA and USC colleges?

2 Which motorcycle stunt man, born in 1938, was known as 'The king of the daredevils'?

3 In the British Navy, which is the higher rank: admiral or lieutenant?

4 Which Scottish actor played the drug addict Mark Renton in the 1996 film *Trainspotting*?

5 In American football, which team won the 2001 Super Bowl: the Baltimore Ravens or the New York Jets?

6 In medicine, a 'contusion' is more commonly known as what *B*?

7 If a man has £1,100 in his bank account and he withdraws £800, how much money is left in the account?

8 If an actor is told to go downstage, would he be going nearer to or further away from the audience?

9 Which country has the maple leaf as its national symbol?

10 The male of which British thrush has an orange beak and all-over black plumage?

11 Queen Victoria succeeded which king to the throne in 1837: William III or IV?

12 The town of Barnstaple is in which English county?

13 In film, what is the real first name of the actor Gary Oldman: Leonard or Howard?

14 What is the name of the system of measurement based on the metre?

15 The full name of Schiphol Airport includes the name of which Dutch city?

16 With which character did Lenny Godber share a cell in the TV sitcom *Porridge*?

17 In maths, if it costs £30 to connect a phone line in an office, how much does it cost in total to connect twenty phone lines?

18 In the name of the meat substitute TVP, for what does the letter *P* stand?

19 In Shakespeare's play *King Lear*, what relation is Lear to Goneril: father or brother?

20 How many members were there in the original line-up of the Spice Girls?

Previous Total

1,000

800

600

450

300

200

100

50

20

Banked

Total

Answers

1 California
2 Evel Knievel (Robert Craig Knievel)
3 Admiral
4 Ewan McGregor (Ewan Gordon McGregor)
5 Baltimore Ravens
6 Bruise
7 £300
8 Nearer
9 Canada
10 Blackbird (*accept Turdus merula*)
11 IV
12 Devon
13 Leonard
14 Metric system
15 Amsterdam
16 Norman Stanley Fletcher (*accept Fletcher/Fletch*)
17 £600
18 Protein (Textured Vegetable Protein)
19 Father
20 Five

Round 132

1 In politics, who has been the longest-serving post-war Chancellor of the Exchequer: Denis Healey, Geoffrey Howe or Nigel Lawson?

2 In history, in which European country was the heir to the throne known as the 'Dauphin'?

3 In TV, which *EastEnders* actress played Saucy Nancy in the 1970s and 1980s children's series *Worzel Gummidge*?

4 What is the full name of the English town where William Shakespeare is buried?

5 Which country is further by air from England: Australia or Thailand?

6 In the human skeleton, there are 206 what?

7 On which Beatles album are the songs 'Eleanor Rigby' and 'Yellow Submarine': *The White Album* or *Revolver*?

8 In computing, what B is an error in a program that is also a common term used to describe insects?

9 Which country lies between Norway and Finland?

10 Which children's TV builder has tools called Scoop the Digger and Travis the Tractor?

11 In nature, what W is the feature generated by the action of the wind on the surface of the sea?

12 Excluding substitutes, how many players are there in a Test cricket team?

13 Which Northern Irish *Schindler's List* actor married Natasha Richardson in 1994?

14 Ascorbic acid is better known as which vitamin?

15 Was the poet Wilfred Owen killed in action, aged 25, in 1918 or 1945?

16 For what do the initials YWCA stand?

17 What is the name of singer Donny Osmond's sister?

18 In tennis, what is it called when a player faults twice on service?

19 Who composed the soundtrack for the film *The Empire Strikes Back*: Julian Bream or John Williams?

20 What *D* is the type of animal that Pavlov used to test his theory of the conditioned reflex?

Previous Total
1,000
800
600
450
300
200
100
50
20
Banked
Total

Answers

1 Nigel Lawson
2 France
3 Barbara Windsor (Barbara Ann Deeks)
4 Stratford-upon-Avon (*accept* Stratford-on-Avon; *do not accept* Stratford)
5 Australia
6 Bones
7 *Revolver*
8 Bug
9 Sweden
10 Bob The Builder (*accept* Bob)
11 Waves
12 Eleven
13 Liam Neeson (William John Neeson)
14 Vitamin C
15 1918
16 Young Women's Christian Association
17 Marie (Osmond)
18 Double fault
19 John Williams
20 Dogs

Round 133

1 In which European country does Chianti wine originate?

2 Which country forms the northernmost part of Great Britain and the UK?

3 In nature, where would you be most likely to find a Brown Dwarf: in the ocean or in space?

4 The dessert 'tiramisu' is from which European country?

5 Which Andrew Lloyd Webber musical features the song 'Mister Mistoffelees'?

6 In which 1967 cartoon film do the characters Mowgli and Baloo appear?

7 In science, on which planet is a year shorter than a day: Mars or Venus?

8 Which female singer left The Go-Gos to launch a solo career, topping the charts in 1987 with 'Heaven is a Place On Earth'?

9 In snooker, if the balls are potted in order, which will be the last to go down?

10 Who plays the male lead in the 1999 film *Notting Hill*?

11 In literature, who does the character Jane Eyre marry in Charlotte Brontë's novel of the same name: Mr Rochester or Mr Winchester?

12 Fashion designer Laura Ashley was born in which country of the British Isles?

13 The first nuclear reactor used for producing electricity was built in which decade?

14 Which of the Brontë sisters wrote the novel *Villette* in the nineteenth century?

15 What is the name of the permanent bony outgrowth on the head of an animal?

16 Which famous children's author wrote *The Tale of Squirrel Nutkin* and *The Tale of Benjamin Bunny*?

17 The monarch's approval of a bill that has been passed by the Houses of Commons and Lords is referred to as the 'royal . . .' what?

18 Who became the 41st president of the United States in 1989?

19 Who discovered penicillin in 1928?

20 What is the surname of Lenny, the singer/guitarist whose albums have included *Let Love Rule* and *Mama Said*?

Previous Total

1,000
800
600
450
300
200
100
50
20

Banked

Total

Answers

1 Italy
2 Scotland
3 Space (it's a star)
4 Italy
5 *Cats*
6 *The Jungle Book*
7 Venus
8 Belinda Carlisle
9 Black
10 Hugh Grant
11 Mr Rochester
12 Wales

13 1950s
14 Charlotte
15 Horn
16 Beatrix Potter (accept Helen Beatrix Potter)
17 Assent
18 George Bush (George Herbert Walker Bush)
19 (Sir Alexander) Fleming
20 Kravitz

Round 134

1 In sport, what is a pugilist?

2 In British politics, what sex were the suffragettes?

3 In which city was the University of Chile founded in 1738?

4 Which type of musician are there normally more of in a symphony orchestra: string or woodwind players?

5 The name of which group of sea creatures means 'crusty ones'?

6 In the USA, the letters HI are used as the postal abbreviation for which state?

7 In literature, which novel did Daniel Defoe write in the eighteenth century about a man's adventures following his shipwreck?

8 In history, Osborne House on the Isle of Wight was built in 1845 for which British Queen?

9 In film, Meg Ryan starred opposite which actor in the 1998 comedy *You've Got Mail*?

10 In human biology, what name is given to the small sac from which a hair grows?

11 In literature, Queequeg was the harpoonist in search of which whale in Herman Melville's 1851 novel?

12 In which African country would you find the Orange River and Table Mountain?

13 On TV, which political satire programme is presented by Angus Deayton?

14 In art, Vincent van Gogh's 1888 series of paintings took which flower as its theme?

15 In rugby, what is it called when a player throws the ball to another member of his team?

16 Which French term is used to describe high-quality fashion design and leading fashion houses?

17 In theatre, of what is RADA the acronym?

18 In sport, which male tennis star was born in Las Vegas in 1970?

19 Culver City and Beverly Hills are both areas of which US city?

20 Which Latin star had a worldwide hit in 1999 with 'Livin' La Vida Loca'?

Previous Total

1,000

800

600

450

300

200

100

50

20

Banked

Total

Answers

1 A boxer	**12** South Africa (Republic of South Africa)
2 Female	
3 Santiago	
4 String	**13** *Have I Got News For You*
5 Crustacea (accept crustaceans)	
6 Hawaii	**14** Sunflower
7 *Robinson Crusoe*	**15** Pass
8 (Queen) Victoria	**16** *Haute couture*
9 Tom Hanks (Thomas J. Hanks)	**17** Royal Academy of Dramatic Art
	18 Andre Agassi
10 Follicle	**19** Los Angeles
11 *Moby Dick*	**20** Ricky Martin

Round 135

1 In nature, what *M* is an insect similar to a butterfly that is mainly nocturnal and commonly breeds inside clothes?

2 Which *Die Hard* actor played Butch Coolidge in the 1994 film *Pulp Fiction*?

3 In biology, what *H* is a term used to describe a creature that has both male and female reproductive organs?

4 In pop music, Huey Morgan is the lead singer of the band The Fun Lovin' . . . what?

5 The word 'cardioid' refers to anything that has the shape of which human organ?

6 In film, what was the sequel to the 1987 comedy *Three Men and a Baby*?

7 According to Greek legend, which ancient city was entered in the thirteenth century BC by soldiers hidden in a wooden horse?

8 The 'Wailing Wall' is a sacred site for which religion?

9 In the *Little Misses* series of children's books, what colour was Little Miss Sunshine?

10 In music, Ronnie . . . [who] opened his jazz club in London's Soho in 1959?

11 Ginza is a world-famous shopping district in which Asian city?

12 What *Q* is one of the most common minerals on Earth?

13 In nature, the climbing wild flower 'Traveller's Joy' is also known as 'Old Man's . . .' what?

14 Which US theme park opened near Paris in 1992?

15 In the 1970s, which pianist was known for wearing beaded tuxedos with diamond buttons spelling out his name?

16 If a bar of chocolate weighs 100 g and you eat a quarter, how many grams are left?

17 Complete the name of the Muslim building in Jerusalem: the 'Dome of the . . .' what?

18 Which band had a 1976 UK hit single with 'Somebody To Love'?

19 What is the name of the feature-length animated film by *Wallace and Gromit* creator Nick Park, released in 2000?

20 The traditional word-guessing game is called 'Animal, Vegetable or . . .' what?

Previous Total

1,000

800

600

450

300

200

100

50

20

Banked

Total

Answers

1 Moth
2 Bruce Willis (Walter Bruce Willis)
3 Hermaphrodite (accept hermaphroditic, hermaphroditical)
4 Criminals
5 Heart
6 *Three Men and a Little Lady*
7 Troy
8 Judaism (accept Jewish)
9 Yellow
10 Scott
11 Tokyo (accept Tokyo–Yokohama Metropolitan Area)
12 Quartz
13 Beard
14 Disneyland Paris (accept Euro Disney)
15 Liberace (Wladziu Valentino Liberace)
16 75 grams
17 Rock
18 Queen
19 *Chicken Run*
20 Mineral

Round 136

1 In nature, which is the tallest living land mammal?

2 In motor racing, what is the name of the track-side area where emergency repairs can take place?

3 In 1986, Sarah Margaret Ferguson became the Duchess of . . . where?

4 In *Alice's Adventures in Wonderland*, to which suit of cards were the king and queen affiliated?

5 In science, an ohm is the measurement of what in an electrical circuit: resistance or current?

6 How many members has girl group Atomic Kitten?

7 In modern history, by what name was the Latin American revolutionary Ernesto Guevara better known?

8 In the animal kingdom, what is a squid: a mollusc or a crustacean?

9 In food, the preserve 'jam' is known as what in the United States?

10 In nature, what *F* is the name given to a large amount of water that has overflowed from a source such as a river or lake?

11 In politics, Ronald Reagan was president of which country between 1981 and 1989?

12 In cockney rhyming slang, to what does the term 'loaf of bread' refer?

13 In Greek mythology, what type of winged animal was Pegasus?

14 In politics, in which decade was the Beveridge Report, which led to the establishment of the Welfare State, released: the 1940s, 1950s or 1960s?

15 In football, which Liverpool striker became the youngest player to win an England cap since 1881, when he played Chile in 1998?

16 In the English language, which vowel is the ninth letter of the alphabet?

17 In TV, Oasis provide the theme music for which sitcom starring Ricky Tomlinson?

18 In literature, which of the following books was written by William Golding: *The Lord of the Rings* or *Lord of the Flies*?

19 In maths, if a golfer plays nine holes and averages four strokes per hole, how many strokes does he take in total?

20 Who is Kirk Douglas's famous Welsh daughter-in-law?

Previous Total

1,000
800
600
450
300
200
100
50
20

Banked

Total

Answers

1 Giraffe	**11** United States
2 The pit	**12** The head
3 York	**13** Horse
4 Hearts	**14** 1940s (1942)
5 Resistance	**15** Michael Owen
6 Three	**16** I
7 Che (Guevara)	**17** *The Royle Family*
8 Mollusc	**18** *Lord of the Flies*
9 Jelly	**19** 36
10 Flood	**20** Catherine Zeta Jones

Round 137

1 In the human body, which *P* is a gland found between the duodenum and the spleen?

2 Which word can follow 'happy' and 'witching' to make new expressions?

3 Which TV gameshow has been presented by Bob Monkhouse, Max Bygraves and Les Dennis?

4 In which year was the State of Israel proclaimed: 1948 or 1949?

5 A lodestone or piece of magnetic rock was an early form of which direction finding instrument?

6 In literature, which John was an English Romantic poet, who died at the age of 25 from tuberculosis?

7 Theodore Roosevelt and Abraham Lincoln are two of the US presidents whose image is carved into the Mount Rushmore – name one of the other two.

8 What *P* is the slang term used for stage properties?

9 Which French singer had a hit in 1970 with 'Raindrops Keep Falling On My Head'?

10 Which flowering plant was named after the French botanist Pierre Magnol?

11 Does the leader in the 'Giro d'Italia' cycle race wear a pink or a yellow jersey?

12 What *O* is the name given to the study of the oceans?

13 Did Samuel Morse send the first Morse code message in the 1830s, 1840s or 1850s?

14 By what name was Marilyn Monroe known before she officially changed it in 1956?

15 In terms of population, which is the largest Scottish City – Glasgow or Edinburgh?

16 Which S is the acid contained in acid rain?

17 What nationality was the painter and engraver Albrecht Durer?

18 What P is the name given to the floor of the auditorium, usually below ground level, and now the place where the orchestra sits?

19 In which city and spa town on the River Avon in south-west England would you find the Royal Crescent and the Assembly Rooms?

20 What G was the ancient region of Europe, which included present day France, Belgium, the Southern Netherlands, South-West Germany and Northern Italy?

Previous Total

1,000

800

600

450

300

200

100

50

20

Banked

Total

Answers

1 Pancreas	**10** Magnolia
2 Hour	**11** Pink
3 *Family Fortunes*	**12** Oceanography
4 1948	**13** 1840s (1844)
5 Compass	**14** Norma Jean Baker
6 John Keats	**15** Glasgow
7 Thomas Jefferson or George Washington (Accept Jefferson or Washington)	**16** Sulphuric (Acid)
	17 German
	18 Pit
8 Props	**19** Bath
9 Sacha Distel	**20** Gaul (accept Gaule / Gallia)

Round 138

1 In the animal kingdom, which collective term describes a hunting group of wolves or hounds?

2 In British politics, with which party is Norman Tebbitt associated?

3 In sport, which Spanish football club is known as 'Barca'?

4 In which US state are Newark and Jersey City?

5 In the Second World War, in which year of the 1940s did Japan surrender?

6 In which English county is Arundel Castle: Dorset or West Sussex?

7 In pop music, at the 2001 Brit Awards, which Irish rock band received an award for 'Outstanding Contribution to Music'?

8 In geography, in which country is the Colorado Desert?

9 What *P* is the name of the oven-proof glassware developed in the US in 1915?

10 In nature, what type of plant is parsley: annual or biennial?

11 The US city of Pittsburgh is most associated with the manufacture of which metal alloy?

12 In pop music, complete the title of Will Smith's 1999 UK hit single 'Wild Wild . . .' what?

13 If a liquid with a lower density than water is mixed with water, what will it do: sink or float?

14 In TV, in which decade was the comedy series *Men Behaving Badly* first broadcast on the BBC?

15 In the animal kingdom, how many species of polar bear are there: one or three?

16 Dragonflies and butterflies have four wings. How many wings does a house fly have?

17 In which century was gunpowder first used in European weapons: the twelfth, thirteenth or fourteenth century?

18 In maths, if you earn fifteen million pounds and spend half of it on a new house, how much is left?

19 According to the phrase, if a space is very small, which animal is there no room to swing?

20 In human biology, the term 'renal' refers to which organs?

Previous Total

1,000
800
600
450
300
200
100
50
20

Banked

Total

Answers

1 Pack	**11** Steel
2 Conservative (accept Tory)	**12** West
3 Barcelona	**13** Float
4 New Jersey	**14** 1990s (1992)
5 1945	**15** One
6 West Sussex	**16** Two
7 U2	**17** Fourteenth
8 United States (accept America)	**18** Seven and a half million pounds
9 Pyrex	**19** A cat
10 Biennial	**20** Kidneys

Round 139

1 In pop music, complete the title of Deacon Blue's 1988 UK hit single 'Real Gone . . .' what?

2 In geography, the west coast of Mexico overlooks which ocean?

3 'Zoophobia' is a fear of what?

4 In basketball, what is it called when play is temporarily suspended at the request of a team to discuss strategy?

5 The oldest quarter of which city is known as the Plaka: Athens or Lisbon?

6 In clothing, what type of men's formal evening suit was designed in the 1880s in America by Pierre Lorillard?

7 In geography, Sardinia is an island off the west coast of which country?

8 In Elizabethan times, Richard Burbage was renowned for his career as what?

9 What is the name of the British charity founded in 1895 which works for the preservation of places of historic interest or natural beauty?

10 In the 1760s, a machine was invented for the mass production of cotton thread called the 'Spinning . . .' what?

11 In Christianity, Holy Week is the week preceding which annual festival?

12 In which 1999 film does Julia Roberts fall in love with Hugh Grant?

Previous Total

13 In the human body, what *H* are tendons that control the bending of the knee?

14 In food, 'whey' is a by-product of the manufacture of which dairy product?

15 When does a Bunsen burner burn gas at its hottest: when the collar is open or closed?

16 Originating in Cuba, what *B* is a pair of small, single-headed cylindrical or conical drums?

17 In football, for which English club did Peter Schmeichel play between 1991 and 1999?

18 In which US state is the Grand Canyon?

19 The name of which type of spirit is derived from the Gaelic for 'water of life'?

20 In wartime, what is the name for the official allowance of food in a time of shortage?

1,000
800
600
450
300
200
100
50
20

Banked

Total

Answers

1 Kid
2 Pacific
3 Animals
4 A time-out
5 Athens
6 Tuxedo (*accept* dinner jacket/DJ)
7 Italy
8 An actor (*accept* thespian/performer)
9 The National Trust
10 Jenny
11 Easter (*accept* Easter Sunday/Easter Day)
12 *Notting Hill*
13 Hamstring(s)
14 Cheese
15 Open
16 Bongos (*accept* bongo drums)
17 Manchester United (*accept* Man U/Man United)
18 Arizona
19 Whisky
20 Rationing

Round 140

1 In the animal kingdom, which sex of lobster has the larger claws: the male or female?

2 On the children's TV show *Rainbow*, what was the name of the large bear character?

3 Which Australian singer and actor had a 1991 UK number-one hit single with 'Any Dream Will Do'?

4 What *H* is the study of garden cultivation?

5 Invented in 1903, the electrocardiograph was designed to monitor what?

6 Who is older: Bill Clinton, Al Gore or George W. Bush?

7 In human biology, 'Otitis media' is a condition more commonly known as 'glue . . .' what?

8 What is the capital of Portugal?

9 In which TV series did Diana Rigg play a character called Emma Peel?

10 Who, after he received the BBC Sports Personality of the Century award said: 'I had a great time boxing, I enjoyed it – and I might come back'?

11 The childhood disease of the parotid salivary glands characterised by a swollen neck or face is commonly known as what?

12 Which British actor won an Oscar in 2000 for his role in *The Cider House Rules*?

13 In food, ricotta, fontina and mascarpone are all varieties of which dairy product?

14 In which century were contact lenses invented?

15 In music, what C is a small, valved brass instrument similar to a trumpet?

16 In nature, what is basil: a herb or a spice?

17 In sport, what is the name for the type of shoes worn by track athletes, so called because of the pointed grips in the soles?

18 In the animal kingdom, a peacock is which gender of the species: male or female?

19 In science, a hydrometer is an instrument used to measure the density of what: solids or liquids?

20 In the military, what G is the American equivalent of a British Field Marshal?

Previous Total

1,000

800

600

450

300

200

100

50

20

Banked

Total

Answers

1 Male

2 Bungle (accept Bungle the Bear)

3 Jason Donovan

4 Horticulture

5 Heartbeats (accept heart/heart rate)

6 George W. Bush

7 Ear

8 Lisbon

9 *The Avengers*

10 Muhammad Ali (Cassius Marcellus Clay)

11 Mumps

12 Michael Caine (Sir Maurice Micklewhite)

13 Cheese

14 Nineteenth

15 Cornet (accept clarion)

16 Herb

17 Spikes (accept running spikes)

18 Male

19 Liquids

20 General

Round 141

1 Which actor played James Bond in the film *Goldeneye*?

2 In which language did Samuel Beckett's play *Waiting for Godot* first appear: French or English?

3 In which century did Louis Pasteur invent pasteurisation?

4 Which type of bird, similar to the finches, shares its name with a general term for small decorative flags?

5 In UK geography, which is further by road from London: Liverpool or Dorchester?

6 In film, the song 'Sixteen Going on Seventeen' is from which 1965 musical?

7 In history, which famous French heroine is also known as the Maid of Orléans?

8 In science, Marie Sklodowska was the maiden name of which famous scientist?

9 Which US city in Louisiana is traditionally called the 'birthplace of jazz'?

10 Which French footballer joined Manchester United from Leeds in November 1992?

11 In literature, the Montagues and Capulets were feuding families in which famous Shakespeare love story?

12 In maths, if you were born on 8 October 1977, what age did you become on the same date in the year 2000?

13 In science, what is the name of the device which produces a beam of high-intensity coherent light?

14 In world geography, the Galapagos Islands are in which ocean?

15 Which French designer created Madonna's bustiers in the late eighties and early nineties?

16 Thunder Bay is a city and port in which North American country?

17 In boxing, which British heavyweight suffered defeats in world title fights against Tim Witherspoon, Mike Tyson and Lennox Lewis?

18 In maths, what is ten per cent of £1.50?

19 In popular culture, Bud Abbott was one half of which comedy duo?

20 In science, which hard metal, with the chemical symbol Co, is used in the preparation of magnetic alloys?

Previous Total

1,000

800

600

450

300

200

100

50

20

Banked

Total

Answers

1 Pierce Brosnan	**11** *Romeo and Juliet*
2 French	**12** Twenty-three
3 Nineteenth	**13** Laser
4 Bunting	**14** Pacific (Ocean)
5 Liverpool	**15** Jean-Paul Gaultier
6 *The Sound of Music*	**16** Canada
7 Joan of Arc (accept Jeanne d'Arc)	**17** Frank Bruno (Franklin Bruno)
8 Marie Curie	**18** Fifteen pence
9 New Orleans	**19** Abbott and Costello
10 Eric Cantona	**20** Cobalt

Round 142

1 'The Scottish Play' is another name for which of Shakespeare's plays?

2 In the 1967 Walt Disney film classic *The Jungle Book*, by what other name was 'the man cub' known?

3 In pop music, in which country did the rock group Bon Jovi originate?

4 Which Greek philosopher wrote *Republic*?

5 In which TV sitcom would you expect to hear the catchphrase 'I don't believe it!'?

6 In which American sport do you have 'linebackers' and 'nose tackles'?

7 Which knighted English actor died in May 2000, aged 96?

8 Which playwright wrote the TV series *The Singing Detective*?

9 In art, willow-pattern crockery is an imitation of traditional designs from which country?

10 What was Elvis Presley's middle name?

11 In which civilisation's mythology was Venus the goddess of love and beauty?

12 In alchemy, the mythical substance supposed to change base metals into gold is known as the 'Philosopher's . . .' what?

13 In nature, the world's largest rainforest surrounds which major river in South America?

14 'Here's one I made earlier' is a catchphrase on which long-running BBC children's TV show?

15 By what name was US president Thomas Wilson better known?

16 In fashion, Mary . . . [who] popularised the miniskirt in the 1960s?

17 In the animal kingdom, 'Great White', 'Tiger' and 'Bull' are all types of which marine fish?

18 In government, the cabinet minister who delivers the annual budget speech in Parliament is known as the Chancellor of the . . . what?

19 In film, which actor played Harry Callahan in the 1971 thriller *Dirty Harry*?

20 Complete the first line from Shakespeare's 'Sonnet 18': 'Shall I compare thee to a . . .' what?

Previous Total
1,000
800
600
450
300
200
100
50
20
Banked
Total

Answers

1 Macbeth	**11** Roman
2 Mowgli	**12** Stone
3 United States	**13** Amazon
4 Plato	**14** *Blue Peter*
5 *One Foot in the Grave*	**15** Woodrow (Woodrow Wilson)
6 American football	
7 Sir John Gielgud	**16** Quant (Mary Quant)
8 Dennis Potter (Dennis Christopher George Potter)	**17** Sharks
	18 Exchequer
	19 Clint Eastwood (Clinton Eastwood Jnr)
9 China	
10 Aaron (accept Aron)	**20** Summer's day

Round 143

1 In law, which country in the British Isles has a civil court called the Court of Session?

2 What W is the bowl-shaped pan used in Chinese cooking for stir-frying?

3 In computing, what does 'IT' stand for?

4 In science, what type of elements make up about 75 per cent of the periodic table: metallic or non-metallic?

5 In UK politics, what symbol is the voter asked to make on a ballot paper to indicate his or her choice?

6 American Prohibition, introduced in 1933, made the manufacture and sale of what substance illegal?

7 In the evolution of man, which came first: *Homo erectus* or *Homo sapiens*?

8 In cosmetics, what M is make-up for eyelashes?

9 In film, which famous animator produced the 1964 musical *Mary Poppins*?

10 Which country of the UK have Lawrence Dallaglio and Rory Underwood represented at rugby union?

11 What W is the West Midlands town that was granted city status in the year 2000?

12 Who became one of the oldest people ever to reach number one when he topped the UK charts in 1999 with 'Millennium Prayer'?

13 What do we call the number the Romans represented by the letter *X*?

14 In nature, papyrus is a grasslike aquatic plant that lends its name to what piece of stationery?

15 In cricket, which famous international ground is owned by the MCC?

16 According to the legend, what was the name of King Arthur's sword?

17 Who was the first Roman Catholic to be elected president of the United States?

18 The Gateway of India is a monumental arch in which city?

19 In law, what is the name for the payment by a tenant for the use of another's property?

20 In science, a 'crith' is a unit of mass for weighing what: liquids or gases?

1,000

800

600

450

300

200

100

50

20

Banked

Total

Answers

1 Scotland
2 Wok
3 Information Technology
4 Metallic
5 Cross (accept X)
6 Alcohol
7 *Homo erectus*
8 Mascara
9 Walt Disney
10 England
11 Wolverhampton
12 Cliff Richard (Sir Cliff Richard/Harry Webb)
13 Ten
14 Paper
15 Lords
16 Excalibur
17 Kennedy (accept JFK/ John F. Kennedy/John Fitzgerald Kennedy)
18 Mumbai (accept Bombay)
19 Rent (accept hire/ lease)
20 Gases

Round 144

1 In food, frankfurter sausages originate from which country?

2 In the animal kingdom, what word describes the fastest pace of a horse?

3 In geography, on which coast of South America is Chile situated: the east or the west?

4 In the TV series *EastEnders*, what did Pauline Beale's surname become when she married Arthur?

5 Which former world heavyweight boxing champion had the nickname 'Smokin' Joe'?

6 In science, what type of electricity does a power station produce: AC or DC?

7 Lyricist Tim Rice collaborated with which composer on the musical *Jesus Christ Superstar*?

8 In which country of the UK would you find the towns of Downpatrick and Portadown: Northern Ireland or Scotland?

9 In maths, what is fifteen times eight?

10 Which famous Russian poet wrote *The Prisoner of the Caucasus*: Alexander Pushkin or Boris Pasternak?

11 In the animal kingdom, a katydid is what type of insect: a grasshopper or a spider?

12 What K is the largest city and chief seaport in Pakistan?

13 On TV, which first name is shared by the actors who play Chandler and Joey in *Friends*?

14 What name is given to an abscess that forms around the base of an eyelash?

15 In the USA, the initials ACLU stand for the 'American Civil Liberties . . .' what?

16 In science, what is the name for a stationary electrical charge which builds up on an insulated object?

17 Which British playwright wrote *Dr Faustus* and *Tamburlaine the Great*?

18 The whale belongs to which order of animals: fish or mammals?

19 After which English duke was the American city of New Amsterdam renamed in the seventeenth century?

20 In how many *Rambo* films did Sylvester Stallone star?

Previous Total

1,000

800

600

450

300

200

100

50

20

Banked

Total

Answers

1 Germany	**12** Karachi
2 Gallop	**13** Matt (*accept* Matthew)
3 West	**14** Stye
4 Fowler	**15** Union
5 Joe Frazier	**16** Static electricity (static)
6 AC	**17** Christopher Marlowe (*accept* Kit Marlowe/ Marlowe)
7 Andrew Lloyd Webber (*accept* Lord Lloyd Webber)	**18** Mammals
8 Northern Ireland	**19** The Duke of York (*accept* York)
9 120	**20** Three
10 Alexander Pushkin	
11 Grasshopper	

Round 145

1 In pop music, complete the title of Slade's 1973 UK number-one hit single 'Come on, Feel the . . .' what?

2 In biology, a tonsillectomy is the surgical removal of which lymphatic tissue found at the back of the mouth?

3 In English superstition, what does a sighting of a single magpie foretell: good or bad luck?

4 In UK geography, which is further by road from Liverpool: London or Aberdeen?

5 For what do the letters RNLI stand?

6 Which leader of the Liberal Democrats was once the youngest member of the House of Commons?

7 In classical music, what is *Coppelia* by Delibes: an opera or a ballet?

8 In food, what *A* are tiny saltwater fish related to sardines that have an intense, briny taste when canned?

9 In the human body, the sternum is more commonly known as the what?

10 On the TV show *Have I Got News For You*, who is Paul Merton's opposing team captain?

11 In the Second World War, what *P* was a German term meaning an armoured division including tanks?

12 Spencer Perceval, the only British prime minister to have been assassinated, was killed in which century?

13 In British politics, what name is given to the area that an MP represents?

14 In tennis scoring, which number comes after fifteen and thirty?

15 What name is given to the branch of medicine that deals with the health and welfare of old people?

16 Of which US state is Denver the capital?

17 The famous Danish fairy-tale author was Hans Christian . . . who?

18 In betting, another name for a bookmaker is a '. . . [what] accountant'?

19 In Australia, what type of fruit did Maria Ann Smith become famous for producing in the nineteenth century?

20 In science, the device which extracts iron from iron ore is called a '. . . [what] furnace'?

Previous Total
1,000
800
600
450
300
200
100
50
20
Banked
Total

Answers

1 Noise
2 Tonsils
3 Bad
4 Aberdeen
5 Royal National Lifeboat Institution
6 Charles Kennedy
7 Ballet
8 Anchovies
9 Breastbone (do not accept chest)
10 Ian Hislop
11 Panzer (accept Panzer Division)
12 Nineteenth (1812)
13 Constituency
14 Forty
15 Geriatrics (accept gerontology)
16 Colorado
17 Andersen
18 Turf
19 Apples (Granny Smith apples)
20 Blast (blast furnace)

Round 146

1 In rugby union, the New Zealand team's first-choice strip is predominantly which colour?

2 In geography, what *H* is a Caribbean country, situated on the western part of the island of Hispaniola?

3 Which part of the body is inflamed in the condition known as 'stomatitis': the mouth or the liver?

4 What is the name of the waterproof overshoes which are usually made of rubber?

5 Complete the title of this 1999 Jim Carrey film: *Man on the . . .* what?

6 In literature, complete the title of George Orwell's 1936 novel: *Keep the Aspidistra . . .* what?

7 'Blues', 'Browns' and 'Coppers' are all British groups of which type of insect?

8 In sport, how many points is the black ball worth in a game of snooker?

9 In which country was the painter Edouard Manet born?

10 In UK geography, Salisbury is a cathedral city in which county?

11 In pop music, who had a 1999 UK hit single with 'That Don't Impress Me Much'?

12 In food, the word 'albumen' refers to which part of an egg?

13 The northern lights are also known as the aurora . . . what?

14 In maths, what is nine times twenty?

15 In politics, in which country of the UK was Robin Cook born?

16 Which racquet game was developed from the children's game of Battledore and Shuttlecock?

17 Who is the spiritual leader of the Church of England?

18 In science, what is the name for the study of the origin, structure and composition of the earth?

19 Which district of Los Angeles has its name spelt out on a world-famous hillside sign erected in 1923 as a real-estate promotion?

20 In history, which of Henry VIII's wives was beheaded in May 1536?

Previous Total

1,000

800

600

450

300

200

100

50

20

Banked

Total

Answers

1 Black (All Black)
2 Haiti
3 Mouth
4 Galoshes
5 *Moon*
6 *Flying*
7 Butterflies (accept *Lepidoptera*)
8 Seven
9 France
10 Wiltshire
11 Shania Twain (accept Eileen Regina Edwards)
12 (Egg) White
13 Borealis
14 180
15 Scotland
16 Badminton
17 The Archbishop of Canterbury (Dr George Carey, Primate of All England)
18 Geology
19 Hollywood
20 Anne Boleyn

Round 147

1 What *F* is a railway with two cars connected by a wire cable wound round a drum at the top of a steep incline?

2 Which country is the venue of motor sport's Acropolis Rally?

3 In the New Testament, how many days after the resurrection did Jesus ascend to Heaven?

4 In finance, the 'Nikkei 225', formerly known as the 'Nikkei Dow', is an indicator of share prices on which city's stockmarket?

5 The American and Horseshoe Waterfalls form which geographical site on the American–Canadian border?

6 In the novel and TV series *Day of the Triffids*, what were the man-eating triffids?

7 In South-eastern India, what was the colonial name of the city of Chennai, which is also the name of a medium to hot curry?

8 Which former member of The Beatles composed the piece 'Liverpool Oratorio' with Carl Davis?

9 Which politician resigned as party leader immediately after the 2001 General Election?

10 'Greenback' is a common nickname for the currency of which country?

11 In 1958, Christopher Trace and Leila Williams became the first presenters of which long-running BBC children's TV show?

12 Which sculptor's works include *The Kiss* and *The Thinker*?

13 In science, what is the name of the small magnetic device which indicates the direction of the earth's poles?

14 The Edinburgh Festival Fringe normally starts in which summer month?

15 The platypus is native to which country?

16 In which century did the verse-writer Edward Lear live and work?

17 Which low-budget film of 1999 saw three young film-makers lost in the woods?

18 In science, the word 'ternary' refers to something consisting of how many parts?

19 Damon Albarn is the lead singer with which UK pop group?

20 Fuerteventura is a popular holiday destination in which island group in the Atlantic?

Previous Total

( )

1,000

800

600

450

300

200

100

50

20

Banked

( )

( )

( )

( )

( )

Total

( )

Answers

1 Funicular
2 Greece
3 40
4 Tokyo('s)
5 Niagara Falls
6 Plants (accept flowers)
7 Madras
8 Paul McCartney
9 William Hague
10 United States
11 *Blue Peter*

12 Rodin (René-François Auguste Rodin)
13 Compass
14 August
15 Australia
16 Nineteenth (century)
17 *The Blair Witch Project*
18 Three
19 Blur
20 Canaries (accept Canary Islands)

Round 148

1 In art, Monet, Renoir and Sisley were leading figures in which nineteenth-century artistic movement?

2 In football, when the ball is in play, who are the only players who can handle the ball?

3 On which island was the TV detective series *Bergerac* set?

4 James I of England was also James VI of which country?

5 In music, how many strings are there on a cello?

6 What is the light-sensitive area at the back of the eye called?

7 The sequel to Roald Dahl's *Charlie and the Chocolate Factory* was *Charlie and the Great Glass . . .* what?

8 Which American actor plays the male lead in the 1999 film *Wild, Wild West*?

9 In motor racing, what is the name given to the position on the starting grid taken by the driver who completed the fastest time in practice?

10 Which unlucky *Peanuts* comic-strip character hit his first ever baseball home run in 1993 after 43 years?

11 In space travel, John Glenn was the first man born in which country to go into outer space?

12 Which famous door-to-door make-up retailer was founded in 1886 in the USA?

13 At the site of which American Civil War battle in 1863 did Abraham Lincoln make his famous address?

14 What *B* is a type of rounded hat stereotypically associated with English middle-class commuters?

15 In children's literature, complete the title of the story by C. S. Lewis: *The Lion, the Witch and the . . .* what?

16 According to the British highway code, what colour are car brake lights?

17 What was the first name of the American paediatrician Dr Spock: Leonard or Benjamin?

18 Predominantly what colour is the fur of an albino animal?

19 Which *Indiana Jones* actor played Bob Falfa in the 1973 film *American Graffiti*?

20 In which part of the body does an orthodontist specialise?

Previous Total

1,000

800

600

450

300

200

100

50

20

Banked

Total

Answers

1 Impressionism	**10** Charlie Brown
2 The goalkeepers (*accept* goalies, keepers)	**11** United States
	12 Avon
	13 Gettysburg
3 Jersey	**14** Bowler
4 Scotland	**15** *Wardrobe*
5 Four	**16** Red
6 Retina	**17** Benjamin
7 *Elevator*	**18** White
8 Will Smith (*accept* Willard Smith Junior)	**19** Harrison Ford
	20 Teeth (*accept* mouth)
9 Pole position	

Round 149

1 In TV, which prehistoric cartoon family were 'a case right out of history', according to their theme song?

2 In modern history, in which country did Winston Churchill deliver his famous 'Iron Curtain' speech in 1946?

3 In history, what was the Russian leader Lenin's first name?

4 In the animal kingdom, which large rodent is also known as the Quill Pig?

5 In maths, if diesel costs sixty pence per gallon, how much do twenty gallons cost?

6 In natural history, mycology is the study of what *F*?

7 In TV, which US sitcom revolved around the Conner family in Lanford, Illinois?

8 Pretoria, Bloemfontein and which other city make up South Africa's three capitals?

9 What G is the name given to the seeds of cereal crops?

10 Which major conflict started on 3 September 1939, when Britain and France declared war on Germany?

11 In science, hematite is the principle ore of which metal?

12 In which country was the car company Jaguar founded?

13 Which of the following is greater: one metre or one thousand centimetres?

14 In human anatomy, what is the name of the horny outgrowths which shield the tips of the fingers?

15 In which 1994 film comedy did Jim Carrey and Jeff Daniels star together?

16 What M is the name of ground almond paste used in cake decoration?

17 Which legendary outlaw had Allan-a-Dale as one of his companions?

18 In pop music, complete the title of Santana's famous song: 'Black Magic . . .' what?

19 In nature, the Earth is composed of three parts: the crust, the mantle and the . . . what?

20 In human biology, the cerebrum is a large part of which organ?

Previous Total

1,000

800

600

450

300

200

100

50

20

Banked

Total

Answers

1 *The Flintstones*
2 United States
3 Vladimir
4 Porcupine
5 £12
6 Fungi
7 *Roseanne*
8 Cape Town
9 Grain
10 Second World War (accept World War II)
11 Iron
12 England (accept Britain)
13 One thousand centimetres
14 Nails
15 *Dumb and Dumber*
16 Marzipan
17 Robin Hood
18 Woman
19 Core
20 Brain

Round 150

1 Complete the title of the following TV series: *Third Rock from the* . . . what?

2 The Red Crescent is the Muslim equivalent of which international relief agency?

3 Which epic film starring Charlton Heston received twelve Oscar nominations in 1960?

4 The American Declaration of Independence was issued in 1776 on which day of the year?

5 In British wildlife, what type of creature is a tench: a bird or a fish?

6 In pop music, what was the surname of Eddie, whose UK hit singles included 'Summertime Blues' and 'C'mon Everybody'?

7 In which city is the 1970 Disney film *The Aristocats* set: Paris or Berlin?

8 In boxing, which famous heavyweight champion was stripped of his title in 1967 for refusing to join the US Army?

9 Complete the title of Edgar Allan Poe's 1839 Gothic horror story: *The Fall of the House of* . . . what?

10 By what name was the 'Black Thursday' crash on the New York stock exchange in 1929 better known?

11 In US film-making, for what do the initials MGM stand?

12 Which comedienne played Edina Monsoon in the sitcom *Absolutely Fabulous*?

13 Which comic-book hero was the best-known creation of Joe Shuster and Jerry Siegel?

14 Complete the title of Bob Dylan's 1969 UK hit single: 'Lay Lady . . .' what?

15 In the 1920s, Hans Wilsdorf designed the first wristwatch to be resistant to what?

16 In entertainment, who is Warren Beatty's actress sister who wrote the 1983 book *Out On A Limb*?

17 Which of the Nobel prizes did George Bernard Shaw win in 1925?

18 In the animal kingdom, what do frogs breathe through: lungs or gills?

19 In the US, the Scopes Trial of 1925 tried a teacher for teaching which scientific theory?

20 What is the capital of Iceland?

Previous Total
1,000
800
600
450
300
200
100
50
20
Banked
Total

Answers

1 *Sun*
2 The Red Cross
3 *Ben Hur*
4 4 July
5 Fish
6 Cochran
7 Paris
8 Muhammad Ali (Cassius Marcellus Clay)
9 *Usher*
10 The Wall Street Crash
11 Metro-Goldwyn-Mayer
12 Jennifer Saunders
13 Superman
14 Lay
15 Water (waterproof)
16 Shirley MacLaine (Shirley MacLean Beatty)
17 Literature (Nobel Prize for Literature)
18 Lungs
19 Evolution
20 Reykjavik

Round 151

1 Who did Ewan McGregor play in *Star Wars Episode I: Obi-Wan Kenobi* or Anakin Skywalker?

2 What *A* is the name for the food of the gods?

3 On TV, what was the zip code in the title of the early nineties American teenage drama set in Beverly Hills?

4 Who won an Oscar for playing the male lead in the 1999 film *American Beauty*?

5 In the animal kingdom, what type of creature is an alligator: a reptile or an amphibian?

6 If *A* is Alpha and *Z* is Zulu, what is *G*?

7 Which foodstuff was invented by a French chemist in 1869 as an alternative to butter?

8 In human biology, how many bones are there between the inner and outer ear: one, two or three?

9 Which American politician married Hillary Diane Rodham in 1975?

10 In theatre, complete the title of the Andrew Lloyd Webber musical: *Jesus Christ . . .* what?

11 What is the name of the playing area in tennis?

12 In computing, what *H* is the obtaining of unauthorised access to files on computers?

13 Of which event in 1969 did President Richard Nixon say, 'This is the greatest week in the history of the world since the Creation'?

14 What was the name of the Motown group of which Diana Ross was a member?

15 In 1972, the famous 'Treasures of Tutenkhamun' exhibition opened at which museum in London?

16 In geography, Edo was the former name of which Japanese city?

17 In nature, from which continent does the grey squirrel originate: Europe or North America?

18 In history, Anne Boleyn was the mother of which English queen?

19 What is the full first name of basketball player Shaq O'Neal?

20 Which type of salesman uses a gavel to indicate when a product has been sold?

Previous Total

1,000

800

600

450

300

200

100

50

20

Banked

Total

Answers

1 Obi-Wan Kenobi
2 Ambrosia
3 90210
4 Kevin Spacey (Kevin Spacey Fowler)
5 Reptile
6 Golf
7 Margarine
8 Three
9 Bill Clinton (William Jefferson Clinton Blythe)
10 Superstar
11 The court
12 Hacking

13 Moon landing (accept man's first landing on the moon/ walking on the moon, etc.)
14 The Supremes (accept Diana Ross and the Supremes)
15 British Museum
16 Tokyo (accept Tokyo-Yokohama Metropolitan Area)
17 North America
18 Elizabeth I
19 Shaquille
20 An auctioneer

Round 152

1 In classical music, with which hand would a right-handed violinist normally hold the bow when playing?

2 Which creamy Italian pasta sauce has bacon and eggs as a basis?

3 In money, what name is given to any small stamped disc of metal used as official currency?

4 Which is the largest wild member of the dog family?

5 In language, which American term means to cross or walk in the road without regard for traffic?

6 In nature, during which season in Europe do deciduous trees shed their leaves?

7 Which US animated TV series is set in Springfield?

8 Which actor plays Captain Billy Tyne in the year 2000 film *The Perfect Storm*?

9 In science, in which strong, bowl-shaped vessel is a substance crushed to a powder using a pestle?

10 In pop music, complete the title of Blondie's 1978 UK hit single: 'Hanging On The . . .' what?

11 The quotation 'Yo-ho-ho and a bottle of rum' is from which children's adventure by Robert Louis Stevenson?

12 In geography, what *K* is both a borough of London and the capital of Jamaica?

13 In which decade of the twentieth century did the American trade unionist Jimmy Hoffa disappear?

14 The real name of which of Elizabeth Taylor's ex-husbands was Richard Walter Jenkins?

15 Opened in 1876, which feature of New York City was designed by landscape architects Frederick Law Olmsted and Calvert Vaux?

16 What is the surname of *Friends* actress Jennifer . . .?

17 The company International Business Machines was founded in 1924 in America. By what name is it better known?

18 Which mathematical symbol consists of two horizontal parallel lines, one on top of the other?

19 In folklore, what is the name for the reanimated corpses who suck the blood of their victims?

20 If you are British, which letter is missing in the American spelling of the word 'colour'?

Previous Total

1,000

800

600

450

300

200

100

50

20

Banked

Total

Answers

1 Right (hand)
2 Carbonara
3 Coin
4 Wolf
5 Jaywalk
6 Autumn (*accept* fall)
7 *The Simpsons*
8 George Clooney (George Timothy Clooney)
9 Mortar
10 Telephone
11 *Treasure Island*
12 Kingston
13 1970s
14 Richard Burton
15 Central Park
16 Aniston (*accept* Pitt: she is Brad Pitt's wife)
17 IBM
18 Equals (equatesor)
19 Vampires
20 U

Round 153

1 Which chain of islands became the fiftieth American state in 1959?

2 Which British actor played Bill Sikes in the 1968 film musical *Oliver*?

3 Deficiency in which vitamin causes rickets?

4 In the title of John Fowles's 1969 novel, what is the nationality of the lieutenant?

5 In US politics, John Adams was the second holder of which office from 1797 until 1801?

6 Who played C. J. Parker in the TV series *Baywatch*?

7 In science, what subjective scale is used to describe the damage caused by earthquakes: Mercalli or Richter?

8 What is the name of the type of race in which the runners must pass a baton to each other in sequence?

9 On which album cover are Paul McCartney and George Harrison wearing their MBEs on brightly coloured uniform jackets?

10 What *L* is a South American mammal, related to the alpaca and used for wool or meat?

11 The official languages of Israel are Arabic and what?

12 What is the most used letter in the English alphabet?

13 Which member of the pig family gets its name from the wartlike lumps on each side of its face?

14 Which former *Monty Python* actor starred in the 1986 film comedy *Clockwise*?

15 Which American who invented the light bulb was born in Milan, Ohio, in February 1847?

16 During the Russian Civil War, the Bolshevik forces organised by Trotsky were known as what colour army?

17 A mercenary can also be known as a 'soldier of . . .' what?

18 In soccer, Atletico Bilbao is a team in the domestic league of which European country?

19 US author and illustrator Theodore Seuss Geisel created the children's book *The Cat In The . . .* what?

20 Which 1994 novel by Louis De Bernières is set on the Greek island of Cephalonia during the 1941 Italian occupation?

Previous Total

1,000

800

600

450

300

200

100

50

20

Banked

Total

Answers

1 Hawaii (accept Sandwich Islands)
2 Oliver Reed (Robert Oliver Reed)
3 Vitamin D
4 French
5 President
6 Pamela Anderson (accept Pamela Anderson Lee/Pamela Lee)
7 Mercalli
8 Relay
9 *Sergeant Pepper's* (*Lonely Hearts Club Band*)
10 Llama
11 Hebrew
12 E
13 Warthog
14 John Cleese
15 Thomas Edison
16 Red (Red Army)
17 Fortune
18 Spain
19 *Hat*
20 *Captain Corelli's Mandolin*

Round 154

1 In maths, if a chicken lays two eggs per week, how many does it lay in twelve weeks?

2 In which 1939 musical does Dorothy Gale get swept away from her Kansas home?

3 Nimbus and cirrus are two types of what?

4 Which famous 1868 book by Louisa May Alcott featured characters called Meg, Jo, Beth and Amy?

5 The upper incisors of the elephant are more commonly known by which name?

6 In maths, if you bought five pencils at six pence each, how much would you have spent?

7 In human biology, pneumonia is the inflammation of which internal organs?

8 In sport, Jonah Lomu is a member of which international rugby team?

9 In the TV soap *EastEnders*, which character is played by Steve McFadden?

10 In maths, if you read 60 pages every day, how many days would it take you to read a 360-page book?

11 In nature, what is wormwood: a fruit or a herb?

12 In science, which metal is harder: brass or copper?

13 According to the proverb, what do birds of a feather do?

14 In fashion, which colour has a shade called 'shocking'?

15 In which major South African city would you find Rand Airport, the Florence Bloom Bird Sanctuary and Turffontein Race Course?

16 According to the saying, when keeping a secret, you keep it under what item of clothing?

17 In human biology, the 'ileum' is the last part of which intestine: small or large?

18 In computing, 'daisywheel' and 'ink jet' are types of what?

19 Who was Humphrey Bogart's female co-star in the 1942 film *Casablanca*?

20 In biology, chloroplasts are only present in which type of cells: animal or plant cells?

Previous Total

1,000
800
600
450
300
200
100
50
20

Banked

Total

Answers

1 24
2 *The Wizard Of Oz*
3 Cloud (formation)
4 *Little Women*
5 Tusks
6 Thirty pence
7 Lungs
8 All Blacks (accept New Zealand)
9 Phil Mitchell (accept Phil)
10 Six
11 Herb
12 Brass
13 Flock together
14 Pink
15 Johannesburg
16 Hat
17 Small
18 Printer
19 Ingrid Bergman
20 Plant (plant cells)

Round 155

1 What is the surname of fashion designer Zandra . . ., who came to the forefront during the early 1970s and also designed for the Princess of Wales?

2 Which flamboyant pop star went to his own 50th birthday party dressed in a massive Louis XIV-style wig?

3 *Columbia*, the world's first reusable interplanetary vehicle in space, was known as a 'Space . . .' what?

4 Which comedian is TV presenter Liza Tarbuck's father?

5 What name is given to the young of a whale?

6 Is Charles Schulz famous as an actor or cartoonist?

7 Which German airport has the international code DUS?

8 Made into a film starring Rita Tushingham and Murray Melvin, Shelagh Delaney's 1958 play was called *A Taste of . . .* what?

9 The Monument, in the City of London, commemorates which event?

10 What *S* is a Berlin prison where Rudolf Hess was held after being found guilty of war crimes?

11 What was the name of the 1985 series featuring Alf Garnett which was a sequel to *Til Death Us Do Part*?

12 Which American state is linked to New York by the George Washington Bridge?

13 In politics, of which party was David Owen a member before leaving to set up the Social Democratic Party in 1981?

14 In which country is the port of Gallipoli?

15 The quote 'That's no moon, it's a space station' is from which 1977 film?

16 In science, in which direction of the compass does the sun rise?

17 Cottonmouth and bushmaster are both types of what animal?

18 In pop music, Beyonce, Kelly and Michelle are members of which American pop band who had a 2001 UK number-one hit single with 'Survivor'?

19 Complete the title of Jimmy Ruffin's 1974 UK hit single 'What Becomes of the . . .' what?

20 In history, which of Henry VIII's wives was Catherine Parr: the first or sixth?

Previous Total

1,000

800

600

450

300

200

100

50

20

Banked

Total

Answers

1 Rhodes (Zandra Rhodes)
2 Elton John (Reg Dwight)
3 Shuttle
4 Jimmy Tarbuck
5 Calf
6 Cartoonist
7 Düsseldorf
8 *Honey*
9 Great Fire of London
10 Spandau
11 *In Sickness and In Health*
12 New Jersey
13 Labour
14 Turkey
15 *Star Wars* (accept *Star Wars Episode IV/A New Hope*)
16 East
17 Snake
18 Destiny's Child
19 Broken-hearted
20 Sixth

Round 156

1 What type of plant is garlic: biennial or perennial?

2 In the Cabinet reshuffle shortly after the 2001 general election, which former Home Secretary was made Foreign Secretary?

3 Which ancient Greek is known as the father of medicine?

4 In science, what M is a prefix added to words to mean 'one millionth'?

5 In literature, complete the title of this 1961 Muriel Spark novel: *The Prime of Miss Jean . . .* who?

6 In mathematics, the ratio of the circumference of a circle to its diameter is represented by which Greek letter?

7 Which is the only spiny, insectivorous mammal native to Britain?

8 In literature, complete the title of the 1932 Stella Gibbons novel: *Cold Comfort . . .* what?

9 In UK politics, in which year did Winston Churchill first become prime minister: 1930 or 1940?

10 Which actress is the eldest daughter of Sir Michael Redgrave and Rachel Kempson?

11 In which children's TV drama have the characters Ziggy Greaves and Zammo appeared?

12 Which famous American heavyweight boxer was known as 'Smokin' Joe'?

13 Did Claude-Michel Schönberg write the music or lyrics for the musical *Miss Saigon*?

14 In French politics, which former general was the first President of the Fifth Republic?

15 In the American Government, for what do the letters NSC stand?

16 In the animal kingdom, in which type of water does the piranha fish live: fresh or salt water?

17 What *Z* is a form of Mahayana Buddhism which began in China in about the sixteenth century AD?

18 By what collective name are the characters Porthos, Athos and Aramis known?

19 What sort of establishment did René Artois run in the TV sitcom *'Allo, 'Allo*?

20 Bioluminescence is the production of what by living organisms?

Previous Total

1,000
800
600
450
300
200
100
50
20
Banked
Total

Answers

1 Perennial
2 Jack Straw
3 Hippocrates
4 Micro
5 *Brodie*
6 Pi
7 Hedgehog
8 *Farm*
9 1940
10 Vanessa Redgrave
11 *Grange Hill*
12 Joe Frazier
13 Music

14 De Gaulle (Charles de Gaulle/Charles Andre Joseph Marie de Gaulle)
15 National Security Council
16 Freshwater
17 Zen (Zen Buddhism)
18 The Three Musketeers (accept musketeers)
19 Café (accept restaurant/bar)
20 Light

Round 157

1 In cricket, which country did Imran Khan represent at international level?

2 Nicknamed the 'King of Twist', which singer was born Ernest Evans in 1941?

3 In art, what *I* describes a figure or image, often religious?

4 Which form of hepatitis used to be known as 'infectious hepatitis': A, B, or C?

5 In which 1994 film does Tom Hanks say the line: 'Stupid is as stupid does'?

6 In pop music, Paul . . . who was formerly a member of the group The Housemartins and now fronts the group Beautiful South?

7 In human biology, the coronary sinus is found in which major internal organ?

8 Which Cumbrian lake is England's largest?

9 In maths, what is four fifths expressed as a percentage?

10 Which person is the commander-in-chief for all branches of the British armed forces?

11 On record players, what is the name for the pointed part of the arm which picks up vibrations by tracing the grooves on the record?

12 What position did Henry Kissinger hold under the presidencies of Richard Nixon and Gerald Ford: vice-president or secretary of state?

13 In UK geography, where is Reading in relation to London: south or west?

14 In children's literature, for what does the C stand in the name of the author C. S. Lewis: Clive or Colin?

15 What is the capital of Argentina?

16 In transport, what is the name of the Eurotunnel's vehicle service?

17 Which Hollywood actor starred as Richard in the year 2000 film *The Beach*?

18 In food, Bird's Nest Soup is a dish originally from which country: China or Egypt?

19 In UK geography, what is the longest river in Ireland?

20 The fifteenth-century battles between the Houses of York and Lancaster were known as the Wars of the . . . what?

Previous Total
1,000
800
600
450
300
200
100
50
20
Banked
Total

Answers

1 Pakistan	**11** Stylus (needle)
2 Chubby Checker	**12** Secretary of state
3 Icon	**13** West
4 A	**14** Clive
5 *Forrest Gump*	**15** Buenos Aires
6 (Paul) Heaton	**16** Le Shuttle (*accept* The Shuttle)
7 The heart	
8 Lake Windermere	**17** Leonardo DiCaprio
9 80 per cent	**18** China
10 The Monarch (*accept* the Queen/Queen Elizabeth II)	**19** Shannon
	20 Roses

Round 158

1 Which Caribbean politician became *de facto* leader of his country in January 1959 and is still in power forty years later?

2 In nature, from which part of a tree is quinine extracted: the bark or the root?

3 In pop music, which female trio had their first number-one hit with 'Whole Again' in 2001?

4 What is the name of the lycra-type material which was often worn as tight trousers by 1970s heavy-metal stars?

5 In which year were the details of the Enigma Code Machine obtained by the British? 1939 or 1944?

6 In TV, actor Joshua Jackson plays the character Pacey in which American series?

7 What *B* is the common name given to the promotional material printed on the back or inside cover of a book?

8 In toys, in which decade was the frisbee introduced: the 1950s or 1970s?

9 Glaucous, Iceland and Herring are all species of which type of sea bird?

10 In geography, in which English county is the coastal resort of Eastbourne: East Sussex or Dorset?

11 In pop music, complete the title of Hot Chocolate's 1982 UK hit single: 'It Started With A . . .' what?

12 In nature, which violent turning wind gets its name from the Spanish word for 'thunderstorm'?

13 In geography, in which European country is the state of Bavaria?

14 Which Brazilian football player was known as 'The Black Pearl'?

15 The noctule and the pipistrelle are British species of which sort of flying mammal?

16 Which former member of the royal family won an Olympic gold medal in 1972?

17 Which retired cricket umpire wrote the book of memoirs *White Cap And Bails*?

18 The city of Jerusalem is situated between the Mediterranean Sea and which salt lake?

19 In the human body, betacarotene is converted into which vitamin?

20 Who wrote the play *As You Like It*?

Previous Total

1,000

800

600

450

300

200

100

50

20

Banked

Total

Answers

1 (Fidel) Castro (Ruz)
2 Bark
3 Atomic Kitten
4 Spandex
5 1939
6 *Dawson's Creek*
7 Blurb
8 1950s
9 Gull
10 East Sussex
11 Kiss
12 Tornado
13 Germany
14 Pele (Edson Arantes do Nascimento)
15 Bat
16 Captain Mark Phillips
17 Harold ('Dickie') Bird
18 The Dead Sea (*accept* Al-bahr Al-mayyit, Yam Ha-melah)
19 (Vitamin) A
20 William Shakespeare

Round 159

1 In finance, if the value of a property falls below the amount of the loan taken out to buy it, the owner is said to be in a situation of 'negative . . .' what?

2 What name is given to a female rabbit?

3 In which European country would you find the region of Alsace?

4 A festival of which composer's work is held annually in Bayreuth, Germany?

5 Which tax replaced Capital Transfer Tax in the UK in 1986 and is levied on the estate of a deceased person?

6 Urdu is a language originating on which continent?

7 In *The Flintstones*, what was the name of Barney and Betty Rubble's adopted son?

8 In football, Hampden Park is a stadium in which country of the UK?

9 In the 1966 film *Born Free*, what kind of animal was Elsa?

10 Which Spice Girl had a UK hit single called 'I Turn To You' in 2000?

11 Which human rights organisation, founded by Peter Benenson, celebrated its fortieth anniversary in 2001?

12 In nature, 'spring', 'pearl' and 'Bermuda' are types of which edible bulb?

13 In golf, what name is given to a hole played in two strokes less than par?

14 Which former Labour MP began presenting a morning chat show on BBC1 in 1987?

15 What type of clothing is a fedora?

16 What is the surname of the former England rugby international brothers Rory and Tony?

17 In film, who starred as Annie Porter in the two *Speed* films?

18 In classical music, which British composer wrote the oratorio *The Dream of Gerontius* in 1900?

19 In literature, the title of Esther Freud's first novel, published in 1992 and later made into a film, is *Hideous . . .* what?

20 Which aquatic worm has historically been applied to the human body for blood sucking?

Previous Total

1,000
800
600
450
300
200
100
50
20

Banked

Total

Answers

1 Equity
2 Doe
3 France
4 Wagner (Wilhelm Richard Wagner)
5 Inheritance Tax
6 Asia
7 Bam Bam
8 Scotland
9 Lion (accept lioness)
10 Mel C (accept Sporty Spice/Melanie Chisholm)
11 Amnesty International (accept Amnesty/AI)
12 Onion
13 Eagle
14 Robert Kilroy-Silk (accept Kilroy)
15 Hat (accept headwear)
16 Underwood
17 Sandra Bullock
18 Elgar (Sir Edward William Elgar)
19 *Kinky*
20 Leech

Round 160

1 What kind of creatures does the RSPB principally aim to protect?

2 In literature, complete the title of the 1959 Laurie Lee novel: *Cider with . . .* who?

3 In TV, what was 'Metal Mickey': a lawnmower or a robot?

4 What is the medical term for German measles?

5 What S is a children's toy that can walk downstairs and is a by-product of Second World War research into springs?

6 For what do the letters 'MA' stand after a university graduate's name?

7 In pop music, according to their 1965 single, The Beach Boys wished all girls were from which US state?

8 In the Bible, which type of bird returned to Noah's ark with an olive leaf?

9 In sport, how many white balls are used in a game of snooker?

10 Who directed the film *2001: A Space Odyssey*?

11 In Roman numerals, what number is represented by the letter C?

12 What is a 'shepherd's purse': a plant or a fish egg?

13 In mythology, Eros is the ancient Greek god of what?

14 In cookery, sauerkraut is a German dish consisting of which vegetable pickled in salt water?

15 Alfred, Lord Tennyson's famous poem is entitled 'The Lady of . . .' where?

16 In inventions, in which country was the motor manufacturing company Fiat founded?

17 By what nickname is the American basketball player Earvin Johnson known?

18 In pop music, with whom did Kylie Minogue sing a duet on the 1988 UK hit single 'Especially For You'?

19 What sort of club is started by Brad Pitt and Edward Norton in the 1999 film of the same name?

20 The Vatican is the headquarters for which religion?

Previous Total

1,000
800
600
450
300
200
100
50
20

Banked

Total

Answers

1 Birds	**12** Plant
2 Rosie	**13** Love
3 A robot	**14** Cabbage
4 Rubella	**15** Shalott
5 Slinky	**16** Italy
6 Master of Arts	**17** Magic (Magic Johnson)
7 California	
8 A dove	**18** Jason Donovan
9 One	**19** Fight club
10 Stanley Kubrick (accept Kubrick)	**20** Roman Catholicism (accept Catholic/ Roman Catholic)
11 One hundred	

Round 161

1 Which South African city is located between Table Bay and Table Mountain?

2 Complete this popular ending to fairy tales: 'They all lived happily ever . . .' what?

3 Which of the following is greater: one centimetre or one hundred millimetres?

4 In nature, which of the following is a type of vegetable: pumpkin, potato or tomato?

5 If you are a diabetic, in which hormone are you deficient?

6 Which maritime measurement of speed is equal to one nautical mile per hour?

7 In the USA, which state is signified by the postal abbreviation AK?

8 In the traditional story of *Jack and the Beanstalk*, the Giant says, 'Fee fie foe fum, I smell the blood of a . . .' what?

9 In UK geography, which is further by road from London: Lincoln or Leeds?

10 'Blackjack', 'brag' and 'bridge' are forms of what type of game?

11 Which actor played the title role in the 2001 film *Captain Corelli's Mandolin*?

12 In sport, which pieces of boxing equipment were originally known as 'mufflers'?

13 In America, what do the initials FBI stand for?

14 In maths, what is twelve times seven?

15 In Christianity, the first day of Lent is commonly known as 'Ash . . .' what?

16 In the animal kingdom, what is the name given to the enlarged pointed front teeth that project from the mouth of a walrus?

17 What name is given to the stick that is passed between runners in a relay race?

18 In money, how many pence are there in a pound sterling?

19 If a bee larva is fed entirely on royal jelly, what type of bee does it mature into?

20 What is the English term used for the item of clothing known as 'pantyhose' in the USA?

Previous Total

1,000

800

600

450

300

200

100

50

20

Banked

Total

Answers

1 Cape Town
2 After
3 One hundred millimetres
4 Potato
5 Insulin
6 Knot
7 Alaska
8 Englishman
9 Leeds
10 Card (card game)
11 Nicolas Cage (Nicholas Coppola)

12 Gloves
13 Federal Bureau of Investigation
14 84
15 Wednesday
16 Tusks
17 Baton
18 One hundred
19 A queen
20 Tights

Round 162

1 In pop music, complete the name of the jazz-rock group formed in the late 1960s: Blood, Sweat and . . . what?

2 In the Warner Brothers cartoons, what type of animal is Taz?

3 In boxing, to what did Cassius Clay change his name in 1964?

4 What G is the name of one of the four accounts of the life and teachings of Jesus Christ that begin the New Testament?

5 In art, what term is used to describe a colour made by mixing together two primary colours?

6 Half, clove and timber hitches are all types of what?

7 What C is a term used by doctors to describe matters connected with the brain?

8 In maths, what is eleven times twenty?

9 Which branch of engineering refers to the building of bridges, harbours and highways?

10 The Hollywood Foreign Press Association Film and Television Awards are known as the Golden . . . what?

11 In the nursery rhyme 'Georgie Porgie', what did Georgie do when the boys came out to play?

12 In nature, what H is a severe tropical storm with torrential rain and winds above 73 miles per hour?

13 In which country was Guccio Gucci, the founder of the Gucci fashion label, born?

14 In music, Catatonia's 1998 UK hit single was 'Mulder and . . .' who?

15 In the animal kingdom, which insect was responsible for transmitting outbreaks of plague during the Middle Ages?

16 What type of military vehicle was the Supermarine Spitfire?

17 In literature, complete the title of the 1937 George Orwell work: *The Road to Wigan . . .* what?

18 In 1953 the Tate Gallery bought which famous sculpture by Rodin?

19 Of which country is Budapest the capital city?

20 In film, which actor and dancer starred as Jerry Travers in the 1935 musical comedy *Top Hat*?

Previous Total

1,000
800
600
450
300
200
100
50
20

Banked

Total

Answers

1 Tears
2 A Tasmanian devil
3 Muhammad Ali
4 Gospel
5 Secondary colour
6 Knots
7 Cerebral
8 220
9 Civil engineering
10 Globes
11 Ran away
12 Hurricane
13 Italy
14 Scully
15 Flea
16 Aeroplane (accept fighter plane/Second World War plane)
17 *Pier*
18 *The Kiss*
19 Hungary
20 Fred Astaire (Frederic Austerlitz)

Round 163

1 In pop music, which group's first album *Please Please Me* was released in 1963?

2 Which actor from *Pulp Fiction* also starred in the films *Get Shorty* and *Primary Colors*?

3 In history, the Nazis described their regime in Germany as the Third . . . what?

4 What *R* is a rolled-up fillet of herring, that has been pickled?

5 In the animal kingdom, the black widow spider is so called because the female eats what after mating?

6 Who wrote the play *Jeffrey Bernard Is Unwell*: Keith Waterhouse or Harold Pinter?

7 In maths, what is two fifths expressed as a percentage?

8 What *H* is an animal that is commonly fitted with a 'throatlatch' and 'stirrup leather'?

9 Which actor starred as racing driver Cole Trickle in the 1990 film *Days of Thunder*?

10 In science, what type of electricity does a battery produce: AC or DC?

11 In the animal kingdom, 'emperor', 'king' and 'gentoo' are all species of which aquatic bird?

12 In maths, how many feet are there in 24 inches?

13 In theatre, complete the title of the Oscar Wilde comedy, *An Ideal . . .* what?

14 Which country has the greater number of borders with other countries: China or Zambia?

15 In money, which British coin was the world's first to have seven curved sides?

16 Ophthalmology is concerned with which organs of the human body?

17 In politics, which party was the result of a merger between the National Party of Scotland, founded in 1928, and the Scottish Party, founded in 1932?

18 In literature, with which form of writing is Allen Ginsberg chiefly associated: Beat poetry or science fiction?

19 In the UK, Tintagel, the legendary birthplace of King Arthur, is in the north of which county?

20 'Tawny', 'barn' and 'long-eared' are British species of which bird?

Previous Total

1,000
800
600
450
300
200
100
50
20

Banked

Total

Answers

1 The Beatles	**11** Penguin
2 John Travolta	**12** Two
3 Reich (accept state)	**13** *Husband*
4 Rollmop	**14** China
5 The male (accept the mate)	**15** Fifty pence piece
6 Keith Waterhouse	**16** The eyes
7 40 per cent	**17** Scottish National Party (accept SNP)
8 Horse	**18** Beat poetry
9 Tom Cruise	**19** Cornwall
10 DC	**20** Owl

Round 164

1 In history, the name of the stereotyped caricature who personified England is John . . . who?

2 Saturday is named after which Roman god?

3 In geography, Wrexham is a town in the north-east of which country of the UK?

4 In money, the US dollar is divided into one hundred what?

5 The 1994 film *Once Were Warriors* was set in which Antipodean country?

6 What is used to hit the ball in a game of polo?

7 What word can mean a horse for breeding and a form of poker?

8 A stretch of road where police monitor the speed of vehicles with electronic equipment is called a 'speed . . .' what?

9 In clothing, which garments are known to the Scots as 'breeks'?

10 Through which English city was Lady Godiva reputed to have ridden naked?

11 The terms 'strike', 'turkey' and 'spare' are used in which sport?

12 Which British queen featured on the Penny Black stamp when it was released in 1840?

13 In cartoons, which character's arch-enemy is known as either Brutus or Bluto?

14 With which American sport are Shaquille O'Neal and Kobe Bryant associated?

15 In which country was there a botched invasion in April 1961 at the Bay of Pigs?

16 In money, which bank is the sole issuer of currency notes in England and Wales?

17 In history, the child Pu Yi became the last emperor of which country in 1908?

18 The 1982 Falklands conflict took place between Great Britain and which South American country?

19 In TV, in which sitcom set on Craggy Island did Ardal O'Hanlon play Father Dougal?

20 In literature, which Shakespearean character was the Prince of Denmark?

Previous Total

1,000

800

600

450

300

200

100

50

20

Banked

Total

Answers

1 (John) Bull
2 Saturn
3 Wales
4 Cents (accept pennies)
5 New Zealand
6 Mallet (accept polo stick)
7 Stud
8 (Speed) Trap
9 Trousers
10 Coventry
11 Ten-pin bowling
12 Victoria
13 Popeye's
14 Basketball
15 Cuba
16 Bank of England
17 China
18 Argentina
19 *Father Ted*
20 Hamlet

Round 165

1 In fashion, what items of clothing are 'mules'?

2 Complete this old English rhyme about cutlery falling on the floor, 'knife falls, gentleman . . .' what?

3 In history, to which country were the Tolpuddle Martyrs transported in 1834?

4 Which racehorse was stolen from a stud farm in February 1983?

5 Which American actor played Edward Lewis in the 1990 film *Pretty Woman*?

6 Which branch of medicine is concerned with providing artificial limbs for the body?

7 In which English county are the towns of Needham Market and Stowmarket?

8 Complete the title of the C. S. Forester novel published in 1935 and later made into a film: *The African* . . . what?

9 In which century did the Hundred Years War begin?

10 In 1961, which Soviet cosmonaut was called the 'New Columbus of the Cosmos'?

11 In the TV sitcom *Friends*, which character is played by Courteney Cox?

12 What sort of fish is used to make the dish 'gravadlax'?

13 Dingos and koalas are native to which continent?

14 What was the name of Gladys Knight's regular backing group?

15 Which position in British government did Neville Chamberlain hold between 1937 and 1940?

16 Which metal alloy, mainly consisting of copper and zinc, is often used in ship fittings?

17 In film, which actor starred as Nick Marshall with Helen Hunt in the year 2000 comedy *What Women Want*?

18 In Tibet and Mongolia, Lamaism is an offshoot of which religion?

19 Complete the title of Glen Campbell's 1975 UK and US hit single: 'Rhinestone . . .' what?

20 On which English island are the towns of Yarmouth, Newport and Ventnor?

Previous Total

1,000
800
600
450
300
200
100
50
20

Banked

Total

Answers

1 Shoes (accept footwear/slippers)
2 Calls
3 Australia
4 Shergar
5 Richard Gere
6 Prosthetics
7 Suffolk
8 *Queen*
9 Fourteenth century (1337)
10 Yuri Gagarin
11 Monica (accept Monica Geller/ Monica Bing/ Monica Geller Bing)
12 Salmon
13 Australia (accept Australasia)
14 The Pips
15 Prime minister
16 Brass
17 Mel Gibson
18 Buddhism
19 Cowboy
20 Isle of Wight

Round 166

1 In Chinese astrology, the year 2001 is the year of which creature?

2 According to the saying, if you agree to take part in a contest, you throw your hat into the what?

3 In British politics, who was Speaker of the House of Commons from 1992 until October 2000?

4 In which decade did skateboards first appear in America?

5 In sport, who was captain of the England rugby union team between 1988 and 1996?

6 Who succeeded Sir John Birt as director-general of the BBC?

7 Humphrey Bogart said about which of his wives: 'She's a real Joe. You'll fall in love with her like everybody else'?

8 In food and drink, Riesling wines have what kind of flavour: sweet or dry?

9 In UK geography, which is further by road from Cardiff: Hull or Glasgow?

10 What is the surname of Sam, the British Oscar-winning film director?

11 Complete the sentence often used by auctioneers when accepting the final bid: 'Going, going, . . .' what?

12 Whist and trumps are types of what sort of game?

13 Complete the title of this popular hymn: 'All Things Bright and . . .' what?

14 If you had a caddy, which sport would you be playing?

15 What name is given to a mixture of beer and lemonade?

16 In pastimes, silver dollars and shillings are examples of which kind of collectible items?

17 In the Bible, complete this quote from the book of Luke. 'Man cannot live by . . . [what] alone'?

18 When trying to minimise the risk of being wrong, you are 'hedging your . . .' what?

19 Complete the title of the novel and 1970s children's TV series about a horse: *Black . . .* what?

20 What C is a fatty liquid product separated from milk, which can be used to make butter?

Previous Total

1,000

800

600

450

300

200

100

50

20

Banked

Total

Answers

1 Snake (accept serpent)
2 Ring
3 Betty Boothroyd
4 1960s (accept sixties)
5 Will Carling
6 Greg Dyke (Gregory Dyke)
7 Lauren Bacall
8 Dry
9 Glasgow
10 Mendes
11 Gone
12 Card (games)
13 Beautiful
14 Golf
15 Shandy (accept lager top)
16 Coins (accept money)
17 Bread
18 Bets
19 (Black) Beauty
20 Cream

Round 167

1 In mythology, which *V* is the Roman goddess of love and beauty?

2 Barbara Woodhouse was mainly associated with training which animals?

3 What colour berets do Royal Marine Commandos wear?

4 In football, Real Madrid is a team in the domestic league of which European country?

5 According to the saying, two people living near each other come from 'the same neck of the . . .' what?

6 In politics, Nigel Lawson is associated with which party?

7 Which five-letter word can be added to 'black', 'goose' and 'straw' to make a soft fruit?

8 What *C* was the surname of the romantic fiction writer Dame Barbara?

9 The *Flying Scotsman* and the *Orient Express* are famous examples of what type of vehicle?

10 In the animal kingdom, chimpanzees, gorillas and orang-utans are all what *A*?

11 In film, the Hollywood star William Bradley Pitt is more commonly known by which name?

12 In geography, in which continent is Austria situated?

13 What *S* are knocked down in a bowling alley?

14 In boxing, what does KO stand for?

15 Which James Bond star appeared in the 1986 film *Highlander*?

16 In science, a rise in average temperatures around the world is described as 'global . . .' what?

17 In the nursery rhyme 'Sing a Song of Sixpence', how many blackbirds were baked in a pie?

18 In theatre, what *B* do they say you tread if you go on stage?

19 In food, 'gardener's delight', 'cherry' and 'beefsteak' are all types of which salad ingredient?

20 In UK politics, what flower does the Labour Party use as its emblem?

Previous Total

1,000

800

600

450

300

200

100

50

20

Banked

Total

Answers

1 Venus
2 Dogs
3 Green
4 Spain
5 Woods
6 Conservative
7 Berry
8 Cartland
9 Trains (*accept* steam trains)
10 Apes (*accept* anthropoids)
11 Brad Pitt
12 Europe
13 Skittles
14 Knockout/knocked out
15 (Sir) Sean Connery
16 Warming
17 Four and twenty (24)
18 Boards
19 Tomato
20 Rose

Round 168

1 In TV, complete the title of this sitcom starring Dawn French: *Murder Most . . .* what?

2 In the animal kingdom, what *F* is a tailless jumping amphibian with long legs?

3 In space, which letter of the alphabet is used to define the crushing forces of take-off in a rocket?

4 In sport, how many pockets does a snooker table have?

5 Which Midlands city has a professional football team nicknamed 'Wolves'?

6 In music, 'Reach Out, I'll Be There' was a 1966 UK number-one single for the Four . . . what?

7 In theatre, which Andrew Lloyd Webber musical tells the story of a ghostly disfigured and deranged composer?

8 In TV, Bamber Gascoigne and Jeremy Paxman have both hosted which long-running quiz show featuring students as contestants?

9 In fashion, what *O* can be worn over clothes to protect them from dirt when working?

10 What type of food is the Scottish dish cock-a-leekie?

11 In maths, if a lift has travelled a quarter of the way up a building and is on the fourth floor, how many floors does the building have?

12 To whom was Nelson Mandela married until 1996?

13 In biology, what *H* is the name given to any chemical that kills plants?

14 In TV, which celebrity was the first to be voted out of the Comic Relief *Big Brother* house in March 2001?

15 With which band did Diana Ross have a UK number-one single in 1964 with 'Baby Love'?

16 What colloquial name is given to someone from Newcastle-upon-Tyne and the dialect of the inhabitants of the north-east of England?

17 In science, what *H* is the more common name for thermal energy?

18 In film, Peter ... who was the star of the *Pink Panther* series?

19 Which Lancashire resort switched on its illuminations for the first time on 18 September 1879?

20 In angling, casters, hemp seeds and maize are all used as what *B*?

1,000

800

600

450

300

200

100

50

20

Banked

Total

Answers

1 Horrid
2 Frog
3 G (accept G-force)
4 Six
5 Wolverhampton (Wanderers)
6 Tops
7 The Phantom of the Opera
8 University Challenge
9 Overalls
10 Soup
11 Sixteen floors
12 Winnie Mandela (Nomzamo)
13 Herbicide
14 Chris Eubank
15 The Supremes
16 Geordie
17 Heat
18 Sellers
19 Blackpool
20 Bait

Round 169

1 In American law, for what do the letters DA stand?

2 In food, what M is a small citrus fruit resembling a tangerine?

3 In musical theatre, which Rodgers and Hammerstein production features 'The March of the Siamese Children'?

4 At Christian weddings, what is the traditional term for a married bridesmaid?

5 The pope and which US president suffered assassination attempts in 1981?

6 What is the official language of Mexico?

7 In the animal kingdom, what animal was the first mammal to have been cloned?

8 In pop music, how many lions featured in the title of the Baddiel and Skinner football song?

9 In nature, what L is a flat structure attached to the stem of a plant?

10 Complete the title of the 1998 film set during the Second World War: *The Thin Red . . .* what?

11 Who designed the cover of the Rolling Stones' *Sticky Fingers* album: Andy Warhol or Roy Lichtenstein?

12 In rugby, in which direction can players not pass the ball?

13 In literature, which type of large sea mammal swallowed Pinocchio?

14 What is the literal translation of Art Nouveau?

15 In modern history, which member of the royal family took part in the 1982 Falklands Conflict?

16 In pop music, complete the title of The Eagles' 1975 UK hit single: 'Lyin' . . .' what?

17 In nature, which *P* is another name for a butterfly's chrysalis?

18 In science, which is bigger: an atom or a molecule?

19 In the animal kingdom, what *H* is a small bird that can beat its wings 75 times a second?

20 In pop music, whose 1991 UK hit album was entitled *Simply The Best*?

Previous Total

1,000

800

600

450

300

200

100

50

20

Banked

Total

Answers

1 District Attorney
2 Mandarin
3 *The King and I*
4 Matron of honour
5 Ronald Reagan
6 Spanish
7 Sheep
8 Three
9 Leaf
10 *Line*
11 Andy Warhol
12 Forward
13 A whale
14 New Art
15 Prince Andrew (Duke of York)
16 Eyes
17 Pupa
18 Molecule
19 Hummingbird
20 Tina Turner (Anna Mae Bullock)

Round 170

1 In science, what *R* is a term that describes how hard it is for current to flow through a conductor?

2 In music, what *C* is a brass instrument similar to a trumpet that is mainly used in brass bands?

3 In music, the Live Aid concert was held in 1985 at which London venue?

4 In geography, which has the greater area: the state of California or the United Kingdom?

5 What *J* is a type of engine that is a form of gas turbine?

6 In history, which Russian tsar was known as 'Ivan the Terrible': Ivan III or Ivan IV?

7 Complete the title of the 1962 film starring Tom Courtenay: *The Loneliness of the Long Distance . . .* what?

8 What *N* is a chemical found in both ammonia and urea?

9 In women's athletics, the pentathlon was replaced by which seven-event contest in 1981?

10 What *N* is the name of the ballet composed by Tchaikovsky in 1892?

11 In theatre, the score for the musical *Chess* was written by Benny Andersson and Bjorn Ulvayuss, former members of which Swedish band?

12 In which decade did the BBC broadcast its first radio programmes?

13 In UK geography, what *D* is an English city on the banks of the River Derwent?

14 The Taj Mahal was built in which century?

15 Who led the English army into the Battle of Hastings in 1066: Harold II or William II?

16 If a train journey covers 100 miles and costs £15, how much does it cost per mile?

17 Which British political party was founded in 1988 through a merger of the Liberal Party and the Social Democratic Party?

18 In science, what is the opposite of expansion?

19 Which British coin are there most of in circulation?

20 What did Jack jump over in the old English rhyme 'Jack Be Nimble'?

Previous Total

1,000

800

600

450

300

200

100

50

20

Banked

Total

Answers

1 Resistance
2 Cornet
3 Wembley Stadium (accept Wembley)
4 California
5 Jet engine (accept jet)
6 Ivan IV
7 *Runner*
8 Nitrogen
9 The heptathlon
10 *The Nutcracker*
11 Abba
12 1920s (1927)
13 Derby
14 17th (1631–53)
15 Harold II
16 15 pence
17 Liberal Democratic Party (accept Liberal Democrats/Lib Dems)
18 Contraction (accept shrinkage)
19 One penny
20 A candlestick

Round 171

1 In travel, in which European country would you be arriving if you flew into Gatwick Airport?

2 In TV, which Australian soap opera is set in Ramsey Street?

3 According to the saying, you wouldn't touch something unpleasant with what kind of pole?

4 In sport, what is the name of the athletics event in which a solid metal ball is thrown from the shoulder, as far as possible?

5 In dance, what sex is a ballerina?

6 Complete the title of the 1976 Thin Lizzy UK hit single, 'The Boys Are Back In . . .' what?

7 What type of food is 'double Gloucester'?

8 A term for someone who watches a lot of TV is a 'couch . . .' what?

9 In politics, what colour is associated with the Liberal Democrats?

10 Which TV presenter had a BBC2 series about his *Weird Weekends*?

11 Complete the title of the 1987 film starring Cher and Jack Nicholson: *The Witches of . . .* where?

12 In children's TV, Valerie Singleton and John Noakes were both presenters of which long-running programme?

13 In snooker, in which shape are the fifteen red balls placed for the start of a frame?

14 What *M* refers to a pole that supports the sails on a ship?

15 What is the international dialling code for Russia: 007 or 001?

16 In food, in which English city did the Chelsea bun originate?

17 In geography, Morocco is situated in the north of which continent?

18 What is the name given to an anchored float that serves as a guide or warning to ships?

19 In nature, what *B* is the onion-shaped base of a daffodil?

20 In science, which colour comes between red and yellow in rainbows?

Previous Total

1,000

800

600

450

300

200

100

50

20

Banked

Total

Answers

1 England (accept United Kingdom/ Great Britain)
2 *Neighbours*
3 Bargepole (accept ten-foot pole [US version])
4 Shot put (accept putting the shot/shot)
5 Female
6 Town
7 Cheese
8 Potato
9 Yellow
10 Louis Theroux
11 *Eastwick*
12 *Blue Peter*
13 Triangle
14 Mast
15 007
16 London
17 Africa
18 Buoy
19 Bulb
20 Orange

Round 172

1 By road, which city is closer to Edinburgh: Birmingham or Sheffield?

2 In the military, what is the abbreviation for someone who is absent without official leave?

3 In food, 'cos', 'little gem' and 'romaine' are all types of what?

4 In the Bible, who killed Abel?

5 In TV, complete the title of this BBC comedy sketch show: *Not The Nine O'Clock* . . . what?

6 In geography, in which continent is Denmark?

7 Which British women's organisation with local branches has the initials WI?

8 By what name is the headquarters in London of the Metropolitan Police known?

9 In the animal kingdom, what *H* is a large wasp that can inflict a severe sting?

10 In children's literature, Laura Ingalls Wilder wrote *The Little House on the* . . . what?

11 In British politics, Kenneth Clarke is associated with which party?

12 For how long was the Eiffel Tower in Paris originally designed to stand: twenty years or sixty years?

13 The comic-strip character Fred Basset was based on what breed of dog?

14 What type of transport across the Mersey features in a song by Gerry and the Pacemakers?

15 In food, what is the main ingredient of compote: fruit or vegetables?

16 Which scientist published his theory of evolution in 1859?

17 In politics, apartheid referred to the racial segregation policy of which country?

18 In cookery, what C is another name for squid?

19 What *T* is a modern ballroom dance of Argentinian origin?

20 Ex-*EastEnders* star Martine McCutcheon is starring as Eliza Doolittle in the 2001 West End version of which musical?

Answers

1 Sheffield
2 AWOL
3 Lettuce
4 Cain
5 *News*
6 Europe
7 Women's Institute
8 New Scotland Yard (*accept* Scotland Yard)
9 Hornet
10 *Prairie* (*accept Big Wood*)
11 Conservative (*accept Tory*)
12 Twenty (years)
13 Basset hound (*do not accept hound*)
14 Ferry
15 Fruit
16 Darwin (Charles Robert Darwin)
17 South Africa (Republic of South Africa)
18 Calamari
19 Tango
20 *My Fair Lady*

Previous Total

1,000
800
600
450
300
200
100
50
20

Banked

Total

Round 173

1 In sport, which country did Carl Lewis represent in track and field?

2 In music, complete the title of Edward Elgar's march: 'Pomp and . . .' what?

3 The international TV channel Cable News Network is more commonly referred to as what?

4 In which British county would you find the towns of Falmouth and Newquay?

5 Which strongman cartoon comic character eats 'cow pies with the horns left in'?

6 In science, which is the higher part of the atmosphere: the exosphere or the stratosphere?

7 In which American state would you find Nashville?

8 What O can be Shakespeare's Moor of Venice and a board game involving black and white counters?

9 Who was US president between 1981 and 1989?

10 Which country is the larger by area: Canada or the United States?

11 What is two fifths expressed as a percentage?

12 Which sportsman is associated with the expression 'You cannot be serious!'?

13 In music, what H is a keyboard instrument resembling a piano, that has strings that are plucked mechanically?

14 In medicine, which of the five senses is a cochlear implant used to stimulate?

15 In nature, what S is the name given to eggs of aquatic animals such as frogs, when they are expelled in a mass?

16 In money, the price at which one currency is bought or sold in terms of other currencies is known as the . . . what?

17 Who wrote the 1904 play *Peter Pan*: J. M. Barrie or E. M. Forster?

18 In literature, which English author wrote the novel *Sense and Sensibility*?

19 What E is the duty levied on certain goods within a country?

20 Which British rock band is associated with the 1982 film *The Wall*?

Previous Total

1,000
800
600
450
300
200
100
50
20

Banked

Total

Answers

1 United States (*accept* US/USA/United States of America/ America)
2 Circumstance
3 CNN
4 Cornwall
5 Desperate Dan
6 Exosphere
7 Tennessee
8 Othello
9 Ronald Reagan (Ronald Wilson Reagan)
10 Canada
11 40 per cent
12 John McEnroe
13 Harpsichord
14 Hearing
15 Spawn
16 Exchange rate
17 J. M. Barrie
18 Jane Austen
19 Excise
20 Pink Floyd

Round 174

1 In human biology, what *I* is found in haemoglobin and has the chemical symbol Fe?

2 In the US, the Golden Gate Bridge connects Marin County on the north side with which city on the south?

3 In which century was the mathematician and physicist Isaac Newton born?

4 In biology, Vitamin B1 is also known as what *T*?

5 In the animal kingdom, what *D* is a one-humped camel?

6 In geography, what *T* is a kingdom in south-east Asia?

7 In motor racing, which Canadian driver won the Formula One World Championship in 1997?

8 In history, the Wars of the Roses took place in which century?

9 In literature, which author wrote the Discworld series that started in 1983 with *The Colour of Magic*?

10 In history, which city was the planned destination of the *Titanic* when she sank in 1912?

11 In the animal kingdom, cheetahs are native to which continent?

12 In cricket, with which discipline is Curtly Ambrose most commonly associated?

13 In Greek mythology, what *S* was a creature with the head and breasts of a woman, the body of a lion and the wings of a bird?

14 In which English county would you find Stoke-on-Trent?

15 Complete the title of this George Bernard Shaw play: *Arms and the . . .* what?

16 In which century did John Milton write *Paradise Lost*?

17 In human biology, what O is the area of the skull around the eyeball?

18 In literature, complete the title of this 1948 Alan Paton novel: *Cry, The Beloved . . .* what?

19 In customs, complete this rhyme recited when picking petals from a daisy: 'He loves me, he loves me . . .' what?

20 The three colours that make up the American flag are red, white and what?

Previous Total

1,000

800

600

450

300

200

100

50

20

Banked

Total

Answers

1 Iron	**12** Bowling (*accept* bowler)
2 San Francisco	
3 Seventeenth (1642)	**13** Sphinx
4 Thiamin	**14** Staffordshire
5 Dromedary	**15** *Man*
6 Thailand	**16** Seventeenth century (*accept* seventeenth)
7 Jacques Villeneuve	
8 Fifteenth (century)	**17** Orbit
9 Terry Pratchett	**18** *Country*
10 New York	**19** Not
11 Africa	**20** Blue

Round 175

1 In politics, John Major was the leader of which party?

2 What is the name given to the pointed projectiles which are fired from longbows?

3 In music, which instrument has a bag and a chanter and is usually associated with Scotland?

4 According to tradition, which type of bird is said to deliver babies to their parents?

5 Tutankhamen was a famous king of which country?

6 Madrid is the capital city of which country?

7 In entertainment, pop star Marvin Lee Aday goes by the name of Meat . . . what?

8 According to superstition, what is the name for a person who turns into a dog-like creature when there is a full moon?

9 In *The Muppet Show*, what is the name of the pig who is Kermit's girlfriend?

10 In law, punishment by death is known as '. . . [what] punishment'?

11 According to the saying, when you are scared, your heart is in your . . . what?

12 In the animal kingdom, which *P* is an endangered mammal that almost exclusively eats bamboo?

13 In TV, Caroline Aherne stars as Denise in which comedy series?

14 In music, how many solo parts are there in a triple concerto?

15 In fashion, a twinset is a matching jumper and what?

16 In food, Neapolitan ice-cream traditionally consists of chocolate, strawberry and which other flavour?

17 In pop music, complete the title of Little Richard's 1958 UK hit single: 'Good Golly . . .' who?

18 In which year of the twenty-first century is it predicted that Halley's comet is due to reappear: 2045 or 2061?

19 In film, Doris Day starred in the 1953 musical *Calamity . . .* what?

20 What is the name of the board game in which players must deduce who killed Dr Black?

Answers

1 Conservative (accept Tory)	**11** Mouth
2 Arrows	**12** Giant panda (accept panda)
3 Bagpipes	**13** *The Royle Family*
4 Stork	**14** Three
5 Egypt	**15** Cardigan
6 Spain	**16** Vanilla
7 Loaf	**17** Miss Molly
8 Werewolf	**18** 2061
9 Miss Piggy	**19** *Jane*
10 Capital	**20** Cluedo

Previous Total

1,000

800

600

450

300

200

100

50

20

Banked

Total

Round 176

1 In politics, Gordon Brown is associated with which party?

2 In tennis, what is the surname of Ivan, the Czech-born player who became an American citizen in 1992?

3 In the 1942 animated film, what sex is Bambi?

4 In Roman numerals, which letter represents the number ten?

5 Complete the title of this 1970s and 80s children's TV series: *John Craven's* . . . what?

6 In a survey of 500 students, 5 per cent had not taken out a student loan. What number of students is this?

7 In the animal kingdom, is the weasel a carnivore or a herbivore?

8 In science, in 1543, Nicolaus Copernicus published his theory that the Earth orbits which celestial body?

9 In film, complete the title of the 1991 thriller starring Julia Roberts: *Sleeping With the* . . . what?

10 In which American state is the town of Unalaska?

11 What *E* is to send goods for sale or exchange in another country?

12 Which word can come before 'fly' to make an insect and before 'cup' to make a common wild plant?

13 The name of which breed of dog, favourites of the royal family, means 'dwarf dog' in Welsh?

14 In maths, if a chicken needs to be cooked for twenty minutes per pound, for how long must you cook a four-pound chicken?

15 In language, what do Americans call a lift?

16 In biology, what O is needed for aerobic respiration to occur?

17 Which office building in Washington, DC gave its name to the scandal that brought down President Nixon?

18 Complete the title of the 1989 film starring Jeremy Irons: *Danny, Champion of the . . .* what?

19 In 1964, the Rockers and which group were involved in gang riots on Brighton beach?

20 In philosophy, what is the name given to Plato's idea of love or friendship which is purely spiritual, not sexual?

Answers

1 Labour (accept New Labour)
2 Lendl
3 Male
4 X
5 *Newsround*
6 25
7 Carnivore
8 The sun
9 *Enemy*
10 Alaska
11 Export
12 Butter
13 Corgi (accept Cardigan Welsh corgi/Pembroke Welsh corgi/Welsh corgi)
14 1 hours 20 minutes (accept 80 minutes)
15 Elevator
16 Oxygen
17 Watergate (Building)
18 *World*
19 Mods
20 Platonic

Previous Total

1,000
800
600
450
300
200
100
50
20

Banked

Total

Round 177

1 Who is the Queen's youngest child?

2 In the animal kingdom, what type of animal is the coypu: a rodent or a crustacean?

3 In music, what does 'tranquillo' mean: quietly or loudly?

4 In Sweden, is the head of state a monarch, president or prime minister?

5 In art, what F is a mural painting technique using water-based paint on wet plaster?

6 Which French phrase, literally translated as 'on the road', is used in English to mean 'during the journey'?

7 In which country was the ballerina Anna Pavlova born?

8 In fashion, what L is the man-made elastic fibre introduced in 1958 by the American company Du Pont?

9 In the animal kingdom, is the badger more closely related to the rabbit or the otter?

10 In music, complete the title of Duran Duran's 1982 UK hit single: 'Hungry Like the . . .' what?

11 In history, was Jane Seymour the third, fourth or fifth wife of Henry VIII?

12 Sudan is the largest country in which continent?

13 In music, a hexachord is a series of how many notes?

14 In science, is oil more or less dense than water?

15 In South America, Brazil is bordered by two countries that begin with the letter P: Paraguay and which other?

16 In science, what R is measured in ohms?

17 In history, what B were the Dutch farmers who colonised South Africa?

18 In geography, in which continent is Cambodia?

19 What was the profession of John Wilkes Booth, the man who assassinated President Lincoln: an actor or a dancer?

20 In music, what A is a song for a solo voice in an opera?

Previous Total

1,000

800

600

450

300

200

100

50

20

Banked

Total

Answers

1 Prince Edward	**11** Third
2 Rodent	**12** Africa
3 Quietly	**13** Six
4 Monarch	**14** Less dense
5 Fresco	**15** Peru
6 *En route*	**16** Resistance
7 Russia (accept USSR)	**17** Boers
8 Lycra	**18** Asia
9 Otter	**19** Actor
10 Wolf	**20** Aria

Round 178

1 What *M* is the process which involves movement of the jaw in order to break up food into small particles?

2 In the New Testament, what *W* was the barren area where the Devil tempted Jesus?

3 Which group are often referred to as The Manics?

4 In mythology, Hades is the god of the Underworld according to which ancient civilisation?

5 In food, what *C* is a seed that is dried and primarily used as a substitute for chocolate?

6 In architecture, what *T* are the supporting beams and bars that strengthen a roof or bridge?

7 In Judaism, what name is given to the first five books of the Old Testament?

8 In literature, whose mandolin features in the title of Louis de Bernières's novel?

9 Which *I* was the son of Abraham and Hagar and the reputed ancestor of a group of Arabian tribes?

10 In mythology, which *J* was the principal Roman god, concerned with oaths, treaties and marriages?

11 In maths, a train journey covers 250 miles and costs £25. How much does it cost per mile?

12 What *B* is the method of trading in which goods or services are exchanged without the use of money?

13 Which *P* are microscopic pipelines that carry sugars and other nutrients around a plant?

14 What *H* is a shark whose head extends into two lobes bearing eyes and nostrils?

15 In eighteenth-century fashion, what *P* were used to extend the width of a dress or skirt at the hip?

16 In the human body, what is the name of the movable shield of skin that protects and lubricates the eyeball?

17 Complete the line of this song from the musical *My Fair Lady*: 'The Rain in Spain Stays Mainly in the . . .' what?

18 In the Bible, what *A* was the name of the ship that Noah built?

19 In language, a sudden large change or advance is known as a 'quantum . . .' what?

20 'HB' and '2B' are gradings of which writing implement?

Previous Total

1,000

800

600

450

300

200

100

50

20

Banked

Total

Answers

1 Mastication	**10** Jupiter
2 Wilderness	**11** 10 pence
3 Manic Street Preachers	**12** Barter (accept bartering)
4 Greek	**13** Phloem
5 Carob	**14** Hammerhead
6 Trusses (accept trussing/trestles/ trestlework)	**15** Panniers
	16 Eyelid
7 The Torah	**17** Plain
8 Captain Corelli's	**18** Ark
9 Ishmael	**19** Leap (accept jump)
	20 Pencil

Round 179

1 Complete the title of Anthony Newley's 1961 UK hit single: 'Pop Goes the . . .' what?

2 In the animal kingdom, 'white admiral' and 'purple emperor' are types of which insect?

3 What G is the slang term used for the gallery seats in the theatre, because they are the highest?

4 Which Australian-born TV personality would you associate with the didgeridoo and the wobble-board?

5 During the late 1970s, what P was a loud and aggressive style of rock music whose fans were characterised by unconventional hair and clothing?

6 In food, what P is a large, orange-coloured fruit with leathery skin, often used in soups and pies?

7 In politics, John Prescott is associated with which party?

8 In football, in which position did Neville Southall play during his professional career?

9 What is the name of the sport in which competitors try to shoot flying discs?

10 In music, the clarinet and bassoon belong to which family of instruments?

11 In TV, Bernard Cribbins narrated which children's programme set on Wimbledon Common?

12 How many seconds are there in one-and-a-half minutes?

13 What S is a fish that feeds in the sea, then returns to rivers to spawn and is often farmed for its meat?

14 In theatre, complete the title of Joan Littlewood's 1963 musical: *Oh, What a Lovely . . .* what?

15 In food, the words 'broad', 'runner' and 'French' can all prefix the name of which vegetable?

16 What is the name of Dr Jekyll's alter ego in Robert Louis Stevenson's 1886 novel?

17 Complete the title of Simply Red's 1986 UK hit single: 'Holding Back the . . .' what?

18 In anatomy, which A is the internal organ that has no known useful purpose in humans?

19 By what name was the artist and film-maker Andrew Warhola better known?

20 What kind of power is generated by an alternator?

Previous Total

1,000

800

600

450

300

200

100

50

20

Banked

Total

Answers

1 Weasel
2 Butterfly
3 Gods
4 Rolf Harris
5 Punk (*accept* punk rock)
6 Pumpkin
7 Labour (*accept* New Labour)
8 Goalkeeper
9 Clay pigeon shooting (*accept* clay pigeons)
10 Woodwind (*accept* wind)
11 *The Wombles*
12 90
13 Salmon
14 *War!*
15 Bean
16 Mr Hyde
17 Years
18 Appendix
19 Andy Warhol
20 Electricity (*accept* electric power/ alternating current/ AC)

Round 180

1 In mythology, a cornucopia is also called the 'horn of . . .' what?

2 What W is the surname of the American brothers who flew their first glider in 1901?

3 In which country of the UK was former Snooker World Champion Steve Davis born?

4 In geography, which G is a major Indian river which flows through Bangladesh into the Bay of Bengal?

5 In which Thomas Hardy novel does a peasant girl learn that she may be a descendant of an aristocratic family?

6 In TV, the 1960s and 1970s sitcom *Please, Sir!* was set where: a school or a prison?

7 In pop music, in the title of Benny Hill's song, Ernie was the fastest what in the west?

8 Equestrian refers to a sport involving which animal?

9 In pop music, complete the title of Paul McCartney's 1984 UK hit single: 'No More Lonely . . .' what?

10 For what does the military term POW stand?

11 In human biology, the shoulder is an example of a . . . [what]-and-socket joint?

12 In science, C is the symbol of which non-metallic element?

13 What institutions can be found at Parkhurst, Long Lartin and Holloway?

14 In plant biology, what is the pistil of a flower: the male or female reproductive organ?

15 What *T* is the word used to describe an act of betrayal or disloyalty against the sovereign or state?

16 In medicine, an electrocardiogram is normally referred to by what abbreviation?

17 Which well-known musical tells the story of the Von Trapp family?

18 In history, who did Lynette 'Squeaky' Frome attempt to assassinate in 1975: President Ford or President Reagan?

19 What *S* is the chemical name for ordinary table sugar, commonly extracted from sugar beet or sugar cane?

20 What *F* is the name given to a trench in the earth made by a plough?

Previous Total

( )

1,000

800

600

450

300

200

100

50

20

Banked

Total

Answers

1 Plenty (horn of plenty)
2 Wright
3 England
4 Ganges (accept Gunga/Ganga)
5 *Tess of the d'Urbervilles*
6 School
7 Milkman
8 Horse (accept pony)
9 Nights
10 Prisoner of war
11 Ball
12 Carbon
13 Prisons
14 Female
15 Treason
16 ECG
17 *The Sound of Music*
18 President Ford
19 Sucrose (accept saccharose)
20 Furrow

Round 181

1 What *D* is a person who makes detailed drawings for buildings, ships, aircraft or machines before they are built?

2 In history, which commodity was thrown into Boston Harbour in 1773?

3 In foreign currency, how many cents are there in a Jamaican dollar?

4 If a woman was born in 1962, in which year did she celebrate her 37th birthday?

5 In science, the abbreviation STP stands for 'Standard Temperature and . . .' what?

6 What is the usual English translation for the German word '*Danke*'?

7 Which G is an abnormal swelling in the human neck that is caused by an enlarged thyroid gland?

8 What is the name of a small marine fish with a head shaped like that of a horse?

9 In chess, which is the only piece that can 'jump' over other pieces?

10 The political scandal that forced President Nixon to resign was known as the . . . [what] Scandal?

11 In TV, the actor Robert . . . who starred in the American series *Hart To Hart*?

12 Which fictional detective, who lived at 221B Baker Street, loved to play the violin?

13 In sailing, what S is the name given to a person in charge of a ship or boat?

14 In which American sport do you have a pitcher?

15 Which star of the film *Pretty Woman* has an actor brother called Eric?

16 In the animal kingdom, which of the following is a crustacean: an eel, a shrimp or an oyster?

17 In clothing, a tricorn hat has how many corners?

18 In food, cumin, turmeric and nutmeg are all types of what S?

19 In maths, how many legs do a spider and a cow have between them?

20 What B is the name of the tactical war game in which players attempt to predict where their opponent's ships are in order to sink them?

Previous Total
( )
1,000
800
600
450
300
200
100
50
20
Banked
( )
( )
( )
( )
( )
Total
( )

Answers

1 Draftsman	**11** Wagner
2 Tea	**12** Sherlock Holmes
3 One hundred	**13** Skipper
4 1999	**14** Baseball
5 Pressure	**15** Julia Roberts
6 Thank you (accept thanks)	**16** Shrimp
7 Goitre	**17** Three
8 Sea horse	**18** Spice
9 Knight	**19** Twelve
10 Watergate	**20** Battleships

Round 182

1 Is the province of Quebec in eastern or western Canada?

2 In music, what C is the common name for the quick waltz tune for piano originally published in 1877 as the 'Celebrated Chop Waltz'?

3 In air travel, 'BKK' is the international airport code for which city's airport in Thailand?

4 In the animal kingdom, 'Persian' and 'Siamese' are both breeds of which domestic animal?

5 In pop music, complete the title of Hear'Say's debut single 'Pure and . . .' what?

6 What is the name given to a dive from a high place using an elastic cord tied to the body as a restraint?

7 In TV, complete the title of the 1980s sitcom starring Paul Nicholas: *Just Good . . .* what?

8 Is calcium classed as a metallic or non-metallic element?

9 In pop music, complete the title of Tom Jones's 1965 UK hit single, 'What's New . . .' what?

10 In which country was the golfer Seve Ballesteros born?

11 Which famous playwright left money in his will in 1950 to develop a more efficient phonetic alphabet: George Bernard Shaw or Oscar Wilde?

12 What is the surname of Malcolm, the musician and producer who managed The Sex Pistols?

13 In the TV series, Pugsley and Wednesday were the children of which ghoulish family?

14 What *H* is the bottom edge of a garment, which is folded under and stitched down?

15 On a 24-hour clock, what time is it seven hours after midday?

16 In the New Testament, in the Sermon on the Mount, Jesus said 'The meek shall inherit the . . .' what?

17 In the British peerage, which is the higher degree of nobility: marquess or viscount?

18 In music, Phil Collins, Tony Banks and Mike Rutherford were members of which band during the 1970s, 1980s and 1990s?

19 In Indian cookery, what is paneer: cheese or egg?

20 Complete the name of this commemorative day in the Christian calendar: Corpus . . . what?

Previous Total

1,000

800

600

450

300

200

100

50

20

Banked

Total

Answers

1 Eastern (Canada)	**12** McLaren
2 Chopsticks	**13** (The) Addams family
3 Bangkok	**14** Hem
4 Cat	**15** 1900 (hours)
5 Simple	**16** Earth
6 Bungee jump	**17** Marquess
7 *Friends*	**18** Genesis
8 Metallic element	**19** Cheese
9 Pussycat?	**20** Christi
10 Spain	
11 George Bernard Shaw	

Round 183

1 In gardening, what *D* is a pointed digging tool used to make holes in soil for bulbs or seedlings?

2 Is the moss stitch used in knitting or embroidery?

3 In art, what was the first name of the artist Cézanne?

4 In the Bible, which people did Moses lead to the border of the Promised Land?

5 How many were in the pop group The Monkees?

6 Which is the only island state in the United States of America?

7 What type of primate is a gorilla: monkey or ape?

8 Which was the first Thomas Hardy novel to be published under his own name: *A Pair of Blue Eyes* or *Desperate Remedies*?

9 In UK geography, what *D* is the name of the English city located on the River Derwent?

10 According to Shakespeare, before the Battle of Agincourt Henry V encouraged his men to cry 'God for Harry, England and Saint . . .' who?

11 In travel, what *F* is the seaside port in Kent which has ferry connections to Boulogne?

12 In the New Testament, what *A* is the name given to the twelve disciples whom Jesus sent forth to preach his gospel?

13 In professional boxing, which is heavier: a super-bantamweight or a super-featherweight?

14 In law, what *D* is an attack on a person's good name, character or reputation?

15 In literature, John . . . who wrote the *Rabbit* series of novels published between 1960 and 1990?

16 In human biology, what is the name of the horny covering that grows on the upper surface of the end of each finger and toe?

17 In comics, what is the name of Batman's masked sidekick?

18 What *W* is a legal document detailing someone's wishes in the event of their death?

19 In which English city is the building known as Canary Wharf Tower?

20 According to the saying, someone inoffensive and harmless wouldn't hurt what type of creature?

Previous Total

1,000

800

600

450

300

200

100

50

20

Banked

Total

Answers

1 Dibber (accept dibble)	**10** George
2 Knitting	**11** Folkestone
3 Paul	**12** Apostles
4 The Israelites (the Chosen People/ Hebrews)	**13** Super-featherweight
	14 Defamation
	15 (John) Updike
5 Four	**16** Nail
6 Hawaii	**17** Robin
7 Ape	**18** Will
8 *A Pair of Blue Eyes*	**19** London
9 Derby	**20** A fly

Round 184

1 In British politics, what sex were the suffragettes?

2 In biology, the coronary artery supplies blood to which organ?

3 In the children's rhyme, how far did the crooked man walk?

4 Complete the lyric from Mud's 1974 hit single: 'That's neat, I really love your tiger . . .' what?

5 In human biology, cataracts cause problems with which part of the body?

6 In nature, what *P* is the name given to the seed of an apple?

7 In fashion, what name is given to a long scarf of feathers or fur worn around the neck?

8 The word 'unilateral' means relating to how many sides?

9 What was the name of the 1968 film starring Dick Van Dyke about a man who invents a flying car?

10 In the animal kingdom, what *P* is the name given to a social group of lions?

11 In human biology, an inability to distinguish between certain colours is known as 'colour . . .' what?

12 What *N* are the spectacular falls which are a tourist attraction in Ontario, Canada?

13 In fashion, trousers that flare from the knee are commonly known as 'bell . . .' what?

14 In history, in which country was the bushranger Ned Kelly born?

15 In card games, another name for 'twenty-one' is 'black . . .' what?

16 In music, the tuba and cornet belong to which orchestral family of wind instruments?

17 Who did Prince Andrew marry in July 1986?

18 Which execution device was adopted as the standard form of capital punishment in France during the Revolution?

19 What *B* is a three-letter word that can mean 'to fight' or 'a container', often made of cardboard?

20 In science, what is measured in watts: power or energy?

Previous Total

1,000

800

600

450

300

200

100

50

20

Banked

Total

Answers

1 Female	**11** Blindness
2 Heart	**12** Niagara (Falls)
3 A crooked mile	**13** (Bell) Bottoms
(accept a mile)	**14** Australia
4 Feet	**15** (Black)Jack
5 Eyes	**16** Brass
6 Pip (accept pippin)	**17** Sarah Ferguson
7 Boa	(accept Fergie/
8 One	Duchess of York)
9 *Chitty Chitty Bang Bang*	**18** Guillotine
	19 Box
10 Pride	**20** Power

Round 185

1 According to the saying, what is stranger than fiction?

2 In theatre, Joseph Grimaldi was known for being what: a clown or musician?

3 In nature, what is a Venus flytrap?

4 What is the surname of the famous American fashion designer Calvin?

5 In which country of the UK is Conwy Castle?

6 In TV comedy, Richard Wilson played which grumpy character in *One Foot in the Grave*?

7 In pop music, which former member of The Beatles had a 1983 UK hit album entitled *Pipes of Peace*?

8 In electrical circuits, what *R* is the name for the device that opposes the current flow?

9 In sport, what is the name of the late Formula One champion Graham Hill's son?

10 In film, complete the title of this 1992 Australian film about dancing: *Strictly . . .* what?

11 In Denmark, is the head of state a monarch, president or prime minister?

12 In which British city would you find the Nightingale School and Home for Nurses, founded by Florence Nightingale in 1860?

13 In biology, the term auditory refers to which sense?

14 In maths, if a used-car salesman buys a car for £1,230 and sells it for £1,750, how much profit has he made?

15 In music, what name is given to a composition for five instruments or voices?

16 Who starred as Catherine Tramell in the 1992 film *Basic Instinct*?

17 In meteorology, 'sheet' and 'forked' are types of what?

18 In the animal kingdom, which is the only species of bear to inhabit the Arctic Sea ice?

19 In human biology, by what name are the deciduous teeth which we lose before adulthood more commonly known?

20 In sport, which Greek city first hosted the modern Olympics in 1896?

Answers

1 Truth
2 Clown
3 Plant (accept carnivorous plant/ insectivorous plant)
4 Klein
5 Wales
6 Victor Meldrew (accept Victor)
7 Paul McCartney
8 Resistor
9 Damon (Hill)
10 *Ballroom*

11 Monarch (Queen Margarethe)
12 London
13 Hearing
14 £520 (accept 42 per cent)
15 Quintet
16 Sharon Stone
17 Lightning
18 Polar bear (accept *Ursus maritimus*)
19 Milk teeth
20 Athens

Round 186

1 The saxophone belongs to which family of wind instruments?

2 An arrangement of elements placed in order of increasing atomic number is known as a periodic . . . what?

3 In the Bible, Jesus's life story is told in the gospels of Matthew, Mark, Luke and who else?

4 What J is the name of Lewis Carroll's nonsense verse about a fictitious monster in the novel *Through the Looking Glass*?

5 What D is a name for a female goat?

6 In geography, on which continent would you find the capital city of Nairobi?

7 In history, was Edward the Confessor king of England before or after the Norman Conquest?

8 What is the first name of Judy Garland and Vincente Minnelli's only daughter?

9 What R is the famous British press agency founded in London in 1851 and among the largest in the world?

10 In art, Hieronymus Bosch painted *The Garden of Earthly* . . . what?

11 In British politics, what name is given to the area that an MP represents?

12 In football, which London Premiership team's ground is in Highbury?

13 In music, what C is to perform songs in a smooth, soft, sentimental style?

14 In the New Testament, the day the angel Gabriel told Mary that she was to conceive a son is known as the Feast of the . . . what?

15 What C is a large city in north-east India and the capital of the state of West Bengal?

16 Which S is the official language of both Kenya and Tanzania?

17 John . . . [who] starred as Fred Flintstone in the 1994 movie version of *The Flintstones*?

18 In Formula One, in which South American country would you find the Interlagos race track?

19 In geography, in which country of the UK is the cathedral city of Brecon?

20 What was the surname of Sergio, the Italian director who made the 1966 western *The Good, the Bad and the Ugly*?

Previous Total

1,000

800

600

450

300

200

100

50

20

Banked

Total

Answers

1 Woodwind	**11** Constituency
2 Table	**12** Arsenal
3 (St) John	**13** Croon
4 'Jabberwocky'	**14** Annunciation
5 Doe	**15** Calcutta
6 Africa	**16** Swahili
7 Before	**17** (John) Goodman
8 Liza (Liza Minnelli)	**18** Brazil
9 Reuters	**19** Wales
10 *Delights*	**20** Leone

Round 187

1 In literature, in which century did Thomas Hardy die?

2 According to the saying, something which spoils success is like a fly in the . . . what?

3 What S is the sport and recreation of riding on a board attatched to rolling wheels?

4 In travel, British traffic lights are green, amber and which other colour?

5 In language, the word 'pooch' refers to which common pet?

6 In nature, how many leaves does a clover have when it is said to bring good luck?

7 What V is the art of producing vocal sounds that seem to come from a puppet or doll?

8 In the TV series *Hi-De-Hi*, what colour coats did the entertainment staff at Maplins Holiday Camp wear?

9 In music, 'Help!' was a 1965 UK number-one hit single for which Liverpudlian band?

10 In the Bible, what food did Jesus say was 'his body' at the Last Supper?

11 Which European city had a tower built for the International Exposition of 1889 by Gustave Eiffel?

12 Who married Lady Diana Spencer in 1981?

13 In France, what meat would you be eating if you were served 'poulet'?

14 In nature, what *B* is a blossom on a flowering plant?

15 In the animal kingdom, the famous English champion Red Rum was what type of animal?

16 In film, complete the title of the 1997 comedy starring Julia Roberts and Cameron Diaz: *My Best Friend's . . .* what?

17 In science, which piece of common laboratory equipment is named after Robert Wilhelm Bunsen?

18 In travel, which American city has an airport with the code 'JFK'?

19 Who was the German leader between 1933 and 1945?

20 What is the sixth month of the year?

Previous Total
1,000
800
600
450
300
200
100
50
20
Banked
Total

Answers

1 Twentieth (century; 1928)
2 Ointment
3 Skateboard (*accept* snakeboard)
4 Red
5 Dog (*accept* mongrel)
6 Four
7 Ventriloquism
8 Yellow
9 The Beatles
10 Bread
11 Paris
12 Prince Charles (*accept* Prince of Wales)
13 Chicken
14 Bloom
15 Horse (*accept* racehorse/steeple chase horse)
16 *Wedding*
17 Bunsen burner (*accept* gas burner)
18 New York
19 Adolf Hitler (*accept* Hitler)
20 June

Round 188

1 In politics, what *T* is a written agreement between two or more countries?

2 In pop music, Benny, Bjorn, Agnetha and Frida were all members of which Swedish group?

3 In sport, which English football league team has the nickname 'Spurs'?

4 Which city in New Zealand shares its name with a type of waterproof boot?

5 According to the nursery rhyme, whose wife could eat no lean?

6 What *T* is a small-scale lottery with tickets drawn from a revolving drum?

7 In nature, what *F* is the name given to any of the rigid outgrowths that form the plumage of birds?

8 In which sport can you score a 'basket'?

9 In travel, Alitalia is the national airline of which country?

10 The Dow Jones Industrial Average is an indicator of share values on which country's stock exchange?

11 What *B* is the name for the breath-testing device first used by British police in the 1960s to deter drink-driving?

12 In nature, what *F* is a very hard stone that produces sparks when struck with iron or steel?

13 The Statue of Liberty and Times Square are landmarks in which US city?

14 In music, 'adagio' is a direction to play or sing a piece at what pace: quickly or slowly?

15 In the animal kingdom what C is a small bird brought to Europe from the Canary Islands during the fifteenth century?

16 On which side of the road do the Japanese drive?

17 In which 1998 war film does Tom Hanks's character attempt to rescue a soldier whose three brothers have been killed?

18 In the animal kingdom, 'greys' and 'reds' are both kinds of what K, native to Australia?

19 In which Italian city would you be most likely to see a gondola?

20 According to the musical and 1954 film, how many brides partnered the *Seven Brothers*?

Previous Total

1,000
800
600
450
300
200
100
50
20

Banked

Total

Answers

1 Treaty
2 Abba
3 Tottenham Hotspur (accept Tottenham)
4 Wellington
5 Jack Spratt
6 Tombola
7 Feathers
8 Basketball
9 Italy
10 United States (accept US/USA/United States of America/America)
11 Breathalyser (accept breath analyser)
12 Flint
13 New York (City)
14 Slowly
15 Canary
16 Left
17 *Saving Private Ryan*
18 Kangaroo
19 Venice
20 Seven

Round 189

1 A tree that is not an evergreen is known as what?

2 In sport, which winter event, held every four years, did the Norwegian town of Lillehammer host in 1994?

3 Martha Washington was married to which American president?

4 In sport, the father of which famous golfer wrote a coaching guide called *Training a Tiger*?

5 In which country was fashion designer Coco Chanel born?

6 What G is a Hindu word for a spiritual teacher?

7 In politics, for which party was James Callaghan elected prime minister?

8 What N is a city in the English county of Norfolk?

9 Actress Annette Bening married which *Dick Tracy* star in 1992?

10 In cookery, what S is a dish consisting of Dublin Bay prawns usually coated in breadcrumbs and fried?

11 In TV, which detective did Sharon Gless play in the US 1980s series *Cagney and Lacey*?

12 At the 1988 Winter Olympics, Eddie 'the Eagle' Edwards represented Great Britain at which ski event?

13 Complete the title of the 1996 romantic comedy starring Uma Thurman: *The Truth About Cats and . . .* what?

14 What *T* is a bird from South and Central America with a large, brightly-coloured beak, which is a relative of the woodpecker?

15 In music, what is the traditional shape of the body of the balalaika: triangular or oval?

16 Which American sprinter won the Olympic 100 metres gold medal in 1984 and 1988?

17 What waterproof item of clothing was first manufactured by a Scotsman and is named after him?

18 In the animal kingdom, what name is given to a young duck?

19 In which country would you find the Ural Mountains?

20 In US politics, of which American political party is Bill Clinton a member?

Previous Total

1,000

800

600

450

300

200

100

50

20

Banked

Total

Answers

1 Deciduous
2 Winter Olympics (accept Olympics)
3 George Washington
4 Tiger Woods (Eldrick Woods)
5 France
6 Guru
7 Labour
8 Norwich
9 Warren Beatty (Henry Warren Beaty)
10 Scampi (accept scampo)
11 Cagney
12 Ski jumping
13 Dogs
14 Toucan (accept toucanet)
15 Triangular
16 Carl Lewis
17 Mackintosh
18 Duckling (accept chick)
19 Russia (accept Russian Federation)
20 Democratic Party (accept Democrats)

Round 190

1 In music, the composer Johann Strauss was known as 'the . . . [what] king'?

2 In music, how many semiquavers make up a quaver?

3 In gardening, what S is a type of pruning shears whose name is an adaptation of a French word?

4 In musical instruments, from what is a 'bassoon' mainly made?

5 In the UK, in which decade was the coronation of Queen Elizabeth II?

6 What is the sum of the number of sides of three octagons?

7 In human biology, what C is a word used to describe an abnormal condition present at birth?

8 In which North American country is the state of Tabasco?

9 Which rock 'n' roll singer, best known for 'Great Balls of Fire', was nicknamed 'The Killer'?

10 In which ocean are the Cook Islands?

11 In biology, the frequency of live births within a population over a set period is referred to as the birth . . . what?

12 In maths, if you were £150 overdrawn and you paid in a cheque for £1,000, what would your new balance be?

13 In TV, which quiz show hosted by Noel Edmonds challenged families about their knowledge of TV?

14 Which income tax payment scheme was first announced in 1943 in the UK?

15 In history, William of where was given the English throne by Parliament in 1689?

16 What was the first name of the Gershwin brother who composed Broadway musicals?

17 What S is the name for the military action when an army attempts to take a town by surrounding it and cutting off all outside communication?

18 In cricket, what is the name for a period of six consecutive balls by the same bowler?

19 If your shopping costs £11.11, how much change would you get from a £20 note?

20 The electric iron was invented in which century?

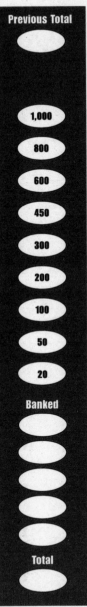

Previous Total

1,000

800

600

450

300

200

100

50

20

Banked

Total

Answers

1 Waltz	**11** Rate
2 Two	**12** £850
3 Secateurs	**13** *Telly Addicts*
4 Wood	**14** Pay-As-You-Earn (*accept* PAYE)
5 1950s (1953)	
6 24	**15** Orange
7 Congenital	**16** George
8 Mexico	**17** Siege
9 Jerry Lee Lewis (*do not accept* Jerry Lewis)	**18** An over
	19 £8.89
10 Pacific Ocean (*accept* South Pacific)	**20** Nineteenth (1882)

Round 191

1 In which country of the UK is the royal yacht *Britannia* berthed?

2 In the animal kingdom, which word must be added to 'lion' to make an alternative name for the puma?

3 Which Hollywood heartthrob appeared as the character Tyler Durden in the 1999 film *Fight Club*?

4 In biology, what name is given to the shortest, thickest digit of the human hand, located next to the forefinger?

5 According to superstition, throwing coins into which water feature entitles you to make a wish?

6 What M is a mythical sea creature with the head and upper body of a woman and the tail of a fish?

7 In music, Neil Tennant is a member of the pop group The Pet Shop . . . what?

8 According to the saying, a declaration that something is in a good condition is like a 'clean bill of . . .' what?

9 The plumage of the magpie is black and which colour?

10 In Christianity, what H is the name of the dwelling place of God and all souls who have been faithful on Earth?

11 In cookery, 'aioli' is made by seasoning which type of dressing with garlic?

12 What W is the fine network spun by a spider to capture prey?

13 The consumer protection organisation known by the initials OFT is the Office of Fair . . . what?

14 In snooker, which colour ball is worth one point?

15 In theatre, complete the title of the Shakespeare play: *A Midsummer Night's . . .* what?

16 What *T* was the nickname of 1960s model Leslie Hornby, because of her thin appearance?

17 What word can mean either a mechanism to regulate the flow of water or a device for listening into telephone conversations?

18 In farming, a swine is more commonly referred to as what kind of livestock?

19 In nature, what *A* is the powdery substance that is left after something has been burnt?

20 In music, the first four of Vivaldi's Opus 8 concertos are known as 'The Four . . .' what?

Previous Total

1,000

800

600

450

300

200

100

50

20

Banked

Total

Answers

1 Scotland	**11** Mayonnaise
2 Mountain	**12** Web (accept spider's
3 Brad Pitt (William	web)
Bradley Pitt)	**13** Trading
4 Thumb (accept pollex)	**14** Red
5 Well (accept wishing	**15** *Dream*
well/fountain)	**16** Twiggy
6 Mermaid	**17** Tap
7 Boys	**18** Pig
8 Health	**19** Ash
9 White	**20** '(The Four) Seasons'
10 Heaven	

Round 192

1 What *T* is another name for an elephant's incisor tooth?

2 In TV, Wendy Richard played Miss Brahms in which BBC sitcom set in a department store?

3 In football, Bayern Munich is a team in the domestic league of which European country?

4 The American actor Patrick . . . who starred in the films *Ghost* and *Dirty Dancing*?

5 In biology, what *N* is the name given to the sweet liquid produced by plants?

6 In government, the Cabinet minister who delivers the annual budget speech in Parliament is known as the Chancellor of the . . . what?

7 What *P* is the name of the collectible brochures which can be purchased at football matches?

8 In aviation, what is the popular name for the unit containing an aeroplane's flight and voice recorders?

9 In the 1960s TV sitcom, Herman, Lily, Grandpa, Eddie and Marilyn were members of which ghoulish family?

10 In Matthew's gospel, who hanged himself because of his guilt over betraying Jesus?

11 In the animal kingdom, which of the following is a species of bird: the yellowhammer or yellownail?

12 In which 1990 film does Johnny Depp's character create ice sculptures using his scissor-like digits?

13 King Charles II had an actress mistress called Nell . . . who?

14 What M is the name given to the first voyage of a ship?

15 In comic books, the alter ego of which of Batman's enemies is the feline-friendly Selina Kyle?

16 In language, which three-letter word can mean both a common insect pest and to travel in an aircraft?

17 In music, a syrinx is a wind instrument more commonly known as the 'pan . . .' what?

18 In British politics, in which of the two Houses of Parliament would you find backbenchers?

19 With which sport is Lance Armstrong associated: cycling or weightlifting?

20 In which European country is the tourist area of Alicante?

Previous Total
⬭
1,000
800
600
450
300
200
100
50
20
Banked
⬭
⬭
⬭
⬭
⬭
Total
⬭

Answers

1 Tusk	**11** Yellowhammer
2 *Are You Being Served?*	**12** *Edward Scissorhands*
	13 Gwynn
3 Germany	**14** Maiden
4 Swayze	**15** Catwoman
5 Nectar	**16** Fly
6 Exchequer	**17** Pipes
7 Programmes	**18** House of Commons
8 Black box	**19** Cycling
9 The Munsters	**20** Spain
10 Judas (Judas Iscariot)	

Round 193

1 What *B* is the name of the woody-stemmed grass plant, found mainly in Asia, which forms the staple diet of the giant panda?

2 In pop music, in which country of the UK were the Bay City Rollers formed?

3 What *F* is the name given to a young female horse?

4 In maths, if a dog chases a cat for 28 metres across a garden, how far is this in centimetres?

5 The term used to describe a large, prestigious company considered a safe investment is 'blue . . .' what?

6 What are rhinoceroses: herbivores or carnivores?

7 What *B* is New York's equivalent of London's West End?

8 In terms of population, which is the largest country in Asia?

9 On standard British cars, what colour are the reversing lights?

10 In language, what *J* do Americans call a caretaker?

11 In a mercury thermometer, when the temperature decreases, does the mercury expand or contract?

12 In modern history, during which World War did the Battle of Britain take place?

13 What kind of creatures are 'bee-eaters'?

14 Complete the title of Rodgers and Hammerstein's 1949 Pulitzer Prize-winning musical: *South . . .* what?

15 In the card game bridge, if you win a rubber, how many games out of three have you won?

16 In music, when a mute is inserted into the bell of a brass instrument, is the sound produced by the instrument louder or softer?

17 What M is a geographical representation, usually of part of the Earth's surface, drawn or printed on paper?

18 In religion, complete the name of this commemorative day in the Christian calendar: Ash . . . what?

19 Who played the Toymaker in the film *Chitty Chitty Bang Bang*: Benny Hill or Bernard Cribbins?

20 In food, okra is also known as 'lady's . . .' what?

Previous Total

1,000

800

600

450

300

200

100

50

20

Banked

Total

Answers

1 Bamboo	**12** Second World War (*accept* World War II)
2 Scotland	**13** Birds
3 Filly	**14** *Pacific*
4 2800 cm	**15** Two
5 (Blue) Chip	**16** Softer
6 Herbivores	**17** Map
7 Broadway	**18** Wednesday
8 China	**19** Benny Hill
9 White	**20** Finger(s)
10 Janitor	
11 Contract	

Round 194

1 In football, which country won the 1966 World Cup final?

2 In fashion, what C is the name given to the upright or turned over neckband of a shirt or blouse?

3 In human biology, dermatitis is a disease that affects which organ?

4 In transport, what H is a vehicle that travels over land or water on a cushion of air provided by a downward blast?

5 In fashion, the sole of a plimsoll shoe is traditionally made of which elastic material?

6 In the USA, which state uses the postal abbreviation FL?

7 In film, complete the title of the 1983 comedy starring Eddie Murphy and Dan Aykroyd: *Trading . . .* what?

8 If it is five degrees Celsius and the temperature drops by twelve degrees overnight, how cold will it be?

9 In sport, for what do the initials RFU stand?

10 In geography, in which continent is Amazonia National Park?

11 In which European country is the city of Utrecht?

12 If a sports stadium has the capacity to seat 40,000 people, how many people would be needed to fill three quarters of it?

13 Who is the actor father of *EastEnders* actress Hannah Waterman?

14 Which region of France takes its name from the Latin *'provincia'*, because it was the first Roman province beyond the Alps?

15 In a playground there are 58 girls and 66 boys: how many children are there in total?

16 In which century was the first parachute jump made from an aeroplane?

17 By what name is the English pop singer Kim Smith better known?

18 In geography, Islamabad has been the capital of which country since 1967?

19 According to the saying, when attending to a person's every need, you are 'waiting on them hand and . . .' what?

20 Solar panels harness energy from what source?

Previous Total

1,000

800

600

450

300

200

100

50

20

Banked

Total

Answers

1 England	**11** The Netherlands
2 Collar	(*accept* Holland)
3 Skin	**12** 30,000
4 Hovercraft	**13** Dennis Waterman
5 Rubber (*accept* latex/	**14** Provence
polymer)	**15** 124
6 Florida	**16** Twentieth (1912)
7 *Places*	**17** Kim Wilde
8 Minus seven	**18** Pakistan
9 Rugby Football Union	**19** Foot
10 South America	**20** The sun

Round 195

1 In golf, what C is the name given to the person who carries a golfer's clubs and offers advice?

2 In travel, buses and trains which are provided for anyone to use are known as what transport?

3 In human biology, the iris, lens and retina can all be found in which sensory organ?

4 In pool and snooker, what colour is the cue ball?

5 If a person is composed and self-possessed, they may be described as 'cool as a . . .' what?

6 In the animal kingdom, what type of animal was the TV star Lassie?

7 What Y is a folk-singing style common in Switzerland?

8 In nature, what name is given to a hanging spike of ice formed from dripping water?

9 In which country would you find the famous Golden Gate Bridge?

10 In sport, who partnered Jayne Torvill to an ice-dancing gold medal at the 1984 Winter Olympics?

11 In chemistry, which two letters are the symbol for the element calcium?

12 In the animal kingdom, what name is usually given to an adult female sheep?

13 In music, what are the foot-operated mechanisms on a piano called?

14 In world politics, of which country was Indira Gandhi prime minister?

15 In English history, who defeated Harold II at the Battle of Hastings?

16 In the Bible, which woman was the first person to eat from the Tree of Knowledge of Good and Evil?

17 What N are the pointed rods used in knitting?

18 What does an audiologist specialise in: sight defects or hearing defects?

19 In British politics, which female prime minister appointed Michael Heseltine as the Secretary of State for the Environment in 1979?

20 What P is a fruit traditionally used to make Jack-o'-lanterns during Hallowe'en?

Previous Total

1,000

800

600

450

300

200

100

50

20

Banked

Total

Answers

1 Caddie
2 Public
3 Eye
4 White
5 Cucumber
6 Dog (accept collie, rough collie)
7 Yodelling
8 Icicle
9 USA
10 Christopher Dean (Christopher Colin Dean)
11 Ca
12 Ewe
13 Pedals
14 India
15 William the Conqueror (accept William, Duke of Normandy)
16 Eve
17 Needles
18 Hearing defects
19 Margaret Thatcher
20 Pumpkin

Round 196

1 In money, the guilder is the currency of which country?

2 What name is given to the small piece of metal, usually shaped like a coin or cross, that is awarded to someone for outstanding achievement?

3 In the Australian TV series, what type of animal was Skippy?

4 Which British boxer's 1987 biography is called *Know What I Mean*?

5 In folklore, what Y is another name for the Abominable Snowman?

6 If a two-and-a-half-hour stage performance starts at 7 p.m., what time will it finish?

7 Followers of which religion face towards Mecca to pray?

8 In science, what G is the pulling force of the earth?

9 In the animal kingdom, which is larger: the harvest mouse or the house mouse?

10 Complete the title of the following Dylan Thomas play: *Under Milk . . .* what?

11 In geography, in which European country is the city of Marseille?

12 In nature, what H is a line of bushes or low trees, trimmed to form a boundary?

13 How many years are celebrated on a golden wedding anniversary?

14 If a company has registered as a public limited company, which three letters must by law appear after its name?

15 The Algarve is the most southerly province of which country?

16 In biology, what *P* is the action of a bird to tidy its feathers?

17 Before embarking on his solo career, George Michael formed which band in 1981 with Andrew Ridgeley?

18 In 1989, the east and west parts of which European country unified?

19 In the Bible, who washed the disciples' feet when preparing for the Last Supper?

20 In theatre, what *B* is the area behind the stage, including the dressing rooms, that is out of the audience's view?

Previous Total

1,000
800
600
450
300
200
100
50
20

Banked

Total

Answers

1 Holland (accept the Netherlands)
2 Medal (accept medallion)
3 Kangaroo (accept bush kangaroo)
4 Frank Bruno (Franklin Bruno)
5 Yeti
6 9.30 p.m. (accept 21.30)
7 Islam (accept Muslim)
8 Gravity (accept gravitation)
9 House mouse
10 Wood
11 France
12 Hedge (accept hedgerow)
13 Fifty
14 Plc
15 Portugal
16 Preening
17 Wham!
18 Germany
19 Jesus (Jesus Christ)
20 Backstage

1 In which Shakespeare play is the line 'To be or not to be, that is the question'?

2 If a hotel room costs £110 per night, how much does it cost in total for three nights?

3 In religion, according to the Book of Genesis, which man was made from the dust of the ground?

4 In traditional costume, what M is a shoe originally worn by Native Americans?

5 In 1993, which royal palace was opened to paying tourists to help fund the cost of refurbishing Windsor Castle?

6 Of which country is Guatemala City the capital?

7 Rowan Atkinson played the character of Father Gerald alongside Hugh Grant in which 1994 British comedy?

8 In science, which colour comes in between green and indigo in the rainbow?

9 What O is a dramatic musical work in which singing takes the place of speech?

10 In human biology, the central nervous system consists of the brain and which cord of nerve tissue?

11 Which British MP was made Home Secretary shortly after the 2001 general election?

12 Which former French footballer appeared in the 1998 film *Elizabeth*?

13 In the novel and film *The Wizard of Oz*, Dorothy lived in which American state?

14 In which country of the UK would you find Caernarvon?

15 Which of the following European capital cities is furthest north: Copenhagen, Moscow or Oslo?

16 In world politics, Adolf Hitler became the Chancellor of which country in 1933?

17 The Christian Revival Association established in 1865 became the . . . [what] Army?

18 In the USA, which state is abbreviated with the letters CA?

19 If an arena has the capacity to seat 40,000 people, how many people would it take to fill one quarter of it?

20 In which year will the next football World Cup be held?

Previous Total

1,000
800
600
450
300
200
100
50
20

Banked

Total

Answers

1 *Hamlet*	**11** David Blunkett
2 £330	**12** Eric Cantona
3 Adam	**13** Kansas
4 Moccasin	**14** Wales
5 Buckingham Palace	**15** Oslo
6 Guatemala	**16** Germany
7 *Four Weddings and a Funeral*	**17** Salvation
8 Blue	**18** California
9 Opera/operetta	**19** 10,000
10 Spinal cord	**20** 2002

Round 198

1 Members of the first organised police force in London were called 'Bobbies' or 'Peelers' after its founder, Robert . . . who?

2 Which Beatle said 'We're more popular than Jesus'?

3 In an orchestra, what K is the English name for the large drums also known as 'timpani'?

4 What D is a term that refers to volcanoes that have not erupted in a long time, but are expected to erupt again?

5 Who was the lead singer of the rock group Queen?

6 In which country was painter Francisco de Goya born?

7 In the TV soap *EastEnders*, who owns the dog Well'ard?

8 In which decade were circle skirts and bobby socks first fashionable?

9 Which British author wrote the novel *A Christmas Carol*?

10 Insulin and adrenalin are types of what H?

11 Mary . . . who wrote the 1818 novel *Frankenstein*?

12 If the area of a greetings card is 42 cm^2 and one side measures 7 cm, how long is the other side?

13 How many faces does an octahedron solid have?

14 Mikhail Gorbachev signed an agreement with which US president in 1987 to destroy all intermediate-range nuclear weapons?

15 What A is the ritual cleansing of a priest's hands, body or sacred vessels during or prior to a religious ceremony?

16 What is the name for the form of horse racing in which the horses do not jump obstacles?

17 In TV, in which decade was the US sitcom *The Monkees* first broadcast in the UK?

18 In music, complete the title of the opera by Mozart: *Così fan . . .* what?

19 In Robert Louis Stevenson's novel, Mr Hyde is the name given to the evil alter ego of which doctor?

20 The engines, wagons and coaches used on a railway are known as 'rolling . . .' what?

Previous Total

1,000

800

600

450

300

200

100

50

20

Banked

Total

Answers

1 Peel
2 John Lennon
3 Kettledrums
4 Dormant
5 Freddie Mercury (Farookh Bulsara)
6 Spain
7 Robbie Jackson (accept Robbie)
8 1950s (accept fifties)
9 Charles Dickens
10 Hormone(s)
11 Mary Shelley (accept Mary Wollstonecroft Shelley/Mary (Wollstonecroft) Godwin)

12 6 centimetres
13 Eight
14 Ronald Reagan
15 Ablutions (accept ablution)
16 Flat racing
17 1960s (1966)
18 *Tutte*
19 (Dr) Jekyll
20 (Rolling) Stock

Round 199

1 In science, of what is botany the study?

2 What G is a breed of dog typically used for racing around a track in pursuit of a mechanical hare?

3 In the TV cartoon *The Simpsons*, what is the name of Homer and Marge's son?

4 In football, which Scottish club won the CIS Insurance Cup against Kilmarnock in March 2001?

5 In US sport, what D is the annual process by which professional teams select young players from colleges?

6 In language, what is the name given to any letter of the alphabet that is not a vowel?

7 Complete the title of Sarah Brightman's 1978 UK hit single: 'I Lost My Heart To A Starship . . .' what?

8 Which word specifically describes a person aged between 80 and 89 years old?

9 In religion, which river in northern India and Bangladesh is considered sacred by Hindus?

10 In the royal family, who became the first heir to the British throne to earn a university degree in 1970?

11 In nature, which colour completes the name of the following butterfly, the 'cabbage . . .' what?

12 Which plant of the mustard family, with red-skinned white roots, is eaten raw in salads?

13 Which scientist is credited with devising the equation 'e equals mc squared'?

14 Which famous organisation owns Lord's cricket ground?

15 Who won a Brit Award for outstanding contribution to British music in 1982, two years after his death?

16 The Wicklow Mountains are south of which Irish city?

17 Daniel Defoe wrote which novel in the eighteenth century about a man and his adventures following his shipwreck?

18 In geography, what *T* is a Japanese city on the Pacific coast of Central Honshu?

19 In pop music, complete the title of The Hollies' 1969 UK hit single: 'He Ain't Heavy, He's My . . .' what?

20 What kind of drill, developed in 1861, works by compressed air?

Previous Total

1,000

800

600

450

300

200

100

50

20

Banked

Total

Answers

1 Plants	**11** White
2 Greyhound	**12** Radish
3 Bart	**13** Einstein (Albert Einstein)
4 Celtic (Glasgow Celtic)	**14** The MCC (accept Marylebone Cricket Club)
5 The Draft (The Draft Pick)	**15** John Lennon
6 Consonant	**16** Dublin
7 Trooper	**17** *Robinson Crusoe*
8 Octogenarian	**18** Tokyo
9 The Ganges (accept Ganga)	**19** Brother
10 Prince Charles	**20** Pneumatic drill

Round 200

1 Which US mammal can be identified by its black mask across the eyes and black band on the tail?

2 What *P* was a coloquial term for a heavy smog in 1950s London?

3 Sir Arthur Conan Doyle wrote a novel entitled *The Hound of the . . .* what?

4 Where in a book would you find the preface: the beginning or the end?

5 What is the surname of Scottish rugby union stars Gavin and Scott?

6 In the TV sitcom *Are You Being Served?*, which character's catchphrase was 'I'm free'?

7 In which South American country did the 1992 Rio Earth Summit on the environment take place?

8 According to the title of the 1979 film, from which famous prison did Clint Eastwood's character escape?

9 In history, what *S* was the name of the bars that sold alcohol illicitly throughout the US Prohibition era?

10 Who painted the Sistine Chapel ceiling from 1508 to 1512?

11 In football, which ex-England manager took over Tottenham Hotspur after George Graham's departure in March 2001?

12 The three branches of the British armed forces are the Army, the Royal Air Force and the what?

13 In football, which country hosted the 1966 World Cup?

14 In TV, which author was played by John Hurt in the 1975 film *The Naked Civil Servant*?

15 In which novel by Lewis Carroll does Alice meet the Mad Hatter?

16 Which is further north: Inverness or Edinburgh?

17 Which device for men was patented and first manufactured around 1930 by Schick Inc.?

18 In the fairy story, which siblings found a house made of bread and cakes in the forest?

19 Bangkok is the capital and chief port of which country?

20 Wenceslas Square is the main square of which European capital city?

Previous Total
1,000
800
600
450
300
200
100
50
20
Banked
Total

Answers

1 Raccoon (accept ringtail)
2 Pea-souper (accept pea-soup)
3 *Baskervilles*
4 Beginning
5 Hastings
6 Mr Humphries (do not accept John Inman)
7 Brazil
8 Alcatraz (accept *Escape From Alcatraz*)
9 Speakeasys
10 Michelangelo (Michelangelo Buonarroti)
11 Glenn Hoddle

12 Royal Navy (accept Navy)
13 England
14 Quentin Crisp
15 *Alice's Adventures in Wonderland* (accept *Alice In Wonderland*; do not accept *Alice Through the Looking Glass*)
16 Inverness
17 Electric razor (accept electric shaver)
18 Hansel and Gretel
19 Thailand (accept kingdom of Thailand)
20 Prague

Round 201

1 The name of which racket sport can also mean to crush or squeeze something?

2 Which is the fastest sprinter of the big cats?

3 In modern history, which country carried out the *Apollo* space missions during the 1960s and 1970s?

4 In the Bible, which boat measured approximately 450 feet in length?

5 On the flag of which former nation would you find a hammer, sickle and star on a red background?

6 From which country does the white or rosé wine retsina originate?

7 Which four-legged animal competes in a gymkhana?

8 In maths, what is 100 divided by 20?

9 Which percussion instrument consists of a circular bronze disc, suspended in a frame, that produces resonant musical notes when struck with a padded mallet?

10 In football, who succeeded Don Revie as Leeds United's manager in 1974?

11 What was the first name of Rowan Atkinson's Scrooge-like character in the TV sitcom *Blackadder's Christmas Carol*?

12 In which country of the UK was the TV pioneer John Logie Baird born?

13 What is the theatrical dance which marks out rhythmic patterns with metal pieces on the shoes?

14 How many ruling monarchs of England have been called Elizabeth?

15 Which river estuary in northern England is formed where the rivers Ouse and Trent join?

16 In England, at which sport do the top teams compete in the Zurich Premiership?

17 In the human body, 'striated', 'smooth' and 'cardiac' are all types of what?

18 Which member of rock band Queen married former *EastEnders* star Anita Dobson in November 2000?

19 In children's literature, which of the Mr Men is coloured blue and wrapped in bandages?

20 What type of fish are used for kippers: herring or mackerel?

Previous Total

1,000

800

600

450

300

200

100

50

20

Banked

Total

Answers

1 Squash
2 Cheetah
3 United States
4 The Ark (accept Noah's Ark/the Ark of Noah)
5 Soviet Union (accept USSR/Union of Soviet Socialist Republics; do not accept Russia)
6 Greece
7 Horse (accept pony)
8 5
9 Gong (accept tam-tam)
10 Brian Clough
11 Ebenezer
12 Scotland
13 Tap dance (accept tap dancing)
14 Two
15 Humber
16 Rugby union (accept rugby; do not accept rugby league)
17 Muscle
18 Brian May
19 Mr Bump
20 Herring

Round 202

1 In nature, what *R* is the grain that forms the staple diet of half the world's population?

2 In football, with which London club did Bobby Moore begin his professional career?

3 In the animal kingdom, what is the woodlouse: an insect or a crustacean?

4 In the 1997 film, which actor starred as Austin Powers, 'International Man of Mystery'?

5 In science, the planets remain in orbit around our sun because of the force of what?

6 In the animal kingdom, the male peafowl is commonly known as the what?

7 In the British royal family, who is Prince Andrew's big brother?

8 In which decade did Martin Luther King deliver his 'I have a dream' speech at the Lincoln Memorial in Washington?

9 Of which wild animal is the male a jack, the female a doe, and the young a leveret?

10 In politics, for what does the initial *T* in NATO stand?

11 In language, complete the phrase 'hook, line and . . .' what?

12 If *A* is Alpha and *Z* is Zulu, what is *D*?

13 In football, which country hosted the 1998 World Cup finals?

14 In British politics, what is the normal maximum lifespan of a parliament?

15 In the United States, what is the capital of the state of Washington?

16 The French scientist Louis Pasteur gave his name to which sterilisation process?

17 In pop music, which British group released their second single 'The Way To Your Love' in 2001?

18 Omega is the last letter of which alphabet?

19 In medicine, what is a soporific drug designed to induce?

20 In geography, what *H* is the German city that has more bridges than Amsterdam and Venice combined?

Previous Total

1,000

800

600

450

300

200

100

50

20

Banked

Total

Answers

1 Rice
2 West Ham (West Ham United)
3 Crustacean
4 Mike Myers
5 Gravity (*accept* attraction)
6 Peacock
7 Prince Charles (*accept* Charles/The Prince of Wales/Earl of Chester/The Duke of Rothesay/Duke of Cornwall)
8 1960s
9 Hare
10 Treaty
11 Sinker
12 Delta
13 France
14 Five years
15 Olympia
16 Pasteurisation
17 Hear'Say
18 Greek
19 Sleep
20 Hamburg

Round 203

1 In sport, which Las Vegas-born tennis star won the 2001 Australian Open?

2 In politics, who became leader of the Revolutionary Command Council of Libya in 1970?

3 At room temperature, in what state does the metal mercury exist: liquid or solid?

4 In which country is the province of Newfoundland?

5 In the Beatrix Potter stories, Flopsy, Mopsy, Cotton-Tail and Peter are all what type of animal?

6 Which Irishman fronted the band The Boomtown Rats?

7 What was the title of the song released by Band Aid in 1984?

8 In geography, in which sea is the island of Menorca?

9 In language, what is the German for 'thank you'?

10 In the animal kingdom, 'mallard', 'eider' and 'canvasback' are all types of which bird?

11 Which TV pundit and former football manager is nicknamed 'Big Ron'?

12 In TV, which presenter of *Top Gear* went on to host his own chat show in 1998?

13 To which British political party does the MP Clare Short belong?

14 Complete the title of Gloria Gaynor's 1979 UK number-one hit single: 'I Will . . .' what?

15 Which word, meaning 'gigantic', is also the name of a prehistoric species similar to an elephant?

16 Complete the title of the musical *42nd* . . .?

17 In zoology, what name is given to a six-legged animal: hexapod or oxypod?

18 In tennis, what is the name of the act of hitting the ball into play at the start of a point?

19 In finance, the Dow Jones Industrial Average is an indicator of share values on which country's stock exchange?

20 'BCN' is the international code for which Spanish airport?

Answers

1 Andre Agassi
2 Colonel Gadaffi (*accept* Gadaffi/ Muammar Colonel Gadaffi/Muammar al-Qadhafi)
3 Liquid
4 Canada
5 Rabbit
6 Bob Geldof (*accept* Robert Frederick Xenon Geldof)
7 'Do They Know It's Christmas?'
8 Mediterranean (Sea)
9 *Danke* (*accept Danke schön/Vielen dank*)
10 Duck
11 Ron Atkinson
12 Jeremy Clarkson (Jeremy Charles Robert Clarkson)
13 Labour (*accept* New Labour)
14 Survive
15 Mammoth (*do not accept* mastodon)
16 *Street*
17 Hexapod
18 Service (*accept* serve)
19 United States
20 Barcelona

Round 204

1 What *S* is the outer garment worn by Hindu women?

2 In clothing, what *P* is a two-piece sleeping suit?

3 How many female Poet Laureates have been appointed in Britain: none, one or two?

4 Which English architect designed and rebuilt St Paul's Cathedral and the Royal Hospital, Chelsea?

5 Which French emperor was exiled to St Helena, where he died in 1821?

6 Which Irish city has a Gaelic name meaning the 'town of the ford of the hurdles'?

7 Which English admiral and lord died on board his ship, the *Victory*, during the Battle of Trafalgar?

8 Which British prime minister was born in 1953 and read law at Oxford?

9 What was the wartime codename given to the first day of the 1944 Normandy landings?

10 Which artist painted *The Hay Wain* in 1821: Joseph Turner or John Constable?

11 Which date is inserted into the calendar in a leap year?

12 In the New Testament, who drove the traders out of the temple in Jerusalem?

13 What was the surname of Harry, the world's most celebrated illusionist and escapologist?

14 In which decade did Sooty first appear on UK TV?

15 Which British twin brother gangsters were convicted of murder and imprisoned for life in 1969?

16 Who is Henry Fonda's actress daughter?

17 In rugby union, Martin Johnson was chosen as the captain of which team's tour of Australia in 2001?

18 Which sports commentator said 'They think it's all over, it is now' at the end of the 1966 World Cup final?

19 In 1876, Wyatt Earp became an assistant marshall in which lawless frontier town?

20 What would you call a native of Glasgow?

Previous Total

1,000

800

600

450

300

200

100

50

20

Banked

Total

Answers

1 Sari
2 Pyjamas
3 None
4 (Sir) Christopher Wren
5 Napoleon Bonaparte (accept Napoleon/ Napoleon I)
6 Dublin
7 Nelson (accept Horatio Nelson/ Viscount Nelson/ Baron Nelson)
8 Tony Blair (Anthony Charles Lynton Blair)
9 D-Day
10 John Constable

11 29th February (accept 29 February/last day of February)
12 Jesus (Jesus Christ)
13 Houdini (accept Weiss)
14 1950s
15 Ronnie and Reggie Kray (accept The Krays/Kray Twins)
16 Jane Fonda (Jane Seymour Fonda)
17 British Lions (The Lions)
18 Kenneth Wolstenholme (Wolstenholme)
19 Dodge City
20 Glaswegian

Round 205

1 Which Walt Disney animated film features the song 'The Bare Necessities'?

2 What *T* is the medical term for ringing or buzzing in the ears?

3 In George Orwell's novel *1984*, what name is given to the figurative head of the Party, who is never seen in person?

4 In TV, Portmerion was the location for which 1960s TV series starring Patrick McGoohan?

5 Blind Pew, Captain Flint and Billy Bones are all characters from which Robert Louis Stevenson novel?

6 In biology, the term 'survival of the fittest' is more correctly called 'natural . . .' what?

7 In pop music, which British duo had hits in the 1980s with 'Shout' and 'Everybody Wants To Rule The World'?

8 The year 2000 film *High Fidelity* was based on which British author's novel of the same name?

9 In literature, what was the nickname of the victimised bespectacled character in William Golding's novel *Lord of the Flies*?

10 In money, which old British coin was nicknamed a 'bob'?

11 In religion, on which day of the week is the Christian festival of Easter celebrated?

12 In geography, in which continent is the city of Pretoria?

13 In pop music, which member of T.Rex was born Mark Feld in 1947?

14 In medicine, what term describes an injury which is caused by the repeated movement of a particular part of the body?

15 What is the capital city of Sweden?

16 In geography, in which East Anglian county is Sutton Hoo, an early Anglo-Saxon burial site?

17 In military history, flamethrowers were first used in which war?

18 In Roman Catholicism, what name is given to a string of beads used while praying?

19 In geography, Hawaii is a Pacific state of which country?

20 Which famous British sprinter set UK and European records for the 100 metres in 1993?

Previous Total

1,000
800
600
450
300
200
100
50
20

Banked

Total

Answers

1 *The Jungle Book*	**13** Marc Bolan
2 Tinnitus	**14** Repetitive strain injury
3 Big Brother	(*accept* repetitive
4 *The Prisoner*	stress injury/RSI)
5 *Treasure Island*	**15** Stockholm
6 Selection	**16** Suffolk
7 Tears For Fears	**17** First World War
8 Nick Hornby	(*accept* World War I/
9 Piggy	Great War)
10 Shilling	**18** Rosary (beads)
11 Sunday	**19** United States
12 Africa	**20** Linford Christie

Round 206

1 In which Hans Christian Andersen fairy tale did a plain-looking bird turn into a beautiful swan?

2 In history, Viscount, later Earl, Mountbatten was the last British viceroy of which country?

3 In human biology, the five senses are touch, hearing, taste, smell and what?

4 In film, which American actor played an Irish gypsy boxer in Guy Ritchie's year 2000 crime comedy *Snatch*?

5 What is the name of the BBC's Birmingham studio?

6 In film, what A is the family name of the sibling actor and actresses David, Rosanna and Patricia?

7 In football, Ajax is a team in the domestic league of which European country?

8 In pop music, Kian, Mark, Nicky, Shane and Bryan are all members of which Irish boy band?

9 In geography, of which country is Kuala Lumpur the capital city?

10 In geography, the towns of Lourdes, Orléans and Limoges are in which country?

11 Which former Take That singer supports Port Vale football club?

12 Which English footballer scored two goals for Liverpool in the 2001 FA Cup final?

13 For which style of dancing was Rudolph Nureyev famous?

14 In rugby union, Scotland's first-choice shirts are predominantly what colour?

15 In the US, what do the fifty stars on the American flag represent?

16 In the Bible, who was the firstborn son of Adam and Eve?

17 In the human body, which nerves transmit impulses from the eye to the brain?

18 In horse racing, in 1956, Devon Loch fell on the run-in to which annual event?

19 In language, what is the seventh letter of the modern Roman alphabet?

20 In the TV soap *EastEnders*, Steve Owen married which character?

Previous Total

1,000

800

600

450

300

200

100

50

20

Banked

Total

Answers

1 *The Ugly Duckling*
2 India
3 Sight
4 Brad Pitt (William Bradley Pitt)
5 Pebble Mill
6 Arquette
7 Netherlands (accept Holland/Dutch)
8 Westlife
9 Malaysia
10 France
11 Robbie Williams (Robert Peter Maximillian Williams)
12 Michael Owen
13 Ballet
14 Blue (accept dark blue/navy; do not accept light blue)
15 The fifty states (accept states/states of the Union)
16 Cain
17 Optic nerves
18 Grand National
19 G
20 Melanie Healy (accept Mel/ Melanie Beale/Mel Beale)

Round 207

1 Which country did footballer Diego Maradona captain to victory in the 1986 World Cup finals?

2 In pop music, complete the title of the Rolling Stones' 1966 UK hit single 'Paint It . . .' what?

3 In the musical *The Sound of Music*, what was the name of the Austrian family who employed Maria as a governess?

4 Which actor played Dudley Moore's butler in the film *Arthur*?

5 In football, at which ground do Liverpool play their home matches?

6 In geography, the peninsula known as Lower California is part of which country?

7 With which character did Lenny Godber share a cell in the TV sitcom *Porridge*?

8 In geography, in which country of the UK is the town of Monmouth?

9 In film, which 1998 comedy starring Jim Carrey had the tagline 'The World is Watching'?

10 In maths, if three CDs cost £21, how much does each CD cost on average?

11 What is the name of Andrew Lloyd Webber's cello-playing brother?

12 Cheryl Baker and Mike Nolan were members of which British pop group?

13 In sport, which equestrian event involves a series of tests involving complicated moves and halts?

14 In geography, the Netherlands borders Belgium and which other country?

15 In pop music, what S is the name of Destiny's Child's April 2001 UK number-one single?

16 In snooker, what is the points value of the red ball?

17 The Booker Prize is awarded for excellence in which field: music or literature?

18 In UK geography, what M is the collective term for the central counties of England?

19 In fashion, for what do the initials NY stand when referring to Donna Karan's company DKNY?

20 In nature, what N is the substance bees collect from flowers in order to make honey?

Previous Total

1,000

800

600

450

300

200

100

50

20

Banked

Total

Answers	
1 Argentina	**11** Julian
2 Black	**12** Bucks Fizz
3 Von Trapp	**13** Dressage
4 Sir John Gielgud	**14** Germany
5 Anfield	**15** 'Survivor'
6 Mexico	**16** One
7 Norman Stanley Fletcher (*accept* Fletcher/Fletch)	**17** Literature
	18 Midlands
	19 New York
8 Wales	**20** Nectar (*do not accept* pollen)
9 *The Truman Show*	
10 £7	

Round 208

1 In finance, the amount of money you can earn each year before being liable for income tax is known as your 'personal . . .' what?

2 In radio, complete the title of the programme created by Roy Plomley in 1942: *Desert Island . . .* what?

3 In the story of Samson and Delilah, which part of Samson is associated with his extraordinary strength?

4 What term means the eating of human flesh by other human beings?

5 In music, in which decade did Rolf Harris release his version of 'Stairway to Heaven'?

6 From which country does Edam cheese originate?

7 Which British monarch died on the Isle of Wight in 1901?

8 Also called Holy Communion, what *E* is a word from Greek, literally meaning 'thanksgiving'?

9 Which American circus owner was famous for his show which was billed as the greatest on earth?

10 Which TV presenter had a 1966 UK hit single with the Burt Bacharach song 'Alfie'?

11 In geography, off the coast of which southern-hemisphere country would you find Kangaroo Island?

12 Of which US state is Juneau the capital?

13 In travel, from which port and resort in Suffolk are there ferry services to Rotterdam and Zeebrugge?

14 In history, Otto and Margot Frank were the parents of which diary author from the Second World War?

15 In travel, which type of British road is known as an *'Autobahn'* in Germany and an *'autostrada'* in Italy?

16 During which World War was the British liner *Lusitania* sunk by a German submarine?

17 In chemistry, which letter is the symbol for the element nitrogen?

18 The medical condition 'hirsutism' refers to an excess of what?

19 In politics, what B is another word for a vote?

20 Which sign of the Zodiac falls between 23 July and 22 August?

Previous Total

1,000
800
600
450
300
200
100
50
20

Banked

Total

Answers

1 Allowance
2 *Discs*
3 His hair
4 Cannibalism (*accept* anthropophagy)
5 1990s
6 The Netherlands (*accept* Holland)
7 Queen Victoria (*accept* Victoria)
8 Eucharist
9 P. T. Barnum (*accept* Barnum/Phineas Taylor Barnum)
10 Cilla Black (Priscilla White)
11 Australia
12 Alaska
13 Felixstowe
14 Anne Frank
15 Motorway
16 First World War (*accept* World War I)
17 N
18 Hair
19 Ballot (*accept* ballot paper)
20 Leo

Round 209

1 In UK politics, which former leader of the Liberal Democrats was dubbed 'Action Man' due to his experience as a commando?

2 In pop music, sharing its name with a type of theme park ride, what was the title of B*witched's 1998 UK number-one hit single?

3 In geography, which of these is one of the Seven Seas: the Bristol Channel or the South Pacific?

4 In football, Ian Wright has played in FA Cup finals for Crystal Palace and which north London club?

5 In nature, what is the mayfly: an insect or a bird?

6 In science, H_2O is the chemical formula for what?

7 In farming, what P is a long-handled fork with two curved prongs for tossing hay?

8 In literature, what was the first name of the Norwegian playwright Ibsen?

9 In human biology, what name is given to the hollow under the arm where it joins the body?

10 In religion, in which month of the Gregorian calendar is Christmas Day celebrated annually?

11 Which city is known to Germans as 'München'?

12 In which 1991 Disney cartoon film do the characters Belle and Beast appear?

13 In 1984, Dawn French married which comedian?

14 What is one quarter of 44?

15 In medicine, as what is 'myopia' more commonly known?

16 What *B* is the national park in South Dakota and a 1973 film starring Martin Sheen?

17 In history, which famous comet is said to have heralded the Norman invasion of Britain in the eleventh century?

18 The comic-strip character Odie the Dog was the sidekick of which lasagne-loving cat?

19 On a record player, a seven-inch record would normally be played at how many RPM?

20 Which northern European capital is famous for its Tivoli Gardens?

Previous Total

1,000
800
600
450
300
200
100
50
20

Banked

Total

Answers

1 (Sir) Paddy Ashdown (Jeffrey John Durham Ashdown)
2 'Rollercoaster'
3 South Pacific
4 Arsenal
5 Insect
6 Water
7 Pitchfork
8 Henrik
9 Armpit (accept axilla)
10 December
11 Munich
12 *Beauty and the Beast*
13 Lenny Henry (Lenworth George Henry)
14 Eleven
15 Short-sightedness (accept near-sightedness)
16 Badlands
17 Halley's Comet
18 Garfield
19 45
20 Copenhagen

Round 210

1 In fashion, what *D* is a pair of trousers with a bib attached?

2 In the animal kingdom, an eaglet is the young of which bird of prey?

3 In pop music, Mick Hucknall is the lead singer in which group?

4 Which actress plays the title character in the year 2000 film *Erin Brockovich*?

5 In nature, what name is given to plants that complete their life cycles in a single year?

6 In cricket, England bowler Darren Gough made his debut for which county in 1989?

7 The national anthem of which country is known as 'La Marseillaise'?

8 In geography, which Pole is in the Arctic Ocean: North or South?

9 What is the name for a type of leather which has a shiny varnished surface and is used to make shoes, handbags and belts?

10 What *M* is the first name of the son of spoof TV interviewer Mrs Merton?

11 In the human skeleton, how many ribs are usually present: 24 or 34?

12 In music, the term flautist refers to a player of which instrument?

13 The Solway Firth partly divides England from which other country?

14 In the British TV sitcom *Absolutely Fabulous*, what was the name of the character played by Jane Horrocks?

15 Which city hosted the 1996 Olympic Games?

16 Roddy Doyle wrote which 1987 novel about a struggling soul band from Dublin?

17 Which radio and TV personality married Billie Piper in May 2001?

18 Which British band had UK hit singles with 'The Love Cats' and 'Friday I'm In Love'?

19 Which breed of dog, usually having white hair and black spots, has been known as a 'coach dog' and a 'firehouse dog'?

20 In which city is the Australian National University based: Sydney, Perth or Canberra?

Previous Total

1,000

800

600

450

300

200

100

50

20

Banked

Total

Answers

1 Dungarees	**11** 24
2 Eagle	**12** Flute
3 Simply Red	**13** Scotland
4 Julia Roberts	**14** Bubble
5 Annuals	**15** Atlanta
6 Yorkshire	**16** *The Commitments*
7 France	**17** Chris Evans
8 North	**18** The Cure
9 Patent leather	**19** Dalmatian
10 Malcolm	**20** Canberra

Round 211

1 In horse racing, in which country is the Prix de l'Arc de Triomphe contested annually?

2 In legend, what was King Arthur's Excalibur: a brooch or a sword?

3 In which 1968 science-fiction film did Charlton Heston star as astronaut Colonel George Taylor?

4 In pop music, whose 1997 UK hit album was entitled *Urban Hymns*: Oasis or The Verve?

5 In pop music, 'Unchained Melody' was a 1965 UK hit single for The Righteous . . . what?

6 Which 1995 animated Disney film featured the characters Mr Potato Head, Woody and Slinky?

7 In sport, for which team is Formula One driver David Coulthard racing during the 2001 season: McLaren or Ferrari?

8 In geography, the Mull of Galloway is the most southerly point of which country of the UK?

9 In food, from which European country does fondue originate?

10 In travel, what C was the main airport for London from 1919 to 1939?

11 In football, Borussia Dortmund is a team in the domestic league of which European country?

12 Which of the following is longer in duration: three minutes or 120 seconds?

13 Which film festival is held annually in May on the French Riviera?

14 Which American Ivy League university is based in the city of New Haven?

15 In nature, what B is the name given to the external tissues of a tree?

16 Which type of elephant usually has smaller ears: Indian or African?

17 Members of which TV comedy team appeared in the film *The Life of Brian*?

18 Which position in British government did Sir Edward Heath hold between 1970 and 1974?

19 In the House of Commons, on which side of the Speaker does the Opposition sit: the left or right?

20 In March 2001, Jim Shekhdar arrived in Australia after becoming the first man to row across which ocean unassisted?

Previous Total

1,000
800
600
450
300
200
100
50
20

Banked

Total

Answers

1 France	**11** Germany
2 Sword	**12** Three minutes
3 *Planet Of The Apes*	**13** Cannes
4 The Verve	**14** Yale
5 Brothers	**15** Bark
6 *Toy Story*	**16** Indian
7 McLaren (Mercedes)	**17** *Monty Python*
8 Scotland	**18** Prime minister
9 Switzerland	**19** Left
10 Croydon	**20** Pacific

Round 212

1 In military history, what *M* is a deep, wide defensive ditch surrounding a castle?

2 In maths, what is nine times twenty?

3 In music, a bass is typically a singer of which sex?

4 In food production, the 'Wiltshire cure' is a method of producing which sort of foodstuff: bacon or eggs?

5 In which year 2000 film did Tom Hanks star as an employee of a courier company, stranded on a desert island?

6 An unseen observer can be called 'a fly on the . . .' what?

7 In sport, what is the name of the 3,000-metre athletics event in which competitors have to jump over water jumps and hurdles?

8 In political history, who was the longest-serving British prime minister of the twentieth century?

9 Which country of the UK is named *'Anglia'* in Latin?

10 In science, from which launch site did *Apollo 11*, the first manned rocket to the moon, take off in 1969?

11 In a theatre, what *F* is the area between the entrance and the auditorium?

12 Which TV soap features the Fowler and Beale families?

13 In which US state are Cleveland and Cincinnati?

14 In literature, Shakespeare wrote a play entitled *The Comedy of . . .* what?

15 In football, for which country did Dino Zoff play at international level?

16 In ice hockey, what name is given to the rubber disc used instead of a ball?

17 In which country was the singer Bryan Adams born?

18 In the animal kingdom, as what are lizards classified: reptiles, amphibians or mammals?

19 In which US city is the Liberty Bell?

20 Which team captain on the TV show *They Think It's All Over* captained England at cricket 32 times?

Previous Total

1,000
800
600
450
300
200
100
50
20

Banked

Total

Answers

1 Moat
2 180
3 Male (accept man)
4 Bacon
5 *Cast Away*
6 Wall
7 Steeplechase
8 Margaret Thatcher (Margaret Hilda Thatcher/Lady or Baroness Thatcher of Kesteven)
9 England
10 Cape Canaveral (accept Cape Kennedy)
11 Foyer
12 *EastEnders*
13 Ohio
14 *Errors*
15 Italy
16 Puck
17 Canada
18 Reptiles
19 Philadelphia
20 David Gower

Round 213

1 In 1981, which US president suffered an assassination attempt?

2 Does the group BBMak have three male members or three female?

3 What sort of animal was Dolly, the first mammal to be cloned from a single adult cell?

4 Which American actor starred in the films *Awakenings* and *The World According to Garp*?

5 Is the Merlot grape used to produce red or white wine?

6 In literature, Nick Stone is the hero of two novels by which former SAS soldier?

7 What is absent in a Manx cat that is present in other cats?

8 In film, which actor played Professor Henry Higgins in the 1964 musical *My Fair Lady*?

9 Which body of musicians is abbreviated to LSO?

10 In the 1971 film *Get Carter*, which actor starred as London gangster Jack Carter?

11 Which 1981 film, set in Scotland, starred Gordon Sinclair as a boy infatuated with a female footballer at school?

12 Which *Only Fools And Horses* actor became a father at the age of 61?

13 In which 1977 science-fiction film did actor Peter Mayhew play Chewbacca?

14 Complete the name of the pop group: S Club . . . what?

15 In football, what is the first name of Brian Clough's son, who was himself an England international?

16 In the Bible, the Promised Land was said to be flowing with milk and . . . what?

17 Shakespeare's Hamlet begins his famous speech 'To be, or not to be, that is the . . .' what?

18 What type of bridge consists of a roadway hanging from cables supported by towers?

19 What is the abbreviation for closed-circuit TV?

20 In TV, Peregrine the Penguin and Louise the Lamb were friends of which puppet mule?

Previous Total

1,000
800
600
450
300
200
100
50
20
Banked
Total

Answers

1 Ronald Reagan (Ronald Wilson Reagan)
2 Males
3 A sheep
4 Robin Williams (Robin McLaurim Williams)
5 Red
6 Andy McNab (Sergeant Andrew McNab)
7 Tail
8 (Sir) Rex Harrison (Reginald Carey Harrison)
9 London Symphony Orchestra
10 Michael Caine (Sir Maurice Joseph Micklewhite)
11 *Gregory's Girl*
12 David Jason
13 *Star Wars* (accept *Star Wars Episode IV: A New Hope*)
14 Seven
15 Nigel (Clough)
16 Honey
17 Question
18 Suspension bridge (*accept* cable-stayed bridge)
19 CCTV
20 Muffin (*accept* Muffin the Mule)

Round 214

1 In film, Bill Murray stars as a sarcastic weatherman in which 1993 comedy co-starring Andie MacDowell?

2 Which former British boxer has the famous catchphrase 'Know what I mean, 'Arry'?

3 In the card game pontoon, what is the lowest number of cards needed to score 21?

4 Complete the title of this 1984 film: *Indiana Jones and the Temple of . . .* what?

5 What is one-quarter of twenty million?

6 Which girl's name is also the name of a hairband?

7 Which US National Park extends across the states of Idaho, Wyoming and Montana?

8 What do Americans call nappies?

9 From which country do amaretti biscuits originally come?

10 In pop music, the band who had a 1963 UK hit single with 'You Were Made For Me' was Freddie and the . . . what?

11 Which famous American actor played Allie Fox in the 1986 film *The Mosquito Coast*?

12 In the 2001 Queen's birthday honours list, which former England football captain received an OBE?

13 In American politics, Rick Lazio opposed which famous woman in the contest to be senator of New York State in 2000?

14 In geography, in which continent is Lake Chad situated?

15 In croquet, what is the name of the wooden, hammer-shaped bat which is used to hit the ball?

16 In 1970, the New English Version of which book reached sales of one million copies a day?

17 In medicine, hepatitis is an inflammation of which organ of the body?

18 Complete the title of the 1999 Matt Damon film: *The Talented Mr . . .* who?

19 In TV, actress Gillian Taylforth played the character Kathy Beale in which long-running soap?

20 In sport, football clubs from which country won the European Cup every year between 1977 and 1982?

Previous Total
1,000
800
600
450
300
200
100
50
20
Banked
Total

Answers

1 *Groundhog Day*	**12** Alan Shearer
2 Frank Bruno	**13** Hillary Clinton
3 Two	**14** Africa
4 *Doom*	**15** Mallet
5 Five million	**16** The Bible
6 Alice	**17** Liver
7 Yellowstone	**18** Ripley
8 Diapers	**19** *EastEnders*
9 Italy	**20** England (accept UK/
10 Dreamers	Britain)
11 Harrison Ford	

Round 215

1 In 1972, President Nixon became the first US leader to make an official visit to which Communist country?

2 In which state of the US is Muscle Beach, which is noted for its bodybuilders: Florida or California?

3 In language, which two letters are used as an abbreviation to indicate the time before noon?

4 What K is Britain's most widespread bird of prey?

5 In UK geography, the town of St Helens is in which part of England: north-west or north-east?

6 Which monkey gives its name to a human blood group system?

7 Which late rock star has a restaurant dedicated to his memory in Memphis, where you can order 'King Wings' and 'Graceland Salad'?

8 In maths, what is one third of 660?

9 Complete Bruce Forsyth's catchphrase: 'Nice to see you, to see you . . .' what?

10 How many ancient wonders of the world were there?

11 What is the 'heavenly' nickname of Southampton football club?

12 Lake Superior is on the border of the USA and which other country?

13 The Roman Catholic belief that the Virgin Mary was conceived without 'original sin' is known as the 'Immaculate . . .' what?

14 Fred Astaire starred opposite which *Wizard of Oz* star in the 1948 musical *Easter Parade*?

15 Which US city has a basketball team called the Celtics?

16 In pop music, Connie . . . who had UK number-one hit singles in the 1950s with 'Who's Sorry Now?' and 'Stupid Cupid'?

17 Where on a jellyfish are the stinging cells?

18 Which TV cartoon sailor sought to avoid the clutches of the evil pirate Cut-throat Jake?

19 Which book, written in 1086, provided a record of the extent, ownership and value of land in England?

20 The names 'black' and 'ship' are types of which rodent?

Previous Total

1,000

800

600

450

300

200

100

50

20

Banked

Total

Answers

1 China (accept People's Republic of China)
2 California
3 a.m.
4 Kestrel (do not accept kite)
5 North-west
6 Rhesus
7 Elvis (Presley)
8 220
9 Nice
10 Seven
11 The Saints
12 Canada
13 Conception
14 Judy Garland (Frances Ethel Gumm)
15 Boston
16 (Connie) Francis
17 Tentacles
18 Captain Pugwash
19 Domesday Book
20 Rat

Round 216

1 In chemistry, the letter H is the symbol for which element in the periodic table?

2 Travelling by road, which is closer to Glasgow: Birmingham or Cardiff?

3 In the 2001 film *Tomb Raider*, which character was played by Angelina Jolie?

4 In politics, Henry Kissinger was the secretary of state for which country between 1973 and 1977?

5 At which annual fringe festival is the Perrier Comedy Award made?

6 In football, which country do Roberto Carlos and Ronaldo represent?

7 In which 1969 film did Robert Redford and Paul Newman star together as two outlaws?

8 What nationality is the contemporary novelist Martin Amis: English or American?

9 What is four plus three plus two plus one?

10 The first programme of which TV music show was presented by Jimmy Savile in January 1964?

11 In 2001, which famous US politician spoke at the Hay-on-Wye Festival of Literature?

12 In which month of 1789 was the Bastille prison in Paris stormed and captured?

13 Which Scottish mountain – the highest in the United Kingdom – reaches over 1,300 metres?

14 What is a condor: an eagle or vulture?

15 In modern history, which country's government was known as the Weimar Republic between 1919 and 1933?

16 In the USA, the dam located on the Nevada–Arizona state border is named after which president?

17 On which island of New Zealand is the city of Wellington: North Island or South Island?

18 In the 1970 film *MASH*, what was the nickname of Donald Sutherland's character?

19 In literature, what S uses humour or irony to ridicule human pretensions?

20 In maths, if a slug travels 36 inches in one day and a snail travels two feet in a day, which animal has travelled further?

Answers

1 Hydrogen
2 Birmingham
3 (Lady) Lara Croft
4 United States
5 Edinburgh
6 Brazil
7 *Butch Cassidy and the Sundance Kid*
8 English
9 Ten
10 *Top of the Pops*
11 Bill Clinton (*accept* Clinton/William Jefferson Clinton)
12 July
13 Ben Nevis
14 Vulture
15 Germany (*do not accept* West Germany/East Germany/GDR/ DDR)
16 Hoover (Herbert Hoover)
17 North
18 'Hawkeye'
19 Satire
20 Slug

Previous Total

1,000
800
600
450
300
200
100
50
20

Banked

Total

Round 217

1 In art, in which Scandinavian country was painter Edvard Munch born?

2 In astronomy, what is the name of Pluto's moon: Charon or Tracey?

3 In the European Union, many food additives are classified using a three-figure number preceded by which letter of the alphabet?

4 In 1960 Rolf Harris had a UK hit single with 'Tie Me Kangaroo Down, . . .' what?

5 In geography, in which sea is the island of St Lucia?

6 In nature, what N is soil that is neither acidic nor alkaline?

7 In biology, if a person is suffering from gingivitis, which part of his body is inflamed?

8 Which small rodent shares its name with a computer accessory?

9 In TV, which *All Creatures Great and Small* actor played The Doctor in *Doctor Who* between 1982 and 1984?

10 What B was the name of the earliest lunatic asylum in Europe and is also a slang word meaning chaos?

11 The Royal Pavilion at Brighton was designed by John . . . who?

12 In maths, what is two cubed?

13 Which of these British mammals hibernates: the dormouse or the fox?

14 Which Swedish Band had a 1979 UK hit single with 'Gimme, Gimme, Gimme A Man After Midnight'?

15 Which comedian's catchphrase was 'Shut that door'?

16 In which northern English city is the National Railway Museum?

17 In Six Nations rugby, which country plays its home matches at the Millennium Stadium?

18 Mrs Boyle and Major Metcalf are characters in which long-running theatrical whodunnit?

19 What S is another name for the American plane tree?

20 In which religion are followers called to prayer by a muezzin in a minaret tower?

Previous Total

1,000
800
600
450
300
200
100
50
20

Banked

Total

Answers

1 Norway
2 Charon
3 E
4 Sport
5 Caribbean
6 Neutral
7 Gums (*accept mouth; do not accept teeth*)
8 Mouse
9 Peter Davison (real name Peter Moffatt)
10 Bedlam
11 (John) Nash
12 Eight
13 Dormouse
14 Abba
15 Larry Grayson (William White)
16 York
17 Wales
18 *The Mousetrap*
19 Sycamore
20 Islam (*accept Muslim*)

Round 218

1 Which American actor links the films *Benny and Joon*, *Chocolat* and *Blow*?

2 In medicine, if you are anaemic, what is the main mineral in which you are deficient?

3 In TV, which quiz show host had the catchphrase 'I've started, so I'll finish'?

4 In dentistry, what *B* is a wire device fitted in the mouth to straighten teeth?

5 In geography, Rossendale is a district within which county?

6 In music, which instrument is associated with the Australian musician John Williams?

7 Which novel by D. H. Lawrence depicts the love affair between the characters Paul Morel and Clara Dawes?

8 What *B* describes any drink other than water?

9 In the nursery rhyme, who couldn't be put back together by 'All the king's horses and all the king's men'?

10 In modern history, Bertrand . . . who was awarded the Order of Merit in 1949, the Nobel Prize for Literature in 1950 and helped found CND in 1958?

11 In pop music, complete the title of the year 2000 single by the group Toploader: 'Dancing in the . . .' what?

12 Of which country was Benazir Bhutto prime minister from 1993 to 1996?

13 What *D* is an animal that traditionally provided rides for children on the beach?

14 In rugby union, how many international teams take part in the annual southern hemisphere Tri-Nations tournament?

15 In which east Asian country is the city of Shanghai?

16 In the 2001 film *Pearl Harbor*, which British actress plays Lieutenant Evelyn Stewart?

17 From which island do you come if you are a Manxman?

18 What *M* is the cereal used to make popcorn?

19 What is the name of the universal system of writing for the blind?

20 In snooker, what is the name of the long sticks which are used to hit the white ball?

Previous Total

1,000
800
600
450
300
200
100
50
20

Banked

Total

Answers

1 Johnny Depp (John Christopher Depp III)
2 Iron
3 Magnus Magnusson (Magnus Sigursteinnson)
4 Brace
5 Lancashire
6 Classical guitar (*accept* guitar, Spanish/nylon-stringed/acoustic guitar)
7 *Sons and Lovers*
8 Beverage
9 Humpty Dumpty
10 Russell (Bertrand Russell)
11 Moonlight
12 Pakistan
13 Donkey
14 Three
15 China
16 Kate Beckinsale
17 Isle of Man
18 Maize
19 Braille
20 Cues

Round 219

1 In theatre, John Osborne's *Look Back In Anger* is the first famous example of drama known as 'kitchen . . .' what?

2 In pop music, Hannah, Bradley and Rachel are members of which pop group?

3 In the human body, in which organ are the 'malleus', 'incus' and 'stapes' bones located?

4 What name is given to the powdery substance, consisting of microscopic grains of male germ-cells, produced in the stamens of flowers?

5 What J was a professional clown employed by a king or a nobleman?

6 What is the name of the delicately woven cotton fabric that was often used to cover butter?

7 Which comedian, born in Brighton in 1894, was known as 'The Cheeky Chappie'?

8 Oscar Wilde's novel is entitled *The Picture of* . . . whom?

9 In which century was the pencil invented: the sixteenth, seventeenth or eighteenth?

10 Which viral disease nearly wiped out Britain's wild rabbit population in the 1950s?

11 In 2001, Silvio Berlusconi became prime minister of where?

12 In pop music, Lionel Richie was the lead singer of which group before going solo?

13 Eric Bartholomew and Ernest Wiseman made up which comedy double act?

14 In cookery, what is the main fruit ingredient of banoffee pie?

15 What is the title of the 1989 film in which Jeff and Beau Bridges play musicians who employ Michelle Pfeiffer as a singer?

16 Which north African country fought a war of independence from France and finally achieved it in July 1962?

17 What is the name for the sign language that bookmakers use to communicate with each other at racecourses?

18 The Strait of Gibraltar separates Europe from which other continent?

19 What type of insect does an apiarist keep?

20 Is a composition for a piano accompanied by an orchestra known as a piano concerto or sonata?

Previous Total

1,000

800

600

450

300

200

100

50

20

Banked

Total

Answers

1 Sink	**12** The Commodores
2 S Club Seven	**13** Morecambe and Wise
3 Ear(s)	
4 Pollen	**14** Banana
5 Jester (accept joker)	**15** *The Fabulous Baker Boys*
6 Muslin	
7 Max Miller (Thomas Henry Sargent)	**16** Algeria
	17 Tic-tac
8 *Dorian Gray*	**18** Africa
9 Sixteenth	**19** Bees (accept honey bees/*Apis mellifera*)
10 Myxomatosis	
11 Italy	**20** Concerto

Round 220

1 Which religious denomination did Queen Elizabeth I of England support: Roman Catholicism or Protestantism?

2 Which poet, born in India in 1865, wrote the poem entitled 'If'?

3 By what nickname was the decade of the 1920s known in the United States: the Roaring Twenties or the Raving Twenties?

4 How many events are there in the modern pentathlon?

5 What A is the world's smallest ocean?

6 In pop music, complete the title of Bobby McFerrin's 1988 UK hit single 'Don't Worry, Be . . .' what?

7 Englishman Arthur Wynne is credited with devising the first of which type of word puzzle in 1913?

8 What is the name of the brief shorts worn by women in a fashion of the early 1970s?

9 In the Hanna-Barbera TV cartoon, the mice who starred alongside Mr Jinks were Pixie and who?

10 Lack of which vitamin causes scurvy?

11 In human anatomy, what T is a fleshy, muscular organ in the mouth?

12 In the USA, Big Cypress Swamp is in which south-eastern state?

13 In pop music, who had a 1973 UK hit single with 'The Laughing Gnome'?

14 In cookery, which part of the liquorice plant is usually used in food preparation: the leaves or the root?

15 In which sport did TV presenter Suzanne Dando compete in the 1980 Olympics?

16 Which American city is located at the mouth of the Hudson river?

17 Which type of grim humour is named after an instrument of execution?

18 On the long-running TV sitcom *Steptoe and Son*, what type of pickled food did Albert Steptoe famously eat in his bath tub?

19 In the animal kingdom, warthogs are originally from which continent?

20 In geography, which line of latitude crosses India: the Tropic of Cancer or Tropic of Capricorn?

Previous Total

1,000
800
600
450
300
200
100
50
20

Banked

Total

Answers

1 Protestantism
2 Rudyard Kipling
3 Roaring Twenties
4 Five
5 Arctic
6 Happy
7 Crossword
8 Hotpants
9 Dixie
10 Vitamin C
11 Tongue
12 Florida

13 David Bowie (David Robert Hayward Jones)
14 Root
15 Gymnastics
16 New York
17 Gallows (*accept* gallows humour)
18 Onions (pickled onions)
19 Africa
20 Tropic of Cancer

Round 221

1 Complete the title of this Chuck Berry song: 'Roll Over, . . .' who?

2 Which *Gone With the Wind* star was called the 'king of Hollywood' during the 1930s?

3 In human biology, what *J* is the point at which two bones meet?

4 What *C* is a kind of chewy sweet, usually in small blocks made from sugar, butter and milk?

5 Which women's group, who used hunger strikes as a form of protest, was affected by the notorious 'Cat and Mouse Act' of 1913?

6 In which English city would you find Lord's cricket ground?

7 What is the official language of Costa Rica?

8 Which *L* is a case worn on a neck chain that often contains a picture of a loved one?

9 In religion, what are the two opposite energies in Chinese thought called?

10 In competitive judo, the main object is to score an 'ippon'. How many points is this worth: ten, twenty or thirty?

11 In the animal kingdom, are hyenas carnivores or herbivores?

12 In which 1983 film did Burt Lancaster star as Happer, a Texan oil tycoon visiting Scotland?

13 What was the first name of the artist Van Gogh?

14 In which US city is the Golden Gate University?

15 In which of Herman Melville's books does Captain Ahab appear?

16 In theatre, when an actor moves towards the front of the stage, is this known as moving downstage or upstage?

17 What piece of hand-held home hairdressing equipment first went on sale to the general public in 1920 in the USA?

18 In maths, what is £9.50 minus £5.30?

19 In film, Glenn Close and Michael Douglas starred together in which 1987 thriller?

20 What *V* is a sweet or dry white wine flavoured with bitter herbs and alcohol?

Previous Total

1,000

800

600

450

300

200

100

50

20

Banked

Total

Answers

1 Beethoven	**12** *Local Hero*
2 Clark Gable	**13** Vincent
3 Joint	**14** San Francisco
4 Caramel	**15** *Moby Dick*
5 Suffragettes	**16** Downstage
6 London	**17** Hairdryer
7 Spanish	**18** £4.20 (accept 420
8 Locket	pence)
9 Yin and Yang	**19** *Fatal Attraction*
10 Ten	**20** Vermouth
11 Carnivores	

Round 222

1 On which side of the road do cars drive in Japan?

2 In education, what is the name of the exam children usually have to pass to go to grammar school?

3 According to the proverb, you can't teach an old . . . [what] new tricks?

4 Which TV magician's well-known catchphrase is: 'You're going to like this – not a lot!'?

5 Which *T* is an ornamental woven textile used for wall hangings, furniture and curtains?

6 Which comedienne and *New Faces* winner had her own sketch show called *As Seen On TV*, which featured Julie Walters?

7 In science, is the speed of sound faster or slower in water than in air?

8 Which real-life blues singer did Diana Ross portray in the 1972 film *Lady Sings the Blues*?

9 Timmy was the dog's name in which Enid Blyton books?

10 In the UK, for what did the initials of the government employment program YTS stand?

11 In sport, who, in 1990, at the age of fourteen, became the youngest-ever seed at Wimbledon?

12 In biology, does a vein carry blood to the heart, or away from the heart?

13 In stringed instruments, what *B* is the name given to the piece of wood that supports the strings?

14 In TV, complete the title of this drama starring Alec Guinness: *Tinker Tailor Soldier . . .* what?

15 Is Kingsford-Smith Airport in Sydney or Cape Town?

16 In food, what name is given to the edible seeds of the pine tree?

17 Complete the title of the Jackie Collins novel: *The World Is Full of Married . . .* what?

18 If the temperature in Prague dropped overnight from 14 degrees Celsius to minus 6 degrees Celsius, what would the difference in temperature be in degrees Celsius?

19 How many southern US states made up the Confederacy: nine, eleven or 22?

20 In computing, what name is given to a portable microcomputer with a compact keyboard?

Previous Total

1,000
800
600
450
300
200
100
50
20
Banked
Total

Answers

1 Left	**12** To the heart
2 Eleven-plus	**13** Bridge
3 Dog	**14** *Spy*
4 Paul Daniels	**15** Sydney
5 Tapestry	**16** Pine nuts (accept pine kernels/pignoli/pinoli)
6 Victoria Wood	
7 Faster	**17** *Men*
8 Billie Holiday	**18** 20 degrees Celsius
9 Famous Five books	**19** Eleven
10 Youth Training Scheme	**20** Laptop
11 Jennifer Capriati	

Round 223

1 Which Beatles film did Richard Lester direct in 1964?

2 Juan Carlos has been king of which country since 1975?

3 What type of animal is an egret?

4 In the animal kingdom, what *T* is a slow-moving land reptile which is enclosed in a shell?

5 In literature, was the poet Philip Larkin English or Irish?

6 In TV, who starred alongside Dudley Moore in the 1960s comedy series *Not Only. . . But Also*?

7 In geography, which is the more easterly of these Canary Islands: Gran Canaria or Lanzarote?

8 In astronomy, the constellation The Plough is also known as The Great . . . what?

9 In medicine, what *L* is the name given to a medicated tablet designed to ease pain in the mouth and throat?

10 In science, rust forms when iron corrodes in the presence of water and which gas?

11 What type of Australian animal was reportedly seen on four different occasions at a golf course in London in October 2000?

12 In geography, there are two cathedral cities in Kent. One is Canterbury. What is the other?

13 Is the London Heliport in Battersea or Barking?

14 In politics, for what do the letters MP stand?

15 Leofric was the husband of which lady who, according to tradition, rode naked through Coventry?

16 The letters LV in gold make up the logo of which fashion company?

17 In maths, how many furlongs are there in a mile?

18 Which art movement came first: Expressionism or Impressionism?

19 In the animal kingdom, which *I* are the teeth that rodents use to gnaw their food?

20 In football, which team won the League and Cup double in 1986: Manchester United or Liverpool?

Previous Total

1,000

800

600

450

300

200

100

50

20

Banked

Total

Answers

1 *A Hard Day's Night*
2 Spain
3 Bird
4 Tortoise (*do not accept turtle: aquatic, not land*)
5 English
6 Peter Cook
7 Lanzarote
8 Bear (The Great Bear)
9 Lozenge
10 Oxygen (*do not accept air*)
11 Kangaroo
12 Rochester
13 Battersea
14 Member of Parliament
15 Lady Godiva
16 Louis Vuitton
17 Eight
18 Impressionism
19 Incisors
20 Liverpool

Round 224

1 In Robert Louis Stevenson's novel *Treasure Island*, what did Long John Silver's parrot keep calling out?

2 The London Stock Exchange has been largely computerised since the 'Big Bang' in which decade?

3 In the pantomime *Ali Baba and the Forty Thieves*, what is the password to open the cave?

4 Which M is produced from the oil of Japanese mint and used to treat nasal catarrh?

5 Which N was a first-century Roman emperor notorious for his crimes and cruelty to Christians?

6 In human biology, is the trachea in the throat or the leg?

7 What C is an abstract art movement dating from the early twentieth century?

8 Which TV comedy character's servant was called Baldrick?

9 Amnesia is a medical term for loss of what?

10 In biology, what G are the so-called 'units of inheritance' in cells?

11 Which political satire magazine is edited by Ian Hislop, who also appears on the TV programme *Have I Got News For You*?

12 In music, which 'Wild West' outlaw is the subject of a ballet by American composer Aaron Copland?

13 Until 1974, administratively, the Isle of Wight was part of which county?

14 Complete this lyric by John Lennon: 'All we are saying, is give . . . [what] a chance'?

15 The lead singer of Scottish band Travis is known by what name: Francis or Neil?

16 With which actor did Katharine Hepburn make ten films and have a secret affair?

17 In which year did the French war minister order the building of a line of concrete forts to protect France against Germany: 1929 or 1939?

18 What European capital city is the name of the novel by Ian McEwan which won the Booker Prize in 1998?

19 The name of which popular cage bird comes from an Australian aboriginal word for 'good cockatoo'?

20 Was Richard Adams's *Watership Down* first published in the 1870s or the 1970s?

Previous Total

1,000

800

600

450

300

200

100

50

20

Banked

Total

Answers

1 'Pieces of eight'	**12** Billy the Kid
2 1980s (1986)	**13** Hampshire
3 'Open Sesame'	**14** Peace
4 Menthol	**15** Francis (Healey)
5 Nero	**16** Spencer Tracy
6 Throat	**17** 1929
7 Cubism	**18** Amsterdam
8 Blackadder	**19** Budgerigar (accept
9 Memory	budgie)
10 Genes	**20** 1970s
11 *Private Eye*	

Round 225

1 In the old Soviet Union, what initials were used for the state security agency formed in 1953?

2 In which year did the Deux Chevaux car first go on sale in France: 1935 or 1949?

3 The name of which South American city means 'river of January'?

4 In what sport would you perform a 'snatch' and a 'jerk'?

5 In medicine, what *H* is the name given to the condition in which the core temperature of the body drops?

6 In film, actor Peter O'Toole has played which British monarch twice: Henry II or Henry VIII?

7 In terms of passengers, which is Britain's busiest airport outside London?

8 In art, was the *Mona Lisa* or the *Venus de Milo* part of François I's original Louvre collection?

9 In literature, which *H* is a figure of speech that contains exaggeration for emphasis?

10 What was the name of the TV charades show which starred Lionel Blair, Una Stubbs and Liza Goddard during the 1980s?

11 Which flightless bird lives in a rookery?

12 Ford's Theatre, where Abraham Lincoln was assassinated, is situated in which US city: Washington, DC or Philadelphia?

13 In sport, which British long-distance race was first run in 1981, resulting in a tie between Dick Beardsley and Inge Simonsen?

14 Which actress separated from her husband Kenneth Branagh in 1995?

15 What *B* were the Russian revolutionaries who took their name from the Russian word for majority?

16 In the Victor Hugo novel, what was the nickname of Quasimodo?

17 In the USA, were electric ovens first marketed by the Carpenter Company in 1890 or 1810?

18 Knock and Bantry Bay are in which country?

19 According to the Bible, who spent three days and nights in the belly of a great fish?

20 When was the so-called 'Window Tax' abolished in Britain: 1845, 1851 or 1900?

Previous Total

1,000

800

600

450

300

200

100

50

20

Banked

Total

Answers

1 KGB	**12** Washington, DC
2 1949	**13** London Marathon
3 Rio de Janeiro	**14** Emma Thompson
4 Weightlifting	**15** Bolsheviks
5 Hypothermia	**16** 'The Hunchback of
6 Henry II	Notre Dame'
7 Manchester	**17** 1890
8 *Mona Lisa*	**18** Ireland (accept Eire/
9 Hyperbole	Republic of Ireland)
10 *Give Us a Clue*	**19** Jonah
11 Penguin	**20** 1851

Round 226

1 What A is a severe pain in the chest caused by narrowing coronary arteries?

2 In mythology, the Egyptian god Ra is shown with the head of which bird of prey?

3 In an alphabetical listing, which Commonwealth country would appear at the end of the list?

4 Which flat fish, popular as food, is instantly recognisable in the sea by the red or orange spots on its back?

5 How did John Evelyn and Samuel Pepys document their experiences in the late seventeenth century?

6 What letters do vehicles from Canada display to identify their nationality?

7 For which political party was Michael Meacher elected MP for Oldham West and Royton in 1997?

8 In football, in what year was the African Nations Cup first played: 1957 or 1977?

9 What S is an organ which acts as a reservoir for red blood cells and helps fight infection?

10 Where did the popular exercise regime t'ai chi originate?

11 In chemistry, what is the most malleable metal?

12 In religion, what is the popular name for the modern Hindu sect the International Society for Krishna Consciousness?

13 Which card game is known in America as blackjack?

14 Which country surrounds San Marino?

15 In football, both Bobby Robson and Alf Ramsey managed which club before managing England?

16 Is Okta a measurement of cloud cover or relative humidity?

17 In literature, which author wrote *The Island of Doctor Moreau*, published in 1896?

18 The jay is a colourful member of which bird family, most of whose members are black?

19 Who, in 1997, became the first Labour Chancellor of the Exchequer since Dennis Healey?

20 In TV, what improvisation show, hosted by Clive Anderson, was first shown in 1988?

Previous Total

1,000

800

600

450

300

200

100

50

20

Banked

Total

Answers

1 Angina (accept angina pectoris)
2 Falcon
3 Zimbabwe
4 Plaice
5 Diaries
6 CDN
7 Labour
8 1957
9 Spleen
10 China
11 Gold
12 Hare Krishna

13 Pontoon (accept twenty-one/vingt-et-un/Van John)
14 Italy
15 Ipswich Town
16 Cloud cover
17 H. G. Wells (Herbert George Wells)
18 Crow (accept Corvidae)
19 Gordon Brown
20 *Whose Line Is It Anyway?*

Round 227

1 In the animal kingdom, what type of creature is a krait?

2 The Ruhr Valley is a major industrial area of which country?

3 In film, Quint and Matt Hooper are characters in which Steven Spielberg blockbuster?

4 In classical music, in which English city is the Halle Orchestra based?

5 In literature, what nationality was the author Marcel Proust?

6 For which political party was Stephen Dorrell elected MP for Charnwood in 1997?

7 What K are tiny crustaceans that are the principal food of baleen whales?

8 In money, £1 sterling was valued at twenty of what pre-decimal coin?

9 In TV, which famous British actress played a siren called Lorelei in the 1960s *Batman* series?

10 In music, which Philadelphia-based trio had a UK hit with the song 'When Will I See You Again' in 1974?

11 In science, photosynthesis removes which gas from the atmosphere?

12 Which 1992 Disney animated film featured the voice of Robin Williams?

13 In anatomy, in which part of the body are the frontal bones?

14 In TV, what Phil Redmond soap is set in a region of Chester?

15 Which fruit is used to make the German pastry *Apfelstrudel*?

16 In music, from which country is the Aviv String Quartet?

17 If a pupil practises the piano for 20 minutes six days a week, how many hours does she practise each week?

18 In the human body, where would you find sebaceous glands?

19 Which author of the book *Congo* also wrote the thriller *Timeline*?

20 A hoastman was a coal merchant that shipped coal from which north-eastern city?

Previous Total

1,000

800

600

450

300

200

100

50

20

Banked

Total

Answers

1 Snake	**12** *Aladdin*
2 Germany	**13** Skull (accept
3 *Jaws*	face/head/
4 Manchester	forehead)
5 French	**14** *Hollyoaks*
6 Conservatives (accept	**15** Apple
Tories)	**16** Israel
7 Krill	**17** Two (hours)
8 Shillings	**18** The skin
9 Joan Collins	**19** Michael Crichton
10 Three Degrees	**20** Newcastle (upon
11 Carbon dioxide	Tyne)

Round 228

1 In which country was England cricketer Andy Caddick born?

2 On what TV comedy did Michael Elphick play an ex-fireman with a courier business called the Texas Rangers?

3 The town of Gettysburg, where Lincoln delivered his famous speech in 1863, is in which US state?

4 In winter sports, in which country is the Cresta Run?

5 In international travel, what three-letter code represents Gatwick Airport?

6 In the animal kingdom, what type of creature is a 'klipspringer'?

7 In which country is the Trans-Siberian Railway?

8 In pop music, Johnny Hallyday was a 1960s rock 'n' roll legend from which European country?

9 In which century did the Industrial Revolution begin in Britain?

10 In mythology, which twins raised by a she-wolf founded the city of Rome?

11 What name is given to a beaver's home?

12 Actor Roddy McDowall played the character Cornelius in which 1968 science-fiction film?

13 Who invented the first air-inflated rubber bicycle tyre in 1887?

14 Which sporting event was the first to be broadcast on British TV in 1931?

15 In the human body, what name is given to the hinge joint between the lower thigh and the lower leg?

16 What was the surname of David and Elizabeth, who designed Princess Diana's wedding dress?

17 The fiftieth anniversary of what historic event was celebrated in Hyde Park in May 1995?

18 Which period of prehistory is distinguished technologically by the use of iron?

19 What *T* is the famous river that runs through London?

20 With which sport would you associate Graeme Hick?

Previous Total

1,000

800

600

450

300

200

100

50

20

Banked

Total

Answers

1 New Zealand
2 *Boon*
3 Pennsylvania
4 Switzerland
5 LGW
6 Antelope (African)
7 Russia (*accept* Russian Federation)
8 France
9 Eighteenth
10 Romulus and Remus
11 A lodge
12 *Planet of the Apes*
13 John Dunlop

14 The Derby
15 Knee
16 Emanuel
17 VE Day (end of the Second World War in Europe/end of war with Germany; do *not* accept the end of the Second World War: that was VJ Day)
18 Iron Age
19 Thames
20 Cricket

Round 229

1 What S is the oily substance secreted by the sebaceous glands that lubricates the hair and skin?

2 In fashion, how is 'baleen', once used to stiffen ladies' corsets, more usually known?

3 In history, which Paris fortress and prison was stormed in the opening days of the French Revolution?

4 Which American rock guitarist developed his reputation with his own band Jimmy James and The Blue Flames?

5 Gabriel Daniel Fahrenheit invented a mercury-filled version of what in 1714?

6 In football, Parma is a team in the domestic league of which European country?

7 What was the family name of Louis XIV of France: Bourbon or Medici?

8 What M is both a model of car made by the former company Morris and the name given to a child under the age of eighteen?

9 In the UK, does the M62 motorway cross the Pennines or the Cotswolds?

10 In Celtic Arthurian legend, what A is known as 'the land of the apples'?

11 A 'patriarchy' is the name given to a society in which women are dominated by whom?

12 In classical music, what is the lowest sounding string on a violin: the C-string or the G-string?

13 Hydrated iron oxide is an orange-brown deposit found on iron and steel. What is it more commonly known as?

14 In food, what F is a long, slender smoked sausage with a very soft, fine texture?

15 In the 1935 Alfred Hitchcock film how many steps were in the title: twelve, twenty-eight or thirty-nine?

16 In US currency, how many cents are there in a nickel?

17 In what year did James Watson and Francis Crick work out the structure of DNA: 1953 or 1973?

18 What I is an injection that causes immunity by inducing a mild form of a disease?

19 An asp is a type of venomous what?

20 Which classic children's stories are set in the Ashdown Forest?

Previous Total

1,000
800
600
450
300
200
100
50
20

Banked

Total

Answers

1 Sebum	**11** Men
2 Whalebone	**12** G-string
3 The Bastille	**13** Rust
4 Jimi Hendrix (Johnny Allen Hendrix)	**14** Frankfurter
5 Thermometer	**15** Thirty-nine
6 Italy	**16** Five
7 Bourbon	**17** 1953
8 Minor	**18** Inoculation
9 Pennines	**19** Snake
10 Avalon	**20** Winnie-the-Pooh

Round 230

1 What *V* is the name often given to a country house in Italy or the south of France?

2 Which of these cities is furthest from London by plane: Manila or Kingston, Jamaica?

3 The duet 'I Know Him So Well' was a UK number-one hit for Barbara Dickson and which other singer?

4 What is the system of sending or receiving text between computers attached to the Internet known as?

5 Which star of silent film comedies was known as 'The Great Stone Face'?

6 In which year did gramophone records made of shellac first go on sale in Europe: 1901 or 1912?

7 In education, whose interests does the NUS represent?

8 In sport, how many balls are used in a game of billiards?

9 What is the name of the three-sided metal instrument that is struck with a metal stick to give a tinkling sound?

10 According to the proverb, there's no . . . what like the present?

11 In the USA, does Logan International Airport serve Baltimore or Boston?

12 What was the name of the string-vested Glaswegian character played by comedian Gregor Fisher?

13 How many countries joined the European Monetary Union when it was first launched in 1999: nine, ten or eleven?

14 In literature, which John was Poet Laureate before Ted Hughes?

15 Was the designer Yves Saint Laurent born in Algeria or South Africa?

16 If a recipe for ice-cream states that one quarter of the ingredients should be milk, what is this in decimal form?

17 'Old Noll' and 'Copper Nose' were among the nicknames of which Lord Protector?

18 Which C is a bird that has the same name as the sound of its two-note call – and is known for laying its eggs in other birds' nests?

19 What name is used for the imaginary line around the Earth which divides it into the northern and southern hemispheres?

20 What A is a fossilised tree resin used to make jewellery?

Previous Total

1,000

800

600

450

300

200

100

50

20

Banked

Total

Answers

1 Villa	**11** Boston
2 Manila	**12** Rab C. Nesbitt
3 Elaine Page	**13** Eleven
4 Email (accept electronic mail)	**14** John Betjeman
5 Buster Keaton	**15** Algeria
6 1901	**16** 0.25
7 Students	**17** Oliver Cromwell (accept Cromwell)
8 Three	**18** Cuckoo
9 Triangle	**19** Equator
10 Time	**20** Amber

Round 231

1 Does Queen Elizabeth II hold a driving licence?

2 American Bobby Fischer defeated Boris Spassky to become which game's world champion in 1972?

3 For which religion is the Koran the scripture?

4 The present London Bridge was completed in which century: nineteenth or twentieth?

5 In literature, was *Our Mutual Friend* the first or the last novel that Charles Dickens completed?

6 In art, was Anthony van Dyke court painter to Charles I or George IV?

7 What word can describe both the basket of a hot-air balloon and a boat associated with Venice?

8 Which Hollywood actor starred in both *The Perfect Storm* and *O Brother, Where Art Thou?* in 2000?

9 In November 2000, Robert Downey Jr made his first TV appearance following his release from prison on which hit American comedy drama about lawyers?

10 In food, which of the following is a root vegetable: parsnip or kale?

11 According to the lyric of a Beatles song, what was the occupation of 'Lovely Rita'?

12 Agoraphobia is a fear of what?

13 In medicine, which S is a drug used to calm and relieve anxiety and tension?

14 In TV, name the drama series centring on the firefighters of Blue Watch, based at Blackwall Station.

15 In education, what do the letters GCSE stand for?

16 Before the First World War, which country was the main car producer in Europe: Britain or France?

17 In the Bible, who were Adam and Eve's first two sons?

18 What was the nationality of the novelist Virginia Woolf: American or English?

19 In maths, how many square inches are there in a square foot?

20 In which English city would you find the 'Bull Ring' market?

Previous Total

1,000

800

600

450

300

200

100

50

20

Banked

Total

Answers

1 Yes	**12** Open spaces
2 Chess	**13** Sedative
3 Islam (accept Muslim)	**14** *London's Burning*
4 Twentieth (1973)	**15** General Certificate of
5 Last	Secondary Education
6 Charles I	**16** France
7 Gondola	**17** Cain and Abel
8 George Clooney	**18** English
9 *Ally McBeal*	**19** 144 square inches
10 Parsnip	**20** Birmingham
11 Metre maid	

Round 232

1 In the animal kingdom, do naked mole rats have hair?

2 In football, which Scottish team won nine League Championships in a row between 1989 and 1997?

3 Who launched the first disposable razor blade in 1901: King Camp Gillette or Frederic Remington?

4 In poetry, what does Keats describe as the 'season of mists and mellow fruitfulness'?

5 In America, what type of sport is played at the Wrigley Field in Chicago and the Camden Yards in Baltimore?

6 Which S is the Greek dramatist who wrote the famous play *Oedipus Rex*?

7 What is the more common name for a fish's caudal fin?

8 In architecture, is the chevron decoration characteristic of Norman or Renaissance architecture?

9 What was the name of the scarecrow character played by Jon Pertwee in the TV series of the same name?

10 By what name is the central solid layer of the Earth, beneath the crust and mantle, known?

11 Did Benjamin Britten compose the opera *Owen Wingrave* for radio or TV?

12 Which island in the United Kingdom is divided into two districts, Medina and South Wight?

13 With which style of music would you associate Garth Brooks: country and western or hip-hop?

14 Genoa and Battenberg are both types of which food?

15 'The Surrey With the Fringe On Top' is a song from which musical?

16 In what year did Germany withdraw from the League of Nations: 1933 or 1938?

17 In the animal kingdom, is the salamander found only in very arid or very damp places?

18 Which *K* is an Israeli collective settlement, usually agricultural but sometimes industrial?

19 Was the author of the children's novel *The Borrowers* male or female?

20 In politics, would you describe socialism as left- or right-wing?

Previous Total

1,000

800

600

450

300

200

100

50

20

Banked

Total

Answers

1 No
2 Rangers (Glasgow Rangers)
3 King Camp Gillette
4 Autumn
5 Baseball
6 Sophocles
7 Tail
8 Norman
9 Worzel Gummidge
10 The core

11 Television
12 Isle of Wight
13 Country and western
14 Cake
15 *Oklahoma!*
16 1933
17 Damp
18 Kibbutz
19 Female (Mary Norton)
20 Left

Round 233

1 In Britain, there are two types of horse racing: National Hunt racing and . . . what?

2 In humans, are the incisor teeth at the front or the back of the mouth?

3 In biology, is maltose a sugar or an enzyme?

4 Vehicles from which country display the letters 'IS' to identify their nationality?

5 In correct spelling, if someone is lying on the floor, are they L-Y-I-N-G or L-I-E-I-N-G?

6 What long-running TV game show has been presented by Larry Grayson, Bruce Forsyth and Jim Davidson?

7 In physics, what E describes an object's ability to return to its original shape after being stretched?

8 In theatre, which M is the French actor associated with the art of mime?

9 Which TV chef is the drummer with rock band Scarlet Division?

10 In which sport, associated with country-house lawns, is the MacRobertson Shield competed for by Australia, Great Britain and New Zealand?

11 What A is the envelope of gases which surrounds the Earth or another celestial body?

12 What H is the name given to a condition of excessive activity in young children?

13 Is the designer Gaultier's first name Jean-Paul or Pierre?

14 A hinny is the offspring of a male horse and a female what?

15 Was Hemingway's novel *For Whom The Bell Tolls* set during the Spanish or American Civil War?

16 What *N* is a type of lighting often used on advertising signs, invented by Georges Claude in 1910?

17 Was the actress Elizabeth Taylor born in England or America?

18 In history, Greece overthrew the rule of which country in the late 1820s?

19 Who played a slave called Lurcio in the 1970s TV sitcom *Up Pompeii*?

20 What *H* describes a small settlement or village, usually without a church?

Answers

1 Flat (racing)
2 Front
3 Sugar
4 Iceland
5 *L-Y-I-N-G*
6 *Generation Game* (accept *The Gen Game*)
7 Elasticity (accept elastic constant)
8 Marcel Marceau (accept Marceau)
9 Jamie Oliver
10 Croquet
11 Atmosphere
12 Hyperactivity (accept hyperactive)
13 Jean-Paul
14 Donkey
15 Spanish Civil War
16 Neon
17 England
18 Turkey
19 Frankie Howerd
20 Hamlet

Round 234

1 In music, who was the lead singer in the groups The Jam and The Style Council?

2 In food, 'bird's eye' and 'jalapeño' are varieties of which vegetable?

3 In religion, what *T* was the portable sanctuary carried by the Israelites during their period in the wilderness?

4 Which famous actress played Dr Chase Meridian in the 1995 film *Batman Forever*?

5 In history, which ancient British queen destroyed London and Colchester before supposedly killing herself?

6 For which political party was Ken Livingstone elected MP for Brent East in 1987?

7 In which sport does the top player in Europe receive the Ballon d'Or award?

8 In the UK, which form of transport is monitored by the CAA?

9 In music, in which religion is the shofar, a wind instrument made of a ram's horn, used?

10 In science, from which mineral is iron extracted?

11 In sport, which Dutch footballer has managed both Chelsea and Newcastle United?

12 In America, what kind of organisation is the Teamsters?

13 Which film director writes a regular restaurant column for the *Sunday Times*?

14 In food, what Q is the name of a fresh curd cheese, popular in Germany?

15 In religion, what does the word Islam mean in Arabic?

16 Commonly used for electrical fittings, bakelite was the first synthetic type of what?

17 In the housing market, what E is the difference between the value of the property and the amount outstanding on any loan secured against it?

18 In the TV series *The Young Ones*, who played the Eastern European landlord, Jerzy Balowski?

19 What type of creature is an avocet?

20 What R is another name for vitamin A?

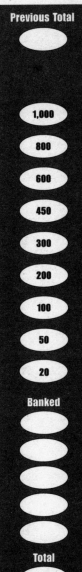

Previous Total

1,000

800

600

450

300

200

100

50

20

Banked

Total

Answers

1 Paul Weller (*accept* John William Weller)
2 Chilli (*accept* pimento/pepper)
3 Tabernacle (*accept* Tabernacle of the Testimony)
4 Nicole Kidman
5 Boudicca (Boadicea)
6 Labour
7 Football
8 Air travel/aviation
9 Judaism (*accept* Jewish)
10 Iron ore
11 Ruud Gullit
12 Trade union
13 Michael Winner
14 Quark
15 Submission (to God)
16 Plastic
17 Equity
18 Alexei Sayle
19 Bird
20 Retinol

Round 235

1 Burt Lancaster, Deborah Kerr and Frank Sinatra starred in which Oscar-winning film based on a James Jones novel?

2 In sport, what is the colour of the blazer given to the winner of the golf US Masters?

3 For what do the initials of the SDLP party stand?

4 When was *The Muppet Show* first broadcast in the UK?

5 In mythology, was Mithras the Persian god of light or darkness?

6 Which Italian artist was named after his father's profession as a dyer?

7 Which British queen died in 1714 and was the last of the Stuart sovereigns?

8 Who wrote the children's classic *The Enchanted Castle*?

9 In 1986, actors Tom Berenger and Charlie Sheen starred in which Oscar-winning Oliver Stone film?

10 'Stag', 'Wasp' and 'Golden Spider' are all types of which insect?

11 Who had a top-ten hit with 'Sledgehammer' in 1986?

12 Which organ receives all the products of food absorption and controls their storage and release?

13 In TV, Troy Tempest was a character in which 1960s puppet programme?

14 What is the name of the railway that links Moscow to Vladivostok?

15 Discovered by Abel Janszoon Tasman, which Australian state was federated with the others into the Commonwealth of Australia in 1901?

16 What *T* is a Japanese name for a colossal ocean wave caused by movements of the sea floor?

17 What animated series of the 1960s and 1970s did Nigel Planer revive and add new narration to in 1992?

18 In theatre, which Norwegian dramatist is known for his social dramas and symbolic plays about modern life?

19 Which Czech-born tennis player partnered Pam Shriver to win five Wimbledon ladies' doubles titles between 1981 and 1986?

20 With which country would you associate the ancient civilisation the Toltecs?

Previous Total

1,000

800

600

450

300

200

100

50

20

Banked

Total

Answers

1 *From Here To Eternity*	**11** Peter Gabriel
2 Green	**12** Liver
3 Social Democratic and Labour Party	**13** *Stingray*
4 1976	**14** Trans-Siberian Railway
5 Light	**15** Tasmania
6 Tintoretto	**16** Tsunami
7 Queen Anne (accept Anne)	**17** *The Magic Roundabout*
8 Edith Nesbit	**18** Henrik Ibsen
9 *Platoon*	**19** Martina Navratilova
10 Beetle	**20** Mexico

Round 236

1 In film, who directed the 1979 film *Apocalypse Now*?

2 Tony Blair was elected to represent which parliamentary constituency in County Durham in 1983?

3 Complete the title of this novel by Arundhati Roy which won the Booker Prize in 1997: *The God of . . .* what?

4 If there are 36 biscuits in a packet, how many, numerically, would be left if a third were eaten?

5 The two-and-a-half-mile 'Freedom Trail' is found in which historic US city of New England?

6 Name one of the two sports that make up a biathlon.

7 In which century did the artist Sir John Everett Millais paint?

8 In biology, what M describes a change in the genetic material of an organism which can result in an altered physical characteristic?

9 What is the principle colour of the Turkish flag?

10 In theatre, in which year of the 1960s was the Royal Shakespeare Company formed?

11 In pop music, what instrument did 1950s rock 'n' roll singer Jerry Lee Lewis usually play?

12 Which Italian explorer went to China and became a diplomat for Kublai Khan?

13 In mythology, which beast was half lion, half eagle and is sometimes shown with a serpent's tail?

14 Which author wrote the book *Gone With The Wind*, which was made into the 1939 film of the same name?

15 In which country was Marie Antoinette, wife of Louis XVI of France, born?

16 What name is given to someone who is born without any pigment in their skin, hair and eyes?

17 In US sports, for what do the initials MVP stand?

18 What number is represented by a figure one followed by nine zeros?

19 What stage musical did Robert Wise and Jerome Robbins direct for the cinema in 1961?

20 In the animal kingdom, what type of animal is a hornbill?

Previous Total

1,000

800

600

450

300

200

100

50

20

Banked

Total

Answers

1 Francis Ford Coppola (accept Coppola)	**11** Piano
2 Sedgefield	**12** Marco Polo
3 *Small Things*	**13** Griffin (accept griffon)
4 24	**14** Margaret Mitchell
5 Boston	**15** Austria
6 Skiing and shooting (accept rifle shooting)	**16** Albino (accept albinism)
7 Nineteenth	**17** Most Valuable Player
8 Mutation	**18** Billion (accept one thousand million)
9 Red	**19** *West Side Story*
10 1961	**20** Bird

1 By what name was daredevil motorcycle stunt-rider Robert Knievel better known?

2 In the human body, the shoulder and what *H* have a ball-and-socket joint?

3 What was the first name of Einstein, the physicist who won the Nobel Prize for Physics in 1921?

4 In the animal kingdom, the name 'dromedary' refers to what type of humped animal?

5 In fashion, are jodhpurs named after a town in India or Egypt?

6 A millennium would be celebrated after how many years?

7 In sport, what *P* is another name for table tennis?

8 In TV, what was the name of the drummer on *The Muppet Show*?

9 In geography, what *M* is the name of the indigenous people of New Zealand?

10 In the traditional children's game of the same name, which animal is 'in the middle'?

11 In science, is water deemed to be hard or soft if it has excessive levels of calcium and magnesium?

12 In film, the surname of Holly Hunter's co-star in *The Piano* is Harvey . . . what?

13 Which *C* is a decorative craftwork created by looping yarn or thread with a specially hooked needle?

14 Is the state of New Hampshire in the east or west of the USA?

15 In what country was the politician Neil Kinnock born and educated?

16 Did Michael Jackson release the album *Dangerous* or *History* in 1995?

17 In food, what *K* is the Turkish word for roast meat?

18 In the animal kingdom, the 'black Molly' is a species of what animal: a bird or a fish?

19 In art, what *P* is a drawing or painting material consisting of a stick of colour made from powdered pigments mixed with gum?

20 In Australia which is further west: Perth or Canberra?

Previous Total

1,000

800

600

450

300

200

100

50

20

Banked

Total

Answers

1 Evel Knievel	**12** Keitel
2 Hip	**13** Crochet
3 Albert	**14** East
4 Camel	**15** Wales
5 India	**16** *History*
6 One thousand	**17** Kebab
7 Ping pong	**18** Fish (*accept* tropical
8 Animal	fish)
9 Maori	**19** Pastel
10 Pig or piggy	**20** Perth
11 Hard	

1 In the fairy tale, who was 'as white as snow, as red as blood and as black as the wood'?

2 In food, what *T* is an open pastry case usually filled with fruit, jam or custard?

3 In the animal kingdom, do krill live on land or in the sea?

4 Which flour-based batter is often traditionally served with roast beef as a side dish?

5 In chemistry, what *O* is formed when most elements react with oxygen?

6 Complete the title of this 1988 film starring Bob Hoskins: *Who Framed . . . what?*

7 What *N* is the name given to the egg of a louse or other parasitic insects?

8 In the James Bond films, who appeared as a Bond girl first: Ursula Andress or Honor Blackman?

9 Which *M* is an embalmed body from ancient Egypt?

10 In classical music, what French word do English audiences sometimes shout at the end of a performance if they wish to hear more?

11 Pedicures are beauty treatments for which part of the body?

12 If you were staying at Butlin's in West Sussex, which English town would you be in?

13 In food, which *B* is an open fire on which meat and vegetables are cooked, often outside?

14 Which C is a crustacean resembling a lobster and only found in fresh water?

15 Complete the title of the following 1970 Frederick Forsyth novel: *The Day of the . . .* what?

16 In geography, is the Isle of Dogs actually an island?

17 What is the next number in the sequence 3, 7, 11, 15?

18 What is the name of the largest bell in the clock tower at the eastern end of the Houses of Parliament?

19 The 1968 album by The Beatles is usually known by what name, because of the colour of its cover?

20 What is the common name given to the female of a domesticated breed of ox?

Previous Total

1,000

800

600

450

300

200

100

50

20

Banked

Total

Answers

1 Snow White
2 Tart
3 In the sea
4 Yorkshire pudding
5 Oxide
6 *Roger Rabbit*
7 Nit
8 Ursula Andress
9 Mummy
10 *Encore* (accept *bis*)
11 Feet (accept toenails)
12 Bognor Regis
13 Barbecue
14 Crayfish
15 *Jackal*
16 No
17 19 (add 4 to previous number)
18 Big Ben
19 *The White Album*
20 Cow

Round 239

1 In which country in the UK is Snowdonia situated?

2 In aviation, what A is the name of the device used to keep a plane flying automatically?

3 What electrically operated, coloured traffic safety measure was first introduced in 1914 in Cleveland, Ohio?

4 Which US state is further north: Nebraska or Montana?

5 Which R is the name applied to the period known as the Golden Age of English Literature between 1485 and the mid-seventeenth century?

6 Which 1999 film, set in the 1950s, starred Matt Damon, Jude Law and Gwyneth Paltrow?

7 What tattoo did wartime prime minister Sir Winston Churchill have: an anchor or dove?

8 In food, what M is a variety of tangerine orange and a form of the Chinese language?

9 Which American teenage pop singer had a massive hit in 1999 with 'Baby One More Time', which became the biggest selling UK single of the year?

10 Which L is the common name of the shrub syringa which has purple or white flowers in May or June?

11 In the Daily Express cartoon strip, Edward Trunk and Bill Badger were pals of which bear?

12 In the human body, what does the term 'tachycardia' mean: a fast heartbeat or a slow heartbeat?

13 In which pair of organs in the human body are air tubes called 'bronchi' located?

14 Which Welsh city was the birthplace of Dylan Thomas, which he celebrated in his poetry?

15 Which syrup, made from the sap of a tree, is a traditional Canadian product?

16 In maths, what *P* means 'at a right angle to'?

17 In the animal kingdom, is the emperor penguin found in the Arctic or the Antarctic?

18 In education, what is the largest university in Britain: Cambridge or London?

19 In 1988, Spurs broke the British transfer fee record by purchasing which player?

20 In literature, Geoffrey Chaucer tells the story of a pilgrimage to which cathedral?

Previous Total

1,000

800

600

450

300

200

100

50

20

Banked

Total

Answers

1 Wales
2 Autopilot (accept automatic pilot)
3 Traffic lights
4 Montana
5 Renaissance
6 *The Talented Mr Ripley*
7 Anchor
8 Mandarin
9 Britney Spears
10 Lilac
11 Rupert the Bear (accept Rupert)
12 Fast heartbeat
13 Lungs
14 Swansea
15 Maple
16 Perpendicular
17 Antarctic
18 London (University)
19 Paul Gascoigne
20 Canterbury Cathedral

Round 240

1 Algernon Moncrieff is a principal character in which Oscar Wilde play: *The Importance of Being Earnest* or *An Ideal Husband*?

2 In religion, what *T* is the cardinal virtue which regulates the desire for pleasure?

3 In the 1964 film *My Fair Lady*, what did Eliza Doolittle sell for a living when Professor Higgins found her?

4 In the novel, was Lady Chatterley's lover a gamekeeper or a policeman?

5 Who played the character Terry McCann in the TV drama of the 1980s, *Minder*?

6 Which cartoon character lives at 1313, Webfoot Walk, Duckburg, Calisota?

7 In music, Papageno is a character in Mozart's opera *The Magic . . .* what?

8 'Goodbye' and 'Viva Forever' were 1998 UK number-one hits for which girl group?

9 What *C* is a confection made from spinning sugar?

10 What nationality is ballerina Sylvie Guillem?

11 In nature, is a lupin a type of plant or a species of bird?

12 'Little Boy' and 'Fat Man' were the nicknames of which bombs, used for the first time during World War II?

13 In literature, Mrs Hudson was the housekeeper of which fictional detective?

14 In the animal kingdom, does the aardvark originate from Africa or Asia?

15 What was the name of Bambi's rabbit friend in the 1942 animated film?

16 In marine life, which *H* is the largest of the flatfish family?

17 In sport, what nationality was cricketer Don Bradman: Australian or South African?

18 Which Buckinghamshire town has a breed of duck named after it?

19 If you had 'Nelly Moser' and 'Ernest Markham' climbing up your wall, what kind of plant would you be growing?

20 What C is the name of the transparent membrane that covers the front of the eye?

Previous Total

1,000

800

600

450

300

200

100

50

20

Banked

Total

Answers

1 *The Importance of Being Earnest*
2 Temperance
3 Flowers
4 Gamekeeper
5 Dennis Waterman
6 Donald Duck
7 *Flute*
8 Spice Girls
9 Candyfloss (accept cotton candy/ fairyfloss)
10 French
11 Plant
12 The atomic bombs (*accept* nuclear bomb; *do not accept* thermonuclear/H-bomb, as didn't exist until 1950s)
13 Sherlock Holmes
14 Africa
15 Thumper
16 (Atlantic) Halibut
17 Australian
18 Aylesbury
19 Clematis
20 Cornea

Head to Head

1a Which northern English city's cultural attractions include the West Yorkshire Playhouse and the Henry Moore Institute?

1b In which 2000 film did Julia Roberts star as an attorney's research assistant?

2a What was the name of the bearded court-jester character on the 1970s TV show *Rentaghost*?

2b In gladiatorial combat, the retiarius would be armed with a net and which other three-pronged weapon?

3a Who was the stage partner of music-hall comedian Chesney Allen, responsible for popularising the song 'Run Rabbit Run'?

3b In food, claret is the term commonly used by the English when referring to red wine from which French region?

4a Which founder member of the SDP was elected Chancellor of Oxford University in March 1987?

4b Which flower lends its name to the annual parade held on New Year's Day in Pasadena, California?

5a In art, the term 'Impressionism' was derived from a painting called *Impression: Sunrise* by which artist?

5b Who was the mascot in the 1970s TV show *Magpie*?

Answers

1a Leeds
1b Erin Brockovich
2a Mr Claypole (Timothy Claypole)
2b Trident
3a Bud Flanagan (accept Flanagan)
3b Bordeaux

4a Lord Jenkins [of Hillhead] (accept Roy Jenkins)
4b Rose (The Rose Parade)
5a Monet (Oscar-Claude Monet)
5b Murgatroyd

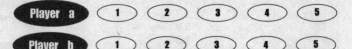

Player a   1   2   3   4   5

Player b   1   2   3   4   5

Head to Head

1a The mandarin, pintail and teal are all species of which bird?

1b In which century did Michelangelo paint the ceiling of the Sistine Chapel?

2a What was the full name of Tom Cruise's character in the *Mission: Impossible* films?

2b Which Beatles song was a UK Christmas number one in 1967?

3a In history, from 1966 Rudolf Hess was the sole inmate of which Berlin prison?

3b Which former leader of the Liberal Party was elected Presiding Officer of the Scottish Parliament in May 1999?

4a Which famous English poet did *Frankenstein* author Mary Wollstonecraft marry in 1816?

4b More usually associated with the theatre, who directed the year 2000 film *Billy Elliot*?

5a Who was the markswoman from Buffalo Bill's Wild West Show who was the subject of a musical by Irving Berlin?

5b What was the German general Erwin Rommel nicknamed during World War II because of his time in North Africa?

Answers

1a Duck
1b Sixteenth century
2a Ethan Hunt
2b 'Hello Goodbye'
3a Spandau

3b (Sir) David Steel (Right Honourable Lord David Steel of Aikwood)
4a Shelley (Percy Bysshe Shelley)
4b Stephen Daldry
5a Annie Oakley
5b 'The Desert Fox'

Player a   1   2   3   4   5

Player b   1   2   3   4   5

Head to Head

1a In Roman numerals, the number 500 is represented by which letter?

1b Which Oscar Wilde play features a character who was found as a baby in a handbag at Victoria Station?

2a In the USA, George Bush Senior was head of which agency in the late 1970s?

2b In football, which European country provided the opposition for Sven Goran Eriksson's first match as England manager?

3a In TV, who provided the original voice for Kermit the Frog?

3b Which singer, born Gaynor Hopkins, had a hit with 'Total Eclipse of the Heart' in 1983?

4a Which Belgian city is known as Anvers to the country's French speakers?

4b Which name was shared by the French kings whose nicknames were 'the Simple', 'the Fair' and 'the Mad'?

5a What was the real name of film star Cary Grant?

5b Jack Lemmon and Walter Matthau starred in which 1993 film comedy about elderly neighbours?

Answers

1a D
1b *The Importance of Being Earnest*
2a CIA
2b Spain
3a Jim Henson
3b Bonnie Tyler

4a Antwerp
4b Charles
5a Archibald Leach (Archibald Alexander Leach)
5b *Grumpy Old Men*

Player a   1   2   3   4   5

Player b   1   2   3   4   5

Head to Head

1a In the sport of grouse shooting, in which month is the so-called 'Glorious Twelfth'?

1b In the 1980s children's TV programme *Roland Rat*, what type of animal was Roland's girlfriend Glenis?

2a Whooper and Bewick's are both breeds of which long-necked bird?

2b In the Bible, which disciple denied Jesus three times following his arrest?

3a Who, in 1999, became the first serving head of state to be formally accused of war crimes?

3b Which US river rises in the state of Minnesota and flows into the Gulf of Mexico?

4a In which month in 1997 was Labour elected to office?

4b In which martial art did Britain's Kate Howey win a silver medal at the Sydney Olympics?

5a What was the name of the 'hippy' rabbit in the children's TV series *The Magic Roundabout*?

5b Which industrial sea port is connected to Liverpool by the Queensway Road Tunnel and the Mersey Rail Tunnel?

Answers

1a August	**3b** Mississippi
1b Guinea pig	**4a** May
2a Swan	**4b** Judo
2b Peter (Simon Peter)	**5a** Dylan
3a Slobodan Milosevic	**5b** Birkenhead

Player a ① ② ③ ④ ⑤

Player b ① ② ③ ④ ⑤

Head to Head

1a On a standard British Monopoly board, name one of the yellow properties.

1b In which French city did European heads of state meet in December 2000 to discuss the issue of vetos?

2a In food, which meat product comes in varieties such as 'Suffolk', 'Bradenham' and 'York'?

2b In the 1960s children's TV show, what was the name of Captain Scarlet's Martian enemies?

3a In the Bible, which Israelite leader was prevented from entering the promised land because of a display of doubt?

3b With which profession would you associate the Spaniard Antoni Gaudí and the Swiss-born Frenchman known as Le Corbusier?

4a The nineteenth-century American President Cleveland shares his first name with which Sesame Street character?

4b Which southern English city on the River Itchen has an eleventh-century Norman cathedral?

5a Which French author wrote the novel *The Count of Monte Cristo*?

5b Who played Max Cady in the 1962 version of *Cape Fear*?

Answers

1a Piccadilly/Coventry Street/Leicester Square
1b Nice
2a Ham
2b The Mysterons
3a Moses
3b Architecture (accept building design)

4a Grover
4b Winchester
5a Dumas (Alexandre Dumas/Dumas père)
5b Robert Mitchum (Robert Charles Durman Mitchum; do not accept Robert de Niro)

Player a 1 2 3 4 5

Player b 1 2 3 4 5

Head to Head

1a Which island's parliament is called the Tynwald?

1b In which game, played on a purpose-built table, are the terms 'winning hazard' and 'losing hazard' used?

2a In the children's cartoon *Jamie and the Magic Torch*, what type of animal was Wordsworth?

2b In nature, aspirin was originally derived from acid found in the bark of which species of tree?

3a In which century did the English artist Thomas Gainsborough live?

3b In geography, the Pump Room and the Abbey Church, completed in 1609, are found in which English city?

4a The name of which Italian cheese translates as 'sweet milk'?

4b In horse racing, what name is given to an ungelded male thoroughbred horse until he reaches five years of age?

5a In art, whose sculpture entitled *The Physical Impossibility of Death in the Mind of Someone Living* features a preserved shark in a tank?

5b In which Charles Dickens novel does Little Nell appear?

Answers

1a Isle of Man

1b Billiards (accept English/pocket billiards; *do not accept* French billiards)

2a Dog (accept old English sheepdog)

2b Willow

3a Eighteenth

3b Bath

4a Dolcelatte

4b Colt

5a Damien Hirst

5b *The Old Curiosity Shop*

| Player a | 1 | 2 | 3 | 4 | 5 |

| Player b | 1 | 2 | 3 | 4 | 5 |

Head to Head

1a Which Manhattan skyscraper, named after a motor-car firm, was briefly the tallest in the world, at 1,048 feet?

1b Which US singer was married to Ava Gardner during the 1950s and Mia Farrow during the 1960s?

2a With which sport are Jahangir and Jansher Khan associated?

2b Which country was formerly known as Portuguese East Africa?

3a In a standard modern symphony orchestra, which instrument is found in greater numbers than any other?

3b Which famous Swansea-born poet began his working life as a reporter at the *South Wales Evening Post* in the 1930s?

4a Christopher Wren designed London's Monument as a reminder of which event?

4b What was the nickname of Eric Moussambani, a swimmer from Equatorial Guinea who took part in the 2000 Olympics?

5a In Dumas's story, d'Artagnan's three musketeer companions were Athos, Porthos and . . . who?

5b In TV, Captain Troy Tempest and Atlanta Shore are characters in which 1960s children's programme?

Answers

1a Chrysler Building
1b Frank Sinatra (Francis Albert Sinatra)
2a Squash
2b Mozambique
3a Violin
3b Dylan Thomas (Dylan Marlais Thomas)

4a The Fire of London (*accept* Great Fire of London/Fire of 1666)
4b 'Eric The Eel'
5a Aramis
5b *Stingray*

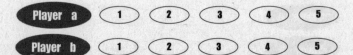

Player a   1   2   3   4   5

Player b   1   2   3   4   5

Head to Head

1a In music, with whose cello concerto is Jacqueline du Pré chiefly associated?

1b In medicine, some doctors still take an oath named after which ancient Greek physician?

2a 'Capelli d'angelo', meaning 'angel's hair', is one of the finest varieties of which foodstuff?

2b In money, how many sides does a twenty-pence coin have?

3a For what did the initials USSR stand?

3b Bantu languages are largely spoken in which continent?

4a In TV, actor Robert Lindsay played which character in the British comedy *Citizen Smith*?

4b In pop music, which 1988 single by Sting about living in America was written for the eccentric Quentin Crisp?

5a In Greek legend, in which war did Agamemnon lead the Greek forces?

5b In geography, on which river is the city of Rome located?

Answers

1a Elgar's
1b Hippocrates
2a Pasta
2b Seven
3a Union of Soviet Socialist Republics
3b Africa

4a Wolfie Smith (accept Wolfie/Walter Henry Smith)
4b 'An Englishman In New York'
5a Trojan War
5b River Tiber

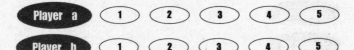

| Player a | 1 | 2 | 3 | 4 | 5 |
| Player b | 1 | 2 | 3 | 4 | 5 |

Head to Head

1a There are two naval bases on the south coast of England. One of them is at Devonport in Plymouth. Where is the other?

1b In food, which type of traditional English sauce contains molasses, vinegar, garlic, onions and anchovies?

2a Which Irving Berlin musical features the song 'I Got The Sun In The Morning'?

2b Which London art gallery houses Van Gogh's *Sunflowers*?

3a How many loaves did Jesus use to feed the five thousand?

3b Which European city hosted the International Exhibition and the Olympic Games in 1900?

4a Which Pulitzer Prize-winning novel by Harper Lee features the characters Atticus Finch and Tom Robinson?

4b In Greek mythology, Minos was king of which Greek island?

5a What is the name of the headland in East Sussex, between Seaford and Eastbourne, famous for its high chalk cliffs?

5b Which Venetian explorer's chronicles of his thirteenth-century travels were entitled, in an early version, *A Description of the World*?

Answers

1a Portsmouth
1b Worcestershire sauce (accept Worcester sauce)
2a *Annie Get Your Gun*
2b National Gallery
3a Five

3b Paris
4a *To Kill A Mockingbird*
4b Crete
5a Beachy Head
5b Marco Polo

Player a   1 2 3 4 5

Player b 1 2 3 4 5

Head to Head

1a During the 1960s, which singer and TV presenter had top-ten hit singles with 'Dick a Dum, Dum' and '1-2-3 O'Leary'?

1b What is the name of the largest lake in Africa?

2a In which English county is Buckfast Abbey?

2b Before decimalisation, what was the name of the large British coin that had a value of two shillings and sixpence?

3a Name the area at the north-east end of Hyde Park renowned for its soap-box orators.

3b In food, which cereal grain is one of the principal ingredients of the dish jambalaya?

4a Which fashionable jazz club opened in Harlem, New York in 1922?

4b In literature, who wrote the novels *Take a Girl Like You*, *The Old Devils* and *That Uncertain Feeling*?

5a Which diminutive Italian-American actor played the role of Leo Getz in the *Lethal Weapon* films?

5b 'Josephine Bruce' and 'Ena Harkness' are varieties of which plant?

Answers

1a Des O'Connor
1b Lake Victoria (accept Victoria Nyanza)
2a Devon (accept Devonshire)
2b Half-crown
3a Speaker's Corner

3b Rice
4a The Cotton Club
4b Kingsley Amis (if answer is Amis, ask to be more specific)
5a Joe Pesci (Joseph Pesci)
5b Rose

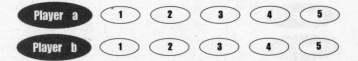

Player a   1   2   3   4   5

Player b   1   2   3   4   5

Head to Head

1a Which letter of the alphabet is often placed as a prefix to medical terms to mean 'without'?

1b What name is given to calculation which uses letters for numbers and takes its name from the Arabic for 're-setting'?

2a Which surname links the nineteenth-century author of *Barchester Towers* and the present-day writer of *The Rector's Wife*?

2b What is the capital of Romania?

3a In travel, the John Wayne Airport in Orange County can be found in which American state?

3b In geography, which long narrow country borders Argentina on the south-west coast of South America?

4a 'Juno' and 'Omaha' were codenames for two of the landing sites for Allied troops in which region of northern France?

4b In TV, Paul Pfeiffer was Kevin Arnold's best friend in which sitcom set in suburban America in the late 1960s?

5a Which hero was the arch-enemy of Ming the Merciless?

5b Which male name features in the title of songs by Pat Boone, John Leyton, and the Fine Young Cannibals?

Answers

1a A
1b Algebra
2a Trollope (Anthony and Joanna)
2b Bucharest
3a California
3b Chile
4a Normandy
4b *The Wonder Years*
5a Flash Gordon
5b Johnny

| Player a | 1 | 2 | 3 | 4 | 5 |
| Player b | 1 | 2 | 3 | 4 | 5 |

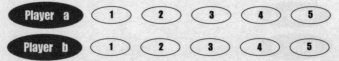

Head to Head

1a Which 1939 musical film includes the line 'Pay no attention to that man behind the curtain'?

1b In literature, who was British Poet Laureate between 1984 and 1998?

2a In Greek mythology, which handsome young man beloved by Aphrodite was killed by a wild boar while out hunting?

2b In which city does the character Freddie spend one night in the song from the musical *Chess*?

3a In the animal kingdom, ichthyology is a field of zoology devoted to the study of which creatures?

3b In economics, what French phrase is used to describe a policy of non-intervention by government in economic affairs?

4a Harvey Keitel played the character Winston Wolf in which 1994 film?

4b In football, how many times did Ronaldo win the FIFA World Player of the Year Award in the twentieth century?

5a In which country are the Balkan Mountains mainly situated?

5b In food, mozzarella cheese is traditionally made from the milk of which animal?

Answers

1a *The Wizard of Oz*	**3b** *Laissez-faire*
1b Ted Hughes	**4a** *Pulp Fiction*
2a Adonis	**4b** Twice (accept two)
2b Bangkok	**5a** Bulgaria
3a Fish	**5b** Water buffalo (accept buffalo)

Player a   (1)   (2)   (3)   (4)   (5)

Player b   (1)   (2)   (3)   (4)   (5)

Head to Head

1a The words 'dung' and 'longhorn' can prefix which insect?

1b With which song did Bucks Fizz win the Eurovision Song Contest in 1981?

2a In computing, how many bits does one byte contain?

2b What was the name of the medieval building material that consisted of interwoven sticks plastered with clay or mud?

3a In film, which 1990 action film featuring stock-car racing starred Tom Cruise and Nicole Kidman?

3b In publishing, which pocket-sized magazine, featuring at least one article for each day of the month, was launched by a husband and wife in February 1922?

4a Which US artist, who died in 1956, was famous for dripping cans of paint on to large canvases on the ground?

4b Which soldiers from Nepal use a curved sword or kukri?

5a Which subject did Tony Blair study at Oxford?

5b Who was the US Army officer commanding Operation Desert Storm in 1991?

Answers

1a Beetle
1b 'Making Your Mind Up'
2a Eight
2b Wattle and daub (accept daub and wattle/mud and wattle)
3a Days of Thunder
3b Reader's Digest

4a Jackson Pollock (accept Pollock/ Paul Jackson Pollock)
4b Gurkhas
5a Law
5b Norman Schwarzkopf (General H. Norman Schwarzkopf; accept 'Stormin' Norman')

Player a	1	2	3	4	5
Player b	1	2	3	4	5

Head to Head

1a In athletics, which British sprinter set up the Nuff Respect management consultancy with Colin Jackson in 1992?

1b In Russia, in the Official Orthodox Church, Christmas falls on the seventh day of which month?

2a In which Russian city is the Cathedral of Saint Basil the Blessed?

2b In botany, the name of which plant is derived from the French word 'pensée', meaning 'thought'?

3a In 1983, Sally Ride became the first woman from which country to go into space?

3b Which British explorer landed at Botany Bay in 1770?

4a Which 1980 film includes the line 'I am not an animal, I am a human being'?

4b In the TV comedy The Good Life, which actress played the role of Margo Leadbetter?

5a Catalan and Valencian are among the dialects or languages spoken in which European country?

5b What is the chemical symbol for nitrogen ?

Answers

1a Linford Christie
1b January
2a Moscow
2b Pansy
3a United States (accept US/USA/ America/United States of America)

3b Captain James Cook
4a The Elephant Man
4b Penelope Keith
5a Spain
5b N

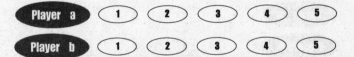

Player a   1   2   3   4   5

Player b   1   2   3   4   5

Head to Head

1a In TV, what was the occupation of Ian McShane's character in *Lovejoy*?

1b The St Leger, The Oaks and The One Thousand Guineas are annual events in which sport?

2a The pulmonary artery connects which organ to the heart?

2b As a child, Drew Barrymore starred in which 1982 science-fiction movie?

3a In which country was Florence Nightingale born?

3b Which alcoholic drink is traditionally added to hot water and sugar to a make a toddy?

4a Whose suffering and passion is depicted in the religious drama known as a passion play?

4b In politics, what term is given to the basic collective entitlements of all citizens?

5a In TV, in which children's comedy series did Una Stubbs play the part of Aunt Sally?

5b Which atoll in the Pacific Ocean was the site of US bomb tests in the 1940s and 1950s, sharing its name with a kind of swimwear?

Answers

1a Antique dealer
1b Horse racing (accept flat racing)
2a Lungs
2b *ET*
3a Italy

3b Whisky
4a Jesus Christ
4b Civil rights (accept human rights)
5a *Worzel Gummidge*
5b Bikini Atoll (accept Bikini)

Player a   1   2   3   4   5

Player b   1   2   3   4   5

Head to Head

1a In medicine, a haemogram is the result of a routine test of what?

1b Which famous Swedish tennis player won the Wimbledon title five times in a row from 1976 to 1980?

2a Which wartime delicacy derived its name from 'spiced ham'?

2b In plants, what is the name of the process prior to fertilisation in which grains are transferred from the male to the female reproductive organ?

3a In film, which ex-footballer won the Best Debut award at the 1999 *Empire* Film Awards?

3b In which sport are there positions called 'props' and 'locks'?

4a Which French national heroine led the French armies against the English during the Hundred Years War?

4b Who is the Queen's eldest grandchild?

5a In geography, in which country is the city of Giza situated?

5b In TV, Charlie Fairhead and Duffy are characters in which long-running medical drama?

Answers

1a Blood
1b Bjorn Borg
2a Spam
2b Pollination
3a Vinnie Jones
3b Rugby (accept rugby union)

4a St Joan of Arc (accept Jeanne d'Arc/ Joan of Arc)
4b Peter Philips
5a Egypt
5b *Casualty*

Player a   1   2   3   4   5

Player b   1   2   3   4   5

Head to Head

1a With what form of transport would you associate the designer Anthony Fokker?

1b Which actor and novelist walked out of the West End play *Cell Mates* in 1995 after poor reviews?

2a In pop music, which British band's UK hit albums have included *Making Movies* and *Brothers In Arms*?

2b Which star of the TV series *Friends* played Gale Weathers in the 1996 horror film *Scream*?

3a Christmas Island, in the Indian Ocean, is a dependency of which country?

3b In medicine, does diabetes mellitus result in high or low levels of sugar in the blood?

4a In Scrabble, *Z* and which other letter are worth 10 points?

4b In athletics, Florence Griffith-Joyner set the women's 100 metres record in 1988. Which country did she represent?

5a What would you buy at London's Billingsgate Market?

5b How many legs does a millipede have in each segment of its body?

Answers

1a Aircraft (accept war planes)
1b Stephen Fry
2a Dire Straits
2b Courteney Cox (Courteney Cox Arquette)
3a Australia

3b High
4a Q
4b United States of America
5a Fish (accept seafood)
5b Four (accept two pairs)

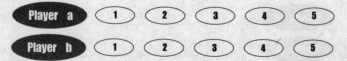

Player a   1   2   3   4   5
Player b   1   2   3   4   5

Head to Head

1a In Six Nations rugby, which country plays its home matches at the Flaminio Stadium?

1b In music, in which country was the composer Johann Strauss born?

2a In film, Danny DeVito played Vincent Benedict alongside Arnold Schwarzenegger in which 1988 comedy?

2b In which English county is Holkham Hall?

3a After the collapse of Communism, who was Russia's first democratically elected president, in 1991?

3b Which species of mouse is Britain's smallest rodent?

4a In literature, which book by William Thackeray features the social climbing of Becky Sharp?

4b With which sport is Tony Jacklin associated?

5a In film, who played Mia Wallace in the 1994 movie *Pulp Fiction*?

5b In pop music, which Canadian singer had UK top-ten singles in 1996 with 'Because You Loved Me' and 'It's All Coming Back To Me'?

Answers

1a Italy	**3b** Harvest
1b Austria	**4a** *Vanity Fair*
2a *Twins*	**4b** Golf
2b Norfolk	**5a** Uma Thurman
3a Boris Yeltsin (accept Yeltsin)	**5b** Celine Dion

Player a   1   2   3   4   5

Player b   1   2   3   4   5

Head to Head

1a Which American president passed the Emancipation Proclamation in 1862?

1b In which classic children's novel, published in 1908, do a mole and a water rat become friends?

2a Complete the title of Sir Arthur Conan Doyle's 1902 bestseller: *The Hound of the . . .* what?

2b What sort of man-made structure on the border of Nevada and Arizona was named after President Herbert Hoover?

3a What is the first name of Serena Williams's tennis-playing sister?

3b What term is used for a person who studies birds?

4a In TV, what is the name of Denise's baby in *The Royle Family*?

4b In pop music, which tartan-clad band had a UK number-one hit single with 'Bye Bye, Baby' in 1975?

5a Which European country has a high-speed rail system called the TGV?

5b What name is given to the colours from which all others can be obtained?

Answers

1a Abraham Lincoln (became effective 1 January 1863)

1b *The Wind in the Willows*

2a *Baskervilles*

2b Dam (for political reasons, known 1933–47 as Boulder Dam)

3a Venus

3b Ornithologist

4a David (accept Baby David)

4b Bay City Rollers

5a France

5b Primary (colours) (accept fundamental/simple colours)

Player a (1) (2) (3) (4) (5)

Player b (1) (2) (3) (4) (5)

Head to Head

1a In the animal kingdom, what animal is a flying fox?

1b In science, which country put the first animal, man and woman into space?

2a In pop music, Jim Kerr is the lead singer with which Scottish band?

2b At which weight do boxers Lennox Lewis and Mike Tyson compete?

3a In TV, who played Queen Elizabeth in the comedy series *Blackadder the Second*?

3b American rock group Survivor had a UK number-one single in 1982 with which song from the film *Rocky III*?

4a What *W* is the Australian term for a solitary nomadic trip into the bush?

4b In the TV comedy *The Good Life*, which character was played by Felicity Kendal?

5a In film, Richard Gere starred opposite which actress in the 1999 romantic comedy *Runaway Bride*?

5b In travel, Acapulco and La Paz are major ports in which country?

Answers

1a Fruit bat (accept bat)
1b Soviet Union (accept USSR/Russia)
2a Simple Minds
2b Heavyweight
3a Miranda Richardson

3b 'Eye Of The Tiger'
4a Walkabout
4b Barbara (Barbara Good)
5a Julia Roberts (Julie Fiona Roberts)
5b Mexico

Player a

Player b

Head to Head

1a In nature, what is the name of the icicle-like spikes of calcium carbonate found on the roofs of caves?

1b In film, which famous American actor had a *Last Tango in Paris* with Maria Schneider in 1972?

2a Complete the title of this play by Tennessee Williams: *The Glass . . .* what?

2b In history, Anschluss was the union between Germany and which other country in 1938?

3a In science, what is the chemical name for table salt?

3b In comic books, Peter Parker is the alter ego of which superhero?

4a On the London Underground, the Central Line is represented by which colour?

4b Who played the role of Doctor Ian Malcolm in the *Jurassic Park* films?

5a In literature, the novel *Agnes Gray* was the first by which of the Brontë sisters?

5b Which Motown singer was born Steveland Morris?

Answers

1a Stalactite(s)

1b Marlon Brando (Marlon Brando Junior)

2a Menagerie

2b Austria

3a Sodium chloride (NaCl)

3b Spider-Man (accept The Amazing Spider-Man)

4a Red

4b Jeff Goldblum (Jeff Lynn Goldblum)

5a Anne

5b Stevie Wonder

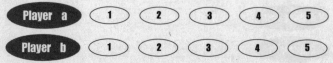

Player a   1   2   3   4   5

Player b   1   2   3   4   5

Head to Head

1a In music, with which song from the musical *Aspects of Love* did Michael Ball have a 1989 UK hit?

1b In human biology, when an ovum is released from an ovary, what is the process called?

2a In fashion, what is the name given to a pair of knee-length trousers which share their name with the rear part of shotguns or rifle barrels?

2b Which novelist wrote the science-fiction books *The Shape of Things to Come* and *The Time Machine*?

3a In food, what *R* is a cooked mixture of fat and flour used as a basis for sauces?

3b In the Bible, who was the first king of Israel?

4a In geography, in which county in the UK is the city of Durham situated?

4b In TV, Kathryn Janeway is the captain of which *Star Trek* ship?

5a In sport, in which country would you find the Formula One race track at Suzuka?

5b In the animal kingdom, what term is used to describe animals who walk upright on two legs?

Answers

1a 'Love Changes Everything'	**3b** Saul
1b Ovulation	**4a** (County) Durham
2a Breeches	**4b** *Voyager*
2b H. G. Wells (Herbert George Wells)	**5a** Japan
3a Roux	**5b** Bipeds

Player a (1) (2) (3) (4) (5)

Player b (1) (2) (3) (4) (5)

Head to Head

1a In which city is the European Union's Council of Ministers based?

1b In music, 'Happy Talk' was a 1982 UK number-one hit single for Captain . . . who?

2a According to mythology, which Roman god of beginnings has two faces?

2b Which actor starred as Dustin Hoffman's brother in the 1988 film *Rain Man*?

3a In history, which Russian leader's name meant 'man of steel'?

3b In medieval history, what was the name of the weapon in the form of a heavy club with a round spiked metal head?

4a What was the name of Stephen King's first published novel, which was made into a film released in 1976?

4b In football, which West Midlands club is nicknamed 'The Sky Blues'?

5a In pop music, which Irish band's 1981 debut UK chart single was 'Fire'?

5b In geography, what is the longest river in Italy?

Answers

1a Brussels
1b (Captain) Sensible
2a Janus
2b Tom Cruise (Thomas Cruise Mapother IV)
3a Stalin (Joseph Stalin)
3b Mace (accept morningstar)
4a Carrie
4b Coventry City (accept Coventry)
5a U2
5b (River) Po

Player a   1   2   3   4   5

Player b   1   2   3   4   5

Head to Head

1a In biology, septicaemia is the poisoning of which fluid found in the body?

1b The holiday resort of Sliema is on which Mediterranean island?

2a Which river in northern England rises in the Pennines and flows to Middlesbrough to join the North Sea?

2b Of which *Apollo* mission was Neil Armstrong a member when he became the first man to walk on the moon in 1969?

3a In history, what C is the name of the peninsula in which the Charge of the Light Brigade took place?

3b What was the surname of the aristocratic sisters Nancy, Unity, Jessica and Diana?

4a In TV, what number Thunderbird vehicle did Virgil Tracy pilot?

4b In food and drink, what flavour is the liquor Triple Sec?

5a Which bridge in northern England opened officially in 1981 and became the longest single-span bridge in the world at that time?

5b Which English actor provided the voice for the evil lion Scar in the 1994 animated film *The Lion King*?

Answers

1a Blood
1b Malta
2a (River) Tees
2b (Apollo) Eleven
3a Crimea
3b Mitford
4a (*Thunderbird*) 2
4b Orange
5a Humber Bridge
5b Jeremy Irons (Jeremy John Irons)

Player a 1 2 3 4 5

Player b 1 2 3 4 5

Head to Head

1a Which adult male singing voice is lower than a tenor, but higher than a bass?

1b In food, Savoy, white and red are all types of which vegetable?

2a In the animal kingdom, the 'red', 'silver' and 'fennec' are all types of which species of mammal?

2b In darts, what does a dart in the outer bull score?

3a In the Hans Christian Andersen story, who exchanged her voice for a pair of legs?

3b In geography, which English university town is situated at the confluence of the River Thames and the Cherwell?

4a Which popular drink, usually served hot, was first publicly sold in London in 1657?

4b In sport, with which team did England footballer Michael Owen sign professionally in 1996?

5a In nature, what is the common name for the fruit of the Cocos *nucifera* palm tree?

5b What is the capital of the American state of Indiana?

Answers

1a Baritone	**3b** Oxford
1b Cabbage	**4a** Tea
2a Fox	**4b** Liverpool
2b 25	**5a** Coconut
3a The Little Mermaid	**5b** Indianapolis

Player a   1   2   3   4   5

Player b   1   2   3   4   5

Head to Head

1a Which 1949 play by Arthur Miller tells the story of Willy Loman, a man destroyed by the values of society?

1b Which US singer's 1975 album was entitled 'Born To Run'?

2a The Faroe Islands belong to which Scandinavian country?

2b According to tradition, at a formal dinner in England, the first toast, known as the Loyal Toast, is proposed to whom?

3a Athletes from which country set a world record for the 4 x 400 metres relay in July 1998?

3b Which US general is remembered for his 'last stand' against Sioux and Cheyenne Native Americans at Little Big Horn?

4a 1 January 2000 saw the first anniversary of the launch of which currency?

4b Which Korean city derives its name from the Korean word meaning 'capital city'?

5a The Order of the Purple Heart is the oldest military decoration given by which country?

5b In the fairy tale, Rumpelstiltskin spun straw into what?

Answers

1a *Death of a Salesman*
1b Bruce Springsteen
2a Denmark
2b The Queen/monarch
3a United States (USA/America/US)
3b Custer (General George Armstrong Custer)

4a Euro (accept Single European Currency)
4b Seoul
5a United States (accept US/USA/America/United States of America)
5b Gold thread (accept gold)

Player a (1) (2) (3) (4) (5)

Player b (1) (2) (3) (4) (5)

Head to Head

1a Born in 1970, what is the name of property tycoon Peter Beckwith's 'It girl' daughter?

1b In geography, which Scottish city is situated at the mouths of the Rivers Dee and Don?

2a In children's TV, which Teletubby is the largest?

2b Which new London landmark was designed by David Marks and Julia Barfield?

3a In film, Tommy Lee Jones and Will Smith starred in which 1997 science-fiction comedy?

3b Which land-based sport was developed by surfers in California when they became bored during the cooler months?

4a In Formula One, in which country would you find the track at Monza?

4b In TV/film, who is Kate Hudson's famous blonde mother?

5a In film, who directed *Blazing Saddles* and *The Producers*?

5b The word for which fuel was coined in 1556 by German mineralogist Georg Bauer from the Latin for 'rock' and 'oil'?

Answers

1a Tamara
1b Aberdeen
2a Tinky Winky
2b London Eye (accept British Airways London Eye/BA London Eye/ millennium wheel)

3a *Men In Black*
3b Skateboarding
4a Italy
4b Goldie Hawn
5a Mel Brooks (Melvin Kaminsky)
5b Petroleum (accept petrol)

Player a 1 2 3 4 5

Player b 1 2 3 4 5

Head to Head

1a By what name are the islands of Guernsey, Jersey, Alderney and Sark collectively known?

1b Which popular comic-strip bear first appeared in the *Daily Express* newspaper in 1920?

2a In which sport is Ian Botham's son, Liam, a professional?

2b Which famous Swedish actress played Mata Hari in the 1931 film of the same name?

3a Which mechanical device for producing a continuous thread from individual fibres was invented in India about two and a half thousand years ago?

3b In pop music, which American folk singer's 1964 UK hit album was entitled *The Times They Are A-Changin'*?

4a In film, who starred as Jimmy Hoffa in the 1992 movie *Hoffa*?

4b Which disastrous financial event took place in the USA in October 1929?

5a A pygmy marmoset is the smallest type of what animal?

5b In sport, who became Britain's youngest ever Formula One driver in the year 2000?

Answers

1a The Channel Islands
1b Rupert Bear
2a Rugby union (accept rugby)
2b Greta Garbo (Greta Lovisa Gustafson)
3a Spinning wheel (do not accept spindle)
3b Bob Dylan (Robert Allen Zimmerman)
4a Jack Nicholson (John Joseph Nicholson)
4b The Wall Street Crash
5a Monkey
5b Jenson Button

Player a   1   2   3   4   5

Player b   1   2   3   4   5

Head to Head

1a In literature, which 1961 Joseph Heller novel features the character Major Major?

1b Which range of hills extends from the Peak District in Derbyshire to the Scottish border and is known as the backbone of England?

2a Where in the British Isles are Port Erin and Port Saint Mary?

2b At which sport do the Thames Valley Tigers and the London Towers compete?

3a Which British prime minister received a vote of no confidence in 1979 and called a general election?

3b In literature, the Authorised Version of the English Bible was agreed at a conference supported by which British king?

4a 'The Ace of Spades' was a 1980 UK hit for which band?

4b In which London art collection is *The Laughing Cavalier* on display?

5a What Stephen King novel was turned into a 1999 film about a miracle that happens on death row?

5b In which US city was 'Tin Pan Alley' in the early twentieth century?

Answers

1a Catch-22
1b Pennines
2a Isle of Man (accept Ellan Vannin)
2b Basketball
3a Jim Callaghan (Leonard James Callaghan)

3b James I (accept James VI of Scotland)
4a Motorhead
4b The Wallace Collection
5a *The Green Mile*
5b New York

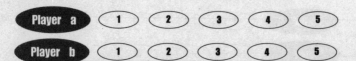

Player a   1   2   3   4   5

Player b   1   2   3   4   5

Head to Head

1a In art, which Spanish Surrealist painter wrote an autobiographical book called *Diary of a Genius*?

1b In medicine, the condition hypoglycaemia is caused by low amounts of what in the blood?

2a Which charity was set up by Prince Charles to help young people increase their confidence and learn new skills?

2b Which famous Irish poet wrote 'Wild Swans at Coole' and 'Sailing to Byzantium'?

3a In aeronautics, which brothers made the aircraft named *Flyer 1* that flew in 1903?

3b In music, what was the surname of the composer George Frederick, whose most famous work is his 1742 oratorio *The Messiah*?

4a In the TV soap *EastEnders*, who does Tamzin Outhwaite play?

4b In children's literature, which Mr Man walks into things?

5a When was William the Conquerer crowned at Westminster Abbey?

5b What name was given to the first artificially cloned sheep, born in 1996?

Answers

1a Salvador Dalí (Dalí; Salvador Felipe Jacinto Dalí)
1b Sugar
2a The Prince's Trust
2b W. B. Yeats (William Butler Yeats)
3a The Wright Brothers
3b Handel
4a Melanie Owen (accept Mel/ Melanie Beale/Melanie Healy)
4b Mister Bump
5a 1066
5b Dolly

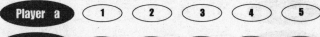

Player a   1   2   3   4   5

Player b   1   2   3   4   5

Head to Head

1a In travel, the resort of St Tropez is in which European country?

1b 'Bottle-nosed' and 'white-beaked' are types of which aquatic mammal?

2a In TV, who did Ainsley Harriott replace as presenter of *Ready, Steady, Cook*?

2b In sport, what is the traditional colour of a cricket ball?

3a In the Bible, what was the name of Samson's female adversary who tricked him into revealing the source of his strength?

3b In maths, how many sides does a rhombus have?

4a Which actor's autobiography is entitled *What's It All About*, a reference to a line from the title song of the 1966 film *Alfie*?

4b What is the name of the table-top game in which coins are 'pushed' up a board to score points?

5a In the Bible, who calmed a violent storm on the Sea of Galilee?

5b In literature, which English town features in the title of a 1937 George Orwell novel?

Answers

1a France
1b Dolphin
2a Fern Britton
2b Red
3a Delilah
3b Four

4a (Sir) Michael Caine (Maurice Joseph Micklewhite)
4b Shove ha'penny (accept shovelboard/shuffleboard)
5a Jesus (accept Jesus Christ)
5b Wigan (*The Road to Wigan Pier*)

Player a   1   2   3   4   5

Player b   1   2   3   4   5

Head to Head

1a In horse racing, Mister Frisk and Bobbyjo have both won which world-famous race?

1b Which ex-*Monty Python* member played the character Archie Leech in the 1988 film *A Fish Called Wanda*?

2a In the animal kingdom, what type of creature is a sandpiper?

2b Henry VIII and Elizabeth I belonged to which English royal house?

3a In UK geography, the town of Lowestoft is in which county?

3b By what first name is the author of *Dracula*, Abraham Stoker, more commonly known?

4a In sport, which British athlete won the 1992 Olympic 100 metres gold medal?

4b In music, which famous American band had UK number-one hits in 1980 with 'Atomic' and 'Call Me'?

5a In the Bible, Moses was placed in which river as a baby?

5b In pop music, who is the lead singer of the Irish band The Corrs?

Answers

1a Grand National (accept Grand National Handicap Steeplechase)
1b John Cleese
2a Bird (accept wading bird/shore bird/sea bird)
2b Tudor
3a Suffolk

3b Bram
4a Linford Christie
4b Blondie (do not accept Debbie Harry)
5a (River) Nile
5b Andrea (Corr)

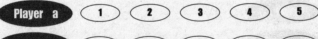

Player a   1   2   3   4   5

Player b   1   2   3   4   5

Head to Head

1a On the London Underground, which tube line is represented with the colour yellow?

1b In sport, who was the highest-ranked British tennis player at the end of the year 2000?

2a In the animal kingdom, the gazelle is a species of which animal?

2b In which African country is the Orange Free State a region?

3a In the American Constitution, Amendment Eighteen refers to the prohibition of what?

3b In which sport do players compete in the Bob Hope Classic?

4a In music, which Andrew Lloyd Webber musical features the song 'Eva, Beware of the City'?

4b Which Asian country officially took on a new constitution and became an Islamic state in 1956?

5a In pop music, the Robbie Williams video 'Supreme' features which sport?

5b In geography, Dartmouth is a fishing port on the estuary of which river?

Answers

1a Circle Line

1b Tim Henman

2a Antelope

2b South Africa

3a Alcohol (accept intoxicating liquors/ alcoholic drinks)

3b Golf

4a Evita

4b Pakistan

5a Motor racing (accept Grand Prix/ Formula One)

5b (River) Dart .

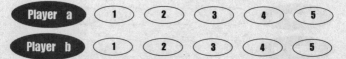

Player a   1   2   3   4   5

Player b   1   2   3   4   5

Head to Head

1a In history, in which capital city is the house where Anne Frank and her family hid from the Nazis during World War II?

1b Which star of the US TV show *Frasier* provided the voice of Stinky Pete the Prospector in the 1999 film *Toy Story 2*?

2a In Greek mythology, which god is represented as a man with the horns, hoofs and ears of a goat, playing the pipes?

2b Who, in 1965, became the first leader of the Conservative Party to be elected by fellow MPs?

3a In football, for which Premiership team did Michael Owen play at the beginning of 2001?

3b In history, what is the name for the northern Spanish region which forms part of the name of Henry VIII's first wife?

4a The chihuahua dog originates from which country?

4b Who wrote the *Dune* science-fiction novels?

5a Which south-western English city grew from a settlement called Brig-Stow?

5b Which US golfer won the 1997 US Masters aged 21?

Answers

1a Amsterdam
1b Kelsey Grammer (Allen Kelsey Grammer)
2a Pan
2b Edward Heath
3a Liverpool
3b Aragon
4a Mexico
4b Frank Herbert
5a Bristol
5b Tiger Woods (Eldrick Woods)

Player a ① ② ③ ④ ⑤

Player b ① ② ③ ④ ⑤

Head to Head

1a What is the British name for the plant which produces May blossom?

1b Which comedienne and actress plays Denise in the TV comedy *The Royle Family*?

2a During the American Civil War, for what did the initials CSA stand?

2b In which Shakespeare play would you find the famous line 'The quality of mercy is not strain'd'?

3a The rock group Queen provided the soundtrack to which 1980 science-fiction film?

3b In which German city were Nazi war criminals famously tried after the Second World War?

4a At which sport were Jo Durie and Annabel Croft both British number ones during the 1980s?

4b With which instrument was the performer Liberace associated?

5a In theatre, which Andrew Lloyd Webber musical features the song 'The Music of the Night'?

5b In which ocean are the Bahamas?

Answers

1a Hawthorn
1b Caroline Aherne (accept Caroline Hook)
2a Confederate States of America
2b *The Merchant of Venice*
3a *Flash Gordon*

3b Nuremburg (accept Nürnberg)
4a Tennis
4b Piano
5a *The Phantom of the Opera*
5b Atlantic (Ocean)

Player a   1   2   3   4   5

Player b   1   2   3   4   5

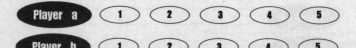

Head to Head

1a In film, which Belfast-born classical actor played Dr Loveless in the 1999 western *Wild Wild West*?

1b Mike Love and Brian Wilson were members of which 1960s band?

2a Which Ben Elton novel and play tells the story of a Hollywood director terrorised by serial killers inspired by his violent films?

2b Which Charles was an English architect whose work includes the neogothic Houses of Parliament?

3a Which inland sea in Asia is the largest lake in the world?

3b What is the name of the region of gold fields in north-western Canada and Alaska?

4a Which internationally acclaimed singer collaborated with the Propellerheads on the track 'History Repeating' in 1997?

4b Who portrayed Nick Leeson in the 1999 film *Rogue Trader*?

5a In mythology, which Roman god of commerce was associated with the Greek god Hermes?

5b How many plagues were inflicted on Egypt in the Book of Exodus?

Answers

1a Kenneth Branagh	**3b** The Klondike
1b The Beach Boys	**4a** Shirley Bassey
2a Popcorn	**4b** Ewan McGregor
2b Charles Barry	**5a** Mercury
3a Caspian Sea	**5b** Ten

Player a   1   2   3   4   5

Player b   1   2   3   4   5

Head to Head

1a In music, what is the highest register of singing voice a woman, girl or boy can have?

1b On a standard British Monopoly board, name one of the orange properties.

2a In TV, which actor played Mr Humphries in the 1970s sitcom *Are You Being Served*?

2b What is the name of the Royal Navy's amphibious infantry?

3a In human biology, the smallest bone in the body, known as the stapes or stirrup bone, is found inside which organ?

3b In food, *pâté de foie gras* originates from which country?

4a In nature, dates, coconuts and sago all grow on which species of tree?

4b What is the name of the animated penguin character who gives his name to the children's TV show made in Norway?

5a In the Bible, who was sentenced to wander the Earth by God for murdering his brother?

5b Which former member of the band Take That won three Brit Awards in February 2001?

Answers

1a Soprano (accept treble)
1b Bow Street/Marlborough Street/ Vine Street
2a John Inman (Frederick John Inman)
2b Royal Marines
3a Ear

3b France
4a Palm
4b Pingu
5a Cain
5b Robbie Williams (Robert Peter Maximillian Williams)

Player a   1   2   3   4   5

Player b   1   2   3   4   5

Head to Head

1a In which London borough did Tony Blair live before moving to Downing Street?

1b Which gangster known as 'Scarface' dominated organised crime in Chicago from 1925 to 1931?

2a In film, which sport featured in the 1996 comedy *Kingpin*, starring Woody Harrelson and Bill Murray?

2b What is the title of Alfred Lord Tennyson's 1854 poem about an ill-fated cavalry charge in the Crimean War?

3a Which British athlete won 1500 metres Olympic gold in 1980 and 1984?

3b Which surname links the footballers Andy, Ashley and Joe, from the England squad that faced Albania in March 2001?

4a What name is given to a major branch of a tree as well as the leg of a human?

4b Which coin was withdrawn as legal tender in 1984?

5a In 1938 Orson Welles announced that New Jersey had been attacked by invaders from which planet?

5b Which British prime minister's father was a shopkeeper who became mayor of Grantham?

Answers

1a Islington
1b Al Capone (Alphonse Capone)
2a Ten-pin bowling (accept bowling)
2b 'The Charge of the Light Brigade'
3a Sebastian Coe (accept Seb Coe)
3b Cole

4a Limb
4b Half penny (accept ha'penny)
5a Mars
5b Margaret Thatcher (Margaret Hilda Thatcher/Baroness or Lady Thatcher)

Player a   (1)   (2)   (3)   (4)   (5)

Player b   (1)   (2)   (3)   (4)   (5)

Head to Head

1a What, in American slang, is your John Hancock?

1b In nature, what is the name of the outer layer of tree bark which is often used as a stopper in wine bottles?

2a In the Book of Genesis, whose name is derived from the Hebrew word for 'man'?

2b In legend, what was the name of the famed court of King Arthur's kingdom?

3a In pop music, which Billy Ocean song did Boyzone release for Comic Relief in 1999 ?

3b In sport, which American tennis player beat Martina Hingis to win her first Grand Slam title at the 2001 Australian Open?

4a Which comedy musical features the song 'Sweet Transvestite'?

4b Martin Scorsese's 1995 film *Casino* is set in which American city?

5a In the TV comedy series *Blackadder The Third*, who played the half-witted Prince Regent?

5b Who played Will Hunting in the 1997 film *Good Will Hunting*?

Answers

1a Signature
1b Cork
2a Adam
2b Camelot
3a 'When The Going Gets Tough'
3b Jennifer Capriati

4a *The Rocky Horror Show* (accept *The Rocky Horror Picture Show*)
4b Las Vegas
5a Hugh Laurie
5b Matt Damon (Matthew Paige Damon)

Player a

Player b

Head to Head

1a With which religion are the Jesuits associated?

1b Who succeeded Barbara Bush as America's First Lady in 1993?

2a Which famous boxer said in 1967: 'I ain't got no quarrel with them Viet Congs'?

2b Which Scottish snooker player became the youngest to win the world championship in 1990?

3a In travel, which European country would you be visiting if you flew into Turin airport?

3b How many wings does a mosquito have?

4a In cricket, how many bails would you find on the field of play?

4b What was the name of the large wooden beams with a metal tip that were used in medieval times to break through doors or castle fortifications?

5a Which veteran British actor delivered the line 'Use the Force, Luke' during the climactic battle of the 1977 film *Star Wars*?

5b What process for treating rubber was invented by the American Charles Goodyear in 1839?

Answers

1a Christianity (accept Roman Catholicism)

1b Hillary Clinton (Hillary Rodham Clinton)

2a Muhammad Ali (Cassius Marcellus Clay)

2b Stephen Hendry

3a Italy

3b Two (accept one pair)

4a Four

4b Battering rams

5a (Sir) Alec Guinness

5b Vulcanisation

Player a   1   2   3   4   5

Player b   1   2   3   4   5

Head to Head

1a Of which Australian state is Perth the capital?

1b In music, 'Supersonic' was the first UK hit single for which Manchester-based pop group in 1994?

2a Which Hollywood actor was credited as Arnold Strong in his 1970 film debut?

2b In folklore, around what type of tree, in the heart of Sherwood Forest, did Robin Hood reputedly gather his Merry Men?

3a The wreck of which famous British liner was discovered in the North Atlantic in September 1985?

3b With which sport would you associate Sean Kerly and Russell Garcia?

4a In pop music, 'Anyone Who Had a Heart' was a UK number-one hit single in 1964 for which British entertainer?

4b In travel, Orly is an international airport in which European city?

5a In cricket, what is the name for the line or rope which marks where the field of play ends?

5b In children's literature, which Mr Men character eats all the time?

Answers

1a Western Australia
1b Oasis
2a Arnold Schwarzenegger
2b Oak
3a The *Titanic*

3b Hockey (accept field hockey)
4a Cilla Black (Priscilla White)
4b Paris
5a The boundary
5b Mr Greedy

Player a   1   2   3   4   5

Player b   1   2   3   4   5

Head to Head

1a In film, Bo Peep, Slinky Dog and Mister Potato Head are all characters from which 1995 comedy animation?

1b Which famous explorer discovered the island of Hispaniola in 1492?

2a In the TV sitcom *Bottom*, which actor played Richie Richard?

2b In geography, in which North American country are the Cariboo Mountains situated?

3a In music, which opera did Verdi write about the conflicts of love and royal duty: *Don Carlos* or *Don Giovanni*?

3b In film, the title of the 1969 musical starring Shirley Maclaine and Sammy Davis Junior is *Sweet . . .* what?

4a Which Irvine Welsh novel features characters named Renton, Sickboy and Begbie?

4b In music, Sheng, Tan, Ching and Chou are the four main character types in traditional opera from which country?

5a What is the general name given to female adult whales?

5b Which singer from Southampton was nominated six times at the 2001 Brit Awards but won nothing?

Answers

1a Toy Story	**3a** Don Carlos
1b Christopher Columbus (accept Cristoforo Colombo/Cristobal Colon)	**3b** Charity
	4a Trainspotting
	4b China
2a Rik Mayall	**5a** Cows
2b Canada	**5b** Craig David

Player a (1) (2) (3) (4) (5)

Player b (1) (2) (3) (4) (5)

Head to Head

1a In which country's military would you find the elite anti-terrorist unit called Delta Force?

1b In which part of the human body are the bones called 'metacarpals' found?

2a In film, which actress and singer played the role of Breathless Mahoney in the 1990 film *Dick Tracy*?

2b Which British actor received a posthumous Best Supporting Actor BAFTA nomination for his role in *Gladiator*?

3a In the animal kingdom, what is the name of the only mammal that is capable of true flight?

3b 'Catch-18' was the working title of which Joseph Heller novel?

4a In 1957, in which Italian city were the treaties signed to establish the European Common Market?

4b Which animal has the scientific name *Panthera leo*?

5a In British geography, in which island group are Stronsay, Westray and Hoy?

5b What is the branch of earth science that uses physics to study the planet?

Answers

1a United States (accept US/USA/ America/United States of America)
1b Hands
2a Madonna
2b Oliver Reed (Robert Oliver Reed)
3a Bat

3b *Catch-22*
4a Rome
4b Lion
5a Orkney Islands (accept Orkneys)
5b Geology (or geophysics)

Player a   1   2   3   4   5

Player b   1   2   3   4   5

Head to Head

1a Who became king of Spain following the death of General Franco in 1975?

1b In religion, according to the Acts of the Apostles, who ascended into heaven at the Mount of Olives?

2a Which 1990 movie starred Julia Roberts and Kevin Bacon as medical students experimenting with near-death experiences?

2b Who wrote 'In Memoriam', and became Poet Laureate in 1850?

3a Which Shakespeare play features a performance of the tragedy *Pyramus and Thisbe*?

3b In sport, which famous footballer was given the freedom of the city of Newcastle upon Tyne in March 2001?

4a In English football, how many leagues are there above the third division?

4b Who defeated Bob Dole and Ross Perot in the 1996 US presidential elections?

5a In TV, who is daughter of *Days of our Lives* star John Aniston?

5b What was the name of the mascot in the 1970s TV show *Magpie*?

Answers

1a Juan Carlos (Juan Carlos Alfonso Victor Maria de Borbon y Borbon)
1b Jesus Christ (accept Jesus or Christ)
2a Flatliners
2b Alfred Lord Tennyson (accept Tennyson)
3a A Midsummer Night's Dream
3b Alan Shearer
4a Three
4b Bill Clinton (William Jefferson Clinton/William Jefferson Blythe III)
5a Jennifer Aniston
5b Benjamin Britten

Player a   1   2   3   4   5

Player b   1   2   3   4   5

Head to Head

1a In history, what is the name of the famous battle of the Second World War in which Montgomery halted Rommel's advance through Egypt?

1b In literature, which fictional detective had a mortal enemy called Professor Moriarty?

2a Jarlsberg is a variety of what food?

2b In religion, by what other name is the Western Wall in Jerusalem known?

3a In pop music, who did Eric Clapton shoot in the title of his 1974 hit single?

3b Which famous American actress starred in *Whatever Happened To Baby Jane?* and *All About Eve?*

4a In theatre, the songs 'Who Will Buy' and 'Boy For Sale' appear in which Lionel Bart musical?

4b In history, which English king married Anne of Cleves in 1540?

5a In snooker, which colour ball has a value of seven points when potted?

5b 'Plié' and 'arabesque' are movements associated with which type of dance?

Answers

1a The Battle of El Alamein
1b Sherlock Holmes
2a Cheese
2b The Wailing Wall
3a The Sheriff

3b Bette Davis (Ruth Elizabeth Davis)
4a *Oliver!*
4b Henry VIII
5a Black
5b Ballet

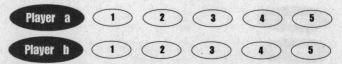

Player a   1   2   3   4   5

Player b   1   2   3   4   5

Head to Head

1a In the animal kingdom, how many wings does a dragonfly have?

1b In which European country would you find the industrial port of Bilbao?

2a What was the first name of the fourteenth-century English poet Chaucer?

2b In TV, which puppet series had the working title 'International Rescue'?

3a In film, Daryl Hannah starred as a mermaid in which 1984 comedy?

3b In modern history, Anzac Day is a commemorative national holiday in Australia and which other country?

4a In fashion, pashmina is a woollen fabric made from the hair of the belly of which animal?

4b Which West End play tells the story of three friends who fall out over a piece of modern art?

5a Which falls on the River Zambezi in Africa were named after a British queen by the explorer David Livingstone?

5b In rugby league, how many points is a try worth?

Answers

1a Four (*accept* two pairs)	**3b** New Zealand
1b Spain	**4a** Goat
2a Geoffrey	**4b** *Art*
2b *Thunderbirds*	**5a** Victoria Falls
3a *Splash!*	**5b** Four (*not* five, which is rugby union)

Player a 1 2 3 4 5

Player b 1 2 3 4 5

Head to Head

1a Which port is situated on the narrow peninsula of Portsea Island in Hampshire?

1b In what type of building was Abraham Lincoln assassinated?

2a In transport, 'disc' and 'drum' are varieties of which safety device on cars?

2b Which famous American had a show called the 'Wild West and Congress of Rough Riders of the World'?

3a In the lower leg of humans, which bone runs parallel with the tibia?

3b Who starred in the title roles of the films *Rob Roy* and *Michael Collins*?

4a In theatre, Iago is a devious character in which Shakespeare play?

4b In pop music, what colour is the ladder in the title of David Gray's year 2000 album?

5a In the UK, which major upland mass extends southward from Northumberland into Derbyshire?

5b In plants, 'lobed' and 'serrated' are both descriptions of the shape of what?

Answers

1a Portsmouth
1b Theatre (accept playhouse)
2a Brakes
2b Buffalo Bill (William Frederick Cody)
3a The fibula
3b Liam Neeson (William John Neeson)
4a *Othello*
4b White
5a Pennines
5b Leaves

| Player a | 1 | 2 | 3 | 4 | 5 |
| Player b | 1 | 2 | 3 | 4 | 5 |

Head to Head

1a Who played Vito Corleone in the 1974 film *The Godfather, Part Two*?

1b What is the name for the soft substance inside some bones that is involved in the production of blood cells?

2a In which decade did the English five-pound note become blue?

2b In sport, what is the name of the indoor game based on lawn tennis, played with small solid bats and a light ball on a table?

3a In bowls, what is the name given to the target ball?

3b In which 1978 film does Robert De Niro's character say 'The deer has to be taken with one shot. I try to tell people that – they don't listen'?

4a In pop music, who released the album *Purple Rain* in 1984?

4b In geography, the Strait of Gibraltar joins the Atlantic Ocean to which sea?

5a 'Klezmer' is a genre of music primarily associated with which religion?

5b In which Bond film did Judi Dench make her debut as 'M'?

Answers

1a Robert De Niro
1b Bone marrow (accept marrow)
2a 1950s (1957)
2b Table tennis (accept ping pong/ whiff-whaff/flim-flam)
3a A jack
3b *The Deer Hunter*

4a Prince (accept 'The Artist'/'The Artist Formerly Known as Prince'/Symbol/ TAFKAP)
4b Mediterranean
5a Judaism (accept Jewish religion)
5b *Goldeneye*

Player a (1) (2) (3) (4) (5)

Player b (1) (2) (3) (4) (5)

Head to Head

1a The name of which Italian volcano translates as 'I Burn' in Greek?

1b In pop music, *Electric Ladyland* was a 1968 UK hit album by which American singer and guitarist?

2a In rugby union, South African Jannie De Beer scored a record five drop goals against which country in the 1999 World Cup?

2b In TV, what was the occupation of Telly Savalas's character in the 1970s US drama *Kojak*?

3a In which country was the 1987 epic film *The Last Emperor* set?

3b Which town in Shropshire is surrounded by a loop in the River Severn and was the birthplace of Charles Darwin?

4a In human biology, 'myopathy' is any disease of which type of body tissue?

4b In history, what was the first name of Napoleon's first wife, whom he divorced in 1809?

5a In history, which famous heroine is the patron saint of France?

5b The locomotive which pulled trains from London to Edinburgh was known as *The Flying . . .* what?

Answers

1a (Mount) Etna	**3b** Shrewsbury
1b Jimi Hendrix	**4a** Muscle
2a England	**4b** Josephine
2b Detective (accept police officer/ policeman/homicide cop/cop)	**5a** Joan of Arc (accept Jeanne d'Arc)
3a China	**5b** *Scotsman*

Player a 1 2 3 4 5

Player b 1 2 3 4 5

Head to Head

1a In sport, which medal did Audley Harrison win for super-heavyweight boxing during the 2000 Olympics?

1b In politics, who did John Smith succeed as leader of the Labour Party?

2a Which 1978 film musical features romances between the 'T-Birds' and the 'Pink Ladies'?

2b In science, the word 'aqueous' describes anything related to which liquid?

3a Which London Underground station shares its name with the long-running BBC children's programme set in a school?

3b In the animal kingdom, what name is given to a male rabbit?

4a In music, which American singer had UK hit singles in the 1970s with 'Woman In Love' and 'You Don't Bring Me Flowers'?

4b What B are read out in church for three Sundays before a wedding?

5a What is the official called in a game of cricket?

5b Frogs, toads and newts are all classed as what type of animal?

Answers

1a Gold
1b Neil Kinnock (Neil Gordon Kinnock)
2a Grease
2b Water
3a Grange Hill
3b Buck

4a Barbra Streisand (Barbara Joan Streisand)
4b Banns
5a Umpire
5b Amphibian (accept amphibia, vertebrates)

 Player a 1 2 3 4 5

Player b 1 2 3 4 5

Head to Head

1a In food, tournedos are thick, round fillet slices of which meat?

1b In British politics, who was Speaker of the House of Commons from 1992 until October 2000?

2a Lisa Scott-Lee is a member of which British pop group?

2b In sport, Hampden Park is the national football stadium of which country?

3a In which European capital city is the musical and film *My Fair Lady* set?

3b In 1533, Henry VIII broke from which religion after failing to obtain a marriage annulment?

4a In geography, which state of the US comprises a group of over twenty islands in the North Pacific?

4b In football, which English club won their first European Cup in 1977?

5a What name is given to a clapperless metal bell that is played as a percussion instrument by being struck with a drumstick?

5b In American politics, which position in government did George Bush Senior hold immediately prior to president?

Answers

1a Beef (accept beef steak)
1b Betty Boothroyd
2a Steps
2b Scotland
3a London

3b Catholic (Roman Catholic)
4a Hawaii
4b Liverpool
5a Cowbell
5b Vice-president

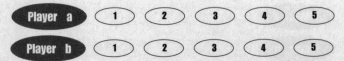

Player a   1   2   3   4   5

Player b   1   2   3   4   5

Head to Head

1a In TV, Nancy Cartwright is the voice of which animated ten-year-old boy?

1b In history, the Hundred Years War took place between England and which other country?

2a In literature, Charles Dickens's novel *A Tale of Two Cities* is set during which eighteenth-century revolution?

2b In pop music, which former *Neighbours* star had a UK number-one single with 'Too Many Broken Hearts' in 1989?

3a In maths, what is found by multiplying the length by the breadth by the height of a cuboid?

3b Prior to decimalisation in the UK, how many shillings were there in a guinea?

4a In history, what *P* was the paper-like writing material used by the ancient Egyptians, Greeks and Romans?

4b What sort of twins have the same information in their DNA?

5a What is the name of the former England goalkeeper who sold his World Cup winner's medal at auction in March 2001?

5b People who participate in which hobby are known as 'twitchers'?

Answers

1a Bart Simpson	**4a** Papyrus
1b France	**4b** Identical (*accept* monozygotic)
2a French Revolution	**5a** Gordon Banks
2b Jason Donovan	**5b** Birdwatching (*accept* 'looking for
3a Volume	rare birds')
3b 21	

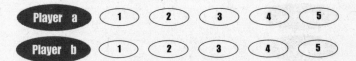

Player **a**   1   2   3   4   5

Player **b**   1   2   3   4   5

Head to Head

1a Which language is most commonly spoken in Switzerland?

1b In pop music, Morten Harket was the vocalist in which band that had a UK hit single with 'Take on Me' in 1985?

2a In rugby union, what is the maximum number of players per team permitted to take part in a scrum?

2b In TV, who was Peter Cook's main male co-star in the comedy series *Not Only But Also*, first shown in 1965?

3a How many sets of chromosomes do diploid cells contain?

3b In pop music, which male singer released the singles 'Never Gonna Give You Up' and 'Together Forever' in the late 1980s?

4a Famous for his prophecies, by what name was the French astrologer Michel de Notredame better known?

4b In fashion, what name is given to the ornamental shoulder strap on a military jacket or coat?

5a Which military rank was Matt Damon's character in the 1998 war film *Saving Private Ryan*?

5b Which monarch is credited with the phrase 'We are not amused'?

Answers

1a German (accept Swiss German)	**3b** Rick Astley
1b A-ha	**4a** Nostradamus
2a Eight	**4b** Epaulette
2b Dudley Moore	**3a** Private
3a Two	**3b** Queen Victoria

Player a   1   2   3   4   5

Player b   1   2   3   4   5

Head to Head

1a In which month is Mothering Sunday celebrated in Britain?

1b In the UK, which Act of Parliament, amended in 1989, prohibits the disclosure of confidential official information in the interest of national security?

2a In TV, Davy Jones starred as the only English member of which 1960s American TV sitcom about a pop group?

2b In history, which Roman general said 'I came, I saw, I conquered'?

3a At which racecourse has the Grand National steeplechase been run since 1847?

3b In musical notation, what does the term 'forte' mean?

4a In music, which American rock band had a UK top-ten hit single in 1986 with 'Living on a Prayer'?

4b In human biology, the word 'dermal' refers to which organ?

5a American jazz musician Edward Kennedy Ellington is better known by what name?

5b In food, from which country does feta cheese originate?

Answers

1a March
1b Official Secrets Act
2a *The Monkees*
2b Julius Caesar (Gaius Julius Caesar)
3a Aintree

3b Loud/loudly/strong
4a Bon Jovi
4b Skin
5a Duke Ellington
5b Greece

Player a   1   2   3   4   5

Player b   1   2   3   4   5

Head to Head

1a What was the name of Annette Crosbie's character in the TV sitcom *One Foot In The Grave*?

1b Which pop icon spoke at the Oxford Union with his foot in plaster in March 2001?

2a In football, with which club did George Best begin his professional career?

2b What is the highest mountain in the UK?

3a In human biology, the superior vena cava delivers blood to which internal organ?

3b In fashion, what is a tam-o'-shanter?

4a In film, Marilyn Monroe, Tony Curtis and Jack Lemmon starred together in which 1959 romantic comedy?

4b In 1927, Charles Lindbergh became the first man to fly solo non-stop across which ocean?

5a In music, which country singer duetted with Kenny Rogers on the 1983 track 'Islands in the Stream'?

5b How long is the current maximum term for a UK parliament?

Answers

1a Margaret (Margaret Meldrew)
1b Michael Jackson
2a Manchester United
2b Ben Nevis
3a Heart

3b Hat (accept cap)
4a *Some Like It Hot*
4b The Atlantic
5a Dolly Parton (Dolly Rebecca Parton)
5b Five years

Player a   1   2   3   4   5

Player b   1   2   3   4   5

Head to Head

1a For which 1995 film, co-starring Kate Winslet, did Emma Thompson win an Oscar for Best Adapted Screenplay?

1b In geography, the South China Sea is a part of which ocean?

2a In TV, which docusoap featured Jeremy Spake as one of its central characters?

2b The 1871 unification of Prussia, Hanover and Saxony helped form which country?

3a Which chemical element has the symbol Cu?

3b In pop music, Denise Van Outen and Johnny Vaughan duetted on what UK top-ten song in 1998?

4a Which human rights organisation was awarded the Nobel Peace Prize in 1977?

4b The Maori people are the original inhabitants of which country?

5a The Grand Canyon was mainly carved by the waters of which river?

5b In sport, at which motor-racing circuit does the British Grand Prix take place?

Answers

1a *Sense and Sensibility*
1b Pacific
2a Airport
2b Germany
3a Copper

3b 'Especially for You'
4a Amnesty International
4b New Zealand (accept Aotearoa)
5a Colorado
5b Silverstone

Player a (1) (2) (3) (4) (5)

Player b (1) (2) (3) (4) (5)

Head to Head

1a In chemistry, what do bases react with to produce salts?

1b What is the name of the arch on the Champs Elysées that commemorates Napoleon's victories?

2a Poldark Mine is a tourist attraction in which English county?

2b The Jerusalem artichoke is related to which flower, widely used as a source of oil?

3a Which famous actor played the angry central character in the 1993 film *Falling Down*?

3b In music, with which famous party song did Black Lace have a UK number-two hit single in 1984?

4a In the Royal Navy, for which rank is the abbreviation PO used?

4b In pastimes, how many picture cards are there in a standard pack of 52 playing cards?

5a In literature, the characters Homily, Arriety and Pod are a family of tiny people who adopt items from their human hosts in which 1952 children's novel by Mary Norton?

5b In which West End musical did comedian and TV presenter Les Dennis appear in the year 2000?

Answers

1a Acid (acids)
1b L'Arc de Triomphe (L'Arc de Triomphe de l'Etoile)
2a Cornwall
2b Sunflower
3a Michael Douglas

3b 'Agadoo'
4a Petty Officer
4b Twelve (accept a dozen)
5a *The Borrowers*
5b *Chicago*

Player a (1) (2) (3) (4) (5)

Player b (1) (2) (3) (4) (5)

Head to Head

1a Which 1955 treaty was signed by eight Communist states in response to West Germany's entry into NATO ?

1b The Republic of Trinidad and Tobago lies just off the coast of which South American country?

2a In the TV soap *EastEnders*, when Cindy fled Britain with her children Stephen and Peter, a private detective discovered she was living in which European country?

2b Which city is home to The Hermitage, the largest public museum and gallery in Russia?

3a In the children's adventure programme *The Littlest Hobo*, what breed was the starring dog?

3b Which 1961 Roald Dahl novel tells the story of a small boy and an enormous fruit?

4a In which country is Kakadu National Park?

4b What was the name of the French monk who is commonly credited with perfecting the method of making champagne?

5a Which comic-strip Viking has a wife called Helga?

5b In rugby league, which Yorkshire club is known as the 'Bulls'?

Answers

1a The Warsaw Pact (Warsaw Treaty of Friendship, Cooperation, and Mutual Assistance)

1b Venezuela

2a Italy

2b St Petersburg (accept Petrograd/ Leningrad)

3a German shepherd (accept Alsatian)

3b *James and the Giant Peach*

4a Australia

4b Dom Perignon

5a Hagar The Horrible

5b Bradford

Player a (1) (2) (3) (4) (5)

Player b (1) (2) (3) (4) (5)

Head to Head

1a In sport, which knock-out football competition was founded during the 1870s by Charles William Alcock?

1b At which cathedral was Thomas à Beckett murdered in 1170?

2a By what name is the internationally successful Irish rock singer Paul Hewson better known?

2b Which actor played the character Dr Richard Kimble in the 1993 film *The Fugitive*?

3a In science, brass and bronze are both alloys that mainly contain which metal?

3b Edvard Eriksen created the statue of which Hans Andersen character that stands in Copenhagen harbour?

4a Launched in 1986 by Eddy Shah, what was Britain's first national newspaper to be printed in colour?

4b In maths, if a circle is divided into twenty equal segments, how many degrees are there in each segment?

5a In Henry Wadsworth Longfellow's 1855 poem, who had a wife called Minnehaha?

5b In the New Testament, which of Jesus's disciples did he describe as a rock on which he would build his Church?

Answers

1a FA Cup (accept FA Challenge Cup)
1b Canterbury
2a Bono (accept Bono Vox)
2b Harrison Ford
3a Copper
3b The Little Mermaid

4a Today
4b Eighteen
5a Hiawatha
5b Peter (accept Simon/Simeon/ Simon Peter)

Player a   1   2   3   4   5

Player b   1   2   3   4   5

Head to Head

1a In music, with which instrument is the Russian composer Sergei Rachmaninov most commonly associated?

1b In football, which South American country did France beat in the 1998 World Cup final?

2a According to Tennyson's poem, with which of King Arthur's knights did the Lady of Shalott have an unrequited love affair?

2b Nancy Sinatra performed a duet with which legendary entertainer on the 1967 UK number one 'Somethin' Stupid'?

3a Where in Europe would you find the River Dordogne?

3b Emperor, snow and Canada are types of which bird?

4a In which Gilbert and Sullivan operetta is a song beginning: 'On a tree by a river a little Tom-Tit sang "Willow, Tit-Willow, Tit-Willow"'?

4b Which UK physicist, born in 1942, is famous for his work on black holes?

5a Which Conservative politician's father was a refugee called Luis who came to Britain at the end of the Spanish Civil War?

5b What is the British dependency on the southern coast of the Iberian peninsula?

Answers

1a Piano
1b Brazil
2a Sir Lancelot (of the Lake)
2b Frank Sinatra (Francis Albert Sinatra; accept 'her father')
3a France
3b Goose

4a The Mikado
4b Stephen Hawking (Stephen William Hawking)
5a Michael Portillo (Michael Denzil Xavier Portillo)
5b Gibraltar

Player a   1   2   3   4   5

Player b   1   2   3   4   5

Head to Head

1a Which English actor and director played the character John Hammond in the *Jurassic Park* films?

1b For which English county did cricketer Geoff Boycott play his first-class career?

2a Who in pop music topped the UK singles chart in 2000 with 'Oops! . . . I did it again'?

2b In comic books, of which superhero is Dr Bruce Banner the alter ego?

3a The blowfly is also known as the 'blue . . .' what?

3b Who starred as Jack Robin in the first 'talkie' film, *The Jazz Singer*, in 1927?

4a In sport, which English football club did Kevin Keegan join from Hamburg in 1980?

4b In children's TV, which type of shop did Mr Benn always go into before going through to another world?

5a Which US TV series featured the Ingalls family?

5b In art, which Spanish Surrealist painter produced the *Burning Giraffe* in 1935?

Answers

1a Richard Attenborough (Lord Attenborough)

1b Yorkshire

2a Britney Spears

2b The Hulk (accept The Incredible Hulk)

3a Bottle

3b Al Jolson (Asa Yoelson)

4a Southampton

4b Fancy-dress shop (accept costume shop)

5a *Little House on the Prairie*

5b Salvador Dalí (accept Dalí/ Salvador Felipe Jacinto Dalí)

Player a   1   2   3   4   5

Player b   1   2   3   4   5

Head to Head

1a In food, with which vegetable would a dish be served if it was described as being 'à la Vichy'?

1b Which prolific writer's autobiography, published in 1969, is entitled *Our Kate*?

2a In pop music, Buster Bloodvessel was the lead singer of which 1980s British band?

2b *The Gremlins* was the first book published by which famous British children's author?

3a In the eighth century, a huge earthwork known as Offa's Dyke was built to mark the boundary between which two countries?

3b Which former American president once held the position of president of the Screen Actors Guild?

4a In the comic strip *Calvin and Hobbes*, what type of animal is Hobbes?

4b In 1982, Prince Charles laid the foundation stone of which library's new home near St Pancras station in London?

5a In finance, the DAX Thirty Index is an indicator of share prices published by which country's stock exchange?

5b On which river in Kent does the town of Maidstone stand?

Answers

1a Carrots
1b Catherine Cookson
2a Bad Manners
2b Roald Dahl
3a England and Wales

3b Reagan (Ronald Wilson Reagan)
4a Tiger
4b British Library
5a Germany('s)
5b (River) Medway

Player a   1   2   3   4   5

Player b   1   2   3   4   5

Head to Head

1a In maths, 'simultaneous' and 'quadratic' are types of what?

1b With which US baseball team did Manchester United football club agree to join in merchandising franchises in February 2001?

2a In the 2001 Six Nations rugby tournament, which country beat Scotland by a record 43 to three scoreline?

2b In science, which type of metal is commonly used as protective material against radioactive substances or X-rays?

3a In music, which rocker had a UK hit single in 1972 with 'School's Out'?

3b In which year is Fritz Lang's futuristic 1926 film *Metropolis* set?

4a During the English Reformation, who was king of England between 1509 and 1547?

4b In music, which instrument is Herb Alpert famous for playing?

5a In the American TV comedy *Friends*, what is the name of the coffee house?

5b In 1917, the Politburo became the decision-making body of which Soviet political party?

Answers

1a Equations
1b New York Yankees
2a England
2b Lead
3a Alice Cooper (Vincent Damon Furnier)

3b 2000
4a Henry VIII
4b Trumpet
5a Central Perk
5b Communist (Party)

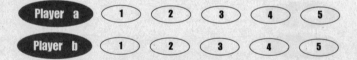

Player a (1) (2) (3) (4) (5)

Player b (1) (2) (3) (4) (5)

Head to Head

1a Which actress plays Dr Sam Ryan in the BBC TV series *Silent Witness*?

1b In the USA, which Amendment guarantees the freedom of speech and worship?

2a In the Book of Genesis, whose sailing vessel was built from gopher wood?

2b What was the profession of Roy Scheider's character in the 1975 film *Jaws*?

3a What name is given to the foam produced in summer on plants by the nymphs of frog-hoppers?

3b In Greek mythology, how many daughters of Zeus made up the Muses?

4a Which Egyptian port shares its name with the canal next to it?

4b In the 1960s, which American band had hits with 'Fun, Fun, Fun' and 'California Girls'?

5a In which country did Winston Churchill make his famous 'Iron Curtain' speech in 1946?

5b At which event did Sally Gunnell win Olympic gold in 1992?

Answers

1a Amanda Burton (Amanda Arnstein)
1b First (Amendment)
2a Noah's (Noah's Ark)
2b Policeman (*accept* sheriff/police chief)
3a Cuckoo spit

3b Nine
4a Suez
4b The Beach Boys
5a United States (*accept* US/USA/ United States of America/America)
5b 400 metres hurdles

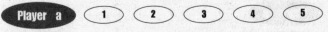

Player **a** (1) (2) (3) (4) (5)

Player **b** (1) (2) (3) (4) (5)

Head to Head

1a A Clydesdale is a large, heavy breed of which mammal?

1b Which Manchester-born artist painted *Coming from the Mill* in 1930?

2a In biology, lactose is the main carbohydrate found in which fluid produced from the mammary glands?

2b In which children's novel by E. B. White does a bashful pig named Wilbur befriend a spider?

3a In Australia, which is the most highly populated city in the Northern Territory?

3b At weddings, what is the name given to the practice of soldiers making a tunnel with their swords for the bride and groom to walk through?

4a What is the literal translation of 'haute couture'?

4b Which actor starred opposite Meryl Streep in the 1995 film *The Bridges of Madison County*?

5a The cooking ingredient miso originates from which Asian country?

5b Which motorway connects Exeter with Birmingham?

Answers

1a Horse
1b Lowry (accept L. S. Lowry/Laurence Stephen Lowry)
2a Milk (accept colostrum)
2b *Charlotte's Web*
3a Darwin

3b Guard of honour
4a High fashion
4b Clint Eastwood (Clinton Eastwood Junior)
5a Japan
5b M5

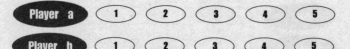

Player a   1   2   3   4   5

Player b   1   2   3   4   5

Head to Head

1a The Iberian Pact was signed in 1939 with Spain and which other European country?

1b What material was invented in 1836 by Frenchman Ignace Dubus-Bonnel, weaving glass with wool or cotton?

2a 'Basic', 'Cobol' and 'Pascal' are examples of what?

2b In literature, what was the nickname of the bespectacled fat boy in William Golding's novel *The Lord of the Flies*?

3a How many fluid ounces are there in an imperial pint?

3b In a 1979 treaty, combat was prohibited from taking place on which natural satellite?

4a The composer Johann Strauss wrote a famous waltz named after which river?

4b Which Canadian singer sang with Peabo Bryson on the 1992 UK hit single 'Beauty and the Beast'?

5a Helios was the ancient Greek god of what?

5b In nature, cayenne and pimento are types of which pungent fruit?

Answers

1a Portugal
1b Fibreglass (*accept* glass fibre)
2a Computer programming languages
2b Piggy
3a Twenty

3b The moon
4a Danube ('The Blue Danube')
4b Celine Dion
5a The sun
5b Pepper

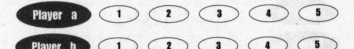

Player **a**   1   2   3   4   5
Player **b**   1   2   3   4   5

Head to Head

1a Which ceremony is held at London's Horse Guards Parade in June each year to celebrate the Queen's official birthday?

1b The West Indian religion Rastafarianism is based on the ideas of Marcus . . . who?

2a Which famous actress and singer did Vincente Minnelli marry in 1945?

2b In science, what term refers to a lens which curves outwards?

3a In tennis, what name is given to a stroke that returns the ball before it bounces?

3b Named after a classical English actor, which is the largest of the three theatres in the National Theatre complex?

4a In travel, the Coffs Harbour area is a popular holiday resort in which country?

4b In TV, which 1990s BBC children's drama series was set in a Newcastle youth club?

5a In which US city is the Lincoln Memorial, which houses a statue of Abraham Lincoln?

5b To which continent is the chinchilla native?

Answers

1a Trooping the Colour

1b Garvey

2a Judy Garland (Frances Ethel Gumm)

2b Convex

3a Volley

3b Olivier

4a Australia

4b Byker Grove

5a Washington, DC

5b South America

Player a — 1 2 3 4 5

Player b — 1 2 3 4 5

Head to Head

1a In cartoons, what is the name of the elderly-looking Smurf with a white beard?

1b Epistaxis is the medical term for bleeding from which part of the body?

2a In geography, Japan's eastern coastline overlooks which ocean?

2b In the Bible, who pushed down the pillars of a temple after being blinded by his Philistine captors?

3a Which 1971 film starred Michael Caine as a London gangster who travels to Newcastle to investigate his brother's murder?

3b A traditional rhyme about which bird often includes the lines 'Three for a girl, and four for a boy'?

4a When eaten with haggis, what type of vegetable are 'bashed neeps'?

4b In geography, Poland has a coastline along which sea?

5a In history, who became prime minister of Italy in 1922?

5b Which term is used to describe a fear of open places?

Answers

1a Papa Smurf	**3b** Magpie
1b Nose	**4a** Turnips (accept swede/rutabaga)
2a Pacific	**4b** Baltic
2b Samson	**5a** Benito Mussolini
3a Get Carter	**5b** Agoraphobia

Player a 1 2 3 4 5

Player b 1 2 3 4 5

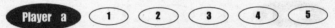

Head to Head

1a In literature, which famous sisters published novels and poems under the pen names of Currer, Ellis, and Acton Bell?

1b What name is given to a straight line that passes from one side of a circle to the other through the centre?

2a In film, Cher and Jack Nicholson starred in which 1987 adaptation of a John Updike novel?

2b The victories of which famous French emperor are commemorated by the Arc de Triomphe in Paris?

3a In pop music, 'Barbie Girl' and 'Doctor Jones' were 1990s UK number-one hit singles for which Scandinavian band?

3b In which ancient civilisation was Ra the god of the sun?

4a 'Destroying angel', 'death cap' and 'fly agaric' are all poisonous species of what?

4b In 1976, Sheffield University maths student Tony Miles became the first British International Grandmaster in what?

5a In America, before becoming president in 1953, Dwight Eisenhower was Supreme Commander of which organisation?

5b Myleene Klass is a singer in which pop group?

Answers

1a The Brontës (Emily, Charlotte and Anne Brontë)
1b Diameter
2a The Witches of Eastwick
2b Napoleon (Napoleon Bonaparte/ Napoleon I)
3a Aqua

3b Egyptian
4a Toadstool (accept fungus, mushroom)
4b Chess
5a NATO (North Atlantic Treaty Organisation)
5b Hear'Say

| Player a | 1 | 2 | 3 | 4 | 5 |
| Player b | 1 | 2 | 3 | 4 | 5 |

Head to Head

1a In religion, Jibrail is the Islamic name for which archangel?

1b For which film did Woody Allen win an Oscar in 1978 for Best Director?

2a In science, malachite is a common ore of which metal?

2b At which sport do the Harlequins and Newcastle Falcons compete?

3a Andrew Lloyd Webber's musical *Cats* is based on a book by which poet?

3b In transport, the *Aaron Manby* was the first steamship to be made of which material?

4a In TV, who interviewed the Beckhams in 2001 for Comic Relief?

4b In history, during which war did the Battle of Little Bighorn take place?

5a What name is given to the white winter fur of a stoat used for trimming ceremonial robes?

5b In art, Annigoni's portrait of whom caused the Royal Academy to break its attendance records in 1955?

Answers

1a Gabriel
1b *Annie Hall*
2a Copper
2b Rugby union (*accept* rugby, *do not accept* rugby league)
3a T. S. Eliot

3b Iron
4a Ali G (*accept* Sasha Baron Cohen)
4b American Civil War
5a Ermine
5b The Queen (*accept* Elizabeth II/The Monarch)

Player a 1 2 3 4 5

Player b   1 2 3 4 5

Head to Head

1a Which disease affecting humans is caused by the tsetse fly?

1b In the *Bob the Builder* stories, what is the name of the woman who works with Bob?

2a In tennis, who won the first of his Wimbledon men's singles titles in 1993?

2b Patras is a port in the west of which country in south-eastern Europe?

3a In fashion design, 'Lincoln' is a shade of which colour?

3b Which company has operated a bus service from 1930 that covered much of the United States?

4a In which 1997 film did Russell Crowe play the character Bud White?

4b Which South African language derives from the language of the Dutch settlers?

5a In which American sport can you score from the 'free throw line'?

5b In which novel and film does Graham Greene describe the life of a seventeen-year-old boy called 'Pinkie'?

Answers

1a Sleeping sickness (accept African trypanosomiasis)
1b Wendy
2a Pete Sampras
2b Greece
3a Green (Lincoln Green)
3b Greyhound Bus Company (accept Greyhound)
4a *LA Confidential*
4b Afrikaans
5a Basketball
5b *Brighton Rock*

Player a   1   2   3   4   5

Player b   1   2   3   4   5

Head to Head

1a In maths, which is further: three feet or 39 inches?

1b Which two-word term describes a state of temporary government by military authorities of a country or region?

2a In pop music, which Australian band's 1987 album was entitled *Kick*?

2b In Greek mythology, who fell in love with his own reflection?

3a In the USA, George W. Bush's brother Jeb was the governor of which state during the year 2000 election campaign?

3b In entertainment, what is the first name of celebrity chef Jamie Oliver's wife?

4a Which American sport is commonly played at Yankee Stadium in New York?

4b Which spiritual figure is believed to have reached enlightenment under a fig tree?

5a In science, what name is given to a small, hot, dying star?

5b In horse racing, what is the name given to a race in which horses carry different weights in order to make it a more equal contest?

Answers

1a 39 inches
1b Martial law
2a INXS
2b Narcissus
3a Florida
3b Jules (Juliette Norton)

4a Baseball
4b Buddha (accept Siddhartha Gotama/Gautama)
5a White dwarf
5b Handicap

Player a   1   2   3   4   5

Player b   1   2   3   4   5

Head to Head

1a Which actor and director starred as Harry Lime in the 1949 film noir *The Third Man*?

1b Which annual festival of music and drama was founded in 1947 by Rudolph Bing?

2a What is the surname of the Harry Enfield TV characters Wayne and Waynetta?

2b Which New York art gallery was designed by Frank Lloyd Wright in the 1960s?

3a In the human body, in which organ is the pineal gland?

3b Which popular American children's programme, which began in 1969, is made by the Children's Television Workshop company?

4a In film, which historical figure did Mel Gibson play in the 1995 epic *Braveheart*?

4b In fashion, tulle is a type of what?

5a The Indian tandoor is what sort of kitchen device?

5b Which south-east Asian country was formerly called Burma?

Answers

1a Orson Welles (George Orson Welles)
1b Edinburgh Festival
2a Slob
2b Guggenheim
3a The brain
3b *Sesame Street*
4a William Wallace
4b Fabric (accept material/cloth)
5a Oven (accept clay oven)
5b Myanmar

Player a   1   2   3   4   5

Player b   1   2   3   4   5

Head to Head

1a Conventions held in which European city govern the rules of war, including the treatment of prisoners?

1b Which female vocal trio had a 1999 UK and US hit single with 'Bills, Bills, Bills'?

2a In American politics, who was Richard Nixon's vice-president, who had to resign in disgrace in 1973?

2b On what road in Chelsea did fashion designer Mary Quant open her first boutique, called Bazaar, in 1955?

3a In religion, 'hajji' is the name given to someone who has made a pilgrimage to which city?

3b In chemistry, which letter is the symbol for the element fluorine?

4a Which Rodgers and Hammerstein musical set in Siam features the song 'Getting To Know You'?

4b Which Disney animation features Flower, the skunk?

5a In transport, the first trains on the London Underground railway ran on which line?

5b In which TV sitcom did Ronnie Corbett play Timothy Lumsden, a forty-year-old who lives with his domineering mother?

Answers

1a Geneva
1b Destiny's Child
2a Spiro Agnew (Spiro Theodore Agnew)
2b King's Road
3a Mecca

3b F
4a The King And I
4b Bambi
5a Metropolitan
5b Sorry!

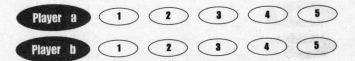

Player **a**   1   2   3   4   5

Player **b**   1   2   3   4   5

Head to Head

1a Which type of blood cell does not contain haemoglobin: white or red?

1b Which animated TV show features Seymour Skinner?

2a Which famous pop star wore a pair of giant Doc Marten-style boots to play the Pinball Wizard in the 1975 film *Tommy*?

2b In which English county is the market town of Marlborough?

3a In 1645, Thomas Fairfax was given command of which Roundhead army in the English Civil War?

3b By what name is the Charles Dickens character Philip Pirrip commonly known?

4a In the Second World War, by what name was the successful German fighter plane, the Me 109, more commonly known?

4b Geri Halliwell's version of 'It's Raining Men' features on the soundtrack of which film from 2001?

5a In the Bible, whose head was brought before Herod on a platter?

5b In science, Marie Curie won a Nobel Prize in 1903 for the discovery of what?

Answers

1a White	**3b** Pip
1b *The Simpsons*	**4a** The Messerschmitt
2a Elton John (Reg Dwight)	**4b** *Bridget Jones's Diary*
2b Wiltshire	**5a** John the Baptist
3a The New Model Army	**5b** Radioactivity

Player a   1   2   3   4   5

Player b   1   2   3   4   5

Head to Head

1a In UK politics, in which year did the regional assemblies in Scotland, Wales and Northern Ireland take power?

1b What is the profession of James Caan's character in the 1990 horror film *Misery*?

2a In the Bible, who washed his hands in a gesture of innocence before delivering Jesus to be crucified?

2b In science, what is the name of the chemical discovered by Samuel Guthrie in 1831 which was used as an anaesthetic?

3a In rugby union, which colour is the first-choice shirt of the British Lions?

3b In which country was playwright George Bernard Shaw born?

4a Which presenter was suspended after the Sex Pistols swore live on his show in 1976?

4b From which genetic blood disease did the son of Tsar Nicholas II suffer?

5a In UK geography, Herne Bay is in which English county?

5b Which city is the most highly populated in the state of South Australia?

Answers

1a 1999
1b Writer (accept author)
2a Pilate (accept Pontius Pilate/the Roman governor)
2b Chloroform
3a Red

3b Ireland
4a Bill Grundy
4b Haemophilia
5a Kent
5b Adelaide

Player a   1   2   3   4   5

Player b   1   2   3   4   5

Head to Head

1a What is the official currency of Denmark?

1b What was the name for the innermost and strongest structure or central tower of a medieval castle?

2a Who directed the films *The Abyss*, *Aliens* and *The Terminator*?

2b In which Jane Austen novel would you find the Dashwood sisters?

3a In music, Levi Stubbs, Renaldo Benson, Lawrence Payton and Abdul Fakir were members of which famous Motown group?

3b Which female star of the year 2000 film *Charlie's Angels* was also a producer on the film?

4a What colour is the centre of a standard British archery target?

4b In the Bible, at what type of ceremony in Cana did Jesus turn water into wine?

5a Which sport is played at The Belfry in the Midlands?

5b In which TV comedy series did Nicholas Lyndhurst play a character with a secret life in wartime Britain?

Answers

1a Krone

1b The keep

2a James Cameron (James Francis Cameron)

2b *Sense and Sensibility*

3a The Four Tops

3b Drew Barrymore (Drew Blyth Barrymore)

4a Gold (accept yellow)

4b A wedding/marriage

5a Golf

5b *Goodnight Sweetheart*

Player a (1) (2) (3) (4) (5)

Player b (1) (2) (3) (4) (5)

Head to Head

1a Which is the largest internal organ of the human body?

1b Which American actor played Santino 'Sonny' Corleone in the *Godfather* films?

2a Which saint, murdered in 1170, is enshrined in Canterbury Cathedral?

2b In history, 'William H. Bonney', Henry McCarty and 'Kid Antrim' were all names used for which nineteenth-century outlaw of the American south-west?

3a Which novel by Charles Dickens features the character Betsey Trotwood?

3b Which Scottish band released the UK hit 'Sing' in 2001?

4a In the New Testament, what is the trade of Jesus's disciple Simon Peter?

4b At which famous rugby union stadium was the 2001 Rugby League Challenge Cup final played?

5a What was the profession of William Shatner's character in the TV series *T. J. Hooker*?

5b In humans, what do the lachrymal glands produce?

Answers

1a Liver
1b James Caan
2a Thomas à Becket
2b Billy the Kid
3a *David Copperfield*
3b Travis

4a Fisherman
4b Twickenham
5a Policeman (accept cop/police officer/police sergeant)
5b Tears

Player a   1   2   3   4   5

Player b   1   2   3   4   5

Head to Head

1a Ho Chi Minh City was formally known by what name?

1b In the 1995 film *Dangerous Minds*, what was the profession of Michelle Pfeiffer's character?

2a In geography, in which English county is the town of Thetford?

2b In geography, in which continent is the River Orinoco?

3a In history, what was the first name of the British soldier known as Lawrence of Arabia?

3b In pop music, who had a 1980 UK hit single with the song 'Fashion'?

4a In boxing, which British featherweight lost his unbeaten record to Marco Antonio Barrera in April 2001?

4b On the London Underground map, which line is coloured brown?

5a In the TV series *Dallas*, what was the name of the Ewings' ranch?

5b In which US city is Gracie Mansion the mayor's residence?

Answers

1a Saigon
1b Teacher (accept ex-marine who becomes a teacher/high-school teacher)
2a Norfolk
2b South America (do not accept America)

3a Thomas
3b David Bowie
4a Naseem Hamed (Prince Naseem)
4b Bakerloo
5a Southfork
5b New York

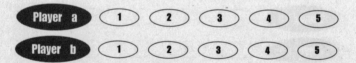

Player a 1 2 3 4 5

Player b 1 2 3 4 5

Head to Head

1a What is the last bone at the base of the spinal column called?

1b Which actor starred as Jerry opposite Julia Roberts in the 2001 film *The Mexican*?

2a Which English city's name is derived from an Anglo-Saxon name meaning 'the hamlet of Snott's people by the water'?

2b Which Rochdale-born singer and comedienne was famous for entertaining troops and for the song 'Sally'?

3a What was the nickname of the nine-man crime-fighting team which was led by Eliot Ness in the late 1920s?

3b Which Spanish football club has been coached by former England managers Terry Venables and Bobby Robson?

4a In *The X-Files*, what kind of seeds are Agent Mulder's favourite snack?

4b In the USA, which city in South Carolina was originally named in honour of Charles II?

5a Which insoluble protein forms a major part of wheat flour?

5b At which football ground did England play their March 2001 World Cup qualifier against Finland?

Answers

1a Coccyx

1b Brad Pitt (William Bradley Pitt)

2a Nottingham

2b Gracie Fields (Dame Gracie Fields/ Grace Stansfield)

3a 'The Untouchables'

3b Barcelona

4a Sunflower (seeds)

4b Charleston

5a Gluten

5b Anfield (accept Liverpool)

Player a   1   2   3   4   5

Player b   1   2   3   4   5

Sudden Death

1a Which football club is nicknamed the 'Cobblers', on account of the area's traditional shoe-making trade?

1b In the 1970s TV sitcom *Are You Being Served?* which actor played the character Mr Humphries?

2a Expressed as a decimal, what is one half plus one quarter?

2b The name of which durable ribbed cotton is thought to be derived from the French for 'cord of the king'?

3a In US politics, Bob Dole ran for US president against which Democrat candidate?

3b The Locomotives and Highways Act of 1865 stated that a man carrying what must walk in front of a motor car?

4a According to the rhyme, children born on which day are fair of face?

4b What is the only Australian state capital that shares its name with a British city?

5a Bacchus and Dionysus were gods of which alcoholic drink?

5b In science the molecule of which chemical compound consists of two hydrogen atoms and one oxygen atom?

Answers

1a Northampton (Northampton Town)
1b John Inman (Frederick John Inman)
2a 0.75
2b Corduroy
3a Bill Clinton (William Jefferson Clinton/William Jefferson Blythe)
3b Red flag or red lamp (accept flag/lamp)
4a Monday
4b Perth
5a Wine
5b Water (accept H_2O)

Player a   1   2   3   4   5

Player b   1   2   3   4   5

Sudden Death

1a By what name is the study of ancestry and descent known?

1b Name one of the three London football clubs for which the commentator Jimmy Greaves played.

2a In the 1963 film *Doctor Strangelove*, which former Goon played three parts?

2b Which Jules Verne character was tracked around the globe by Inspector Fix in the novel *Around the World in 80 Days*?

3a Which is the only one of the Seven Wonders of the Ancient World to remain substantially in existence?

3b Which Scottish vocalist was born Marie Lawrie in 1948?

4a Which children's book by Dick King-Smith featured a pig called Babe, who was brought up by a sheepdog?

4b Name either of the British cathedrals that hold a copy of the Magna Carta from 1215.

5a In which 1958 Hitchcock film does the detective played by James Stewart have a fear of heights?

5b Which entertainer and former husband of Cher was elected to the US House of Representatives in 1994?

Answers

1a Genealogy

1b Chelsea, Tottenham Hotspur or West Ham United (accept Spurs/ Tottenham/West Ham)

2a Peter Sellers (Richard Henry Sellers)

2b Phileas Fogg (Phileas T. Fogg)

3a The Pyramids

3b Lulu

4a *The Sheep Pig*

4b Lincoln/Salisbury

5a *Vertigo*

5b Sonny Bono (accept Salvatore Bono/Sonny/Bono)

Player a 1 2 3 4 5

Player b 1 2 3 4 5

Sudden Death

1a In the USA, what is the state capital of Mississippi?

1b In `Baa Baa Black Sheep`, where does the little boy live?

2a In food, a chorizo, a highly seasoned sausage containing pork and paprika, originates from which European country?

2b In finance, which tax is known by the initials C.G.T?

3a In music, which Cardiff born composer wrote the song popularly known as `Keep the Home Fires Burning` in 1914, and has song writing awards named after him?

3b On a standard clock face, how many degrees is the angle between 1 o`clock and 7 o`clock?

4a The city of Chicago lies on the shore of which American Great Lake?

4b In Henry Fielding`s novel of the same name, what is the name of the baby that Squire Allworthy finds on his bed?

5a In football, to what did the East London club, 'Thames Iron Works', change their name in 1900?

5b In science, which metal was known by the Latin name 'plumbum'?

Answers

1a Jackson
1b Down the lane
2a Spain
2b Capital Gains Tax
3a Ivor Novello (accept David Ivor Davies, Ivor Novello Davies)

3b 180 (degrees)
4a Lake Michigan
4b Tom Jones
5a West Ham United (accept West Ham)
5b Lead

Player a 1 2 3 4 5

Player b 1 2 3 4 5

Sudden Death

1a In the animal kingdom, what is the largest of all living birds?

1b Which of Henry VIII's wives is said to appear as a ghost at her son Edward the VI's birthplace at Hampton Court Palace?

2a Which major US river's name is derived from the Algonquin for 'Big River'?

2b The film *The Green Mile* is based on a novel by which American horror writer?

3a With which sport is the TV commentator Peter Alliss famously associated?

3b In geography, St Peter's Basilica is a landmark in which European capital?

4a What is the more common name for the Strategic Defence Initiative, initiated by Ronald Reagan in 1983?

4b In human biology, in which part of the body are the radius and ulna bones?

5a Holly Hunter stars as Ada McGrath in which 1993 romantic drama set in New Zealand?

5b American Gangster Al Capone was jailed for what offence in 1931?

Answers

1a Ostrich	**3b** Rome
1b (Lady) Jane Seymour	**4a** Star Wars
2a Mississippi	**4b** Arm (accept Forearm)
2b Stephen King	**5a** The Piano
3a Golf	**5b** Tax Evasion

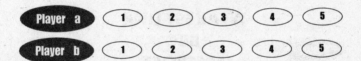

Player **a** — 1 2 3 4 5

Player **b** — 1 2 3 4 5

THE WEAKEST LINK

CONGRATULATIONS!

You have taken the first step towards becoming a contestant on **THE WEAKEST LINK**. All you need to do is fill in this form and send it back to us. Before you start, here are a few points to remember:

- **Please attach a recent photo of yourself (this is non-returnable).**
- **Please write clearly using an ink pen – if we cannot read your details, we won't be able to consider you.**
- **Please ensure that any information you give us about yourself is accurate.**
- **This form can be photocopied should you require to do so.**

AUDITIONS

Due to the amount of correspondence we receive, unfortunately we cannot acknowledge receipt of application forms. We also cannot audition everyone who applies to the programme. If you are invited to attend an audition we will contact you with details of when and where it will take place.

Please note that guests will **NOT** be permitted to watch the audition session. They will be asked to wait in the reception area.

We regret that we are not able to reimburse travelling expenses to attend the audition, but if you are selected to take part in the show your travel and accommodation expenses for the filming **only** will be covered.

Please return the completed form to:

WEAKEST LINK
BBC
FREEPOST

*ATTACH PHOTO
HERE*

'WEAKEST LINK'
CONTESTANT APPLICATION FORM

TITLE (MR, MRS, MS, MISS): ....

FIRST NAME(S): .... **SURNAME:** ....

ADDRESS: ....

DATE OF BIRTH: .... **AGE:** ....

TEL NOS & CONTACT DETAILS (please include STD Codes):

Day/Work:........................... **Eve/Home:** ....

Mobile: .... **Email address:** ....

Fax: ....

CAN YOU ACCEPT CALLS AT WORK? *YES / NO*

How long have you been resident in the UK? ....

Marital status: .... **Occupation:** ....

Previous jobs (please include temporary jobs, student jobs etc.): ....
....
....

Please list six words which best describe you: ....
....

**What other TV shows have you appeared on or been interviewed for
before? (please give name of show and approximate dates)**

....
....

**What types of competitions or quizzes have you won or taken part
in other than television shows?**

....
....

What is your main active hobby or interest? ....

What other hobbies and interests do you have? ....
....

What are your favourite TV programmes & quiz shows? ....

....

If you won the *Weakest Link* prize money what would you spend it on?

....

How competitive are you? (please give an example)

....

....

Do you regard yourself as a team player? (please give an example)

....

....

Please circle the 3 most convenient locations for audition on the list below, indicating order of preference with a 1, 2 or 3 (1 being the most convenient).

BELFAST	**BIRMINGHAM**	**BRISTOL**	**CAMBRIDGE**
CARDIFF	**EDINBURGH**	**GLASGOW**	**INVERNESS**
LEEDS	**LIVERPOOL**	**LONDON**	**MANCHESTER**
NEWCASTLE	**NOTTINGHAM**	**PLYMOUTH**	**SHEFFIELD**
SOUTHAMPTON	**YORK**		

Please write here any dates on which you will *not* be available between now and May 2002: ....

....

Do you have an undischarged criminal record? *YES / NO*

If YES, please give details ....

I acknowledge that this criminal conviction information may be held on the Weakest Link Contestant Database.

I acknowledge that I am neither a BBC employee or contractor, nor a close relative of a BBC employee or contractor.

I confirm that all information provided on this application form is correct and I agree for it to be held on the Weakest Link Contestant Database until I advise that I no longer wish to be considered as a contestant. If any of the above information changes I will inform the Production Team.

SIGNATURE: .... **DATE:** ....

PLEASE NOTE THAT YOUR APPLICATION CANNOT BE PROCESSED WITHOUT YOUR SIGNATURE TO THE ABOVE CLAUSES.